The Global Crisis of Violence

The Global Crisis of Violence:
Common Problems, Universal Causes, Shared Solutions

Dorothy Van Soest

NASW PRESS

National Association of Social Workers
Washington, DC

Jay J. Cayner, ACSW, LISW, *President*
Josephine Nieves, MSW, PhD, *Executive Director*

Linda Beebe, *Executive Editor*
Nancy Winchester, *Editorial Services Director*
Patricia D. Wolf, Wolf Publications, Inc., *Project Manager*
Donna Verdier, *Copy Editor*
Beth Gyorgy, *Proofreader*
Melissa D. Conroy, Wolf Publications, Inc., *Proofreader*
Robert Elwood, *Indexer*

Library of Congress Cataloging-in-Publication Data
Van Soest, Dorothy.
    The global crisis of violence : common problems, universal causes, shared solutions / Dorothy Van Soest.
        p.   cm.
    Includes bibliographical references and index.
    ISBN 0-87101-276-6
    1. Violence.   2. Political violence.   3. Sustainable development.
    4. Child abuse.   5. Drug abuse and crime.   I. Title.
HM281.V293   1997   97-1076/
303.6—dc21   CIP

Dedicated to Eileen McGowan Kelly (1946–1996), who created an international network that now connects a global community of social workers.

Contents

Part 6: Healing
Coauthored by Arline Prigoff, PhD

Part 7: Epilogue

Preface and Acknowledgments

This book grew out of a four-year initiative of the National Association of Social Workers (NASW) called the Violence and Development Project, which was launched in 1993 by NASW's Peace and International Affairs program with funding from the United States Agency for International Development. The Violence and Development Project was aimed at educating U.S. social workers about a topic new to them and to international development educators: the interrelatedness of violence and development.

The project showed how to build grassroots capacity for globalizing the context within which social workers address social problems by fostering partnerships between schools of social work and NASW chapters, which are both invested contributors to and actors in the initiative. The talents of hundreds of NASW members at the grassroots level in six chapter-based project centers covering 11 states were engaged in conducting research, developing educational materials, and educating their constituencies locally and regionally on violence and development issues in workshops and conference presentations. Through the International Commission of the Council on Social Work Education (CSWE), dedicated social work educators participated in all aspects of the project, with a special contribution in the area of curriculum development. This book could not have been completed without the collective work of all the NASW and CSWE participants in the project, and their contributions are gratefully acknowledged.

A week-long teach-in organized in the third year of the project drew the participation of hundreds of colleges and universities in 41 states, Puerto Rico, and the U.S. Virgin Islands. Scheduled events included symposia, panels, film festivals, special class lectures, displays of materials, and workshops for students and faculty. Thirty colleges and universities organized hunger banquets, and more than 2,000 students, faculty, social work practitioners, and community representatives participated. Two videoconferences on "The Challenges of Violence Worldwide," hosted by renowned CBS broadcast journalist Charles Kuralt, were produced during the teach-in week at the University of North Carolina at Chapel

Hill School of Social Work and shown live at 375 sites with approximately 20,000 viewers for each broadcast. The two videoconferences were edited into one-hour videotapes for classroom use, which would make good accompaniments to this book.

Six briefing papers were produced by the Violence and Development Project and compiled in the book *Challenges of Violence Worldwide: An Educational Resource*, which serves as a student guide that introduces students to ideas about violence as a global affliction and sustainable human development as a global antidote. The companion guide for faculty, *Challenges of Violence Worldwide: Curriculum Modules*, includes course objectives, discussion questions, and various class activities and course assignments. It also includes the full text of *An Educational Resource*. Both books, published by the NASW Press, have been used in undergraduate and graduate courses on Human Behavior in the Social Environment, Social Work Theory and Practice, Social Welfare Policy, Research, and the Field Practicum. They are useful complements to this book.

As director of the Violence and Development Project for its first two years and, later, content consultant and member of its national advisory committee, I have been intimately involved in all aspects of this movement to establish an extended network of people knowledgeable about and committed to the involvement of social workers in global development issues. Through this experience, I further developed my own conceptualization about violence in collaboration with my colleague and friend, Shirley Bryant, as well as a philosophical and practical perspective about the connections between violence and development. I amassed a tremendous amount of information from numerous sources and collected hundreds of case studies from communities in both the United States and the global South that point to potentially successful strategies from which U.S. social workers might learn. It became apparent that there was much more to be said about the issues. Hence, this book was born. Its aim is to provide an in-depth look at the issues introduced in the briefing papers produced by the project.

Contributors who wrote the case studies that are used throughout the book gave their permission with a willingness and desire to contribute to social workers' understanding of global interrelatedness. Their work enhances the book's usefulness and relevance. The contributions of Arline Prigoff, who co-authored the part on trauma, improved the original draft 10-fold.

Special thanks are extended to Toni Johnson, who reviewed every single chapter of the manuscript and was always eager to get the next one. Hundreds of people reviewed portions of the original manuscript and provided materials that ultimately resulted in the book becoming a reality. Special acknowledgment goes to three focus groups of BSW and MSW students who read the first draft of the first three parts and provided extremely thorough and valuable feedback that helped shape subsequent revisions, including Miriam Alpern, Aimee Arcuni, Susan Azeka, Sarah Edmunds, Anne Hoffman, Elizabeth Hoffman, Andrea Link, Yasmin Lluveras, Cheri Roe, Philip Rozario, Laurie Strongin, Anne Sturgis, and Christine Vercellino. Margee Ensign, Ken Kusterer, and Sam Samarasinghe from the Development Studies Program reviewed original drafts of the manuscripts and provided helpful information. Others who reviewed material at various stages included Shantha Balaswamy, James O. Billups, Lorraine Blackman, Bruce Ellsworth, Charles Figley, Beverly Flanigan, Joe Gallegos, Gerald Gray, Chris Herman, Marie Hoff, Arleen B. Kahn, Kenneth Kazmerski, Allie Kilpatrick, Diane Knust, Janet Kusyk, Pat Leahan, Rosemary Link, Rosemary Merrigan, Marilynn Moch, Mary Mussell, Arline Prigoff, Chathapuram Ramanthan, Beth Rosenthal, Debbie Ruboyianes, JoAnne St. Clair, Krishna Samantrai, Judy Smith, Jennifer Stucker, Maura Sullivan, Ellen Thursby, Daniel Tovar, Linda Vinton, Jack Wall, and Marilyn Zide.

In addition to the hundreds of NASW and CSWE members who contributed to this book by submitting written materials for the Violence and Development Project, many others supported the idea for this book and contributed to its completion. Eileen Kelly (1946–1996), director of NASW's Peace and International Affairs program, supported the original idea for this book as an outgrowth of the project's activities. Jane Crosby, who served on the national advisory committee to the project during its first two years and then became project director, has been a joy to work with and a source of constant inspiration. Lucy Sanchez, NASW's director of public affairs, who was involved with the project from the beginning, has been a consistent source of encouragement and moral support. Linda Beebe, former associate executive director of communications for NASW, provided essential encouragement and support to bring the idea to fruition. Nancy Winchester, editorial services director, expedited the production process in a consistently positive and helpful manner. Donna Verdier copy edited the manuscript, and Patricia Wolf and the staff at Wolf Publications shepherded it through the production process.

The constant support and encouragement I received from Dean Barbara White made it possible to see this endeavor through to the end. The able assistance of Mario Cortez, Suzanne Ewing-Brethé, Mary Alice Fuller, Kelly Larson, and Griselda Ponce, who tracked down essential information and were always willing to provide whatever help was needed, is gratefully acknowledged. And finally, my greatest appreciation to Susan Seney, my greatest advocate and supporter.

—*Dorothy Van Soest*

Foreword

People acting as a strong, cohesive community can achieve more than individuals. When people work together in community, strategies for change that are sustainable are possible. When people identify with their community, they want to see it survive, which encourages a long-term perspective.

The alternative—when instead of seeking community, people engage in individualistic, self-seeking behavior—forms a vicious circle that leads to greed, violence, and crime. The stubborn persistence of violence in the United States and throughout the world is related to a loss of community. This is the case whether we are talking about the United States, Bosnia, Rwanda, Palestine, or anywhere else where violence is endemic.

When violence is an expression of powerlessness, isolation, and exclusion, participatory community development from the bottom up has the potential to counter it. Community development at the grassroots level taps into and builds the integrity and leadership of members of the community and has the potential to break the cycle of violence. Social workers must become involved with communities at this level by learning from them and allowing themselves to be influenced and changed by them.

The National Association of Social Workers is committed to bringing a deeper analysis and more lasting solutions to the crisis of violence facing many U.S. communities. We are committed to exploring new paradigms and models in community building and violence prevention.

The Global Crisis of Violence: Common Problems, Universal Causes, Shared Solutions is a valuable contribution to this commitment. It expands the context within which the social work profession addresses violence and its attendant problems. It reflects NASW's investment in training social workers to be better informed and more sensitive "global professionals" so that they might develop more effective strategies for reducing violence through promoting development. It highlights home-grown strategies to address violence so that social workers can learn about what works and why. Finally, it makes clear social work's and NASW's appreciation for the increasingly cross-border nature of the systemic problems that give rise to violence by expanding the search for solutions to our social problems beyond U.S. borders.

It is anticipated that faculty, students, and practitioners who read this book will be stimulated to stretch their understanding about violence and its relationship to development, renew their commitment to community practice, and expand their global consciousness.

—*Josephine Nieves, MSW, PhD*
Executive Director
National Association of
Social Workers

Introduction

> It is a new world, a different world, a world that demands new responses and major changes on the international, national, professional and personal levels. . . . We have come to live, as some have said, in a global village. The earth has become small and the peoples of the world so intimately cross-joined that all of us are deeply affected by events occurring in distant corners of the world, and people in those corners are affected by us. . . . Economic, social, political, domestic, international, and ecological issues are intricately bound in an ever-escalating, lethal cycle. (Hartman, 1994, p. 66)

Sophisticated communications and transportation networks make the world seem smaller. The technologies that have helped unify the world have made us aware that the world is increasingly interdependent: many social problems are no longer personal or local or national—they are global in scope. Human distress caused by crime, drugs, terrorism, pollution, war, poverty, and disease knows no national borders.

Violence, in particular, is a pervasive, growing problem of critical importance. From the teenager in Los Angeles or El Salvador to the mother in Washington, DC, or the Sudan to the infant in New York City or India, violence affects millions of people worldwide. Like other social problems, violence cannot be solved without acknowledging and understanding the complexities of global interdependence. This book emphasizes the importance of working for global peace and development by examining parallel conditions of violence in the United States and in less economically developed countries and by identifying issues of interdependence and common solutions.

The book is based on the following convictions:

- Global interdependence is a fact of life that cannot be ignored.
- Violence—whether in Baltimore or Bangladesh—must be conceptualized in systemic and not just individual terms, because a cycle of violence operates through a complex of cultural and institutional arrangements.
- Preventive investments that shore up social infrastructures are more fiscally and ethically responsible than crisis management or punishment-oriented approaches to problems of violence.

- Breaking the cycle of violence requires development strategies that are holistic, multidimensional, community based and directed, and, ultimately, sustainable by local people.
- Homegrown strategies to address the causes and effects of violence must be retrieved and exchanged and new methods must be devised to share learning and tell stories about what works and why. Internationally, for example, we can learn from projects such as the Self-Employed Women's Association in India, which is based on the premise that, instead of welfare, poor women need to organize for empowerment and access to credit; a grassroots community's approach to healing from the trauma of civil war in Nicaragua; a microenterprise program in Kenya that has been used as an example followed by the mayor's office in Baltimore; and a community development center for Palestinian and Arab children and young parents in East Jerusalem that has survived despite ethnic conflict and fragile political sensibilities.
- An informed, professional social work voice for social and economic justice is critical in a political climate characterized by a drawbridge mentality toward the rest of the world and a short-sighted view of issues ranging from crime and violence to poverty and foreign aid.

Grounded in the above tenets, this book seeks to expand the frame of professional social work discourse within which violence is defined, its contexts analyzed, and its prevention and amelioration explored. To that end, it broadens the definition of violence and links it with individual, social, and economic development; focuses on violence as a global affliction; examines the parallel conditions and causes of violence in the United States and in less economically developed countries; and proposes the development of communities—using sustainable human development strategies—as a powerful antidote to violence.

The book is primarily about making connections: between the United States and less economically developed countries, between violence and development, and among different levels of violence. The themes of connectedness and interdependence are emphasized throughout. "Lessons without borders" is the phrase that best represents the book's approach to shared solutions to violence. Sustainable human development strategies that provide evidence of promising practices and problem-solving techniques, both in the global South and in the United States, are showcased.

This book is divided into parts that explore relationships between violence and development or maldevelopment within specific contexts: poverty, gender violence and violence against children, ethnicity, drugs, and trauma. One chapter in each part addresses the global link of problems and what we know from observing those problems in the United States and in less economically developed countries; other chapters examine what the United States can learn from other countries' experiences with those problems and what role social workers can play in addressing the problems. In particular, these questions are asked and answered:

- What are the similarities and differences between social problems in the United States and those in less economically developed countries?
- How do problems in less economically developed countries affect the United States and vice versa?
- What lessons can we learn from the efforts of other countries to solve problems similar to ours?
- What can social workers do to help?

The "resources" section at the end of the book, which lists organizations and publications concerned with the subjects addressed throughout the book, can be consulted for further information.

Reference

Hartman, A. (1994). Our global village. In A. Hartman (Ed.), *Reflection and controversy: Essays on social work* (pp. 65–70). Washington, DC: NASW Press.

Part 1

Violence and Development

Chapter 1

The Global Crisis of Violence and Maldevelopment: Overview and Framework

Violence is an affliction that threatens both local communities and the global community. Its ties to development are complex, but it is clear that social, economic, and human development is a global need that must be met before the crisis of violence can be stemmed. This chapter seeks to provide the framework for understanding the connections between violence and development by defining the key concepts that will be addressed throughout the book, focusing particularly on a reconceptualization of violence that examines the various levels at which it occurs.

Key Concepts Defined

Development

Although development takes place at many levels (among individuals, organizations, communities, or whole societies, for example), its meaning is much the same at any level: *development* is people's capacity to accomplish what they want to accomplish. On a personal level, it usually refers to individual growth and fulfillment of one's potential throughout the life cycle. Conversely, *maldevelopment* or *distorted development* refers to any process that blocks the natural growth process of the individual and interferes with the fulfillment of potential.

Development on a societal level is generally defined as "meeting the basic needs of all and extending to all the opportunity to fulfill their aspirations for a better life" (Shuman, 1994, p. 2). Broadly defined, development is a people-centered process aimed at improving the requisites of a better life, including income level, equity, human rights, democracy, environmental protection, and peace (Korten, 1981; Shuman, 1994).

3

McAfee (1991) defined development as a process that

- enables people to meet their essential needs
- goes beyond aid and emergency relief to enable people to become more self-reliant, less dependent on outside aid, and less vulnerable to disasters
- reverses the process of impoverishment and helps stop the drain of wealth from the poor to the rich within nations and from the world's poorer countries to the wealthier ones
- enhances democracy
- makes possible a balance between populations and resources by alleviating poverty and thus reducing the pressure on families to have many children
- improves the well-being and status of women; respects local cultures; sustains the natural environment
- measures progress in human—not just monetary—terms.

In short, development requires the empowerment of poor people by challenging political and economic structures that perpetuate inequities, and it promotes the interests of most people worldwide, in the global North as well as in the global South. Development encourages the use of resources in ways that help sustain the global environment, and it rights economic and social injustices, thus creating a less violent and more secure world for all. Maldevelopment or distorted development on a societal level refers to any process that does not meet the basic needs of all and does not extend to all the opportunity to fulfill their aspirations for a better life.

Development must take place in three areas for people and societies to accomplish their goals: (1) economic development, (2) human development (building of knowledge, skills, experience), and (3) social development (often thought of as building organizations, networks, and relations of trust among people so they can work together).

Social Development

Social development is a concept and set of practices that has evolved into a comprehensive, multidimensional approach to seeking social advancement and improving the quality of life for both individuals and the broader society (Lowe, 1995). Social development—a concept widely used and accepted in the social work profession—emphasizes such values as distributive justice, cooperation, grassroots participation, and equity. It recognizes the need to address the social dimensions of economic development, brings together individual and community notions and strategies for change, and links traditional social welfare and community development with economic development (Billups, 1994; Khinduka, 1987; Lowe, 1995; Midgley, 1994; Pandey, 1981; Sanders, 1982). Social development has two interrelated dimensions, according to Paiva (1982): (1) developing the capacity of individuals to improve their own and society's welfare and (2) altering or changing society's institutions so that they better meet human needs. Midgley (1994) defined social development as "a process of planned social change designed to promote people's welfare within the context of a comprehensive process of economic development" (p. 3).

Midgley (1993) identified three normative ideologies for social development: (1) the individualistic view, which posits that social betterment is attained through the cumulative effect of individual improvement; (2) the collectivist or statist view, which advocates the involvement of governmentally based bureaucratic organizations in social welfare; and (3) the populist or communitarian approach, which emphasizes the centrality of participation by citizens and recipients of services in the process of change. Each of these three perspectives has some value, but this book adopts the populist beliefs of the third view of social development, based on Korten's (1981) concept of people-centered development. An important role in social work is to promote and guide grassroots participation in efforts to effect social change; community workers who facilitate such participation may be employed either by government or by private organizations.

Billups (1994) maintained that the social development perspective gives the social work profession a far-reaching vision and holds considerable promise as a "principal organizing framework for guiding social work as a practice and a profession" (p. 25). Work to promote social development requires long-term strategies that balance services with supports and empowerment opportunities, not the short-term, service-heavy strategies of formal delivery systems. The promotion of sustainable human development, a new concept of development that will be discussed in chapter 2, is a powerful strategy that the social work profession can use to help alleviate the problem of violence worldwide.

Community Development

The word "community" is naturally evoked as part of development and social development processes. Community life is a fundamental aspect of individual development, and the community is a key to promoting larger-scale social and economic development. Just as people do not develop in isolation, a society or nation cannot develop properly without the development and participation of communities. Although community development can mean many different things, each definition addresses the idea of taking planned action to deal with the common concerns of people who share a geographic locality, cultural or philosophical identity, or crucial social and economic relationships (Harrison, 1995).

Community development involves the growth and strengthening of the structures and functioning of social networks and economic arrangements. When these networks and arrangements are robust, important aspects of the life that people have in common can be improved, thus enhancing the quality of life (Harrison, 1995). Rivera and Erlich (1995) gave this definition: "Community development refers to efforts to mobilize people who are directly affected by a community condition (that is, the 'victims,' the unaffiliated, the unorganized, and the nonparticipating) into groups and organizations to enable them to take action on the social problems and issues that concern them. A typical feature of these efforts is the concern with building new organizations among people who have not been previously organized to take social action on a problem" (p. 3).

This book addresses the significance of community for individual, social, and economic development and explores the kinds of violence that can endanger community. Oppression, disenfranchisement, withdrawal of social supports and services, and crime threaten to destroy the ties that hold people together in communities both in the United States and in other countries. Yet the case studies presented in this book illustrate people's tenacity as they sustain themselves and fulfill their needs in collective human systems by reconstructing communities when changes are necessary. They demonstrate that "no matter how destroyed a community may appear to be, some members are willing to rebuild their lives and the life of their community to obtain a better situation for themselves and their families" (Pantoja & Perry, 1995, p. 227).

⌈The chapters that follow take the viewpoint that community development is a crucial component of development strategies aimed at reducing violence.⌉They emphasize grassroots participation and empowerment and acknowledge that economic development is often central to the work of community development in addressing problems of violence. As Pantoja and Perry (1995) pointed out, "Without the right to work, to be productive, . . . community members are rendered economically impotent and dependent with some subsequently internalizing this dependency and abandoning their rights and privileges to be in charge of their own communities" (p. 225). Community development work with members of economically dependent and politically disenfranchised communities has to help people understand the forces and processes that create and maintain their oppressed condition, mobilize and organize their internal strength, abolish the mythology that makes them participants in their own powerlessness, and act to restore or develop new functions to increase community competence for the well-being of its members (Pantoja & Perry, 1995). Common characteristics of the community development models presented in this book include a bottom-up, grassroots emphasis; a strengths paradigm that taps into recognized capacities and assets of individuals, families, organizations, and communities; and a recognition of the interconnectedness of systems and the need for collaboration, cooperation, and empowerment.

Global North and Global South

The term *global North* (and, alternatively, North or countries in the North) refers to industrialized, relatively rich countries. The *global South* (and South or countries of the South) refers to the relatively poor countries of the world. Although these terms characterize the enormous gap between rich and poor countries in an increasingly interdependent world, they are merely descriptive. It is important to note that some countries north of the equator are relatively poor (India and Pakistan, for example) and some countries south of the equator are relatively rich (for example, Australia and New Zealand). Moreover, every country in the North has people living in poverty, and every country in the South has people who are very wealthy (Shuman, 1994). These terms are nonetheless preferable to those such as the *Third World* and the *Developing World,* which are used to contrast poorer, nonindustrialized countries with the *First World* of Western industrialized countries and the *Second World* of the former Soviet Union and its satellites. Many believe such terms to be not only inaccurate since the collapse of the Soviet Union in 1991 but condescending to the world's poorest nations.

The World Bank (1995) uses data on per capita gross national product (GNP) to divide the world into three sectors: high, middle, and low income. According to World Bank figures, 24 countries (including the United States, Switzerland, and Japan), with 15 percent of the world's population, are in the high-income category; 63 countries, with 29 percent of the world's people, are middle income (the Philippines, Romania, and Iran are in this group); and 45 countries (including Guatemala, Somalia, and Bangladesh)—with 56 percent of the world's population— are low income (World Bank, 1995, pp. 162–163).

Development Needs in the Global South

An estimated four-fifths of the earth's 5 billion people live in the global South in low- and middle-income countries (Kerschner, 1991), yet this segment of the world's population accounts for only about one-fifth of the world's GNP (United Nations Development Programme [UNDP], 1994). Many in the North view countries of the South almost exclusively in terms of persistent poverty; low standards of living; widespread malnutrition; disease; insufficient medical services; and high levels of illiteracy, unemployment, and hopelessness (Contee, 1987). What many do not know is that some development programs have resulted in spectacular improvements worldwide over a relatively short time. For example, in just 30 years infant mortality per 1,000 births has dropped by almost half, and the average life span even in the poorest regions of the world has been lengthened by 12 years or more. More than 100 million more children are enrolled in primary school than were enrolled just 15 years ago, and, in the 1980s, 1.6 billion additional people had access to safe water (Sivard, 1993; United Nations Children's Fund [UNICEF], 1994). Although these figures illustrate significant development gains, it is still a fact that one person in four in the global South is unable to satisfy such basic needs as adequate nutrition; safe and sufficient water; clean air; proper sanitation; and access to health care, vaccines, family planning, and elementary education (Sivard, 1993; UNDP, 1994).

However, economic progress is clearly not everything, as analyses of social development trends in 124 nations show (Estes, 1984, 1988). The diversity of economic and social progress among nations of the global South proves that the link between a country's economic level and the well-being of its people is not automatic. For example, Vietnam's record for reducing child deaths is considerably better than that of Algeria, where per capita income is approximately seven times higher than that of Vietnam. Sri Lanka and Zimbabwe both have a per capita income of less than $600, but both manage to provide 90 percent of their children with at least four years of primary schooling, whereas Brazil, with a per capita income of almost $3,000 a year, cannot boast half that figure. Many of the world's poorest nations have achieved 80 percent immunization coverage; several richer nations, including regions of the United States, lag behind that rate (UNICEF, 1994). The point is that economic and social programs must be mounted simultaneously or, inevitably, one will hold the other back.

Development Needs in the United States

Although it is generally acknowledged that development is needed in the global South, it is less widely recognized that in many parts of the United States—both urban and rural—poverty and inequities stubbornly persist (Hollister, 1982; Midgley, 1991; Sharkansky, 1975). The United States is economically the richest and militarily the most powerful country in the world, but its socioeconomic standing is only ninth among 140 nations, and its infant mortality rate puts it in 21st place (Sivard, 1993). Serious weaknesses in U.S. social and economic development are evident: The economic resources of a large, poverty-burdened population are increasingly remote from the soaring incomes of the top segment of the population; the system of free public education through the secondary level still somehow leaves half the adult population functionally illiterate; and the most expensive health care system in the world provides no insurance protection at all for 37 million people (Sivard, 1993).

Shared Solutions

Achievements in many parts of the United States and other countries of the North are praiseworthy, but U.S. social workers have much to learn from their colleagues in the global South who have established programs targeted specifically at social and economic development. These workers understand the need for deliberate social intervention that focuses on changing social institutions rather than individuals (Midgley, 1990). There is much that we can learn together about how to address the universal problems of violence, which cross national borders and require shared solutions.

Violence: A Global Affliction

The threat to life by sudden, unpredictable violence—as well as by more insidious, covert violence—is a growing problem for rich and poor countries alike. Threats to personal security come from several sources: social and economic systems (deprivation, lack of access to resources, oppression), the state (physical torture, repression, police brutality, official neglect), other states (war, colonization), other groups of people (ethnic tension, hate crimes, discrimination), and individuals or gangs (homicides, street violence, gang warfare, muggings). The focus of violence also takes several forms: against women (rape, domestic violence), against children (child abuse, neglect), against oppressed populations (hate crimes, genocide), and against self (suicide, substance abuse).

This section offers a reconceptualization of violence that takes into account these many and diverse forms of violence.[1] The reconceptualization seeks to broaden the traditional perspective on violence, and it provides a framework for the discussions of violence in the following chapters.

Violence Conceptualized

Violence is undoubtedly a pervasive phenomenon that creates substantial anxiety, yet we react to it with considerable ambivalence and inconsistency. Traditional social science definitions of violence—which

---

[1]This section ("Violence: A Global Affliction") is adapted from Van Soest, D., & Bryant, S. (1995). Violence reconceptualized for social work: The urban dilemma. *Social Work, 40,* 549–557.

imply intent and address motivation on the part of a perpetrator, exclude self-destructive behaviors, and limit harm to physical injury—are inadequate. Under traditional definitions, some forms of violence go unchallenged, and some are even regarded as legitimate and acceptable. For example, killing by the prison executioner; by the soldier at war; by the police officer; or by an individual in defense of self, family, or property is often considered to be necessary and even honorable, moral, and expected. In short, undeniably destructive behavior is often tolerated or considered legitimate, and objections are reserved for illegitimate violence. In fact, some destructive behaviors are not considered to be a form of violence at all.

If social work is to play an effective role in addressing the global crisis of violence without inadvertently perpetuating it, the nature of violence must be better understood. The organizing framework for this book, then, is a conceptual model that considers the multilevel character of violence and its manifestations within conditions of oppression. This model is based on a synthesis of several theoretical perspectives (Bulhan, 1985; Dasgupta, 1968; Gil, 1990; Keefe & Roberts, 1991; Nagler, 1982; Salmi, 1993).   Def. of Violence

Violence is defined here as any act or situation that injures the health and well-being of others, including direct attacks on a person's physical or psychological integrity, as well as destructive actions that do not necessarily involve a direct relationship between the victim and the institution or person responsible for the harm (Bulhan, 1985; Salmi, 1993). This definition broadens traditional behavioral science perspectives about violence in several ways by

- emphasizing the consequences from the perspective of the victim
- treating all types of violence equally, regardless of whether the perpetrator is an individual, group, institution, or society in general
- permitting examination of the many and various manifestations of violence without excluding socially sanctioned (legitimate) violence, unintended violence, actions causing nonphysical harm, subtle or covert forms of violence, or actions causing long-term consequences

- including any avoidable action that violates a human right in the broadest sense or that prevents the fulfillment of a basic human need (Salmi, 1993).

As this broad definition indicates, violence comes in many forms and its victims and survivors bear indelible, but often unrecognized or disregarded, scars. To understand the complexity of violence as a social phenomenon, several considerations must be addressed: the multilevel nature of violence; the links among the individual, institutional, and structural or cultural levels of violence; and violence in the form of omission, repression, and alienation.

Multilevel nature of violence.   Figure 1-1 illustrates the trilevel nature of violence. At the pinnacle of the pyramid are individually oriented harmful actions against people or property. These actions are what most people think of, and quickly condemn, as violence. Violence at this level is more visible and easier to assess than at other levels because it usually involves direct actions and means and immediate consequences. The perpetrator (and motivations) and the victim (and injuries) are often easily identified.

The individual level of violence, however, is only a small part of the structure. Institutional violence is submerged from view, so that its forms are almost completely invisible. Violence at this level includes harmful actions within social institutions and their organizational units, actions that can obstruct the spontaneous unfolding of human potential. It occurs in institutions such as prisons, governmental bodies, and the military. Such violence is often produced by bureaucratic functionalism or oppressive social policy that is considered to be a necessary means of social control. Because institutional violence may be subtle, indirect, and covert, it is more complex than individual violence and its consequences may be long term.

The foundation of the pyramid holds the normative and ideological roots of violence that undergird and give rise to the institutional and individual levels. Explanations for this structural and cultural level of violence abound, but for whatever reasons it exists, the result is that the structure of social reality, conventional values, and the everyday practice of social relations eventually form a collective way of thinking

Figure 1-1
Social Workers Redefine Violence

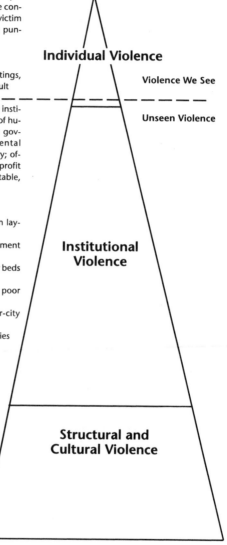

Individual Violence. Harmful actions against people or property; visible, easy to condemn, immediate consequences; perpetrator (and motivations) and victim (and injuries) are easy to identify; considered a punishable crime.

Examples

- murders, rape, gang fights, drive-by shootings, terrorism, spouse abuse, child abuse, assault

Institutional Violence. Harmful actions within institutions that obstruct the spontaneous unfolding of human potential; occurs in bureaucracies such as government agencies, businesses, prisons, mental institutions, welfare systems, schools, the military; often caused by policies considered necessary for profit or control; usually subtle, indirect, covert, regrettable, but not a crime.

Examples

- ✓ leveraged buyout by corporation results in layoffs and reduced wages
- company defaults on pensions and retirement health coverage
- nursing home patients are strapped to their beds because the home lacks sufficient staff
- development assistance is withheld from poor communities and countries
- ✓ banks fail to make loans in certain inner-city neighborhoods
- wars between countries and within countries
- female genital mutilation practices

Structural and Cultural Violence. Harmful actions that result from the way society thinks, conventional values, everyday practice; often sinister, difficult to discern; usually accepted as "normal."

Examples

- avoidable differences between groups within a country/between countries: infant mortality rates, premature death rates, cancer rates, little political representation, few development opportunities
- passively accepting deprivations and inequities such as poverty, racism, sexism
- denigration of minorities, refugees, unfamiliar cultures and countries, ethnic groups, women, gay men and lesbians, people with disabilities
- the easy acceptance of violence or threat of violence as a solution to problems

that becomes part of both individual and societal psyches (Gil, 1990). Williams (1979) described how "value orientations, repeatedly experienced and reformulated by large numbers of persons over extended periods, will eventually become intellectualized as components of a comprehensive world view. . . . A given subset of value orientations may so monopolize attention and legitimacy as to constitute the very context (or framework) within which more particular ideologies and major societal and political issues are defined, discussed and fought over" (p. 45). This comprehensive world view provides the cultural foundation for institutions that, in carrying out their functions, perpetuate the race and gender programming that ensures structural inequality. Change at this level involves especially strong psychological tensions and ambivalence and accentuated polarization between advocates of change and defenders of deeply held values.

The structural and cultural foundation of violence is all the more sinister because it is difficult to grasp (Bulhan, 1985). It manifests itself in passive acceptance of inequalities and deprivations. Seldom are social, economic, and political indicators of inequality (for example, differential infant mortality rates, premature death, lack of political representation, and other avoidable differences between populations or countries) perceived accurately as symptoms of violence. Ultimately, the structural and cultural level reveals itself in an easy acceptance of the threat or use of violence as a form of social control and an appropriate solution to problems. The general public's acquiescence to those who would "look first of all for military solutions to issues which could be solved by other means" indicates the permeation of militaristic values in collective thinking at the structural and cultural level (Giddens, 1985, p. 328). Shachter and Seinfeld (1994) captured the essence of this level of violence in the United States:

> The American culture of violence is reflected in the history, attitudes, belief systems, and coping styles of the population in dealing with conflicts, frustration, and the quest for wealth and power. Historically, violent traditions have made a clear imprint. Recall the genocidal wars against Native Americans by the early settlers; the lawlessness of the American frontier; the violence of slavery; the fratricidal Civil War; the massacres of early union organizers; the long history of violence against racial, ethnic, and political minorities; the violence against women; the romanticizing of the gangsters of the Roaring Twenties;

[handwritten margin note: American Culture's love affair w/ violence; Violence as the cure all of social problems]

and the imperialistic wars against Third World countries. . . . In addition, manifestations of violence on television and film have grown. Violence sells. . . . Furthermore, the United States was also the first country to use atomic weapons on populated areas and has maintained an enormous stockpile of nuclear weapons for more than four decades. (p. 347)

Links among levels. The individual, institutional, and structural and cultural levels of violence are interrelated and cannot be understood apart from one another. The violence of societal institutions and individuals gives expression to the dominant beliefs and values embedded in the structural and cultural foundation. Violence at the individual level is considered a punishable crime—unless it has institutional sanction. Violence on the institutional level, however, takes on its own logic and thrust and becomes what Keefe and Roberts (1991) called "the violence not seen as such" (p. 28).

Oppression is inherent at all three levels. Any ideology at the structural and cultural level that presumes the superiority of one group over another rationalizes institutional violence and depersonalizes personal violence. When oppression continues for generations, the original violence becomes obscured within an entire system of institutional arrangements— the law, education, religion, work relations, the media, economics (Gil, 1990). As a result, at the individual level of violence, "people are not condemned in a neutral, objective, and systematic way, but are dealt with in a discriminatory fashion according to hidden social criteria" (Salmi, 1993, p. 12). For example, African Americans, who constitute 12.5 percent of the U.S. population, account for 54.2 percent of prison admissions and are given longer sentences than white criminals imprisoned for identical crimes (Gavzer, 1995; Gaylin, 1974; Hacker, 1992).

The three levels form an intractable cycle of violence that demonstrates the adage that "violence breeds violence." The structural and cultural foundation of violence supports the institutional level, which in turn can give rise to individual-level violence. Complex risk factors for violent behavior at the individual level—including individual biological and psychosocial traits—obviously have to be figured into the violence equation. However, according to Gil (1990), individual forms of violence, which may appear to be senseless and irrational if studied as isolated occurrences, often reveal their "inner logic as counterviolence to violent societal practices and conditions" (p. 307) when viewed in the context of oppressive history. When people experience unresolved emotional trauma as a result of being victimized by overt or covert violent actions or situations, the long-term destructive effects may include violent, abusive, or self-destructive behaviors. For example, life histories of perpetrators of violence provide evidence of learned and repeated patterns of behavior, such as alcohol and other substance abuse, child abuse, spousal battering and other forms of domestic violence, as well as physical assault with a deadly weapon (California NASW Center, 1994).

The institutional response of the police or military to individual acts of violence is often increased repressive violence, thus completing the cycle of violence shown in Figure 1-2. In highly repressive situations—in which the police deploy tanks, mortars, and machine guns to control civilian populations physically—the distinction between the police and the military disappears; the dominance of militaristic values at the structural and cultural level then perpetuates the cycle of violence (Giddens, 1985).

Types of violence.   Salmi's (1993) description of three types of violence— omission, repression, and alienation—further broadened our under-

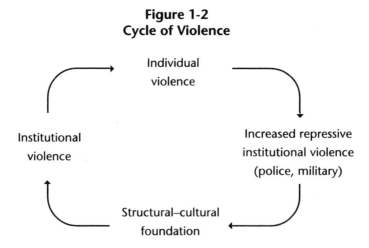

Figure 1-2
Cycle of Violence

Source: Reprinted from Van Soest, D., & Bryant, S. (1995). Violence reconceptualized for social work: The urban dilemma. *Social Work, 40,* 552.

standing of violence. The types overlap in some instances and operate on all three levels—individual, institutional, and structural and cultural.

The violence of omission involves not giving help to people in need or danger. At the individual level, it is the passive behavior of people or groups who refuse or neglect to help someone in need. On the institutional level, it is the passive failure on the part of societal institutions to intervene when people are threatened by harm that is technically avoidable or controllable by society (for example, failing to remedy unhealthy urban conditions, such as poor housing, lack of access to medical care, or exposure to high levels of pollution and toxic waste). On the structural and cultural level, it is conventional thinking that passively accepts inequality and deprivation as normal.

Repressive violence includes infractions of civil, political, economic, and social rights of individuals or groups. Ultimate examples of repressive violence on the individual level are murder, physical assault, and mob violence, which deny the right to life and safety of individuals and entire communities. On the institutional level, examples of repressive violence include capital punishment, torture, infringements of a person's right to equality before the law, and infringements on certain groups' rights to participate democratically in the political life of their area. On the structural and cultural level, conventional thinking related to group superiority provides justification for and gives rise to institutionalized repressive violence.

Alienating violence deprives people of higher rights, such as the right to emotional, cultural, or intellectual growth. Inclusion of this type of violence is based on recognition of the importance of certain nonmaterial human needs such as well-being and self-esteem. On the individual level, an example of alienating violence is denigration of a person's culture or language. "Ethnocide" or cultural oppression occurs at the institutional level; it is a form of alienating violence that affects the cultural identity of a group or community, as when immigrant or refugee children are taught only in a language other than their own and stripped of their cultural traditions. Underlying the individual and institutional levels of alienating violence is the structural and cultural foundation, which consists of a deeply embedded belief in the superiority of one group over another.

Parallel Conditions and Interdependent Causes of Violence in the United States and in the Global South

As the model described previously indicates, the forms of violence addressed throughout this book take a universal perspective. From that perspective, several observations are obvious: Violence can be both legitimate and illegitimate and overt and covert. Individual and domestic forms of violence can be intimately connected with institutional and international violence. Deep, structural inequalities can produce violence, and legitimate violence (that is, force used by established authorities to control people) can provoke illegitimate violence on the part of those harmed and marginalized, inevitably usurping the violence of the legitimate and escalating the destructive cycle of violence.

The examples that follow introduce the forms and levels of violence that are discussed more specifically in other chapters. They illustrate two main themes reiterated throughout: (1) global interdependence, or how problems and issues in the United States affect problems of violence in the global South and vice versa; and (2) comparative insights, which can be gained from exploring similarities and differences of problems in the United States and countries of the global South and which can suggest the best practices for solutions.

Violence of militarism.   Militarism is defined as a system of beliefs and values—inseparable from patriarchal systems—at the structural and cultural level of violence and a way of thinking and acting at the institutional level. Official, organized violence has taken the form of a pervasive military ethos in countries worldwide in this century; whole societies have become militarized (UNDP, 1994). In the United States the development of expensive, sophisticated weapons has meant that technological and military progress have become increasingly intertwined (Sivard, 1993). Weapons exports have become an important factor in the U.S. economy, accounting for an estimated 5 percent of all U.S. exports and supporting several hundred thousand jobs (Hartung, 1994). By 1992 the United States controlled nearly 60 percent of the weapons trade to countries in the global South, and cumulative evidence indicates that arms sales practices of the past 25 years have helped fuel terrorism and war on four continents (Hartung, 1994).

In countries with weakly developed democratic systems, the armed forces have generally been better funded and more organized than other institutions, which puts them in a strong position to direct the political process and subvert democracy (UNDP, 1994). The military currently controls political power in more than half of the nations of the global South; its control is associated with both militarization of the economies and repressive violence against the citizens (Sivard, 1993). At any given time, dozens of military conflicts are taking place in trouble spots around the world. From the end of World War II to 1989, 127 wars—all but two of which occurred in the global South—claimed the lives of 22 million people (Sivard, 1989). These conflicts are increasingly a threat not only to the lives of military personnel but also to civilian populations, who now constitute 90 percent of war casualties (UNDP, 1994). Another legacy of war is the 105–110 million antipersonnel mines that lie in the ground in 62 countries, killing and maiming 26,000 people each year—90 percent of whom are women, children, and noncombatant men—and driving refugees from their homes and farmlands ("Dangerous Ground," 1996; UNDP, 1994).

Violent crime.   For many people in the United States, the greatest source of anxiety since the mid-1980s has been violent crime. Although overall U.S. crime rates have not increased substantially, the United States still has the highest homicide rate of any country in the global North. At current rates, 25,000 citizens are murdered annually, making homicide the 10th leading cause of death in our country (American Psychological Association, 1993). Moreover, the victimization of youth by violent crime has increased significantly within the past decade: homicide is now the most common cause of death for young African American females and males, children can buy handguns on street corners in many communities, the intensity of violence involving children and youths has escalated dramatically, and children are becoming involved in violence at ever younger ages (American Psychological Association, 1993).

Crime and violence are also a concern in the global South. For example, four children are murdered every day in Brazil, where the killing of minors has increased by 40 percent in the past year. In Kenya, 3,300 car thefts were reported in 1993, and in China violent crime and rape are on the rise (UNDP, 1994).

What people in the United States and the global South face in their own communities—more guns and more violence—bears comparison with the unchecked proliferation of small arms worldwide. A huge influx of modern firearms results in higher levels of ethnic, religious, and criminal violence around the globe. The rising curve of human casualties generated by such violence is the same in Los Angeles, Moscow, Bombay, and Mogadishu (Klare, 1994). U.S. lawmakers' lack of response to the growing gun trade is mirrored on international fronts: "U.S. lawmakers have been slow to impose any sort of restrictions on domestic gun sales—and global policymakers are only now beginning to talk about the need for international controls" (Klare, 1994, p. 15).

Violence against women.   Gender violence is widespread throughout the world. Routinely, significant numbers of the world's population are subjected to torture, terrorism, humiliation, mutilation, and murder simply because they are female (Heise, 1989). In all societies physical violence stalks girls and women from cradle to grave. In the United States, every six minutes a woman is raped; worldwide, one woman in every 2,000 is reported to have been raped (Koop, 1989; UNDP, 1994). Statistics from around the world indicate that violence against women in the home is a common problem in most countries, leading to the conclusion "that violence is part of the dynamics of many family situations, with women being murdered, assaulted, sexually abused, threatened, and humiliated within their own homes by [their male partners] . . . and that this does not seem to be considered as unusual or uncommon behavior" (United Nations, 1989, p. 20). In addition, when compared with boys throughout the global South, girls are given much less food, denied access to education and health care, forced into hard labor sooner, denied any kind of economic return on their labor, forced into marriage as young teens, regularly raped throughout their lives, often bought and sold like slaves for prostitution and labor, victimized by genital mutilation, and even killed by sex-selective abortions and female infanticide (Minnesota NASW, 1994). Undoubtedly, there are important connections among gender violence, militarism, and the torture of women (Wetzel, 1993).

Violence against children.   Children, who should be the most protected people in any society, are instead the subject of violence in all societies. In the United States, one in five children is living in poverty, 8 million lack health care coverage, and about 3 million a year are reported to be neglected or physically or sexually abused. Also, the United States—along with the former Czechoslovakia—has the highest incidence of infant death from abuse (UNICEF, 1994). In 1992 nearly 7,000 U.S. children (20 a day) died from gunshot wounds (Carnegie Corporation, 1994; UNDP, 1994; UNICEF, 1994).

In the global South, poverty compels many children to take on heavy work at too young an age, often at great cost to their health (UNDP, 1994). In Brazil more than 200,000 children spend their young lives on the streets, surviving by prostitution and begging and often falling prey to drug abuse, violence, and death (Dimenstein, 1991). The sex tourism industry is growing: There are more than 1 million child prostitutes in Asia alone, and conservative estimates put the combined number of child prostitutes in Thailand, Sri Lanka, and the Philippines at 500,000 (UNDP, 1994).

Ethnic violence.   A large proportion of the world's countries have sizable ethnic populations, many of which face discrimination. In several nations, ethnic tensions are on the rise, often over limited access to opportunities and resources. Interethnic strife takes the form of an increase in reported hate crimes in the United States and ethnic clashes in countries of the global South, particularly where national conflict was exacerbated by cold war rivalry (UNDP, 1994). The results are often brutal. For example, in Sri Lanka more than 14,000 people have died since 1983 in the conflict between the Tamils and the Sinhalese; since 1981 in former Yugoslavia, more than 130,000 people have been killed and more than 40,000 women raped in what has been named "ethnic cleansing"; and in Somalia in 1993, there were up to 10,000 casualties—about two-thirds of them women and children—from clashes between rival factions or with United Nations peacekeepers (UNDP, 1994).

Violence and Development: Making the Connections

"The world can never be at peace unless people have security in their daily lives. Future conflicts may often be within nations rather than between

them—with their origins buried deep in growing socio-economic deprivation and disparities. The search for security in such a milieu lies in development, not in arms" (UNDP, 1994, p. 1). Whatever their causes, the
violence and social disintegration that fill the newspapers daily and engage the energies of social workers in their practices are often accompanied by a silent crisis of underdevelopment, chronic and growing poverty,
and unfulfilled potential. Without understanding that maldevelopment
or distorted development is a major part of the problem—and that development is a necessary ingredient of the solution—it is unlikely that violence prevention or even amelioration can be achieved and sustained. The
connections between various forms of violence and development are undoubtedly complex and multifactorial. The next chapter introduces some
of these links and suggests how a new paradigm—sustainable human
development—might help prevent and reduce violence.

References

American Psychological Association. (1993). *Violence and youth: Psychology's response: Vol. I. Summary report of the American Psychological Association Commission on Violence and Youth*. Washington, DC: Author.

Billups, J. (1994). The social development model as an organizing framework for
social work practice. In R. G. Meinert, T. Pardeck, & P. Sullivan (Eds.), *Issues in
social work: A critical analysis* (pp. 21–37). Westport, CT: Auburn House.

Bulhan, H. A. (1985). *Frantz Fanon and the psychology of oppression*. New York:
Plenum Press.

California NASW Center on Violence, Development, and Trauma. (1994). *Healing
a traumatized community: Lessons from the Atlantic Coast of Nicaragua* (report
submitted to the Violence and Development Project). Sacramento, CA: Author.

Carnegie Corporation. (1994, April). *Starting points: Meeting the needs of our youngest children* (report of the Carnegie Task Force on Meeting the Needs of Young
Children). New York: Author.

Contee, C. E. (1987). *What Americans think: Views on development and U.S.–Third
World relations*. Washington, DC: InterAction and the Overseas Development
Council.

Dangerous ground. (1996, May 13). *Nation, 262*, 5.

Dasgupta, S. (1968). Gandhian concept of nonviolence and its relevance today to
professional social work. *Indian Journal of Social Work, 29*(2), 113–122.

Dimenstein, G. (1991). *Brazil: War on children*. London: Latin America Bureau.

Estes, R. J. (1984). *The social progress of nations.* New York: Praeger.

Estes, R. J. (1988). *Trends in world social development: The social progress of nations, 1970–1987.* New York: Praeger.

Gavzer, B. (1995, August 13). Life behind bars. *Parade Magazine,* pp. 4–7.

Gaylin, W. (1974). *Partial justice.* New York: Alfred A. Knopf.

Giddens, A. (1985). *The nation-state and violence.* Berkeley: University of California Press.

Gil, D. G. (1990). *Unravelling social policy: Theory, analysis, and political action towards social equality.* Cambridge, MA: Schenkman.

Hacker, A. (1992). *Two nations: Black and white, separate, hostile, unequal.* New York: Charles Scribner's Sons.

Harrison, W. D. (1995). Community development. In R. L. Edwards (Ed.-in-Chief), *Encyclopedia of social work* (19th ed., Vol. 1, pp. 555–562). Washington, DC: National Association of Social Workers.

Hartung, W. D. (1994). *And weapons for all.* New York: HarperCollins.

Heise, L. (1989, March–April). Crimes of gender. *World Watch,* pp. 12–21.

Hollister, D. (1982). The knowledge and skill bases of social development. In D. S. Sanders (Ed.), *The developmental perspective in social work* (pp. 31–42). Honolulu: University of Hawaii Press.

Keefe, T., & Roberts, R. E. (1991). *Realizing peace: An introduction to peace studies.* Ames: Iowa State University Press.

Kerschner, H. K. (1991). *A primer on international development.* Washington, DC: American Association for International Aging.

Khinduka, S. K. (1987). Development and peace: The complex nexus. *Social Development Issues, 10*(3), 19–30.

Klare, M. T. (1994, June 13). Armed and dangerous. *In These Times,* pp. 14–19.

Koop, E. (1989). *Violence against women: A global problem.* Presentation by the Surgeon General of the United States, Public Health Service, Washington, DC: U.S. Government Printing Office.

Korten, D. (1981). Social development: Putting people first. In D. Korten & F. B. Alonso (Eds.), *Bureaucracy and the poor: Closing the gap* (pp. 201–221). West Hartford, CT: Kumarian Press.

Lowe, G. R. (1995). Social development. In R. L. Edwards (Ed.-in-Chief), *Encyclopedia of social work* (19th ed., Vol. 3, pp. 2168–2173). Washington, DC: National Association of Social Workers.

McAfee, K. (1991, winter). What is development? *Oxfam America News,* p. 8.

Midgley, J. (1990). International social work: Learning from the Third World. *Social Work, 35,* 295–301.

Midgley, J. (1991). Social development and multicultural social work. *Journal of Multicultural Social Work, 1*(1), 85–100.

Midgley, J. (1993). Ideological roots of social development strategies. *Social Development Issues, 15*(1), 1–14.

Midgley, J. (1994). Defining social development: Historical trends and conceptual formulations. *Social Development Issues, 16*(3), 3–16.

Minnesota NASW Chapter Center on Violence, Development, and Family Structure. (1994). *Analysis of the linkages between violence and development/underdevelopment within the context of family structure* (report submitted to the Violence and Development Project). St. Paul, MN: Author.

Nagler, M. N. (1982). *America without violence: Why violence persists and how you can stop it.* Covelo, CA: Island Press.

Paiva, F. J. (1982). The dynamics of social development and social work. In D. S. Sanders (Ed.), *The developmental perspective in social work* (pp. 1–11). Honolulu: University of Hawaii Press.

Pandey, R. (1981). Strategies for social development. In J. F. Jones & R. Pandey (Eds.), *Social development: Conceptual, methodological, and policy issues* (pp. 33–49). New York: St. Martin's Press.

Pantoja, A., & Perry, W. (1995). Community development and restoration: A perspective. In F. G. Rivera & J. L. Erlich (Eds.), *Community organizing in a diverse society* (pp. 217–242). Needham Heights, MA: Allyn & Bacon.

Rivera, F. G., & Erlich, J. L. (Eds.). (1995). *Community organizing in a diverse society.* Needham Heights, MA: Allyn & Bacon.

Salmi, J. (1993). *Violence and democratic society.* London: Zed Books.

Sanders, D. S. (Ed.). (1982). *The developmental perspective in social work.* Honolulu: University of Hawaii Press.

Shachter, B., & Seinfeld, J. (1994). Personal violence and the culture of violence. *Social Work, 39,* 347–350.

Sharkansky, I. (1975). *The United States: A study of a developing country.* New York: David McKay.

Shuman, M. (1994). *Towards a global village: International community development initiatives.* Boulder, CO: Pluto Press.

Sivard, R. L. (1989). *World military and social expenditures 1989.* Washington, DC: World Priorities.

Sivard, R. L. (1993). *World military and social expenditures 1993.* Washington, DC: World Priorities.

United Nations. (1989). *Violence against women in the family.* New York: Author.

United Nations Children's Fund (UNICEF). (1994). *The progress of nations 1994.* New York: United Nations.

United Nations Development Programme (UNDP). (1994). *Human development report 1994.* New York: Oxford University Press.

Van Soest, D., & Bryant, S. (1995). Violence reconceptualized for social work: The urban dilemma. *Social Work, 40,* 549–557.

Wetzel, J. W. (1993). *The world of women: In pursuit of human rights.* New York: New York University Press.

Williams, R. M., Jr. (1979). Change and stability in values and value systems: A sociological perspective. In M. Rokeach (Ed.), *Understanding human values: Individual and societal* (pp. 15–46). New York: Free Press.

World Bank. (1995). *World development report 1995* (pp. 162–163, table 1). New York: Oxford University Press.

Chapter 2

Violence and Development: Understanding the Connections

Violence impedes development. It is inevitable that development is impeded when, for example, national military expenditures exceed public expenditures for education, as was the case in the United States and in 34 countries of the global South in 1993 (Sivard, 1993). Global military spending in 1994, despite the end of the cold war, equaled the combined income of half of humanity (United Nations Development Programme [UNDP], 1994). The poorest billion people in the world, who subsist on a tiny fraction (1.6 percent) of the income commanded by the richest billion, bear the brunt of inadequate spending for development. It is clear that in a world where there are so many inessential weapons, people go hungry and children do not live to enjoy their childhoods.

Effects of War and Militarism on Development

During the cold war, the major powers fought their proxy battles on the territory of the global South, precipitating catastrophic wars and leaving a legacy of militarized societies, many of which have used their armed forces to repress their own people (Hartung, 1994; UNDP, 1994). Wars, political instability, and arms spending have profoundly hampered economic growth and poverty alleviation. Spending limited resources on weapons undermines human security, eating up precious resources that could be used for human development. For example, even though the chances of dying from malnutrition and preventable diseases are 33 times greater than the chances of dying in a war caused by external aggression, military expenditures in the global South rose three times as fast as those of the global North between 1960 and 1987; on average, there are about 20 soldiers for every physician (UNDP, 1994). In 1993 countries in the global South spent as much on military power as the world's poorest 2 billion people earned in total income (Sivard, 1993).

Military assistance to the global South during the cold war also helped sustain the arms industry by subsidizing exports and unloading outdated weaponry. In recent years several industrial countries of the North, fearing job losses in defense industries, have increased their subsidies to arms exporters and encouraged them to increase sales to countries of the South. Arms traders sell sophisticated jet fighters or nuclear submarines to countries where millions of people lack the most basic means of survival (Hartung, 1994). The United States leads the list of the top five exporting countries, which sell 86 percent of all conventional weapons sent to developing countries; two-thirds of the arms these countries sell go to 10 countries of the South—among them some of the poorest in the world, such as Afghanistan, India, and Pakistan. Arms dealers continue to ship weapons to potential trouble spots, thus fanning the flames of conflict (UNDP, 1994). Not only have the weapons wrought havoc within the buying countries, but they have also sometimes been turned against soldiers from the supplying nations, as in recent conflicts involving Iraq and Somalia (Hartung, 1994). Military bases, like military assistance, have contributed to the militarization of the global South and distorted social and economic development (UNDP, 1994).

Because the world is more interconnected than ever before, wars anywhere—within countries or between countries—impose global costs on development. Shuman and Harvey (1993) offered six reasons why no country has the luxury of indifference to other nations' wars: (1) wars disrupt global trade and investment activities; (2) wars sever international transportation and communications links; (3) wars cause environmental damage that crosses national boundaries; (4) wars force people to flee to nations thousands of miles away (34 million people, according to United Nations estimates, have been displaced by current wars and civil strife, and half of them have crossed one or more international borders); (5) wars waste precious time, energy, and resources that nations need to advance development; and (6) wars give neighboring nations an incentive to acquire more armaments, which in turn causes more wars, thus ensuring the continuation of the cycle of violence.

The effects of wars and militarism are far reaching, impeding social development in the United States as well as in the countries most directly affected. Increased military spending in the United States during the1980s paralleled the draining of resources from human services programs, resulting in a widening gap between the haves and have-nots and increased social problems in underdeveloped regions of the country (Iatridis, 1988; Korotkin, 1985). Although the cold war has ended, the U.S. Congress and the administration continue to seek billions of dollars for investment in new weapons each year; in 1996 the administration reportedly proposed more than $73 billion for new weapons for 1997, more than any other country spends on its entire military budget ("Bravehearts," 1996). Meanwhile, already threadbare domestic programs continue to be under budget-cutting attack. The result? low-birthweight babies, children without child care, children who cannot read or write, schools without textbooks, and water that is unsafe to drink, among other problems.

Obstructed Development through Effects on Children and Families

Wars, conflicts, and other forms of violence have devastating effects on children and families and retard progress in countries of both the global North and the global South. In many U.S. cities, families are raising children in what has been described as "inner-city war zones." Even very young children experience extreme violence (assaults, homicides, and rapes) and everyday aggression (shoving, punching, and kicking) as both victims and witnesses (Carnegie Corporation, 1994). In one survey, 47 percent of mothers reported that their children had heard gunshots in their neighborhood, and one in 10 of these young children had witnessed a knifing or shooting before the age of six. Half of the violence occurred at home and half in the streets (Taylor, Zuckerman, Harik, & Groves, 1994).

Repeated exposure to violence is a threat to children's healthy physical, intellectual, and emotional development. Children who are exposed to violence often have difficulty sleeping and show increased anxiety and fearfulness. Young children withdraw, become depressed, and have difficulty paying attention. Parents' ability to provide a safe, reassuring environment is diminished when their children must play below the windowsill or sleep in a bathtub to avoid random bullets or when everyone knows a neighbor's child who was killed or who is a gang member. Parents often are so traumatized that they lose confidence and find it difficult to be emotionally responsive to their children, further impeding normal human development (Carnegie Corporation, 1994).

In situations of war, conflict, and other chronic violence, families of the global South also experience fear that thwarts normal life. Women and children—who are often the victims of abduction, rape, and physical abuse—are the most vulnerable. Orphaned and unaccompanied children often become children of the streets, without care or nurturing from adults or local organizations.

Even when wars end, violence might not. Ex-combatants must be demobilized and reintegrated into society. Their transition to civilian life and reintegration into home communities are critical to peace processes, conflict prevention, and economic and social development. This transition is especially critical for the child soldiers in the global South, who are triply handicapped by separation from their families, schools, and the environment in which normal children grow up; by the distorted values they receive through military training; and by traumatic experiences encountered during war (InterAction, 1994b).

Conditions of violence, poverty, and war—wherever they may be found—undermine the development of children, families, communities, and societies. Economists refer to a nation's people as its *human capital*, a term that encompasses our collective ideas, labor, knowledge, and problem-solving skills. The sum of human capital largely determines a nation's economic and social progress. The effects of poverty and violence on the development of a nation's human capital are described in a report on the needs of young children: "It is not just the families and their children who pay the price, but the nation as a whole. Parents pay the price in anxiety, in lost wages, in missed opportunities. Children pay in poor health, in delayed development, in a clouded future. And the nation pays twice—now, in reduced productivity and increased social disruption, and in the future in a workforce unequal to the demands of the twenty-first century" (Carnegie Corporation, 1994, p. 22).

Effects of Lack of Development Opportunities on Violence

Even though the connections are not widely understood, there is no question that poverty and environmental debasement result in economic decline, which is often followed by political instability and violence. When more people must share fewer resources, peaceful communities can become ethnic battlegrounds. In recent years several nations in the global South, as well as communities in the United States, have disintegrated. Threats to survival can materialize on several fronts—ethnic, religious, and political—but the underlying cause can frequently be traced to the lack of socioeconomic progress and the limited participation of people in development programs (UNDP, 1994). If the basis of people's livelihood erodes—access to water in parts of central Asia and in the Arab states, for example—political conflict can result (UNDP, 1994). The violence can also be turned against self in the form of despair, suicide, and substance abuse. Dom Helder Camara, Archbishop of Olinda and Recife in Brazil, eloquently expressed the connection between underdevelopment and violence in human terms: "Those who cannot earn bread for their families, those who must sleep on an empty stomach, those forced to listen to their children crying with hunger either turn to extremism and violence or lapse into fear, cowardice, silence. When shall we have the courage to see that at the bottom of all relations between rich and poor there is a problem of justice?" (Costain, 1994, p. 2).

Maldevelopment and Violence

Development does not necessarily go hand in hand with a decrease in violence, however. Development programs that are not gender sensitive or committed to equity and empowerment may, in fact, lead to violence or increased violence. Such maldevelopment can disempower the majority if it enables a few people in a given country to control most of the wealth, the political system, and the media. The outcome is gross exploitation and violence (Shuman, 1994).

First, failed or restricted human development causes an accumulation of human deprivation: poverty, hunger, disease, or persisting disparities between ethnic communities, between men and women, or between regions. Continued lack of access to power and economic opportunities can then lead to violence, and oppression and injustice can provoke violent protest against authoritarianism (UNDP, 1994). In some cases, frustration over inequality can take the form of religious fundamentalism or even international terrorism. *Violence is not isolated*

Violence related to maldevelopment or distorted development is not limited to isolated countries; it has global ramifications in our increasingly interdependent world. For example, when distorted development of the world economy results in severe inequities among countries, millions of people are driven to leave their homes in search of a better life, whether receiving countries want them or not (UNDP, 1994). Disparities in economic opportunities encourage overconsumption and overproduction in the global North and perpetuate the link between poverty and environment in the global South, which inevitably breeds resentment and fosters migration from poor countries to rich ones (UNDP, 1994). The cycle of violence continues as new arrivals face life as refugees or immigrants and the receiving countries face the social development needs of a new population.

Another global consequence of disparities in economic opportunity: Farmers in countries of the global South who cannot support themselves and their families any other way can be drawn into the production of drugs. Most users of the drugs are in the United States, where consumer spending on narcotics reportedly exceeds the combined gross domestic product of more than 80 countries in the South. Drug trafficking is one of the most corrosive threats to the development of individuals, communities, and society (UNDP, 1994).

Shared Solutions: Reducing Violence through Sustainable Human Development

"Behind the blaring headlines of the world's many conflicts and emergencies, there lies a silent crisis—a crisis of underdevelopment, of global poverty, of ever-mounting population pressures, of thoughtless degradation of the environment. This is not a crisis that will respond to emergency relief. Or to fitful policy intervention. It requires a long,

quiet process of sustainable human development" (UNDP, 1994, p. iii).
⌈A basic premise of this book is that the solution to problems of violence lies in development, not in weapons, and furthermore, that it is
more humane and cost efficient to meet threats of violence early—
through long-term development—rather than after crises have occurred (UNDP, 1994). Just as short-term humanitarian assistance to
meet immediate crises can never replace long-term development support for countries of the global South, neither can crisis intervention
or punitive measures replace long-term development strategies for violence prevention in the United States.⌋

A new development paradigm—sustainable human development—
provides a powerful strategy for preventing and reducing violence
through the promotion of sound social and economic development
(UNDP, 1994). Sustainable human development is pro-people, pro-
nature, pro-jobs, and pro-women. It is consistent with Korten's (1981)
people-centered model of social development in that it makes people
the central focus; regards economic growth as a means and not an end;
not only generates economic growth but also distributes its benefits equitably; regenerates the environment rather than destroying it; empowers people instead of marginalizing them; gives priority to poor people,
enlarging their choices and opportunities and providing for their participation in decisions that affect their lives; values human life for itself,
not merely because people can produce material goods; and judges one
person's life to be just as valuable as another's.

Sustainable human development is based on several principles (Bread
for the World, 1995):

- meeting basic human needs for food, clean water, shelter, health
  care, and education
- expanding economic opportunities for people, especially the poor,
  to increase their productivity and earning capacity in ways that
  are environmentally, economically, and socially viable over the
  long term
- protecting the environment by managing natural resources in ways
  that take into account the needs of current and future generations
- promoting democratic participation, especially by poor women and
  men, in economic and political decisions that affect their lives

- encouraging adherence to internationally recognized human rights standards.

Requirements for sustainable human development strategies include (1) meaningful participation, which includes the freedom of people to choose their own leaders and to speak, assemble, publish, and travel so they can become masters of their own destiny; (2) environmental sustainability, which includes maximizing use of renewable resources and minimizing consumption of depletable resources through recycling and simpler lifestyles, as well as eliminating the release of pollutants and toxins into the global environment; (3) equity, which requires redistribution of resources to give the weakest members of society a modicum of control over their future; and (4) demilitarization, which would cut military spending to free up resources for development (Shuman, 1994).

The fourth requirement, demilitarization, involves specific imperatives along with continued reduction in global military spending. The poorest regions of the world also must cut their arms spending and establish a firm link between reduced arms spending and increased social spending (UNDP, 1994). In addition, the major suppliers of arms, including the United States, must phase out their military assistance and their military bases, regulate the shipment of sophisticated arms, and eliminate subsidies to their arms exporters. Foreign assistance also must give the right signals: Rather than reward high military spenders, as happens now, donor countries should reduce allocations of official development assistance if a recipient country insists on spending more on its armies than on the social welfare of its people (UNDP, 1994).

Just as sustainable human development is needed in the global South, it is needed in the United States to address persistent poverty and inequity. In the United States, sustainable human development programs in underdeveloped regions must be accompanied by strategies that remove all guns from communities except those lawfully registered under stringent controls; reduce military forces, military expenditures, and the production of weapons; shun the use of violence as a solution to problems; and meet human needs by focusing on provision of services rather than responding to unmet needs with punishment-oriented measures.

Impoverished communities need assistance for sustainable human development programs both in the United States and in the global South. Although foreign aid and domestic social programs are much criticized, assistance to poor communities and poor countries has resulted in significant progress. Since 1960, for example, development assistance has helped reduce infant mortality rates in the global South by 50 percent, increase life expectancy from 46 years to 63 years, and raise primary school enrollment from 48 percent to 78 percent. In some cases, development achievements in poor countries have surpassed those of richer nations. For example, the immunization rate of children younger than age five in Mexico is 90 percent, whereas in Baltimore, the rate is less than 50 percent (NASW, 1995).

One criticism leveled at assistance is that the United States is spending too much on foreign aid and social welfare programs. A variant is that the United States allocates more of its gross national product to foreign aid than it does to welfare expenditures at home. The reality is that only 1 percent of the federal budget in 1992 went to welfare, and even less went to foreign aid; in fact, the United States ranks last in proportional spending for foreign assistance among the wealthiest 20 countries of the Organization for Economic Cooperation and Development (Kerschner, 1991; Schwenninger, 1996). In 1994, $14 billion went to foreign assistance; of that amount, only 15 percent ($2.1 billion) funded long-term projects to help people in poor countries better their lives. The rest was for military and security aid; food, exports, and other economic aid; and emergency humanitarian assistance (NASW, 1995). Some maintain that U.S. foreign aid has declined so much in both quantity and quality as to be almost irrelevant to the economic development of the global South (Isbister, 1993).

Hundreds of U.S.-based charitable organizations for international development, called private voluntary organizations (PVOs) or nongovernmental organizations (NGOs), supplement official U.S. foreign assistance. PVOs and NGOs receive approximately $4.5 billion per year from individuals and businesses for the support of relief and development efforts in the poorest nations and communities of the world. Some of the better known of these organizations are Save the Children, CARE, Oxfam, and the American Red Cross (NASW, 1995).

⌈An underlying premise of this book is that, because the world is interdependent, people in rich communities and rich countries must accept the responsibility of being helpful to people in poor communities and countries.⌉Rich people in the United States are affected in fundamental ways by poor communities in the United States and by poor countries in the global South, just as poor people are fundamentally affected by those who are rich.

Although most North Americans may not realize it, the global South matters to the United States and to the rest of the world, and it will matter even more in coming decades. The people, problems, and promise of the global South are paralleled by those of underdeveloped communities in the United States: Supporting sustainable human development efforts around the world is an integral part of addressing problems at home. U.S. support for the global South is important for other reasons, too:

- Aid is critical to maintaining our position of world leadership in a positive sense.
- Aid is our best defense against threats to global stability, including rapid population growth, forced migration, and environmental degradation.
- Aid can produce significant benefits for North Americans, including billions of dollars in export growth and tens of thousands of jobs.
- Aid has a proven record of success, including millions of lives saved.
- Aid is the right thing to do. Most North Americans believe the United States has a moral obligation to help the global South (Alliance for a Global Community, 1995).

Why Does the Global South Matter to Social Workers?

Social workers have much to offer to the field of international development. Their interest in countries of the global South and sustainable human development has two important motivations. One is self-interest—the impulse to take care of one's own—as captured in the following quote: "[The global South] matters—not only in its own right, but also in the impact it has on the everyday lives of people who live in the United States. In our increasingly interdependent global community, the seemingly distant nations of [the South] are in fact our neighbors—and 'foreign' aid is really world aid" (Alliance for a Global Community, 1994, p. 1).

A second motivation for social workers' interest in the global South and people-centered development is a moral and ethical imperative to help those most in need—an urge to altruism—as the following statement signifies: "Individuals are entitled to some share of the wealth produced by a society, simply by virtue of being members of that society, and irrespective of any individual contributions made or not made to the production of that wealth" (Joy, 1990, p. 25).

Practical Self-Interest

Social work support for nations of the South is important because the future of the United States is intertwined with that of poor countries. The global South matters to social workers because, when human security is under threat anywhere, it affects people in the United States. The following facts are illustrative:

- Political instability and war arising from disparities in wealth cause immigrants and refugees to flee to the United States, arousing anti-immigrant sentiment, hate crimes, and pressures on social services resources; social work in this country is thereby hampered.
- Because poor farmers in Peru lack any other way to support their families, they grow drug crops; U.S. social workers must struggle here with the effects of drug use.
- Because the wages of the 1 billion people living in absolute poverty in the global South are low and working standards are poor, jobs flow out of the United States to them; social workers must then struggle with the effects of unemployment in the United States.

Reducing poverty and violence in the global South is in our own interest in other concrete ways (Kerschner, 1991). Improving health in the global South saves us money, as illustrated by the successful effort to eradicate smallpox, which saves the United States approximately $300 million a year in vaccines and border checks. The eradication of polio could provide similar savings. Similarly, sustainable human development, conflict mediation, human rights protection, arms control, and other programs could help prevent migration and refugee explosions and reduce the number of wars in which U.S. soldiers are killed and maimed. Moreover, development of the global South could bring economic gain to the United States because people who are healthy and have more income are in a position to buy more of our goods.

Furthermore, the global South matters because we can learn much from successful, low-cost programs that were developed there, often with the help of foreign aid, to combat problems such as infant mortality, environmental pollution, and chronic unemployment. Successful problem-solving techniques used in countries of the global South serve as "lessons without borders" that can be applied in underdeveloped regions of the United States. For example, only 39 percent of inner-city children in the United States were immunized against measles in 1990, yet in Egypt the immunization rate is 90 percent and in many other countries of the global South the rate is at least 80 percent. Such success is attributable in part to the skills of those in the South who propagate the importance of inoculations at the grassroots level. Another success story is oral rehydration therapy (ORT), a lifesaving technique that has saved millions of children in the global South from dying of diarrhea; for the hundreds of children with the disease who are hospitalized in the United States each year, ORT is a practical, low-cost, and painless alternative treatment (InterAction, 1994a, p. 7).

Moral and Ethical Imperative

Countries of the global South matter to social workers because we have a responsibility, as global citizens, to the world community. Curriculum standards for schools of social work, developed and implemented by the Council on Social Work Education (1994), state that effective social work education programs recognize the interdependence of nations and the need for worldwide professional cooperation. Furthermore, the social work values and ethics are based on an ethic of care that requires that there be no distinction between "our" poor and "their" poor—or even between rich and poor (Imre, 1982). Social work values advance a moral and ethical imperative to serve those members of the community most in need of help, with the understanding that the elimination of problems of violence—poverty, crime, and war, for example—depends on changing social systems.

The social justice tradition of social work provides the moral justification for changing the lifestyles of rich nations and communities in such a way that all people share in the world's wealth. There can be no social justice or peace in a world that is one-fourth rich and three-fourths poor, that is half democratic and half authoritarian, and that denies poor nations equal access to global economic opportunities. Consider these facts: The income disparity between the richest 20 percent and the poorest 20 percent of the world's population has doubled during the past three decades, one-fourth of the world's people are unable to meet basic human needs, and the rich nations of the world consume four-fifths of humanity's capital without being obliged to pay for it (UNDP, 1994). The global North has roughly one-fifth of the world's population and four-fifths of its income, and it consumes 70 percent of the world's energy, 75 percent of its metals, and 85 percent of its wood (UNDP, 1994).

Redistributing resources to poor people by improving their health, education, and nutrition is intrinsically important because it enhances their capabilities to lead more fulfilling lives and it has a lasting influence on the future. Social justice values support sustainable human development programs that do not perpetuate current inequities and that do provide equal access to development opportunities now and in the future. Without global social justice, effective development will remain an elusive goal (UNDP, 1994).

What Social Workers Can Offer in the Field of International Development

U.S. social workers are in a unique position to participate in international efforts to promote global security and development (Rosenthal, 1990, 1991; Watson, 1994). They bring several strengths to the work:

- Social workers know how to develop and implement successful interventions for social problems. They are educated to consider a problem at the individual, family, community, organizational, and national levels. There is a growing awareness of the need for comprehensive inclusion of an international perspective as well.

- Social workers understand the connection between a client's well-being and the political, social, and economic context within which the client lives. Social workers have a natural affinity with issues related to underdevelopment, such as the reproductive health of women, literacy (especially for girls), access to credit for women, empowerment of minorities, and the rights of children.
- With rapid urbanization of the global South, social workers' expertise in inner-city development issues is of critical importance.
- Social workers adhere to principles that mirror those of successful development, including confronting the basic unmet needs of people first; listening to people and helping them define their own needs; facilitating the empowerment of people and adhering to the precept of self-determination; promoting leadership skills; and encouraging democratic participation.

What Social Workers Can Do

We as social workers are summoned to a deeper understanding of ourselves and our profession, an understanding that goes beyond an "us versus them" mentality. We are called to value and respect the connectedness of all people, not to perpetuate false dichotomies and artificial separations. Because all of life is interconnected, it is indeed in our own self-interest to promote and support development both at home and abroad. If we want to stop violence, we must work for sustainable human development. We already have many of the necessary skills and perspectives, and the chapters in the rest of this book will provide new ones. Here are some beginning suggestions for focused actions to address problems related to violence and development:

- Learn more about nations of the global South. Use the resources provided in this book as a start, talk with people from the global South who are in the United States, join a study or travel group, and find out all you can about our interdependence with countries of the South.
- Join organizations that are committed to reducing gun violence and militarization. Read their literature and respond to their calls for action in areas such as banning land mines, arms control

legislation, trade restrictions on weapons, gun control in the United States, economic conversion, and diverting military spending by both the global North and the global South to the social needs of people.

- Learn more about U.S. foreign aid. Read a variety of materials (the resources list at the end of the book and the references in this chapter are a good place to start) and support foreign assistance aimed at sustainable human development.

- Become an activist against excessive violence in television and film. Learn how the media and U.S. culture socialize us to use violence as the solution to problems; research conflict resolution strategies as an alternative to violence; and send letters of complaint to television and film-industry executives, your local stations, and commercial sponsors of violent shows.

- If you have children, monitor their television viewing, teach them about people from other countries and cultures, explain to them that the physical aggression they see in the movies is not the smart way to solve problems, and educate them about real-world consequences. Push for conflict resolution and peer mediation groups in your local schools.

- Support the Code of Conduct Campaign, which aims to reduce arms exports to human rights abusers or aggressor nations. The campaign calls for a new policy whereby the United States would not export weapons to a government that abuses human rights, denies democratic rights, attacks its neighbors or its own people, or undermines international efforts to control weapons. For more information, contact the Federation of American Scientists Fund (307 Massachusetts Avenue, SE, Washington, DC 20002).

- Learn what happened at the World Summit for Social Development held in Copenhagen in the spring of 1995, the International Women's conference held in Beijing in fall 1995, and the World Summit on Children in 1995. Become informed about international summits through the United Nations and the media and plan to attend.

- Although world peace may be more of a possibility in this new era than it has been for a long time, do not be lulled into believing that problems of militarism and nuclear threat have disappeared. Social workers can support NASW's Social Workers for Peace and Justice and other groups to demand that national resources be diverted from preparation for war to the support of development programs for people (Hartman, 1994).

References

Alliance for a Global Community. (1994, September). *Connections, 1*(1).

Alliance for a Global Community. (1995). *Connections, 2*(2). (Available from Alliance for a Global Community, 1717 Massachusetts Avenue, NW, Washington, DC 20036)

Bravehearts. (1996, May 13). *Nation, 262,* 4.

Bread for the World. (1995). *Hunger 1995: The causes of hunger.* Washington, DC: Author.

Carnegie Corporation. (1994, April). *Starting points: Meeting the needs of our youngest children* (report of the Carnegie Task Force on Meeting the Needs of Young Children). New York: Author.

Costain, P. (1994). Human rights in the new global community. *Connection to the Americas, 11*(6), 2.

Council on Social Work Education. (1994). *Handbook of accreditation standards and procedures.* Washington, DC: Author.

Hartman, A. (1994). Our global village. In A. Hartman (Ed.), *Reflection and controversy: Essays on social work* (pp. 65–70). Washington, DC: NASW Press.

Hartung, W. D. (1994). *And weapons for all.* New York: HarperCollins.

Iatridis, D. S. (1988). New social deficit: Neoconservatism's policy of social underdevelopment. *Social Work, 33,* 11–15.

Imre, R. W. (1982). *Knowing and caring.* Lanham, MD: University Press of America.

InterAction. (1994a, July 18). AID shares techniques that can help communities in the US. *Monday Developments, 12,* 7.

InterAction. (1994b, July 18). Strategies for families in war zones of Africa. *Monday Developments, 12,* 13.

Isbister, J. (1993). *Promises not kept: The betrayal of social change in the Third World* (2nd ed.). West Hartford, CT: Kumarian Press.

Joy, C. (1990). *Believing is seeing: Attitudes and assumptions that affect learning about development.* New York: National Clearinghouse on Development Education.

Kerschner, H. K. (1991). *A primer on international development.* Washington, DC: American Association for International Aging.

Korotkin, A. (1985, July–August). Impact of military spending on the nation's quality of life. *Social Work, 30,* 369.

Korten, D. (1981). Social development: Putting people first. In D. Korten & F. B. Alonso (Eds.), *Bureaucracy and the poor: Closing the gap* (pp. 201–221). West Hartford, CT: Kumarian Press.

National Association of Social Workers (NASW). (1995). *Stop violence, promote development.* Washington, DC: Violence and Development Project, Peace and International Affairs Program, NASW.

Rosenthal, B. (1990). U.S. social workers' interest in working in the developing world. *International Social Work, 33,* 225–232.

Rosenthal, B. (1991). Social workers' interest in international practice in the developing world: A multivariate analysis. *Social Work, 36,* 248–252.

Schwenninger, S. R. (1996, May 13). How to save the world: The case for a global flat tax. *Nation, 262,* 16–18.

Shuman, M. (1994). *Towards a global village: International community development initiatives.* Boulder, CO: Pluto Press.

Shuman, M., & Harvey, H. (1993). *Security without war: A post–cold war foreign policy.* Boulder, CO: Westview Press.

Sivard, R. L. (1993). *World military and social expenditures 1993.* Washington, DC: World Priorities.

Taylor, I., Zuckerman, B., Harik, V., & Groves, B. (1994, cited in Carnegie Corporation, 1994, April). Witnessing violence by children and their mothers. *Journal of Developmental and Behavioral Pediatrics.*

United Nations Development Programme (UNDP). (1994). *Human development report 1994.* New York: Oxford University Press.

Watson, D. (1994, April 8). *Social work and foreign assistance?* Comments prepared for the Meeting of the Chapter Violence and Development Project Centers at the Annual Leadership Meeting of the National Association of Social Workers, Washington, DC.

Part 2

Poverty, Violence, and Development

Chapter 3

Poverty as a Form of Violence

> A poverty curtain has descended right across the face of our world, dividing it materially and philosophically into two different worlds, two separate planets, two unequal humanities— one embarrassingly rich and the other desperately poor. (Ul Haq, 1976, p. xv)

Conditions have greatly improved for the world's people since 1950, as measured by indicators such as increased life expectancy, decreased infant mortality, increased educational attainment, and improved nutrition. Yet despite such unprecedented human development, the chasm remains and grows deeper between the wealth of the global North and the poverty of the global South (Isbister, 1993; United Nations Development Programme [UNDP], 1994). Similarly, in the United States the gap is widening between rich and poor—the United States now has the most unequal distribution of income of any country of the global North (United Nations, 1995d). Both in the United States and in the global South, levels of poverty, violence, and intergroup tension are increasing while levels of resources allocated to public service programs are declining.

The poverty faced by poor people in the United States differs in some ways from the mass poverty experienced by people in the global South, but poor people worldwide share this characteristic: Very few North Americans know anything substantial about them. In a survey of 1,200 U.S. voters, for example, 27 percent of the respondents said that foreign aid was the biggest item in the federal budget and 19 percent said it was welfare. In truth, the federal share of welfare costs in 1992 was only 1 percent of the total federal budget and foreign aid constituted less than 1 percent ("Brief News Item," 1995). Nevertheless, the loudest cries for budget cuts in the 1995 U.S. Congress were directed at these two minuscule budget items aimed at helping poor people at home and abroad.

This chapter examines similarities and differences in poverty and inequity in the United States and in less economically developed countries. It discusses insights drawn from the comparison, focusing particularly on the relationship between poverty and violence. It also looks at the complex links among poverty, violence, and development issues and illustrates the profound, multifarious ways in which global and domestic problems interact.

Poverty and Inequity: A Global Problem

What Is Poverty?

The term *absolute poverty* means the inability to obtain goods and services sufficient to meet socially defined minimum needs. In the most severe conception of absolute poverty, this package of economic goods and services consists of some form of shelter and the minimum caloric intake necessary for sustaining human existence (Schiller, 1989). The official government measure of poverty in the United States is based on a definition that identifies the minimum amount of money required to sustain a family (the 1994 poverty standard for a family of three was $11,821). The World Bank (1992) has established two poverty lines. According to the first, anyone whose annual consumption fell below the equivalent of $350 a year in 1985 was considered poor. The second and more severe line was drawn at $275. By the higher measure, about one-third of the population of the global South is poor; in Africa and India, the figure is closer to one-half. Such absolute approaches to defining poverty are vague and subject to change, depending on who is doing the defining and on geographic location and other variables.

A relative definition of poverty—which makes the subjectivity of the absolute approach more explicit—states that a person is poor when his or her income is significantly less than the average income of the population. This puts the emphasis on inequality of income rather than on absolute needs (Schiller, 1989). Poverty in the relative sense is found in every nation around the globe. In the United States, millions of people live in abject poverty, although their income may be much greater than that of the typical person in Asia or Africa. A homeless family of four living on the sidewalks of Washington, DC, with $5,000 annual income and no other resources is deeply impoverished and constrained in its choices, but in the global South—where the average income per person was $320 in 1988—a family of four with $5,000 is privileged.

The contrast between relative and absolute measures of poverty constitutes a basic policy issue that is beyond the scope of this book. Nor do these two measures exhaust the ways in which the poor might be identified. For example, a holistic definition of poverty would include lack of money, lack of spirit, and lack of hope for a better life—in other words, complete material and spiritual deprivation. Rather than debate diverse definitions and measurements of poverty, this chapter focuses on the conditions of hardship and inequality that envelop poor people; those conditions are considered to be a basic form of violence that harms people in many ways (New York City NASW Center, 1994). Conditions of poverty include lack of access to material goods or social services, disempowerment, social marginalization, and lack of choices (Yarrow, 1995). As Michael Harrington (1962) warned, we should "not allow statistical quibbling to obscure the huge, enormous, and intolerable fact of poverty" (p. 10).

Inequities Abound

The gap between haves and have-nots is increasing nationally and internationally. The inequities are startling. From 1960 to 1991, the share of world income for the richest 20 percent of the global population rose from 70 percent to 85 percent. Over the same period, all but the richest quintile saw their share of world income fall, and the meager share for the poorest quintile declined from 2.3 to 1.4 percent (UNDP, 1994). Figure 3-1 shows the widening gap between rich and poor people worldwide. Another way to look at the extent of global inequity is to consider the actual income accruing to each fifth of the world's population. As shown in Table 3-1, the poorest fifth of the population in 1985 received 1.6 percent of the world's income; the richest fifth received 74.2 percent.

The tremendous difference in wealth between the global North and the global South is demonstrable in countless other ways. For example, the annual income of the United States and Canada is greater than the annual income of all the poor countries of the global South put together. Although wealthy nations have almost tripled their per capita incomes

Figure 3-1
The Widening Gap between Rich People and Poor People

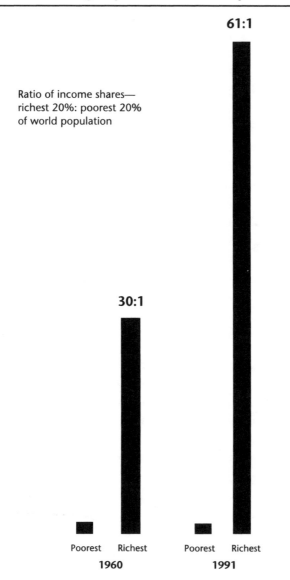

61:1

Ratio of income shares—
richest 20%: poorest 20%
of world population

30:1

| Poorest | Richest | | Poorest | Richest |

1960 | | | **1991**

Source: Adapted with permission from United Nations Development Programme. (1994). *Human development report 1994* (p. 35). New York : Oxford University Press.

Table 3-1
Distribution of the World's Income, by Quintile

Quintile	Millions of U.S. Dollars	Percentage of Total
Poorest fifth	230,396	1.6
Second fifth	316,254	2.2
Third fifth	497,128	3.5
Fourth fifth	2,595,577	18.5
Richest fifth	10,448,828	74.2
World total	**14,088,184**	**100.0**

Source: Reprinted with permission from Isbister, J. (1993). *Promises not kept: The betrayal of social change in the third world* (2nd ed., p. 18). West Hartford, CT: Kumarian Press.

over 1950 levels, per capita income in the poorest countries—where more than three-fourths of the world's population live—has stagnated, ensuring the maintenance of widespread misery (Epstein, Graham, & Nembhard, 1993). Such disparities drive millions of people to migrate to other countries in search of work. At least 35 million people from the global South have taken up residence in the global North in the past three decades, and approximately 1 million join them each year (UNDP, 1994).

Distribution of income in the United States also is becoming increasingly inequitable. In 1987 the average income of families in the top quintile of the U.S. population was nearly 10 times larger than that of the lowest quintile. As Table 3-2 shows, the top fifth got 43.7 percent of all income in the United States; by contrast, the 20 percent of the U.S. population in the lowest quintile got only 4.6 percent of all income (Schiller, 1989). Current figures show a greater disparity: one-fifth of households earn nearly 50 percent of income, the bottom fifth earns 3.6 percent, and half of all U.S. citizens earn less now than they did 10 years ago (Renshaw, 1995). By government measures, 37 million people in the United States currently live in poverty, more than in any year since 1962, and one of four children is now born into poverty. The richest half of 1 percent of families (comprising 500,000 families) was worth $2.5 trillion in 1983; by 1989 their wealth reached $5 trillion (David R. Obey [D-WI] as quoted in "Notes on Budget Balancing," 1996). When all sources of wealth—income, property, investments, and so on—are taken into account, the combined wealth of the top 1 percent of American families is about the same as that of the entire bottom 95 percent (Sklar, 1994).

Table 3-2
U.S. Income Distribution, 1987

Income Quintile	Family Income	Mean Income	Percentage of Total Income
Top fifth	More than 52,910	79,900	43.7
Second fifth	36,600–52,909	44,063	24.1
Third fifth	25,100–36,599	30,900	16.9
Fourth fifth	14,450–25,099	19,746	10.8
Lowest fifth	0–14,449	8,410	4.6
Average		36,568	100.0

Source: Reprinted with permission from Schiller, B. R. (1989). *The economics of poverty and discrimination* (5th ed., p. 8). Englewood Cliffs, NJ: Prentice Hall. Used with the permission of Prentice Hall.

Obviously poverty and inequity are ubiquitous in the world—at least one-fifth of all human beings live in absolute poverty and lack adequate food, clothing, and shelter. About 1.3 billion of these people live in countries of the global South. Most poor people worldwide still live in rural areas, but more and more are moving to the cities in search of jobs and sustenance, thus leading to the increasing urbanization of poverty (United Nations, 1995c).

Poverty is inequitably distributed by gender as well as by location. The "feminization of poverty" is a global reality. Worldwide, women receive less health care than men and thus have higher death rates; the work they perform is more tedious and of lower status than that of men; and they receive less compensation than men for their work, even though they work more hours (Isbister, 1993). Even in the United States, one of the world's richest countries, increasing numbers of women are "sliding inexorably for the first time below the subsistence level" (United Nations, 1995e, p. 1). Women make up 65 percent (23 million) of the poor in the United States. More than half of poor women are white and about one-third are African American (Civil Rights Project, 1995).

Poverty is also inequitably distributed by race; more people of color are poor, proportionately, than white people. Most people living in the global South—where most poor people live—are people of color. In the United States, 15 percent of white children are poor, but rates of poverty are particularly high for ethnic minority groups: 38 percent of Hispanic, 44 percent of Asian and Pacific Island American, 45 percent of African

American, and up to 90 percent of Native American children grow up in poverty.

Poverty and Violence

Social workers are in a unique position to understand that violence takes many forms, from murder in the streets to physical abuse in the home to hunger and homelessness. Most people, however, think of violence only as crime. Although people become concerned and outraged when a child is murdered, with almost no comment 12,000 infants die every year in the United States because of poverty. Horrifyingly, 24,500 people were murdered in the United States in 1992; at the same time, however, 100,000 people died as a result of occupational illnesses and another 100,000 died because they could not afford health care when they needed it (Chasin, 1996).

This book's conceptualization of violence provides a framework for two propositions aimed at revealing the relationship between economic inequity and violence: (1) poverty itself is a form of violence and (2) conditions of poverty give rise to and are linked with other forms of violence in an intractable cycle. Issues of poverty and violence interact in unremitting, multifarious, and widening spirals with dynamic consequences that cannot be neatly captured in linear relationships. The discussion in this section therefore seeks to broaden perspectives, stimulate new ways of thinking, and open doors to further exploration.

Violence Redefined

In chapter 1 violence was defined as any act or situation that injures the health and well-being of others. Accordingly, violence includes actions that do not necessarily involve a direct relationship between the victims and institutions or people responsible for the harm (Bulhan, 1985; Salmi, 1993). The consequences of violence are viewed from the perspective of the victim, and all types of violence are treated equally. This definition of violence, unlike most others, does not exclude either harm that is socially sanctioned or avoidable actions that violate a human right in the broadest sense or that prevent the fulfillment of a basic human need (Salmi, 1993). Violence is seen as a trilevel phenomenon. It occurs at

individual, institutional, and structural and cultural levels, and at all three
levels are three types of violence: (1) omission, or not providing help to
people in need; (2) repression, or infractions of civil, political, economic,
and social rights; and (3) alienation, or depriving people of higher rights
such as emotional, cultural, or intellectual growth (Salmi, 1993).

Poverty as Violence

"Poverty *is* violence—violence against people. Physical, mental, spiritual, psychological, intellectual, emotional, social, legal, political, you-
name-it violence. It is ugly and angry and everywhere. It, with racism,
[sexism], and war, is our major mental health problem" (Lourie, 1968).
Poverty is easily conceived as a form of violence when its consequences
for its victims are understood. The following discussion illustrates ways
in which poverty conforms to the new violence model. It fits the broadened definition of violence; it is characterized by all three types of violence (omission, repression, and alienation); and it occurs on three interrelated levels (individual, institutional, and structural and cultural).

Poverty fits the new definition of violence.   Conditions of poverty
constitute a situation that injures the health and well-being of others.
Poverty injures those who suffer under its conditions in both the United
States and the global South, although direct links to obvious perpetrators usually cannot be made. How do poor people suffer from poverty?
The violence of poverty and inequity destroys life, not with a single blow
as does physical violence but by blocking the full development of the life
potential of millions of people (Van Soest, 1992). Although the consequences of poverty vary in the global South and in the United States,
and no uniform pattern of consequences is apparent, the effects of poverty are the same for many people.

[Poor people often go hungry and suffer from undernourishment
(insufficient caloric intake) and malnourishment (insufficient protein
and vitamin intake).] As a result, many poor children do not achieve
full physical and mental development. Compared with other children,
they are more vulnerable to disease, they have much higher infant
mortality rates, and their life expectancy is reduced (Isbister, 1993).
Half a billion people each year—mostly women and children—face

starvation (Tessitore & Woolfson, 1992), and 786 million people are chronically undernourished (UNDP, 1994). The two places where hunger has most obviously increased are Africa and the United States (InterAction, 1994). Although food has been more available in recent years than it used to be in Sub-Saharan Africa, 240 million people (about 30 percent of the population) are undernourished. In South Asia, 30 percent of babies are born underweight, a sad indication of inadequate access to food, particularly for women, who are often the last in the household to eat (UNDP, 1994). In addition, poor women often die giving birth: Maternal mortality is about 18 times greater in the global South than elsewhere (UNDP, 1994).

Poverty undermines health; poor people get sick and die from disease at far higher rates than do their better-nourished counterparts. In both the global North and the global South, threats to health security are usually greater for the poorest people, particularly children in rural areas. In the global South the major causes of death are infections and parasitic diseases, which kill 17 million people annually. Most of these deaths are linked to poor nutrition and an unsafe environment, particularly polluted water, which contributes to nearly 1 billion cases of diarrhea a year. In 1990 safe water was available to 85 percent of urban dwellers but to only 62 percent of rural people in the global South (UNDP, 1994).

In the global North poor people, particularly poor people of color, are more exposed to disease. For example, in the United States one-third of white people live in areas polluted by carbon monoxide, but the figure for African American people is nearly 50 percent (UNDP, 1994). The effects of poverty on health among Native American people in the United States are more severe than for any other group. Statistics show that they have the worst health and the highest disease rate of all the major ethnic groups in the United States; their health statistics are comparable to those for many people in the global South. Native American deaths from curable diseases such as tuberculosis, influenza, and dysentery are more than 400 times the national average (Harris, 1992).

Poor people live in inadequate housing under crowded, hazardous conditions. This is particularly true in urban areas, where more and more of the world's population now lives. Every year more than 80 million people move—driven mainly by poverty—from rural areas in the global South to cities; by 2030, an estimated two-thirds of the global South's population will live in urban areas (United Nations, 1995a, 1995c). In an increasingly urban United States, many poor families—60 percent in 1987—live in central cities of metropolitan areas (Schiller, 1989). The shelters that poor people are forced to seek are one of the most visible characteristics of urban poverty. Adequate shelter implies more than a roof over one's head; it means adequate privacy, space, security, lighting, ventilation, and infrastructure at a location that allows access to work and basic facilities. By 1990 at least 600 million people in urban areas of the global South were living under life- and health-threatening conditions. In some cities, more than half of the population lives in slums and squatter settlements (United Nations, 1995c). Bombay, India, is a prototype of urban decay: "One-third of the city's 20 million people are homeless, either living on the streets or in squatters' camps built atop putrid landfills. The clammy air is thick with oily black smoke and industrial poisons. . . . The drinking water is fetid. Last [year], a radioactive leak at the city's nuclear power plant contaminated the drinking water of outlying villages for more than forty-five days" (Friedman, 1996, p. 12).

Poor quality, unsafe housing is characteristic of urban poverty pockets in the United States as well, where the severest shelter problem is caused by homelessness. Nearly a quarter of a million people in New York City—more than 3 percent of the city's population, and more than 8 percent of its African American children—stayed in shelters between 1989 and 1994. In the global South the situation is much worse. For example, more than 25 percent of the people in Calcutta and Mexico City constitute what is sometimes called a "floating population" (UNDP, 1994).

Not surprisingly, poverty conditions often inflict great stress on poor people. Annette Sanchez captured some of the anguish of poverty she experienced in the United States in these words: "Ask us what it's like to try and survive on $488 a month plus $230 in food stamps for a family of four. Out of that, I spend $100 on child care and $50 on transportation. Could you survive on that? . . . Could you survive on $338 a month [plus food stamps] for you and your child? You need to know that we're dying out there!" (Shepherd, 1994).

The consequences of poverty for children are particularly cruel. World-wide each year, 13 million children under the age of five die from easily preventable diseases and malnutrition; nearly 200 million children younger than age five—36 percent of all children in this age group—are moderately to severely malnourished, with 69 million severely malnourished; 130 million children, almost two-thirds of them girls, lack access to primary education; increasing numbers of children—estimated at 200 million—work for their own and their families' survival, often in dangerous and exploitative conditions (United Nations, 1995b).

Poverty has severe consequences for children and families in the United States, too. According to the Children's Defense Fund (1996), 21.8 percent, or 15.3 million, of the children in the United States live in poverty. The overall poverty rate for children in many urban areas is higher than 35 percent; for African American children, the figure is more than 50 percent. Ten million children have no health insurance, and 31 percent of young families work at or below poverty-level pay. Moreover, among the 15 most industrialized countries of the global North, the United States ranks highest in infant mortality and lowest in health care coverage and preschool and day care attendance.

According to Sherman (1994), poverty threatens good nutrition and healthful housing conditions; directly limits children's resources for learning both at home and at school; strains the capacity of parents to provide warmth, guidance, and steady discipline for their children by heightening parental stress and depression; restricts poor children to noisy, polluted, crime-infested neighborhoods; influences child health directly by making it difficult for families to afford health services and supplies; affects opportunities for play, physical exercise, and healthy socializing; and hampers access to good child care, recreational activities, medical care, and other services. All of these effects add up and interact to create a cumulative impact that can be overwhelming. Poverty exposes children to greater risks, and it tips the odds against their survival, growth, and development toward their full potential. According to the Children's Defense Fund, "Across an astonishing range of outcomes—including premature death, stunted growth, physical impairment, injury, learning disability, low educational achievement, school failure, abuse and neglect, extreme behavioral problems, and delinquency—poor children fare worse than children who grow up in families that are able to meet their basic needs" (Sherman, 1994, p. 16).

The violence of poverty can be categorized. [As the preceding discussion demonstrates, the slow grind of poverty can be seen as a form of
violence in itself, based on injuries suffered by its victims. That violence
can be put into the three categories described by Salmi (1993): omission, repression, and alienation. Each type has several dimensions that
relate to the perpetrator of harm: interpersonal—a person or small group
doing harm to others; intrapersonal—a person doing harm to self; and
collective—an organized group or an unorganized mob doing harm to
others. The categories of violence, and the perpetrators, may sometimes
overlap, as the following examples show.

[Poverty as violence of *omission* means not providing help to people
in need or danger. For example, a passerby may ignore a homeless person's
request for a sandwich; a hospital emergency department may refuse to
treat a deathly ill person because he or she is destitute; poor people may,
out of a sense of hopelessness and desperation, engage in actions or conditions that harm themselves (alcohol and drug abuse, unsafe sexual
behavior, or sharing of intravenous drug needles, for example); societal
institutions may fail to intervene when people are threatened by harm
that is avoidable (by not providing adequate housing or access to medical care, for example, or by allowing hunger or exposure to high levels of
pollution, toxic waste, or lead paint to continue).

Hunger is a particularly insidious form of violence of omission because the general perception is that the problem of hunger is insolvable.
However, the overall availability of food in the world is not the root of
the problem. There is enough food to offer everyone in the world approximately 2,500 calories a day, which is 200 calories more than the
required minimum. Even in the global South, per capita food production increased by 18 percent on average in the 1980s. Nevertheless,
800 million people go hungry because food is poorly distributed and
because they lack purchasing power (UNDP, 1994).

Failure on the part of societal institutions to provide access to health
care for poor people constitutes a form of organized collective neglect.
(Lack of health care access is an endemic problem in the global South,
where there is approximately one physician for every 7,000 people.)
People in the United States in general are more likely to have access to
health care, but the disparities among groups are sharp and getting

worse: between 1989 and 1992, the number of people in the United States without health insurance increased from 35 million to 39 million (UNDP, 1994).

Failure to provide adequate government support can be viewed as a collective form of neglect of omission. When their incomes are low and insecure, many people look for support from their governments. However, most countries of the global South lack even the most rudimentary forms of social security. In the global North, budgetary problems have unraveled social safety nets. For example, in the United States between 1987 and 1990, the real benefits per pensioner declined by 40 percent (UNDP, 1994). Furthermore, support to poor families under the Aid to Families with Dependent Children (AFDC) program amounts to just 20 percent to 60 percent of poverty-level income in 40 states ("A Million More Poor Kids," 1995).

The failure to alleviate the harmful conditions of poverty is sometimes attributed to lack of resources. In part, however, governments neglect the physical and social needs of people because they give greater priority to military spending. Many nations spend two to three times more on military weapons than they do on meeting the domestic needs of their citizens (UNDP, 1994). The World Commission on Environment and Development (1987) noted that the poorest billion of the world's poorest people could have received $1,000 each from the $900 billion that was spent on military resources worldwide in 1985.

Repressive violence deprives people of their civil, political, economic, and social rights. At its worst, poverty kills, the ultimate violation of civil rights. Poverty deprives people of basic human needs. Conditions of poverty arise from infringements of a person's right to equality before the law (evidenced in the United States, for example, by differential incarceration rates for poor and rich people and African American and white people),[1] as well as infringements of the rights of poor people and people of color to participate democratically in the political life of their area (for example, through restrictive voter registration systems and electoral practices that dilute minority voting strength).

---

[1] Moreover, there are a disproportionate number of African American men on death row, and virtually all death row inmates are poor.

The 1948 Universal Declaration of Human Rights (United Nations, 1988) set out certain rights as basic to people's health and well-being: "Everyone has the right to a standard of living adequate for the health and well-being of himself and his family, including food, clothing, housing and medical care and necessary social services, and the right to security in the event of unemployment, sickness, disability, widowhood, old age or other lack of livelihood in circumstances beyond his control" (article 25). Even the most cursory examination reveals that poverty deprives people of these rights around the globe, and thus can be viewed as a form of repressive violence.

The declaration also states that "everyone has the right to work, to free choice of employment, to just and favorable conditions of work and to protection against unemployment" (article 23). Yet it is clear from all accounts that the right to employment and just work conditions is routinely denied to millions of people around the world. Estimates of global unemployment range from a half billion people to more than 1.2 billion, which equals approximately 20 percent of the world's population (UNDP, 1994; Wolpin, 1986). Another infraction of this right occurs worldwide: Many people are working more and getting paid less. The global shift from manufacturing jobs to jobs in the service sector—where employment is more likely to be temporary or part-time and to be less protected by trade unions—is accompanied by increasing insecurity of incomes. Modest wages have remained stagnant or risen only slowly, and inflation has sharply eroded their value. Consequently, real wages in many parts of the world fell by 20 percent or more (80 percent in Sierra Leone, for example). Women, who typically receive wages 30 percent to 40 percent lower than those of men, are harmed the most (UNDP, 1994). The worst examples of violation of women's rights in this area are the thousands of poor women—many of them young girls—who are sold into sexual slavery in the global South (Friedman, 1996).

Income insecurity has also hit countries in the global North. In the United States real earnings fell by 3 percent throughout the 1980s, with minority ethnic groups being the hardest hit (UNDP, 1994). One of the most troubling trends in the U.S. economy is a sharp increase in the number of people who work full-time but who still cannot, by themselves, lift their families out of poverty; that number rose 50 percent

from 1981 to 1994 (DeParle, 1994). According to the Institute for
Women's Policy Research (IWPR, 1994), the problem for many poor
mothers is not that they do not work but that the work they can get does
not pay enough, last long enough, or provide enough health insurance
to enable them to support their families. IWPR research studies found
that 40 percent of U.S. women who receive welfare over a two-year period also work, so that in many cases welfare functions as a supplement
to wage income.

"Working in the Garment Industry" is a composite of stories that illustrate the kind of deplorable and unjust conditions under which millions of people around the world work.

Working in the Garment Industry

Claudia is 17 years old and Judith is 15 years old. They are among thou-
sands of workers who make clothing for U.S. labels such as The Gap, J. C.
Penney, and Eddie Bauer. During their 14- to 18-hour work days, the girls
are allowed to go to the bathroom only twice. They must get a ticket for each
bathroom visit, which is restricted to five minutes. The girls make a maxi-
mum of about $43 for an 88-hour week. To make them work faster, manag-
ers at the company scream at workers and pipe in loud music.

Pregnant women and union sympathizers are fired or threatened.
Judith's sister was fired for her connection to a union. The workers have no
protections.

Claudia and Judith work in large plants called maquiladoras *(factories*
built, in part, with U.S. funds in free-trade zones with favorable tax and
tariff policies). The number of workers in maquiladoras—*most of them*
young women and girls—exploded in the 1990s; meanwhile, the United
States lost about 35,000 garment industry jobs in a little more than a year.
In addition, sweatshop labor began to be uncovered in the mid-1990s in the
United States, from California to New York.

Consider this statement from article 21 of the Universal Declaration of Human Rights: "Everyone has the right to take part in the government of his country, directly or through freely chosen representatives. Everyone has the right of equal access to public service in his
country" (United Nations, 1988). At the very root of poverty is a question of power. Poor people are poor because they are powerless. Poor
people have traditionally been denied fair access to the halls of power
in both the United States and the global South. Much of the political

frustration and alienation that afflict poor communities can be traced
to lack of political power and inability to elect a fair share of representatives to political office.

Alienating violence deprives people of higher rights, such as the rights
to emotional, cultural, or intellectual growth and to self-esteem. Being
poor too often means low educational achievement—poor children seldom have access to quality education—and school failure. Being poor
for children of color means experiencing a form of ethnocide in school,
where one's cultural identity is denigrated or ignored in textbooks and
in class. Children who are immigrants or refugees are the subject of anti-
immigrant sentiment that would deny them any education at all. When
one is poor and marginalized in societies that value economics over
people, it is difficult to develop and maintain a positive sense of self.
Conditions of poverty by definition deprive people of opportunities for
cultural and intellectual development. When productive work is organized solely on the basis of profitability, the inherent dignity and worth
of each human being go unrecognized, and people without economic
roles are discounted and treated with neglect or contempt (Prigoff, 1996).

Poverty as violence operates at three levels.   The three categories of
poverty as violence—omission, repression, and alienation—operate on
the individual, institutional, and structural and cultural levels shown
in Figure 3-2. The structural and cultural level is the firmly embedded
foundation that contains the normative and ideological roots of poverty and inequality (R. M. Williams, 1979). This submerged level provides the structure of social reality, which includes a collective way of
thinking based on an ideology of race and gender superiority, values
of individualism and economic power, an easy acceptance of the use
and threat of violence as a way to maintain power and control, and
militaristic values that purport that there must be winners and losers
in any conflict.

Property and profit are valued highly at the structural and cultural
level, just as they are in U.S. and multinational systems of corporate
production. Hoff (1996) maintains that several major systemic elements
intertwine at the structural level of the world economy, which ensures
poverty and promotes inequity between the global North and the global
South. For example, international monetary institutions entrap poor

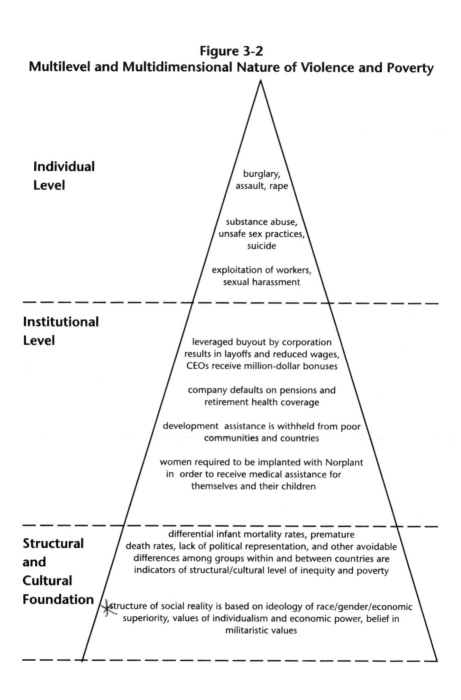

Figure 3-2
Multilevel and Multidimensional Nature of Violence and Poverty

Individual Level

burglary, assault, rape

substance abuse, unsafe sex practices, suicide

exploitation of workers, sexual harassment

Institutional Level

leveraged buyout by corporation results in layoffs and reduced wages, CEOs receive million-dollar bonuses

company defaults on pensions and retirement health coverage

development assistance is withheld from poor communities and countries

women required to be implanted with Norplant in order to receive medical assistance for themselves and their children

Structural and Cultural Foundation

differential infant mortality rates, premature death rates, lack of political representation, and other avoidable differences among groups within and between countries are indicators of structural/cultural level of inequity and poverty

structure of social reality is based on ideology of race/gender/economic superiority, values of individualism and economic power, belief in militaristic values countries in a cycle of lending and debt, producing increased wealth for rich people; free-trade agreements with inherently unjust structures are drawn up and concluded; international trading in weapons is poorly restrained, and the weapons are often used to suppress the economic and political demands of citizens in their own countries; and agriculture is incorporated into the world capitalist system, and thus food is exported to countries of the North for profit while people in the exporting countries starve. Moreover, international institutions lack shared values and standards for upholding human rights.

Violence at the structural and cultural level manifests itself as passive acceptance of inequalities and deprivations. Statements such as "poor people will always be with us" illustrate the point. At this basic level, people with economic roles count; others do not. Cultural beliefs at this level lead naturally to a victim-blaming mentality and to a steadfast confidence in the superiority of Western culture over different cultures. Social, economic, and political indicators of inequality (for example, differential infant mortality rates, premature death rates, lack of political representation, and other avoidable differences among groups within the United States and between the global North and the global South) merely reinforce predominant cultural beliefs in racial, gender, and economic superiority.

Violence at the institutional level also is submerged from view. The harm caused by governmental bodies, schools, the military, welfare bureaucracies, corporations, and other institutions is complex, subtle, indirect, and covert, and its consequences are long term. Unjust social arrangements are themselves a kind of extortion, even violence, as St. Augustine noted long ago (Moch, Rosenthal, & Goldberg, 1995). Yet violence at this level is not universally condemned; it is, in fact, sometimes viewed as a legitimate, necessary form of social control and thus becomes "the violence not seen as such" (Keefe & Roberts, 1991, p. 28).

Examples of poverty as violence at the institutional level include a state welfare bureaucracy that refuses to provide financial assistance for a child born to a mother who was receiving assistance when she became pregnant; a state law that requires women to have birth-control implants as a condition for medical assistance for themselves and their children; English-language-only laws that do not allow immigrant or refugee children to speak their native tongue in schools; a legislative body that eliminates services necessary to sustain people's basic needs or that withholds assistance to or otherwise represses certain groups; corporations that seek to maximize their profits by downsizing and moving production to countries in the global South with no minimum wage laws or adequate working standards; international lending institutions that make their loans contingent on a country's adoption of a structural adjustment program,[2] which calls for a poor country to cut basic social services to its people; and a congressional decision that withholds development assistance from poor communities and countries.

Harmful actions taken by individuals or groups against others or against self constitute the third level of poverty as violence. That is the violence that we see. Although individual-level violence takes various forms, it usually involves direct actions, means, and immediate consequences. The perpetrator's motives and the victim's injuries are more readily apparent and easily assessed than at other levels. For example, when someone out of a sense of superiority or sadism beats up a homeless person, the immediate harm is obvious. The harm a drug abuser does to himself or herself is visible. Some harm at this level may even be considered legitimate or at least understandable, as when a police officer beats a suspect in so-called self-defense.

It is illegitimate violence that is most quickly condemned. However, cultural beliefs and norms at the structural level ensure that people doing harm at the individual level "are not condemned in a neutral, objective, and systematic way, but are dealt with in a discriminatory fashion according to hidden social criteria" (Salmi, 1993, p. 12). For example, stealing committed by a poor person is harshly punished, yet corporate exploitation of cheap refugee labor—which amounts to stealing—is not usually punished as stealing, although it may sometimes be labeled an unfair or unjust business practice.

---

[2]Structural adjustment programs (SAPs) are measures designed by the World Bank and the International Monetary Fund and imposed on almost 90 countries of the global South. They include reduced government spending, privatization of state-run enterprises, currency devaluation, elimination or reduction of subsidies, deregulation and trade liberalization, and incentives to promote production for export. The harm fostered by SAPs is discussed extensively in chapter 4.

A Cycle of Violence

Gandhi spoke of the need to understand two distinct aspects of violence: It can be either physical or passive, with passive violence taking the form of discrimination, oppression, and exploitation. He characterized poverty as the worst form of violence. According to Gandhi, the subtle forms of violence give rise to physical violence (Dasgupta, 1968).

Research supports Gandhi's proposition. Several studies show that the combination of poverty and other variables reflecting inequity, racism, and discrimination are correlated with higher rates of violence (Hawkins, 1986, 1990; McLloyd, 1990; Sampson, 1985; Sampson & Lauritsen, 1994; K. R. Williams, 1984). The greatest predictor of physical violence, in fact, has been found to be poverty (Centerwall, 1984, 1995; Sampson, 1993). The absence of sufficient income by itself, however, is not primarily implicated in violence (Hawkins, 1990). Rather, increased violence may be accounted for by insufficient income within a given geographical context, compounded by inequity and lack of access to resources resulting from discrimination and institutionalized oppression (Eron, Gentry, & Schlegel, 1994). Hawkins (1990) emphasized these links: "Despite some findings to the contrary, a significant correlation has been shown to exist among societal inequality, discrimination, and homicide.... Deprivation, whether relative or absolute, is linked to high rates of homicide. Among all groups in the United States regardless of race, homicide is found disproportionately among the lowest socioeconomic groups" (p. 160).

The American Psychological Association (1993), in a report on youth and violence in the United States, maintained that many social science disciplines have firmly established that poverty and its contextual life circumstances are major determinants of violence. Violence is most prevalent among poor people, regardless of race, and it is very likely that socioeconomic inequality—not race—facilitates higher rates of violence among ethnic minority groups.

In sum, conditions of poverty form an intractable cycle of violence. Figure 3-3 illustrates that the seemingly senseless and irrational forms of violence at the individual level—when viewed in the context of poverty, discrimination, and inequity—reveal their inner logic as a form of

**Figure 3-3
Cycle of Violence and Poverty**

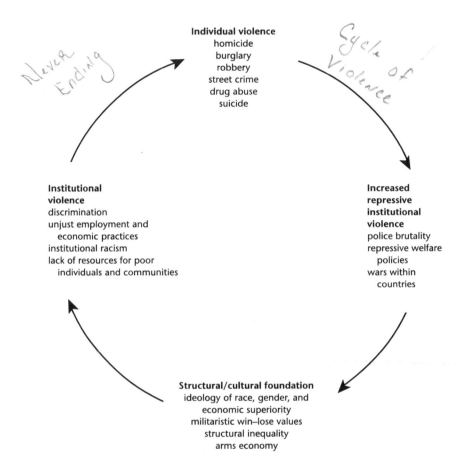

counterviolence to oppressive societal practices and conditions (Gil, 1990). It is within the context of a cycle of severe impoverishment that violence on the individual level can best be understood. Because of chronic unemployment, racism and discrimination, a personal sense of displacement, and cultural conflict, for example, Native American people have the highest rates of suicide, fetal alcohol syndrome, infant mortality, accidental death, and increasing human immunodeficiency virus seroprevalence of any group in the United States (Harris, 1992).

Gandhi pointed out that actions to eliminate passive violence (that is, poverty and other forms of "violence not seen as such") must be taken to rid society of the physical violence that we do see (Dasgupta, 1968; Keefe & Roberts, 1991). Development of individuals and societies, without which peace is unattainable, constitutes such actions. The next chapter explores the links between that development and the promotion of peace.

References

American Psychological Association. (1993). *Violence and youth: Psychology's response: Vol. 1. Summary Report of the Commission on Violence and Youth.* Washington, DC: Author.

Brief news item of interest. (1995, March). *NASW News, 40,* 11.

Bulhan, H. A. (1985). *Frantz Fanon and the psychology of oppression.* New York: Plenum Press.

Centerwall, B. S. (1984). Race, socioeconomic status, and domestic homicide, Atlanta, 1971–72. *American Journal of Public Health, 74,* 813–815.

Centerwall, B. S. (1995). Race, socioeconomic status, and domestic homicide. *Journal of the American Medical Association, 273*(22), 1755–1758.

Chasin, B. H. (1996). *Casualties of capitalism: Violence and inequality in the United States.* New York: Monthly Review Press.

Children's Defense Fund. (1996). *State of America's children 1996.* Washington, DC: Author.

Civil Rights Project. (1995). *America's war on poverty: A discussion and viewer's guide to the PBS series.* Boston: Author.

Dasgupta, S. (1968). Gandhian concept of nonviolence and its relevance today to professional social work. *Indian Journal of Social Work, 29*(2), 113–122.

DeParle, J. (1994, March 31). Sharp increase along the borders of poverty. *New York Times,* p. A18.

Epstein, G., Graham, J., & Nembhard, J. (Eds.) (1993). *Creating a new world economy: Forces of change and plans for action.* Philadelphia: Temple University Press.

Eron, L. D., Gentry, J. H., & Schlegel, P. (1994). *Reason to hope.* Washington, DC: American Psychological Association.

Friedman, R. I. (1996, April 8). India's shame: Sexual slavery and political corruption are leading to an AIDS catastrophe. *Nation, 262,* 11–20.

Gil, D. (1990). *Unravelling social policy: Theory, analysis, and political action towards social equality.* Rochester, VT: Schenkman.

Harrington, M. (1962). *The other America.* New York: Macmillan.

Harris, C. (1992, June). Presentation made at the International Social Work Forums by activists with the American Indian Community House in New York.

Hawkins, D. F. (1986). Devalued lives and racial stereotypes: Ideological barriers to the prevention of family violence among blacks. In R. L. Hampton (Ed.), *Violence in the black family* (pp. 189–205). Lexington, MA: D. C. Heath.

Hawkins, D. F. (1990). Explaining the black homicide rate. *Journal of Interpersonal Violence, 5*(2), 151–163.

Hoff, M. (1996). Poverty, environmental decline, and intergroup violence: An exploration of the linkages. In J. S. Ismael (Ed.), *International social welfare in a changing world* (pp. 163–179). Calgary, Canada: Detselig Press.

Institute for Women's Policy Research (IWPR). (1994). *IWPR program highlights, 1994.* Washington, DC: Author.

InterAction. (1994, October 17). Report says hunger rooted in values breakdown. *Monday Developments, 12,* 1.

Isbister, J. (1993). *Promises not kept: The betrayal of social change in the Third World* (2nd ed.). West Hartford, CT: Kumarian Press.

Keefe, T., & Roberts, R. E. (1991). *Realizing peace: An introduction to peace studies.* Ames: Iowa State University Press.

Lourie, N. V. (1968, September 28). *Poverty is violence.* Speech prepared for the Women's International League for Peace and Freedom, Philadelphia.

McLloyd, V. C. (1990). The impact of economic hardship on black families and children: Psychological distress, parenting, and socioemotional development. *Child Development, 61,* 311–346.

A million more poor kids. (1995, March). *NASW News, 40,* 11.

Moch, M., Rosenthal, B., & Goldberg, T. (1995). [Concept paper for curriculum modules, submitted by the New York City NASW Center on Poverty, Violence, and Development to the Violence and Development Project.]

New York City NASW Center on Poverty, Violence, and Development. (1994). [Report submitted to the Violence and Development Project]. New York: Author.

Notes on budget balancing. (1996, April 8). *Nation, 262*(14), 7.

Prigoff, A. (1996, February 15). *International content in social work education: Global dimensions in policy and practice.* Paper presented at the Annual Meeting of the Council on Social Work Education, Washington, DC.

Renshaw, L. (1995). *The impact of structural adjustment on community life: Undoing development.* Boston: Oxfam America.

Salmi, J. (1993). *Violence and democratic society.* London: Zed Books.

Sampson, R. J. (1985). Neighborhood and crime: The structural determinants of personal victimization. *Journal of Research in Crime and Delinquency, 22,* 7–40.

Sampson, R. J. (1993). The community context of violent crime. In W. J. Wilson (Ed.), *Sociology and the public agency* (pp. 259–268). Newbury Park, CA: Sage.

Sampson, R. J., & Lauritsen, J. (1994). Violent victimization and offending: Individual, situational, and community-level risk factors. In A. T. Reiss, Jr., & J. Roth (Eds.), *Understanding and preventing violence: Social influences* (Vol. 3, pp. 1–114). Washington, DC: National Academy Press.

Schiller, B. R. (1989). *The economics of poverty and discrimination* (5th ed.). Englewood Cliffs, NJ: Prentice Hall.

Shepherd, D. (1994, June–July). We're dying out there! Consumers challenge welfare reformers to action. *Currents, 35.* (Available from the New York City Chapter of the National Association of Social Workers)

Sherman, A. (1994). *Wasting America's future: The Children's Defense Fund report on the costs of child poverty.* Boston: Beacon Press.

Sklar, H. (1994). *Jobs, income, and work: Ruinous trends, urgent alternatives.* Philadelphia: American Friends Service Committee.

Tessitore, J., & Woolfson, S. (Eds.). (1992). *A global agenda: Issues before the 47th General Assembly of the United Nations.* Lanham, MD: University Press of America.

Ul Haq, M. (1976). *The poverty curtain: Choices for the Third World.* New York: Columbia University Press.

United Nations. (1988). *The international bill of human rights* (Fact sheet no. 2). Geneva: Centre for Human Rights, United Nations.

United Nations. (1995a). *Agriculture and social development* (World Summit for Social Development Issue Paper, Institutions and Agrarian Reform Division). New York: United Nations Department of Public Information.

United Nations. (1995b). *Families: The heart of society* (World Summit for Social Development Issue Paper). New York: United Nations Department of Public Information.

United Nations. (1995c). *Shelter, employment and the urban poor* (World Summit for Social Development Issue Paper, United Nations Centre for Human Settlements). New York: United Nations Department of Public Information.

United Nations. (1995d). *Towards full employment.* (World Summit for Social Development Issue Paper, International Labour Organisation). New York: United Nations Department of Public Information.

United Nations. (1995e). *Women: Investing in the future* (World Summit for Social Development Issue Paper, Fourth World Conference on Women). New York: United Nations Department of Public Information.

United Nations Development Programme (UNDP). (1994). *Human development report 1994.* New York: Oxford University Press.

Van Soest, D. (1992). *Incorporating peace and social justice into the social work curriculum.* Washington, DC: National Peace and Social Justice Committee, National Association of Social Workers.

Williams, K. R. (1984). Economic sources of homicide: Reestimating the effects of poverty and inequality. *American Sociological Review, 49,* 283–289.

Williams, R. M., Jr. (1979). Change and stability in values and value systems: A sociological perspective. In M. Rokeach (Ed.), *Understanding human values: Individual and societal* (pp. 15–46). New York: Free Press.

Wolpin, M. D. (1986). *Militarization, internal repression, and social welfare in the Third World.* London: Croom Helm.

World Bank. (1992). *World development report 1992.* New York: Oxford University Press.

World Commission on Environment and Development. (1987). *Our common future.* New York: Oxford University Press.

Yarrow, A. L. (1995). Mandate: Eliminate poverty by 2010. In *IDC conference news: Achieving global human security.* Washington, DC: International Development Conference.

Chapter 4

Poverty, Violence, and Development: Making Connections

Development on a personal level refers to growth and fulfillment of one's potential throughout the life cycle, and development on a societal level is generally defined as meeting basic needs and extending to all the opportunity to fulfill aspirations for a better life. Both personal and societal development are attendant on the development of communities. For authentic development to take place, we must be able to "connect the dots"—that is, see the relationships between development and peace (Boulding, 1995, p. 8). Answers to three questions help clarify these complex relationships and their abstruse patterns of cause and effect: (1) How are poverty, violence, and development linked? (2) How is militarism linked with poverty, violence, and development? (3) How are economic institutions and structures linked with poverty, violence, and development?

Links among Poverty, Violence, and Development

The framework of poverty and violence discussed in previous chapters allows us to identify three links among poverty, violence, and development.

The First Link: Poverty as an Impediment to Individual and Societal Development

Poverty is a condition that damages the physical and psychological integrity of people, even though no direct relationship between its victims and perpetrators may be discernible. As an insidious form of violence, poverty injures its victims by blocking their normal development. It stacks the odds against the normal development of children even before their birth by decreasing their chances of being born healthy and of normal

70

birthweight. At its worst, poverty kills, thereby terminating all development. Low-income children in the United States are two times more likely to die from birth defects, three times more likely to die from all causes combined, four times more likely to die in fires, five times more likely to die from infectious diseases and parasites, and six times more likely to die from other diseases (Edelman, 1994). For those who survive, poverty stunts physical and educational development; erodes resilience and emotional reserves; saps spirits and sense of self; and crushes hopes and devalues aspirations. Time after time—and over time—poverty exposes children to physical, mental, and emotional assault, injury, and indignity (Edelman, 1994).

Societal development is inevitably impeded when individual development is restrained by poverty. As Edelman (1994) succinctly stated, "Poverty steals children's potential and in doing so steals from all of us" (p. xv). For example, according to estimates compiled by the Children's Defense Fund (1996), poverty's toll on the lifetime earnings and economic output of poor children will amount to about $192 billion; the loss of those earnings accrues to society as well for each year that the current high level of child poverty continues in the United States (Sherman, 1994).

The Second Link: Poverty and Other Forms of Violence

Conditions of poverty give rise to other forms of violence that impede development. Evidence was cited earlier that a combination of poverty, inequity, and oppression is correlated with higher rates of violence. As economic hardship increases, so too do parents' signs of stress and depression. In extreme cases, poverty-related distress may trigger or exacerbate child abuse. Although child abuse and neglect exist in families at all income levels in the United States, there is growing agreement that they occur at a higher rate among poor families. Studies show that low-income children suffer more abuse of all types and are more likely to be seriously injured or impaired by abuse than nonpoor children, although such findings may partly reflect underreporting among wealthier families and greater scrutiny of poorer families (Sherman, 1994).

Child abuse and neglect also appear to contribute to juvenile delinquency, crime, and violence in later life. In fact, according to the American

Psychological Association (1993), "the strongest developmental predictor of a child's involvement in violence is a history of previous violence" (p. 17). According to a study of intergenerational violence conducted for the National Institute of Justice, a child who is abused or neglected is 53 percent more likely to be arrested as a juvenile and 38 percent more likely to be arrested as an adult than children who do not suffer such treatment (Sherman, 1994).

Juvenile delinquency has become a major global problem in the 1990s. The rising incidence of youth-perpetrated crime in many countries seems to be precipitated by certain socioeconomic problems often associated with underdevelopment. Among these problems are poverty, inadequate shelter and housing, youth unemployment and underemployment, insufficient social services, and poor education (United Nations, 1995c). These difficulties are particularly destructive because youths constitute the main human resource for societal development; in many sectors they are the key agents for social change and technological innovations (United Nations, 1995c).

Several U.S. studies show that the effects of poverty on adult and youth crime can be almost immediate. Crime and poverty often go hand in hand, with the highest-poverty neighborhoods tending to have the most crime. For example, the poorest part of Washington, DC, has a violent crime rate 13 times higher than the part with the least poverty. In fact, if overall DC crime rates were as low as those in the area with the lowest rate of poverty, violent crime in the nation's capital would drop by 90 percent (Sherman, 1994).

Conditions in poor communities that are unstable are especially ripe for increased violence and crime. When hundreds of thousands of jobs in U.S. cities were demolished as factories moved to other countries where labor was cheaper and profits larger, many people moved out of the inner cities in search of jobs. Communities were destabilized, social networks fractured, and essential institutions closed, leaving those who were left—the poorest of poor people—bereft and disenfranchised. Sampson (1993) found that such communities, which are characterized by poverty and high mobility, have significantly higher rates of violent crime. High crime rates, in turn, discourage the development of communities—institutions and businesses do not want to take the risk of operating in a violent environment.

Poverty is a tremendous threat to social cohesion at the larger societal level also. Evidence about the connection between poverty caused by unemployment and violence is mounting. In 1984 the Joint Economic Committee of the U.S. Congress quantified the historical link between unemployment and economic inequality on the one hand and rising rates of arrest, imprisonment, and violence on the other. Holding other factors constant, a one-tenth increase in unemployment was associated with a significant rise of more than 400,000 arrests a year (Sherman, 1994). Such facts are particularly distressing in light of a report by the International Labour Organisation (1995), which estimated that 30 percent of the global labor force—about 820 million people—were unemployed or underemployed in 1994, in what was called the worst employment crisis since the Great Depression of the 1930s. In industrialized countries, about 35 million workers are without jobs.

Unemployment has also been indicted as a factor underlying political tensions and ethnic violence in several countries (United Nations Development Programme [UNDP], 1994). As Boulding (1995) maintained,

> violence . . . does not spring naturally from ethnic difference. . . . The peoples now struggling through civil wars are not warrior clans; they have lived productively on the land, lived cooperatively with one another, lived histories shaped by strong traditions of independent conflict resolution. Modern states, however, create an economic barrier between mainstream populations— the rich and the educated—and ethnic populations—the poor and the marginalized. The ensuing power struggles generate the sorts of violent civil conflict that many observers attribute to some sort of natural hostility. But the ten thousand societies are not predetermined enemies, and when these peoples have adequate space and autonomy, their basic capacity for respect and problem-solving will flourish. (p. 9)

People in societies are not natural Born Enemies.

The Third Link: Maldevelopment, Poverty, and Violence

Maldevelopment or distorted development thwarts authentic development and creates conditions of poverty that give rise to other forms of violence, thus further impeding individual and societal development. Economic growth and development are not synonymous. Maldevelopment or distorted development refers to growth that dramatically increases income inequalities, diverts resources from social programs such as education and public health, and threatens the survival of people. It is not development. Inequities of enormous magnitude—such as current ones—will confront future generations for as long as distorted development continues (UNDP, 1994).

Development may increase the per capita income of a country, but more than income matters—the use that is made of the income determines whether people have the resources to achieve their full potential. Countries can seriously limit their citizens' choices by spending more on soldiers than on teachers and more on entrenched elitist groups than on marginalized poor people (UNDP, 1994). Thus, although economic growth can help reduce poverty and violence, it cannot serve as the basis for human development. A country's economic growth will enhance the living conditions of poor people only if they get their fair share of the additional income and the added resources are used to finance social services for those who would otherwise be deprived of them. Distorted development that promotes aggregate growth while overlooking the interests of the community often is accompanied by decreased personal security—rising crime rates, continuous uncertainty about how to survive, and increasing numbers of female-headed households and abandoned children.

Distorted development can also hinder rather than help the development of countries. During the 1950s and 1960s, ambitious projects that used Western technology and aid were aimed at modernizing and bringing prosperity to the global South. However, efforts to develop countries based on Western experience ultimately disrupted the lives of many people. For example, the introduction of farm technology in Iran put many laborers out of work and hence caused massive unemployment. Displaced workers and their families therefore migrated to overcrowded cities, which were unable to support them (Rohr, 1989).

Development efforts that value human life only insofar as people can produce profits—the "human capital" approach—"can easily lead to slave labor, forced child labor, and the exploitation of workers by management" (UNDP, 1994, p. 17). Such exploitation of the global South by the North has been exemplified in Africa, which is often considered to be underdeveloped. In reality, as early as the 1400s, Nigeria, Mali, and the Guinea coast were making some of the world's finest fabrics and leathers; Katanga, Zambia, and Sierra Leone produced copper and iron; Benin had a brass and bronze industry; the Amharic culture of Ethiopia produced finely illuminated books and manuscripts; and impressive stone palaces stood in Zimbabwe. Under the political and military force of colonial rule, however, African countries were soon exporting raw materials and importing manufactured goods from Europe at unequal exchange. Arms superiority also allowed Europeans to impose a slave trade that decimated certain parts of Africa, set African leaders against one another in the procurement of slaves, and further retarded the continent's economic development (Parenti, 1989).

This history suggests to some that the global South, rather than being "underdeveloped" or "developing," may in fact be overexploited and maldeveloped by the North in its quest for its own development. According to this perspective, industrial investment in the nations of the South is attractive because of a "relative lack of competition, a vast cheap labor pool, the absence or near absence of environmental and safety regulations and corporate taxes, and the opportunity to market products at monopoly prices" (Parenti, 1989, p. 20). Bolstering this perspective is the fact that from 1970 to 1980, the flow of investment capital from the United States to the South amounted to about $8 billion, while the return flow from the South to the United States in the form of dividends, interest, branch profits, management fees, and royalties was $63.7 billion. Furthermore, researchers maintain that multinational corporations and banks worldwide take as much as $200 billion each year from nations in the South (Parenti, 1989).

"Exploitation in the Global South" illustrates how people can be marginalized and exploited by distorted development and how those in the United States are interconnected with people in nations of the South.

Exploitation in the Global South

The November 1990 issue of Bobbin, *the trade journal of the apparel business, ran an ad featuring a photo of a woman sewing a man's shirt. In bold type the caption read: "Rosa Martinez produces apparel for United States markets on her sewing machine in El Salvador. You can hire her for 57 cents an hour." And then, in smaller type: "Rosa is more than just colorful. She and her coworkers are known for their industriousness, reliability, and quick learning. They make El Salvador one of the best buys." The ad urged U.S. textile companies to "find out more about sourcing in El Salvador."*

It was an invitation for U.S. firms to relocate their production or, in industry double-speak, to "outsource."

Rosa Martinez's pitiful wage and diligent work ethic did not come about because the people of El Salvador like to work long hours for little pay. Readers of Bobbin probably did not need to be reminded that over the previous 10 years the government of El Salvador had brutally repressed trade unionists, priests, and any others who spoke out against the exploitation of workers like Martinez. According to Salvadoran Catholic church sources, more than 5,000 trade unionists had been killed and many more otherwise silenced or run out of the country. During this period the U.S. government had spent $4 billion supporting the government of El Salvador, offering as justification the threat of communism in the region. In August 1991, the Bobbin ran an almost identical advertisement, but this one said Martinez could now be hired for $0.33 an hour. It was an offer that many U.S. garment businesses would find hard to refuse.

In the United States, garment workers averaged $5.77 an hour in 1989 for sewing men's shirts. U.S. garment workers are among the most productive in the world, producing on the average more than four shirts an hour. But productivity is not that much different in El Salvador, Sri Lanka, Bangladesh, or wherever shirts are made. A sewing machine is a sewing machine, and skilled stitchers are about as good whether their names are Martinez or Rahman or Rankin. In Bangladesh, for example, workers average about two and a half shirts an hour; they are paid about what Rosa Martinez gets.

In 1980 there were 1.25 million garment workers in the United States. Nine years later there were barely 1 million: 190,000 jobs had been lost. This was despite the fact that the average wage in the U.S. garment industry, like Rosa Martinez's wage, was not keeping up with inflation. The buying power of the average garment worker's wage in the United States fell 10 percent in just nine years.

Particularly galling to U.S. textile workers is the fact that they have been forced to pay for their own undoing. Although the fortunate few who work full-time take home less than $10,000 a year (well below the poverty line for a family of four), as a group they gave up more than $20 million of their tax dollars to support the repressive government of El Salvador. Their tax dollars paid for the death squads that eliminated leaders of the Salvadoran trade-union movement, crushing Rosa Martinez's hopes for a decent wage. Some of their tax dollars may well have paid for the ad in the Bobbin seeking to lure their employers to the business-friendly environment to the south.

The Amalgamated Clothing and Textile Workers Union in the United States has taken up the cause of people such as Rosa Martinez, defending the rights of trade unionists in Central America and successfully pressuring *the U.S. Congress to cut off financial support to the government of El Salvador. Other unions, churches, environmental groups, and ordinary citizens have done the same.*

Source: Adapted from Bowles, S. (1993). Foreword. In G. Epstein, J. Graham, & J. Nembhard (Eds.), *Creating a new world economy: Forces of change and plans for action* (pp. xv–xx). Philadelphia: Temple University Press. Reprinted by permission of Temple University Press. ©1993 Temple University.

Besides showing development connections between the United States and the global South, the case study illustrates links between economic exploitation and militarism, a topic that is explored in the next section. It also shows that, even though unemployment is a major cause of poverty, employment does not automatically lift a person out of poverty. For example, according to an analysis of Census Bureau data conducted by the National Center for Children in Poverty, a full-time minimum wage job in the United States ($4.25 per hour) pays about $7,440 per year, well below the poverty line of $11,180 for a family of three ("A Million More Poor Kids," 1995).

Distorted development that undermines family and community, makes individuals and countries more vulnerable to the world economic market, violates people's rights, and does not value culture or ethnicity is ultimately a destructive force; when it further impoverishes people, it is a form of violence. Conditions of violence give rise to other forms of violence, which impede development more. In particularly oppressive situations, distorted development results in violent rebellion. Local tribesmen, for example, mounted an insurrection with sticks, spears, and arrows against Freeport-McMoRan, a U.S. multinational corporation that operates the world's largest gold mine and third-largest copper mine in Irian Jaya. The media reported three dead and 15 injured in the uprising. The protesters' statement captures the links among distorted development, poverty, and violence: "We fight because our rights are not recognized, our resources are extracted and destroyed while our lives are taken. You [U.S. executives] and your workers live in luxury on our property. We, who own the rights to the property . . . sleep on rubbish. Therefore, from today, we don't give you the permission for this company and close it" (Yosepha Alomang, tribal spokesperson, as quoted in Cockburn, 1996).

The Links among Militarism and Poverty, Violence, and Development

There are many conceptual as well as practical connections between structural and cultural tenets of militarism (a win–lose posture and a belief that violence is an acceptable solution to problems, for example) and its institutional manifestations (governmental support for military spending and sales of arms, for example). In other words, militaristic ideology at the structural level undergirds and gives rise to institutional policies and programs that accord priority to military expenditures. Exorbitant military spending around the world eats up resources that could be used for social development programs to alleviate suffering and to develop and restore communities. Figure 4-1 illustrates how military spending in the global South undermines human security and consumes resources that could have been used for human development (UNDP, 1994).

Figure 4-1
The Human Cost of Military Spending in Developing Countries

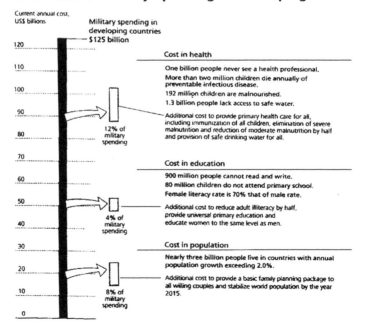

Source: United Nations Development Programme. (1994). *Human development report 1994* (p. 50). New York: Oxford University Press. Used with permission.

Militaristic values are apparent in the United States not only in the priority afforded to arms expenditures but in our national love affair with guns. The U.S. weapons economy is booming, and the links between guns and violence and death both in U.S. inner cities and in poor countries of the global South—major importers of U.S. arms—are both direct and indirect. Edelman (1994) succinctly made the connections:

> We have been preparing for and waging the wrong wars over the last three decades and still are. Between 1979 and 1991, nearly 50,000 American children were killed by guns. And when 1.2 million Americans lost their lives to guns and other violence at home between 1968 and 1991, in a period when 31,000 American soldiers died in wars abroad, does it make sense that we spend $767 million a day, or $23 billion a month, on our defense budget while we ignore needed investments in Head Start, child health, and nutrition? (p. xxv)

Another way to make the connections is to compare countries with low military spending and relatively high outlays for human development with those that put their resources heavily into militarism. For example, compared with Iraq, Myanmar, and Somalia, which spend heavily on arms, Botswana, Costa Rica, and Mauritius have been more successful at defending their national sovereignty and have been more peaceful (UNDP, 1994). Obviously, the armed conflicts of militarized societies around the world seriously undermine progress toward improving human conditions and threaten future development (United Nations, 1995a). Similarly, the easy availability of handguns in U.S. communities seriously undermines the development of those communities.

The Links among Economic Institutions and Structures and Poverty, Violence, and Development

> Never before has the world had the opportunity to adopt an international system built on law, in which the weak and strong are treated equally, and where all have a chance to benefit from an open, market based, global economy. . . . Pushed together by technology and collapse of statist ideologies, the world's economies are now integrated not merely through trade in goods, but also through trade in services, finance and multinational products. (Sachs, 1994, p. 1)

Sachs, a renowned Harvard economist, wrote those words in a celebratory essay marking the anniversary of the Bretton Woods Institutions—the International Monetary Fund (IMF) and the World Bank—whose central task, he argued, was to consolidate the achievement of "an open, market based, global economy." These two multilateral lending institutions were established in 1944 by leaders of England and the United States. For more than 50 years these two institutions have garnered the extraordinary power to determine which countries receive international loans (Danaher, 1994).

An international coalition, called the "50 Years Is Enough Campaign," does not agree with Sachs's glowing appraisal. To the contrary, the coalition denounces IMF and World Bank policies for producing extremely negative effects on the development of countries around the globe. The campaign, which includes more than 135 U.S.-based nongovernmental organizations, seeks to transform the IMF and the World Bank into accountable, participatory institutions that foster sustainable, people-centered development. The following description of structural adjustment programs (SAPs), one policy instituted by the World Bank and the IMF, shows how economic institutions and structures in our global economy are linked with poverty, violence, and development.

What Are Structural Adjustment Programs?

Although most U.S. citizens have never heard of SAPs, poor people in every part of the world are talking about them, and many speak of the ways in which SAPs undermine communities and families and undo the development progress that millions of people have struggled to achieve. SAPs are a series of measures intended to bring about monetary stabilization and structural changes in the economy. Since 1980 the IMF and the World Bank have required almost 90 countries of the global South to implement SAPs to qualify for loans. The programs have directly affected almost 4 billion people (Renshaw, 1995). Under SAPs, which are designed to facilitate repayment of debt, poor countries of the Global South must privatize state enterprises, promote exports, liberalize trade, deregulate the private sector, cut wages, and reduce spending for social welfare services such as health care and education.

Effects of SAPs on Poverty and Inequity

According to Danaher (1994), the consequences of structural adjustment policies have been devastating for the poor majority: "Money that could have been invested in health, education and housing has instead been transferred to wealthy bankers. . . . Infant mortality rates [have] increased, schools and housing [have] deteriorated, unemployment [has] skyrocketed and the general health of the people [has] declined" (p. 2). Danaher used Africa to illustrate: 30 of the 47 governments in Sub-Saharan Africa were pressured into implementing structural adjustment reforms; as early as 1988 the United Nations concluded that those who were severely and adversely affected were the most vulnerable people, especially women, disabled people, and elderly people. Moreover, the programs did not reduce debt burdens: By 1992 Africa's external debt was two and a half times greater than it was in 1980. Narda Melendez, coordinator of Asociacion Andar in Honduras, spoke of the injury to his country:

> What has structural adjustment meant for our people? Greater poverty, greater inflation, and greater unemployment. According to data from the Honduran College of Economists, poverty grew from 68 to 73 percent, over 54 percent of the economically active population is unemployed, and inflation has increased 63.4 percent since 1990. Misery is reflected in the faces of men, children, women, and old people, who must wander through the city in search of food, housing, and work. The World Bank officials who have visited the country must have seen this misery from the moment they disembarked from the plane, since at the airport, as much as in the streets of the city, it is evident that many people subsist only thanks to the few pennies they manage to collect by begging. (Danaher, 1994, p. 151)

SAPs Perpetuate Oppression

It is clear that SAPs have caused suffering for people in the global South (Bello, 1994; Danaher, 1994; George, 1994), but it is not clear that they have had any effect on reducing debt. George (1994) maintained that debtor countries were more in debt in 1990 than they were in 1982, although corporations became more profitable and Southern elites became richer. At the same time, wages and the power of unions were reduced. For many in the South, the imposition of structural adjustment strategies by the IMF and World Bank is reminiscent of the oppression of colonial times:

> Structural adjustment is a policy to continue colonial trade and economic patterns developed during the colonial period, but which the Northern powers want to continue in the post-colonial period. Economically speaking, we [countries in the South] are more dependent on the ex-colonial countries than we ever were. The World Bank and the IMF are playing the role that our ex-colonial masters used to play. (Martin Khor, director of the Third World Network in Malaysia, quoted in Danaher, 1994, p. 28)

The following passage expresses sentiments in Trinidad and Tobago about oppression:

> During the 1980s under structural adjustments, instead of flowing North to South through loans and aid investment, more money flowed from South to North in debt servicing, capital flight, and profits from transnational corporations and the privatization of state-owned companies. In truth and fact, the countries of the South are subsidizing the countries of the North. We are helping to subsidize the United States deficit. (David Abdullah, Oilfield Workers' Trade Union, Trinidad and Tobago, quoted in Danaher, 1994, p. 145)

Violence is inherent in the experience of poor people with SAPs. The two people quoted below come from different countries, but they express a common distress over the violent consequences of SAPs:

> The third world war has already started. It is a silent war. Not, for that reason, any less sinister. This war is tearing down Brazil, Latin America, and practically all the Third World. Instead of soldiers dying, there are children. It is a war over the Third World debt, one which has as its main weapon interest, a weapon more deadly than the atom bomb, more shattering than a laser beam. (Luis Inancio Lula da Silva, head of Brazil's Workers' Party, quoted in Danaher, 1994, p. xiv)

> The rise in vagrancy, the rise in crime, the rise in the prison population, all of those are results of imposed structural adjustment programs. . . . Violence against women increases. Men are being fired in the thousands, and their frustration contributes to this. It is a very unfortunate, natural human response to take out your frustration on somebody who is perceived as weaker. Women and children are bearing the brunt of the frustration of men caused by structural adjustment imposed by agencies external to our society. Women are under a lot of stress. (Professor at the University of the West Indies, St. Augustine campus, quoted in Hodge, 1994, p. 124)

Parallels between the United States and the Global South

The SAPs of the 1980s went hand in hand with policies of the new Republican administration in the United States. When Ronald Reagan came to power in 1980, his agenda was based on an ideology of economic individualism, unfettered private enterprise, and a very limited role for government. He applied that ideology with equal vigor to the global South and to the United States. Reagan set out to discipline the global South, and he used foreign aid policy as his weapon (Bello, 1994); parallel strategies were instituted in the United States (Bell, 1983).

From the perspective of Reaganism, most countries of the global South were economic failures because they had mismanaged their economies through state intervention in the economy; their demands for redistribution of resources, according to this view, were aimed at making up for their own failure to produce wealth. The conclusion of the administration was that "foreign aid [is not only] patently not required for development, it is in actual fact much more likely to obstruct it" (Bauer & Yamey, 1982, p. 57). Similarly, domestic aid for poor people in the United States—welfare programs—was thought to harm them and to exacerbate rather than alleviate the poverty problem (Trattner, 1994). A common perspective was that we tried to do more for poor people and instead produced more poor people (Murray, 1984).

A cornerstone of Reagan administration policy was supply-side economics, which was translated into tax reform that made deep cuts in federal taxes for some taxpayers. The result was a windfall for the rich, the top 1 percent of whom saw their tax share drop by 14 percent, while the bottom 10 percent of the U.S. population saw their taxes rise by 28 percent (Bello, 1994). This upward redistribution of income through tax reform was accompanied by a selective assault on what was considered by the Reagan administration to be the interventionist powers of government related to the New Deal state. By 1985 funds for entitlement programs such as food stamps, employment and training programs, Aid to Families with Dependent Children (AFDC), and social security benefits had been cut by close to $30 billion; by the end of the Reagan–Bush era, welfare benefits (AFDC and food stamps) were down about 40 percent from their levels in the early 1970s (Prowse, 1992). At the same time, the military–industrial complex, designed to roll back global communism, was strengthened; defense spending increased by $35 billion (Harrison & Bluestone, 1988).

Other aspects of the Reagan philosophy included deregulation and attempts to break labor's resistance to corporate policies that would increase profits only at the expense of workers. The success of the assault on organized labor is apparent in wage trends: Between 1979 and 1989 the hourly wages of 80 percent of the U.S. workforce declined, and the median wage fell by nearly 5 percent in real terms. By the end of the 1980s, the top 20 percent of the U.S. population had the largest share of total income ever recorded, and the bottom 60 percent had the lowest share (Bello, 1994). Under the Republican rule, 20 million people in the United States went hungry, and the child poverty rate topped that of any other country of the global North.

> Structural adjustment Republican-style was beginning to give the United States a Third World appearance: rising poverty, widespread homelessness, greater inequality, social polarization. But perhaps it was the condition of infants that most starkly captured the "Third Worldization" of America. The infant mortality rate for African Americans now stands at 17.7 infant deaths per 1,000 live births. This figure compares unfavorably not only to those for most other industrial countries but even to figures for some of the developing countries of the Caribbean, such as Jamaica (17.2 per 1,000), Trinidad (16.3), and Cuba (16). (Bello, 1994, p. 97)

Structural adjustment under the Reagan and Bush administrations triggered severe social stresses and strains, which have been linked with increased violence in both the United States and the global South (Bello, 1994; United Nations, 1995b; Wright & McManus, 1991). Wright and McManus (1991) gave a particularly vivid illustration of an event in Brazil—the global South's biggest debtor—that exemplifies the link between adjustment policies and rising lawlessness: "In 1991, the kidnappers of Francisco Jose Coeho Vierira, a Brazilian businessman, demanded a ransom of thirty-two thousand dollars—in food. When twenty tons of meat, sugar, pasta, beans, rice and milk were left near a Rio shantytown, a line of slum dwellers half a mile long battled for the goods. After fifteen minutes, everything was gone; five people were injured in the melee" (p. 163).

The dismantling of stabilizing social mechanisms in the United States unleashed considerable discontent and disaffection, which were addressed largely through punitive measures. U.S. expenditures on criminal justice increased four times faster than the budget for education and twice as fast as outlays on health and hospitals. The number of people in prison increased threefold between 1970 and 1990; the United States could claim the dubious distinction of imprisoning a larger share of its population than any other nation (Bello, 1994).

Similarly, the response of the global North to growing misery, anger, and strife in the global South was largely punitive in character. Draconian responses began to gain some popular support among Northern elites and, more seriously, among the Northern masses. For example, it became acceptable to propose that famine relief should be withheld from places like the Horn of Africa so that recipients could not reproduce and thus increase the number of starving and diseased people in countries that had exceeded their carrying capacity. If development aid was given, it "should be offered on condition that contraceptives and vasectomies go with the groceries" (Fletcher, 1993, pp. 44–45).

Shared Consequences in an Interdependent World

As shown in this chapter and in the preceding one, the causes and conditions of poverty and other forms of violence interconnect and are interdependent in the United States and in the global South. Danaher (1994) summed up four other ways in which issues in the United States and the global South are interdependent:

1. Keeping wages suppressed in the South causes companies to move jobs from high-wage countries such as the United States and relocate to the global South, thus creating unemployment here while exploiting Southern workers at starvation wages. We would gain from increased exports if Southern workers earned decent pay.

2. Loans from the World Bank and IMF prop up undemocratic and repressive regimes without requiring them to democratize, which foments a spiral of violence and creates refugees, many of whom seek refuge in the United States.

3. Poverty in the global South forces people to migrate in search of jobs and survival for their families; this mass migration of people in search of work in rich countries is often met with racist attacks that debase the entire spectrum of social discourse.

4. There is a built-in contradiction between poverty and sustaining the environment. Countries desperate to pay off their debts pillage their natural resources to gain new income, thus promoting global warming and water pollution, which endanger us all (pp. 186–187).

The next chapter explores how sustainable human development might be used to address these and other issues that concern poverty and other forms of violence.

References

American Psychological Association. (1993). *Violence and youth: Psychology's response: Vol. 1.* Summary report of the Commission on Violence and Youth. Washington, DC: Author.

Bauer, P., & Yamey, B. (1982, summer). Foreign aid: What is at stake? *Public Interest,* p. 57.

Bell, W. (1983). *Contemporary social welfare.* New York: Macmillan.

Bello, W. (1994). *Dark victory: The United States, structural adjustment and global poverty.* London: Pluto Press.

Boulding, E. (1995, February). The many dimensions of peace-building. *Hunger TeachNet, 6*(1), 8–11.

Bowles, S. (1993). Foreword. In G. Epstein, J. Graham, & J. Nembhard (Eds.), *Creating a new world economy: Forces of change and plans for action* (pp. xv–xx). Philadelphia: Temple University Press.

Children's Defense Fund. (1996). *State of America's children 1996.* Washington, DC: Author.

Cockburn, A. (1996, April 8). Beat the devil. *Nation, 262,* 9.

Danaher, K. (Ed.). (1994). *50 years is enough: The case against the World Bank and the International Monetary Fund.* Boston: South End Press.

Edelman, M. W. (1994). Introduction. In A. Sherman (Ed.), *Wasting America's future: The Children's Defense Fund report on the costs of child poverty* (pp. xv–xxix). Boston: Beacon Press.

Fletcher, J. (1993). Chronic famine and the immorality of food aid: A bow to Garrett Hardin. *Focus, 3*(2), pp. 44–45.

George, S. (1994). The debt boomerang. In K. Danaher (Ed.), *50 years is enough: The case against the World Bank and the International Monetary Fund* (pp. 29–34). Boston: South End Press.

Harrison, B., & Bluestone, B. (1988). *The great U-turn.* New York: Basic Books.

Hodge, M. (1994). Women, structured adjustment and empowerment. In K. Danaher (Ed.), *50 years is enough: The case against the World Bank and the International Monetary Fund* (pp. 124–127). Boston: South End Press.

International Labour Organisation (ILO). (1995). *World employment 1995: An ILO report.* Geneva: Author.

A million more poor kids. (1995, March). *NASW News, 40,* 11.

Murray, C. (1984). *Losing ground: American social policy, 1950–1980.* New York: Basic Books.

Parenti, M. (1989). Imperialism causes Third World poverty. In J. Rohr (Ed.), *The Third World: Opposing viewpoints* (pp. 17–25). San Diego: Greenhaven Press.

Prowse, M. (1992, May 8). America's poor are very different. *Financial Times,* p. 12.

Renshaw, L. (1995, April). *The impact of structural adjustment on community life: Undoing development.* Boston: Oxfam America.

Rohr, J. (Ed.). (1989). *The Third World: Opposing viewpoints.* San Diego: Greenhaven Press.

Sachs, J. (1994, October 1). Beyond Bretton Woods—A new blueprint. *The Economist,* pp. 2–4, 27.

Sampson, R. J. (1993). The community context of violent crime. In W. J. Wilson (Ed.), *Sociology and the public agency* (pp. 259–268). Newbury Park, CA: Sage.

Sherman, A. (1994). *Wasting America's future: The Children's Defense Fund report on the costs of child poverty.* Boston: Beacon Press.

Trattner, W. I. (1994). *From poor law to welfare state: A history of social welfare in America.* New York: Free Press.

United Nations. (1995a). *Children are our future* (World Summit for Social Development Issue Paper, UNICEF). New York: United Nations Department of Public Information.

United Nations. (1995b). *Crime goes global* (World Summit for Social Development Issue Paper). New York: United Nations Department of Public Information.

United Nations. (1995c). *Youth: Shaping society's future* (World Summit for Social Development Issue Paper, Social Policy and Development Division, Sub-Programme on Youth). New York: United Nations Department of Public Information.

United Nations Development Programme (UNDP). (1994). *Human development report 1994.* New York: Oxford University Press.

Wright, R., & McManus, D. (1991). *Flashpoints: Promise and peril in a new world.* New York: Alfred A. Knopf.

Chapter 5

Sustainable Human Development: A Way to Reduce Poverty and Related Forms of Violence

> We commit ourselves to the goal of eradicating poverty in the world, through decisive national actions and international cooperation, as a moral, political, and economic imperative of humankind. (Draft Declaration of the World Summit for Social Development, March 6–12, 1995, Copenhagen, Denmark)

Social change is possible, and not just theoretically—much positive change has already occurred in the world as a result of development assistance. In the past 50 years, world income increased seven times in real gross domestic product (GDP), income per person more than tripled in per capita GDP, and health conditions improved more than in all prior human history (United Nations Development Program [UNDP], 1994). Worldwide, life expectancy is up 33 percent, and infant and child death rates have been reduced by 50 percent (Atwood, 1995). Such remarkable human progress gives hope, but much remains to be accomplished. One of the basic challenges facing us now is the more equitable redistribution of human gains.

The global crisis of poverty cannot be resolved unless we first reject the pernicious claim that rising joblessness and homelessness is the fault of poor people, poor women, and poor countries rather than the result of insufficient income and meager opportunity, both of which are attributable to inadequate structures (Long-Scott, 1992). A fundamental premise of this book is that only through social, human, and economic development can poverty and other forms of violence be effectively reduced. Sustainable human development is people-centered development. It is nonexploitative, and it ensures that all people have food, shelter, education, and health care; it also does away with social exclusion and facilitates empowerment.

Three essential strategies that form the core of sustainable human development, as embodied in the Universal Declaration of Human Rights, are presented in this chapter: (1) reducing poverty, (2) creating employment, and (3) increasing citizen participation and social integration (UNDP, 1994). The chapter also explores how communities around the globe are mobilizing themselves to engage in those strategies, the role of nongovernmental organizations in community building, and grassroots economic alternatives.

Poverty Reduction

To reduce poverty is to reduce violence and to ameliorate conditions that seem to give rise to other forms of violence, such as crime. The experience of many countries shows that strategies to reduce poverty must encompass all facets of national and international policy; such strategies must include the following components (UNDP, 1994):

- Basic social services to poor people must be widely distributed. This step is important not only because it enhances people's capabilities to lead more fulfilling lives but also because it has a lasting influence on the future.
- Education must have a central place in development efforts. Everyone has the right to education, according to article 26 of the Universal Declaration of Human Rights (United Nations, 1988); moreover, no lasting progress toward reducing poverty and violence is possible without providing educational opportunities for all (United Nations, 1995a). For example, it has been proved that educated women have fewer children and that those children tend to live longer; statistically, each additional year of a mother's schooling translates into a 5 percent to 10 percent decline in child mortality. Also, many studies verify a link between education and improved production; countries such as South Korea and Malaysia, for example, are now reaping the benefits of heavy investments in raising the overall educational level of their workforces (United Nations, 1995a). Evidence is beginning to accumulate in the United States that prevention programs aimed at encouraging disadvantaged, high-risk youths to finish school may be far more effective than tough prison terms in reducing the crime rate.

- Land and agricultural resources in rural areas must be more equitably distributed.
- Criteria for creditworthiness must be changed, and credit institutions must be decentralized to allow equal access to credit.
- Productive employment opportunities must rapidly expand and a framework must be created to ensure a sustainable livelihood for everyone.
- Poverty reduction strategies must be decentralized to ensure participation of poor people in their design.
- Approaches to economic growth must seek to preserve the world's raw materials and energy and increase people's capacity to use resources in a sustainable manner.

Because women experience poverty differently than men, policy measures to alleviate poverty should take their reality into account. Reducing poverty for women will require creating an environment in which they, in their own right as full citizens of their societies, can exercise greater control over resources. The state and the community must provide social support systems for health, family planning, education, and care of elderly people to relieve the multiple burdens on women (United Nations, 1995d).

Employment Creation

The only meaningful and long-term solution to poverty and other forms of violence is to make decent jobs available to all who seek them (Schiller, 1989). The International Labour Organisation (ILO, 1995) holds that restoring full employment in most parts of the world is feasible, although it is complex and difficult. The ILO maintains that a renewed commitment by all nations to the objective of full employment could facilitate cooperative international action to achieve higher growth in the world economy; in turn, higher growth, coupled with expanded trade and investment flows, would foster worldwide job creation (ILO, 1995).

Basing its recommendations on the experience of several countries, UNDP (1994) proposes that those elements of employment strategy most likely to be fruitful are the following:

- heavy investment in educating, training, and skill development
- creation of a market environment that facilitates new employment opportunities, including fair and stable macroeconomic policies, an equitable legal system, sufficient physical infrastructure, and an adequate system of incentives for private investment
- more equitable distribution of land, credit, and information
- encouragement of labor-intensive employment
- public works programs that enable people to survive when the private market consistently fails to provide sufficient jobs
- targeted interventions or programs to counter discrimination against particular ethnic groups and women
- innovative and flexible working arrangements, such as job sharing.

In addition, it is essential that productive employment for youths be expanded and that effective means be developed to prepare young people for entry into the workforce as competent and responsible workers (United Nations, 1995e). The collapse of the unskilled labor market in the United States during the 1980s and 1990s greatly diminished work opportunities for youths and very likely contributed to increases in criminal activity. Providing job training and job opportunities for youths is a necessary strategy for preventing youth violence.

Social Integration

Conflicts often occur between groups of people who are disenfranchised and powerless and must fight over scarce resources. UNDP (1994) called the following actions essential for avoiding violent social dislocations, particularly conflicts between ethnic groups:

- Ensure that each person enjoys the same basic rights before the law.
- Ensure that ethnic groups are accorded specific legal rights that are upheld in practice, including the right to maintain their own culture.
- Enact firm measures to counter discrimination and apply stiff penalties for violations.
- Ensure that everyone has access to basic educational opportunities that respect diverse cultures and traditions.

- Enact affirmative action measures that favor the most disadvantaged and marginalized groups, including women.
- Decentralize government to bring it closer to the people and promote grassroots organizations and create other avenues for direct participation.

What is needed is meaningful participation of people in underdeveloped communities in the United States and in countries of the global South so they can become masters of their own destiny. This strategy requires fair and equitable participation in the political process of choosing leaders, and it requires that people be free to speak, assemble, publish, and travel. In other words, people must be empowered to define and steer a democratic development process.

Tackling Poverty through Community Mobilization

It is easy to lament over the plight of the poor. . . . But for the poor, despair is a luxury which they can ill afford. And throughout the South, there are seeds of hope. These are sown by citizens' groups. Against all the odds, tenacious people have started small projects—even some big ones. Out of the bankruptcy and poverty of failed international and national development strategies, a new set of organizations have emerged among the poor. (De Silva, 1989, p. ii)

Change and development are taking place in local communities around the world as women's groups, peasant groups, ethnic groups, religious organizations, consumer campaigners, union organizers, and environmental protection societies work to break the poverty trap and interrupt the cycle of violence. People in the South Bronx in New York City, for example—through struggle and determination and against all odds—reclaimed their communities from four decades of "wracking social changes, misguided urban policies and the scourge of drugs" (Breslin, 1995, p. 102).

In many countries of the global South, individuals, families, and communities frequently join forces to cope with poverty. Tellingly, in many parts of Sub-Saharan Africa, the term for being poor is synonymous with lacking kin or friends (United Nations, 1995b). The Green

Belt Movement in Kenya is a particularly poignant example of how the actions of an individual can grow into a community development approach that empowers people to reduce poverty and other forms of violence (Maathai, 1988; Wallace, 1992).

The Green Belt Movement

On June 5, 1977, World Environment Day, 36-year-old Wangari Maathai went into her own backyard and planted seven small trees. She told a U.S. radio audience, "I realized that when you talk about the problems, you tend to disempower people. You tend to make people feel that there is nothing they can do, that they are doomed, that there is no hope. I realized that to break the cycle, one has to start with a positive step, and I thought that planting a tree is very simple, very easy—something positive that anybody can do. . . . We have hunger [but] the answer isn't to give people food, but to plant trees for firewood. . . . Poverty and need have a very close relationship with a degraded environment" (Maathai, 1988, p. 1).

As a member of the National Council of Women of Kenya, Maathai got the farmers, mostly women, to also plant trees. At first she went to Mobil Oil for funding for tree nurseries. Now the funding comes mostly in the form of small checks from women all over the world and from not-for-profit organizations. The nurseries, which grow indigenous trees, are located in rural areas where they provide jobs for local people who then train other local people.

The people not only get the benefit of the trees and make a living; they also take responsibility for their environment and for themselves. As Maathai told the radio audience, "The Green Belt Movement is a movement to empower people, to raise their consciousness, to give them hope, to give them a feeling that they can do something for themselves that does not require much money, does not require much technology or information. The power to change their environment is within them and within their own capacities" (Maathai, 1988, p. 1).

The Green Belt Movement moved into other fields: it began to train local women in nutrition and family planning, and it proceeded to take on other social conditions. Finally, in successfully challenging the construction of a large apartment and business complex in Nairobi that would have destroyed a large urban park, the movement had its first protracted (1989–91) clash with the government and drew international attention.

When the Green Belt Movement took its concern for the environment, for human rights, and for empowerment of poor women and unemployed men to the national scene, clashes with the police and imprisonment of activists accelerated. Finally, in 1992, a group of rural mothers whose sons had been put into prison without trial staged a hunger strike in the same urban park—Uruhu Park—that they had previously saved. They appealed to Wangari Maathai for leadership, and she joined them. Government soldiers attacked the strikers, clubbing Maathai into unconsciousness. She has nearly recovered, and the Green Belt Movement continues.

Empowerment is a key to social change. People who are poor and marginalized at the bottom of society tend to internalize their own oppression; they begin to believe themselves what the dominant culture says about them, that they are inferior and worthless. Those beliefs can be changed through empowerment. Helping illiterate poor people learn to read and write is an effective instrument of empowerment and social transformation. By increasing their awareness of their plight and the reasons for it, poor people can develop a new consciousness. Paulo Freire and his adherents, who conducted literacy campaigns among peasants in northeast Brazil in the late 1950s (and, later, among poor people on four continents) relied on words such as "hunger" and "land"—chosen for their relevance to the pupils' own political and social situation—to teach peasants and workers to read and write. The objective is to develop a critical comprehension of reality, from which action for social change can emerge. Freire's theories are popular in countries of the global South, where focus on political consciousness strikes a sympathetic chord among governments that wish to establish a national identity or ideology distinct from their colonial past. Freire's methods have been adapted for use among oppressed populations in the United States (Rohter, 1986).

The Role of Nongovernmental Organizations

Nongovernmental organizations, or *NGOs,* is the term most commonly used to describe private groups involved in development issues ranging from disaster relief and child nutrition to literacy and agricultural programs; such groups are also known as *private voluntary organizations* (PVOs) in the United States. Sometimes NGO is used to refer to groups in the global North that work on the behalf of countries in the global South. But whether PVO or NGO, these private organizations when taken together present an impressive picture of sources of development assistance, as shown in Figure 5-1. Through the empowerment of local citizens and through international advocacy, thousands of NGOs play an important role in addressing problems related to poverty and other forms of violence.

During the past decade, NGO involvement in development activities has increased spectacularly; they have reached 250 million needy people in underdeveloped regions, more than two and a half times the number served 10 years ago (United Nations, 1995c). Moreover, NGOs provided concrete assistance to about one-fifth of the 1.3 billion of the world's people living in absolute poverty, especially those in remote rural and poor urban areas, where government services may be scarce or nonexistent. NGOs often operate beyond the periphery of the public sector to reach groups that governments and development agencies find it difficult to help.

De Silva (1989) reported that projects in India, Tanzania, Bangladesh, Kenya, Sri Lanka, Indonesia, and Zambia are helping people not only to

Figure 5-1

The Big Picture

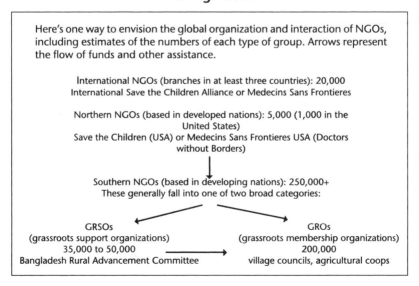

Here's one way to envision the global organization and interaction of NGOs, including estimates of the numbers of each type of group. Arrows represent the flow of funds and other assistance.

International NGOs (branches in at least three countries): 20,000
International Save the Children Alliance or Medecins Sans Frontieres

Northern NGOs (based in developed nations): 5,000 (1,000 in the United States)
Save the Children (USA) or Medecins Sans Frontieres USA (Doctors without Borders)

Southern NGOs (based in developing nations): 250,000+
These generally fall into one of two broad categories:

GRSOs
(grassroots support organizations)
35,000 to 50,000
Bangladesh Rural Advancement Committee

GROs
(grassroots membership organizations)
200,000
village councils, agricultural coops

Source: Alliance for a Global Community. (1995, April). *Connections, 1*(7).

make material gains but also to take control of their lives as they find solutions to seemingly intractable problems. Their experiences are relevant to people in other parts of the world, including underdeveloped regions of the United States. Vital lessons can be learned from approaches that yield long-term benefits by building the confidence of communities so that they can do things for themselves and realize that they themselves hold the key to their future. For example, the Community Development Trust Fund (CDTF) provides funds only to projects that are initiated and carried out by the recipients, because CDTF believes that the strength of an endeavor lies in the villagers' commitment to self-help. In Tanzania, CDTF helped an impoverished village set up a village clinic that has transformed people's health. CDTF's executive director called the success of the project a "living testimony" to a strategy that "shows the way" to people in rural areas so that they can direct development themselves. "After all," he continued, "it's the wearer who knows where the shoe pinches" (Ngaiza, 1989, p. 40). This project illustrates two important ideas: (1) participatory development, in which the beneficiaries of development funds show the initiative and identify the areas where they need help, and (2) sustainability, in that people see the project as their own and maintain it as their property.

Economic Alternatives at the Grassroots

> A society is more human or developed, not when its members have more, but when all are enabled to have enough in order to be more, to be fully human. Material growth and quantitative increase are doubtless needed for genuine human development, but not any kind of growth nor increase obtained at any price. The world as a whole remains underdeveloped so long as a small number of nations or privileged groups remain alienated in an abundance of luxury at the expense of the many who are deprived thereby of their essential subsistence goods. . . . As Fromm put it, "alienation in mindless affluence is just as dehumanizing as alienation in misery." (Goulet, 1995, p. 6)

According to the Global Exchange (n.d.), a San Francisco–based organization that promotes grassroots development, a new wave of grassroots organizations is redefining development to incorporate principles of equity, democratic participation, and environmental sustainability. A movement is growing across the global South and in the United States that aims to rebuild the world economy from the bottom up, with justice and sustainability replacing greed as the key principle. Many different institutions, described below, make up this movement:

- *Cooperatives:* In countries as diverse as Zimbabwe and Mexico, family farmers have formed cooperatives to produce and market their products. For example, in the mountains of Mexico's Guerrero Province, *campesinos* have organized a regional alliance of co-ops to manage their exports of coffee and honey. The co-ops also support communal health projects, education, housing, and political organizing.
- *Revolving credit schemes:* Most of the world's poor people lack access to credit. Many groups—the most successful being the Grameen Bank in Bangladesh—have been pooling capital and lending small amounts to poor people to start a small business or to improve farming practices. Recipients are usually part of a small group that has joint responsibility for repaying the loan. "Credit for All" describes the microenterprise concept in several parts of the world. It is also being used more and more extensively in the United States.

Credit for All

Study after study on credit schemes for poor people confirm that they are creditworthy:
- *Poor people can save, even if only a little.*
- *Poor people have profitable investment opportunities to choose from, and they invest their money wisely.*
- *Poor people are reliable borrowers and hence a good risk. Repayment rates of 90 percent and more are not rare.*
- *Poor people are able and willing to pay market interest rates, so that credit schemes for them stand a good chance of becoming viable, self-financing undertakings.*

The reason credit schemes for poor people work is that they significantly improve the incomes of this population—typically by more than 20 percent, and at times even by more than 100 percent.

Smaller loans are administratively more costly than larger ones. Yet the literature on credit schemes for poor people abounds with examples of how some organizations and programs manage to keep their administrative costs low. Among the successful measures: Lending to peer groups, standardizing loan terms, collaborating with community-based and other developmental nongovernmental organizations, eschewing traditional banking requirements and procedures, and being located in the community and knowing local people and local investment opportunities.

Many savings schemes for poor people currently do mobilize the modest funds that poor communities have to spare. But rarely do they reinvest the money only in poor neighborhoods. Just the opposite should be the case. Not only should poor people's savings be reinvested in poor neighborhoods, the savings of rich people should also be encouraged to flow into these neighborhoods.

Governmental incentive policies can help. For example, governments could subsidize, for a defined interim period, the increased overhead costs that banks would incur in lending to poor people. If the aim were to serve about 120 million poor people a year—every tenth poor person—this could cost some $10 billion.

Poor people know best their opportunities for productive and remunerative work. What they really need are modest amounts of start-up capital for their microenterprises.

As one study put it, the old parable about feeding the people for a day by giving them a fish or feeding them for life by teaching them how to fish needs a 20th-century postscript; what really matters is who owns the pool.

Small credit can make a difference, as shown in these examples:
Integrated Rural Development Programme (IRDP), India
  - *Among beneficiaries, 64 percent increased their annual family incomes by 50 percent or more.*
  - *Seventy percent of the assisted families belonged to the poorest group; however, their share in the benefits of IRDP was only 29 percent.*
  - *In 71 percent of cases, the assets procured by the IRDP beneficiaries were found to be intact after two years.*

Metro Manila Livelihood Programme, Philippines Business for Social Program, Philippines
  - *The average increase in income from an average loan of $94 was 41 percent.*
  - *Women received 80 percent of loans.*
  - *Borrowers had an average of 5.7 dependents.*

Revolving Loan Fund, Dominican Republic
  - *The average increase in income from 101 loans was 27 percent a year.*
  - *The job creation rate among borrowers was more than 20 times that of the control group of nonborrowers.*

Revolving Loan Fund, Costa Rica
- *The average increase in income from 450 small loans was more than 100 percent a year.*
- *A new job was created for every $1,000 lent.*

Source: United Nations Development Programme. (1994). *Human development report 1994* (p. 40). New York: Oxford University Press. Used with permission.

- *Contract farming:* Under this alternative, found mainly in the global North, a group of families contracts with a farmer to grow organic produce to suit their needs. The farmer gets a guaranteed market at a set price, and the families know that their food is being produced without chemicals.

- *Trade union solidarity:* Trade unions in the global North have increased their solidarity with organizations in the global South. In some cases, as in the strike by Guatemalan Coca-Cola workers, international trade union support has been key to challenging corporate elites successfully. Global labor solidarity was clearly evident when more than 60 representatives of unions and popular organizations from South and Central America, Mexico, Canada, and the United States attended a forum in Oaxtepec, Mexico, in March 1994 to discuss the effect of economic integration and restructuring and common strategies to confront the new reality. The forum concluded with unanimous agreement on a declaration of commitment to joint action ("Woman to Woman," 1994).

- *Fair trade organizations:* Promoters of fair trade alternatives are looking for a way out of the trade trap, in which a profit-oriented world economy pays smaller and smaller amounts for exports from the global South while prices of manufactured goods from industrial countries continue to soar. The fair trade movement is based on an understanding that marketing products from the global South directly to consumers in the global North—eliminating the "middle people"—will enable the producers to make a better living. Fair trade also seeks to educate consumers about the working and living conditions of those producers in the global South and to explain how these conditions could be improved by changing the foreign policies and consumption patterns of the global North. Those who promote fair trade alternatives are driven by a sense of justice; they feel that empowering poor people to earn their way out of poverty and to control their own production processes is better than any aid scheme. "A Thread of Hope" exemplifies a fair trade alternative.

A Thread of Hope

A Thread of Hope is a nonprofit organization supporting fair trade be-tween a Guatemalan weavers' cooperative of Mayan women and thousands of North American consumers. A Thread of Hope helps the Mayan commu-nity develop its design, marketing, and grant-writing skills.

The Mayan women use traditional back-strap looms to weave some of the most beautiful cloth in the world. The cloth is then sewn into shirts, vests, jackets, children's clothing, and bags; the products are marketed by partners in the United States. What began as a self-help project with just 17 weavers has grown to include more than 200 women, most of them wid-owed by the political violence of the Guatemalan military against the In-dian majority.

The cooperative has built a 1,000-square-foot building that serves as a workshop and a meeting hall. In 1990 the members of the cooperative elected a board of directors consisting of seven women, and this directiva has taken on more and more responsibility for running the expanding enterprise.

The co-op is now making enough money to be able to pay end-of-year dividends—equivalent to about three months' wages—to each member. The co-op also started a medical emergency fund for the families of its members.

Many more widows would like to join the co-op, which would be possible if the market for the co-op's products increased in the global North.

Source: Global Exchange, n.d.; for more information on this partnership, contact A Thread of Hope at Box 1902, Eugene, OR 97440, or telephone 503-687-6865.

Two Final Requirements: Reduce Consumption and Militarism

Historically, the environment has been treated as a free resource, and rich nations have helped themselves to the bounty; they have consumed vast quantities of the world's resources and emitted most of the world's pollution. Those who subscribe to sustainable human development models, however, do not consider natural resources to be free goods that can be pillaged at will by any individual, nation, or generation. They believe that there is a better, more equitable way for rich and poor nations to share the common heritage of humankind. If the goal of strategies for sustainable human development—the reduction of global poverty—is to be achieved, the lifestyles of the rich nations will clearly have to change (UNDP, 1994).

World disarmament is also required, and reduction of military spending is an essential first step. Special attention must also be paid to higher levels of cooperation between the global North and the global South in such matters as establishing forums for disarmament; defusing tensions around the globe; phasing out military assistance, including U.S. military bases, to countries of the South; regulating the arms trade; initiating dialogue about an aid policy that would divorce foreign aid from military spending; agreeing on criteria for United Nations mediation in conflicts within nations; and creating more effective information systems for finding out where and how arms flows are going so that they can be slowed or halted (UNDP, 1994).

Implications for Social Workers

We in the social work community have to begin to grapple with our response professionally to issues of violence and what it means for practice. . . . Agency practice and social work education need to deal with the implications of working with people who are literally surrounded by violence 24 hours a day. What does that do to people's ability to nurture, to people who are trying to make sure that not only is there enough food on the table but that their children are in fact safe? (Davis, 1992)

Social workers hold conflicting roles in relationship to poverty and other forms of violence and to development issues. On the one hand, social workers are agents of a society that in general oppresses and controls disadvantaged populations; in particular, social workers and social agencies are often involved in the care, control, and containment of people who respond to intolerable social conditions with deviant and sometimes abusive and violent behavior. On the other hand, social workers must be advocates for those disadvantaged populations. It is essential that social workers learn to recognize—and help clients recognize—the systemic roots of problems; they must also work to help clients empower themselves to change abject social conditions (Social Action

Network, 1993). This advocacy is particularly important when one considers that most of the moral, social, and political reforms that have happened in Western society have occurred through the struggles of people who were oppressed, demanding changes (New York City NASW Center, 1994).

Social Workers' Orientation to Development

The approach that social workers take toward development, and their philosophy about it, must be consistent with the profession's tradition of social change and social justice. Goulet (1995) suggests four general orientations to development. The fourth orientation is most consistent with the profession's emphasis on multiculturally competent practice, but others may be more appropriate in particular contexts.

1. The growth strategy seeks to maximize aggregate production by promoting investment and productivity tactics that foster rapid economic expansion. Inequality is seen as an inevitable byproduct of the process, but the benefits of growth are expected to eventually trickle down to poor people; if they do not, the state can institute a system of safety nets through corrective welfare measures.
2. The redistribution strategy is based on a belief that equity must be planned as a direct goal of development and that distributive justice is not compatible with high levels of growth. Investments in education, jobs, and health and nutrition are seen as productive.
3. A basic human needs strategy moves beyond the redistribution model by specifying what is needed to satisfy the basic needs (goods and services relating to nutrition, health, housing, education, and access to jobs) of people in poverty. True development is measured not by economic growth but by the economic welfare of large numbers of people. Basic-needs advocates target scarce resources toward providing for the poorest people first.
4. A "development from tradition" strategy departs radically from the first three orientations. It refuses to borrow Northern development goals and advocates instead that each society seek its particular and proper development imperatives within indigenous value systems (traditional beliefs, local institutions, and popular practices, for

example). Although the strategy does not automatically reject "modern" ideas, behavior, and technology, it holds that those ideas need to be judged critically to determine whether they can contribute to the sound development of people and communities as defined by their own traditions. Development must thus address a people's cultural identity and self-worth and contain a "full-life" dimension that incorporates traditional beliefs concerning the ultimate meaning of life and history (Goulet, 1995, p. 6).

Focus on Communities

> You cannot have healthy families in sick communities. Therefore, [we need to] build into our responsibilities a strong community organizing, community response part, with the use of the community as a resource for families as well as working in concert with others in the community to address those issues which are injurious to community and family health. (Davis, 1992).

Much can be learned from case studies of communities that have attempted to overcome powerlessness, whether such approaches to economic and social development were taken by people in the Americas, India, Africa, the Philippines, or other places. Their stories prove that efforts to overcome poverty are worldwide and that much of the requisite structure, skills, and will already exist in poor communities. The idea is to work with such communities, to listen to them, to learn from them, and to form alliances that use both their knowledge and skills and ours to gain access to the resources necessary to overcome poverty (Moch, Rosenthal, & Goldberg, 1995). The following guidelines are offered to help social workers focus on community development as an antidote to poverty and other forms of violence.

- Consistent with the "development from tradition" strategy discussed previously, focus should be on critical development needs identified by the community itself. This strategy requires staying as close as possible to the voices in the community, which requires deliberate attempts to obtain information from the person whom the community appears to accept as articulating their reality; that person can then be a bridge from the community to the outside (Moch, Rosenthal, & Goldberg, 1995).

- Social workers must understand the role that exploitation and repression play in the existence and continuation of poverty; they
  should be aware of the temptation to "support efforts to eradicate
  poverty that ignore the existing structures and skills in the community, including those developed to counter exploitation, and
  thereby merely inflict further violence on communities" (Moch,
  Rosenthal, & Goldberg, 1995, p. 4).
- Social workers, who often do not share the class, racial, or other
  attributes of the communities in which they work, must be aware
  of the complexities involved in trying to relate to the people in
  those communities. It is essential that social workers continually
  examine their attitudes and belief systems, in particular to determine whether they think a particular culture or group is inferior
  (New York City NASW Center, 1994). Whenever prejudice is uncovered, social workers have an obligation to educate themselves
  to change such attitudes.
- Particular attention must be paid to the issue of trust. Social workers
  should be aware that some clients—for example, refugees from
  Panama, El Salvador, or Guatemala—may direct considerable anger
  toward a social worker, whom they see as an agent of a government
  whose military "advised" the people who bombed and tortured them;
  they might believe that such a social worker would not only refuse
  aid but also report refugees for deportation (Davis, 1992).

Social Workers as Activists

It seems to me that it is very, very difficult to be a social worker and not to be
an activist of some sort. I cannot see people graduating from a school of
social work and not having some understanding of the fact that their work
is going to involve some degree of activism, some degree of political and
social activism. As social workers, understanding our role, our potential social and political role comes first, and then everything else. (Wallace, 1992)

Bombyk (1994) identifies several strategies used by U.S. welfare
consumers—labeled "self-defense tactics against the violence of poverty"—
and classifies them based on whether they can be done alone or whether
they are most feasible and politically effective when done with others at

different levels of social organization, including small groups, organizations, coalitions, and social movements (Table 5-1). All of the strategies have various "jumping in" points for social work activists. Bombyk (1994) notes that the most visible activism currently seems to be at the organization level. In general, the major thrust of the tactics is education and advocacy for immediate survival needs in income maintenance and welfare centers; education and organization of welfare consumers and others for actions related to welfare policies; and resistance lobbying and activism in legislative and other policy arenas against repressive welfare proposals. What is needed is work toward a larger-scale social movement for social and economic justice—"a poor people's movement for social change" (Bombyk, 1994, p. 4).

What You Can Do

Here are some things that you can do to become more informed, to take actions to reduce poverty and other forms of violence, and to promote sustainable human development:

- To develop a philosophical grounding for social work's commitment to advocacy for higher standards of life and greater personal fulfillment, learn about the United Nations human rights instruments and the principles and standards embodied in them. The Universal Declaration of Human Rights, adopted by the United Nations in 1948, is the first major international statement of the fundamental rights of all human beings. It defines human rights as inherent in human nature and essential for a truly human existence. The declaration has acquired universal acceptance, and its provisions have been incorporated into laws and constitutions in many countries, as well as in many other human rights conventions and treaties concluded since 1948. Among them are the Declaration on the Right to Development (1986), which provides a philosophical basis for a "people-centered" concept of development by establishing the right of all people to participate in, contribute to, and enjoy economic, cultural, and political development; the International Covenant on Economic, Social and Cultural

Table 5-1
Organizing against the Violence of Poverty:
Self-Defense and Empowerment Tactics of Welfare Consumers

Levels of Resistance	Self-Defense and Empowerment Tactic
Individual	Self-advocacy to welfare workers and system
	Initiating fair hearings
	Seeking legal counsel
Small Group	Consciousness-raising (resisting stigmatization, identifying and analyzing the dysfunctional welfare system, finding affirmation and support)
	Educating (about the nature and rules of the system, the chain of command, and the rights of people seeking public assistance)
	Training (to advocate for others; to perform acts of civil disobedience in welfare offices)
Organization	Bearing witness: sharing stories and experiences at conferences, clubs, congregations, civic associations, classrooms, and other public forums to educate and win support
	Testifying in legislative hearings and to other policy makers
	Lobbying legislators
	Organizing and participating in rallies, marches, and demonstrations
	Running welfare simulation games for community groups to educate the public about the experience of welfare and poverty
	Providing services (helping with transportation and child care to facilitate participation, acting as a liaison or broker with the welfare system)
	Convening and staffing a Consumer Advocacy Committee for the local welfare office to identify consumer concerns to agency and offer policy and procedure alternatives
Coalition	Forming congresses with other welfare rights groups, joining with National Welfare Rights Organization, creating nationally circulated publications for advocacy, education, and publicity
	Identifying common ground and collaborating with other antipoverty organizations (for example, housing and hunger) for legal challenges, lobbying, and public education campaigns
	Enlisting support of mainstream organizations to broaden political and resource base (churches, labor unions, professional social services associations) for initiating or opposing legislation of social welfare benefits
Social Movement	Broadening issue from welfare rights to human rights and economic and social justice by joining with other social movements (for example, feminism, labor, and civil rights) to support similar objectives such as jobs with benefits and decent pay, universal health care, universal child care

Source: M. Bombyk, Professor of Social Work, Eastern Michigan University. This framework is based on an earlier memo sent by the author to the New York City NASW Center on Violence, Development, and Poverty, August 23, 1994.

Rights (1966); the International Covenant on Civil and Political Rights (1966); the Convention on the Prevention and Punishment of the Crime of Genocide (1951); the International Convention on the Elimination of All Forms of Racial Discrimination (1969); the Convention on the Elimination of Discrimination against Women (1981); the Convention on the Rights of the Child (1990); and the International Convention on the Protection of the Rights of All Migrant Workers and Members of Their Families (1990).

- Read *Teaching and Learning about Human Rights: A Manual for Schools of Social Work and the Social Work Profession,* published by the United Nations in 1992. For information about how to obtain materials, contact the United Nations Center for Human Rights, United Nations Office at Geneva, Palais des Nations, 8-14, Avenue de la Paix, CH-1211 Geneva 10, Switzerland; (41 22) 917-1530 or 4326.
- Become involved with the Universal Declaration of Human Rights Project, which aims to create a "human rights culture" to raise awareness of the declaration, monitor movements toward compliance, and suggest ways to overcome violations. Universal rights to shelter, health care, and employment are absent in U.S. federal and state constitutions. To get involved, contact Joseph Wronka, Department of Social Work, Springfield College, Springfield, MA 01109.
- As advocates for change, social workers are subject to repression and abuse. Become involved in advocating for social workers around the world whose human rights have been violated. Join the Committee for International Human Rights Inquiry and become involved in letter-writing campaigns to stop human rights violations against social service workers. For information, contact the New York City NASW chapter at 545 8th Avenue, 6th Floor, New York, NY 10018; (212) 947-5000; fax (212) 947-5311.
- Educate yourself about the issues and advocate for actions aimed at alleviating poverty, such as revisions of structural adjustment policies; implementation of a code of conduct for transnational corporations; and curbing of arms trade worldwide, along with a decrease in military expenditures.

- Organize a teach-in on your college or university campus like the one held in June 1994 at Fordham University Graduate School of Social Service on the politics of welfare reform. Attendees gathered to express indignation over recent welfare reform proposals that blame social problems on poor families, to dispel myths surrounding the current debate over welfare reform, and to mobilize for action.
- Learn about SAPs of the World Bank and the International Monetary Fund (IMF) and their consequences. A good place to start is to read *50 Years Is Enough: The Case against the World Bank and the International Monetary Fund,* edited by Kevin Danaher (1994) (see the suggestions for further reading at the end of the book). Join in some of the activities of the "50 Years Is Enough" campaign, which is pushing for fundamental restructuring of the IMF and World Bank. The campaign calls for a halt to SAPs; a reorientation of lending that is people-oriented, with particular attention to those who are marginalized; an embracing of full citizen participation; and implementation of immediate debt relief. To find out more about the campaign and to get a quarterly newsletter and action alerts, contact Global Exchange, 2017 Mission Street, Room 303, San Francisco, CA 94110; (415) 255-7296.
- Support the Global Exchange Fair Trade Campaign to foster grassroots development. For information, contact Global Exchange. Discrimination in education and the labor market produce distinct disadvantages for racial and ethnic groups, women, and poor people that result in less income and poverty conditions. Thus, it is important to advocate for the elimination of all forms of discrimination.
- Join the National Jobs for All Coalition formed in New York City in June 1994. The coalition aims to put on the public agenda the elimination of unemployment and underemployment in the United States; it considers this to be a necessary step toward overcoming many social problems that are directly or indirectly linked to people's exclusion from the work system. Read the coalition plan in *Jobs for All* (Collins, Ginsburg, & Goldberg, 1994). The goals of the coalition are consistent with the policy statement of NASW on

full or equitable employment, which was adopted by the NASW Delegate Assembly in August 1990. For more information, contact David Gil at (617) 736-3827.

- Advocate for world demilitarization by joining peace organizations and engaging in actions for peace. As Elise Boulding (1995), international chair of the Women's International League for Peace and Freedom, stated, "In order to do all the other things that are necessary for the well being of the planet it is absolutely essential that we keep pushing along these endless treaty processes and [disarmament] negotiations with the clear goal in mind of zero nuclear arms: simply, no guns in my home, my neighborhood, my world" (p. 9).

- Moderate your own consumption patterns—take shorter showers, avoid taking more than you need of anything, and so on—in keeping with Gandhi's emphasis on material simplicity. Contribute personally to solving the problem of overconsumption of resources by the North. As Goulet (1995) argued, "[Sustainable development] requires simple living in which consumption and resource use are limited" (p. 4).

- Share your abundance with the desperately needy people of the world and join with others to relieve the suffering and to support people-centered development in these lands. Contribute to the NGOs of your choice.

- Find ways to put your skills to work in international development organizations by seeking employment opportunities in NGOs or by considering international fieldwork assignments. Read the articles by Rosenthal (1990, 1991) for further information about the role of social work in international practice in the global South.

References

Alliance for a Global Community. (1995, April). *Connections, 1*(7).

Atwood, B. (1995, January 25). Opening remarks at the Meeting of the U.S. Agency for International Development Advisory Committee on Voluntary Foreign Aid, Washington, DC.

Bombyk, M. (1994, August 23). *Organizing against the violence of poverty: Self-defense tactics of welfare consumers.* Memorandum to Marilynn Moch, coordinator of the New York City NASW Center on Poverty, Violence, and Development.

Boulding, E. (1995, February). The many dimensions of peace-building. *Hunger TeachNet, 6,* 8–11.

Breslin, P. (1995, April). On these sidewalks of New York, the sun is shining again. *Smithsonian, 26,* 100–111.

Collins, S. O., Ginsburg, H. L., & Goldberg, G. S. (1994). *Jobs for all: A plan for the revitalization of America.* New York: Apex Press.

Danaher, K. (Ed.). (1994). *50 years is enough: The case against the World Bank and the International Monetary Fund.* Boston: South End Press.

Davis, R. (1992, June). *Responses of African Americans to European political and economic dominance of the Americas beginning in 1492.* Paper presented at the International Social Work Forums, New York.

De Silva, D. (Project Coordinator). (1989). *Against all odds: Breaking the poverty trap.* Washington, DC: Panos Institute.

Global Exchange. (n.d.). GATT and NAFTA: How trade agreements can change your life. (Available from the Global Exchange, 2017 Mission Street, Room 303, San Francisco, CA 94110.)

Goulet, D. (1995, February). Authentic development: Is it sustainable? *Hunger TeachNet, 6,* 3–8.

International Labour Organisation (ILO). (1995). *World employment 1995: An ILO report.* Geneva: Author.

Long-Scott, E. (1992). "Sistuhs with an *attitude*": Women taking a stand! *Economic Justice Speakout, 6*(2), 1.

Maathai, W. (1988). *The Green Belt Movement.* Nairobi, Kenya: Environment Liaison Center International.

Moch, M., Rosenthal, B., & Goldberg, T. (1995, February 21). Concept paper for curriculum modules, prepared by the New York NASW Center on Poverty, Violence, and Development.

New York City NASW Center on Poverty, Violence, and Development. (1994). [Report submitted to the Violence and Development Project]. New York: Author.

Ngaiza, A. (1989). Tanzania: A life-saving clinic in remote Chanika. In D. De Silva (Project Coordinator), *Against all odds: Breaking the poverty trap* (pp. 27–42). Washington, DC: Panos Institute.

Rohter, L. (1986, August 19). Radical theorist takes his message to the world. *New York Times,* C1.

Rosenthal, B. S. (1990). U.S. social workers' interest in working in the developing world. *International Social Work, 33,* 225–232.

Rosenthal, B. S. (1991). Social workers' interest in international practice in the developing world: A multivariate analysis. *Social Work, 36,* 248–252.

Schiller, B. R. (1989). *The economics of poverty and discrimination.* Englewood Cliffs, NJ: Prentice Hall.

Social Action Network. (1993). Violence and victimization in our midst: Issues for contemporary social work. (The proposal for the Social Action Network was prepared at Adelphi University School of Social Work, Garden City, NY.)

United Nations. (1988). *The international bill of human rights* (Fact Sheet no. 2). Geneva: United Nations Center for Human Rights.

United Nations. (1995a). *Education empowers* (World Summit for Social Development Issue Paper, UNESCO). New York: United Nations Department of Public Information.

United Nations. (1995b). *Helping the poor to help themselves* (World Summit for Social Development Issue Paper, World Bank). New York: United Nations Department of Public Information.

United Nations. (1995c). *NGOs: Partners in social development* (World Summit for Social Development Issue Paper). New York: United Nations Department of Public Information.

United Nations. (1995d). *Women: Investing in the future* (World Summit for Social Development Issue Paper, Fourth World Conference on Women). New York: United Nations Department of Public Information.

United Nations. (1995e). *Youth: Shaping society's future* (World Summit for Social Development Issue Paper, Social Policy and Development Division, Sub-Programme on Youth). New York: United Nations Department of Public Information.

United Nations Development Programme (UNDP). (1994). *Human development report 1994.* New York: Oxford University Press.

Wallace, S. (1992, June). Paper presented at the International Social Work Forums, New York.

Woman to Woman, Mujer a Mujer. (1994, May). *Correspondicia, 16,* 2–5.

Part 3

Gender Violence and Violence against Children

Chapter 6

Connecting the Dots between Development and Violence against Women and Children

> Jesus was a 9-year-old Mexican child who was shipped to New York City to be a prostitute. Maria was a 5-year-old who was blinded by her parents to be a beggar in India. . . . Fifteen-year-old Remy was beaten to death by Bolivian police when he refused to help produce cocaine. . . . Lisa Steinberg and the millions of other abused and neglected children in the United States have less money spent to investigate their cries of horror than is spent on pets in this nation. (Herrmann, 1990)

> Violence against women . . . is perhaps the most pervasive yet least recognized human rights issue in the world. It is also a profound health problem sapping women's physical and emotional vitality and undermining their confidence—both vital to achieving widely held goals for human progress. (Heise, 1989, p. 12)

Violence is a pervasive and dangerous fact of life for women and children in virtually every country in the world, yet only recently have gender violence and violence against children emerged as topics of worldwide debate. Not until 1975, at the Mexico City World Conference of the International Women's Year, did the issue of violence within the family arise as a global concern; 10 years after that women came together for the first time as activists against gender violence in a broader sense at the 1985 World Conference on Women in Nairobi (Mann, 1994). In 1989 the United Nations General Assembly called on nations to protect children from all forms of violence and exploitation by passing the Convention on the Rights of the Child (United Nations Children's Fund [UNICEF], 1994).

This chapter is based on the premises that gender violence and violence against children must be understood as pervasive global problems with multiple and complex manifestations, causes, and consequences; that these problems do not develop within the isolation of the individual family, nor are they confined to that institution; and that solutions to

115

gender violence and violence against children need to be linked to processes of human, social, and economic development. The chapter also holds that, in turn, development strategies are doomed to failure if they do not make central the issues of violence against women and militarism in societies.

Within the context of the conceptualization of violence presented in chapter 1, this chapter first discusses conditions of violence facing women and children in the United States and the global South, including an examination of similarities and differences. This examination is followed by discussion of how such conditions affect development processes and vice versa.

Violence against Women and Their Children: Beyond a Family Affair

Violence Reconceptualized

This section illustrates the magnitude and types of violence against women and children all over the world. The discussion goes beyond the types of violence at the individual level, however, to include forms of violence that are legitimized by societal institutions and are most often considered to be necessary forms of social control. Also addressed is the even more deeply submerged level of violence at the structural and cultural level, which contains the roots of violence at other levels. For example, the norms and ideologies underlying the structural relationships of power, domination, and privilege that exist between women and men in different societies are one of the root causes of gender violence included at the bottom of the triangle in Figure 3-2. The experiences of women and girls in different countries reveal common threads that show "why the threat of male violence is a fundamental experience that unites women across barriers of race, culture, and class throughout the world" (Davies, 1994, p. vii).

Violence at the Individual Level

Violence at the individual level involves harmful actions taken by individuals or groups against women or children. Violence at this level takes different forms—rape, wife-beating, sexual harassment, child abuse, or incest, for example—and it usually involves direct actions, means, and immediate consequences.

Violence against women.   Individual-level gender violence crosses class, race, age, and national lines, whether it appears as domestic violence, sexual assault and coercion, sexual harassment, rape, or female sexual slavery (United Nations, 1989). Rape of women is a reality in virtually every country of the world—in the United States a rape occurs about every six minutes—and violence against women, ranging from assault to homicide, is a significant pattern within the family in probably all countries of the world (Davies, 1994; Koop, 1989; United Nations, 1989). Empirical evidence cannot capture the true dimensions of domestic violence, but the following statistics illustrate its pervasiveness and pattern both in the United States and in the global South:

- Battery is the leading cause of injury to adult women (Koop, 1989).
- Seventy percent of all crimes reported to police in Peru involve women who are beaten by their partners; in Lima alone, 168,970 rapes were reported in 1987 (Portugal, 1988).
- Eight of every 10 wives in India are victims of domestic battery, dowry-related abuse, or murder (United Nations, 1989).
- Domestic violence occurs in an estimated 70 percent of Mexican families (Carrillo, 1991).
- A retrospective study of 170 women murdered in Bangladesh between 1983 and 1985 revealed that half of the murders occurred within the family (United Nations, 1989).

Although violence is a common reality for women worldwide, it takes unique forms in several countries because of traditional practices regarding dowry, widowhood rites, sati (widow burning), and genital mutilation. Gender violence has emerged as a pervasive theme for women in India, for example, where comparative statistics suggest that hundreds of thousands of women are "missing" because of such violence. Ratios in North America, Europe, and Africa range from 1,020 to 1,060 females per 1,000 males; the female-to-male ratio in India is 935:1,000 (Sen, 1987). The uniqueness of the situation for women in India is addressed by Omvedt (1990), who documented the increasing focus of women's organizations on gender violence: "First it was the horrifying, rising toll of fire in the growing numbers of 'dowry deaths'; then from 1980 . . . the problem of rape burst out of the shadows to stand as the symbol of women's oppression. Finally, the last few years have seen dramatic revivals of the ancient custom of sati as well as female infanticide—and at the same time the advent of 'ultramodern' medical forms of violence against females through bio-medical practice, such as amniocentesis" (p. 2).

Violence against children.   Like domestic violence against women, violence against children within the home is a global problem. Some individual forms of violence against children are universal (physical abuse, sexual abuse, rape) and some are unique to regions and countries (genital mutilation, sexual slavery). The precise incidence of child abuse is unknown, but the American Humane Association estimates that 2.1 million U.S. children in 1986 were victims of abuse and neglect, and Childhelp USA estimates that one in three girls and one in eight boys are sexually abused before the age of 18 (Rohr, 1990). A 1985 nationwide poll of the extent of child molestation in the United States conducted by the *Los Angeles Times* found that at least 27 percent of women and 16 percent of men were sexually victimized during childhood (Dziech & Schudson, 1990). Most of child sexual abuse in the United States is perpetrated by someone known to the child—very often the father, stepfather, or father substitute; information from some countries of the global South (the Philippines, Sri Lanka, and Thailand) suggests a similar pattern (Center for Protection of Children's Rights [CPCR], 1991; Doek, 1991). Mounting evidence suggests that, outside the home, male children may be sexually molested by adult males as often as are female children (Dziech & Schudson, 1990).

    Gender violence begins even before birth in some cases (female infanticide), and it continues throughout life. The reality of gender violence for females in the global South is that girls are given less food and forced into hard labor sooner than boys, denied adequate economic return on their labor, denied access to education and health care, forced into marriage as very young teens, raped throughout their lives and often forced to marry their rapists, bought and sold like slaves for prostitution and labor, exploited and violated at military bases and during wartime as "comfort women" for soldiers, and even killed by sex-selective abortions and female infanticide (Davies, 1994; Minnesota NASW Center, 1994).

Violence at the individual level may be institutional. Increasingly, individual-level violence against women and children is being recognized and dealt with. Still, such violence is too often hidden and vastly underestimated everywhere: Violence within the family is a well-kept secret most of the time; rape is still very much a hidden problem, one that is difficult to prosecute even when the will is there; and frequently people refuse to see sexual harassment as violence, even when it is overt and blatant.

Nevertheless, the problem has been put on local and national political agendas in countries near and far, from the United States to France in the global North and from Zimbabwe to Brazil and the Philippines in the global South (Davies, 1994). Intervention efforts at the individual level, such as setting up shelters for battered women and children and providing counseling, are essential for ensuring the safety of women and children, yet such efforts often encounter difficulties at the institutional level. The next section explains why.

Violence at the Institutional Level

Violence against women and children at the individual level is insufferable, but it is only the tip of the iceberg. At the level below individual violence, less-visible institutional arrangements operate normatively to rationalize, support, and depersonalize individual acts of violence. When viewed as a normative part of the traditional hierarchical, patriarchal family, beating of wives and children is institutionalized. Legal institutions have a long history of supporting such violence against women as a form of social control:

> Legal systems, which are a reflection of cultural values, often gave a husband the right to chastise, or even kill his wife, if she was regarded as sufficiently disobedient. . . . The husband was empowered to correct the wife in the same moderation that a man is allowed to correct his apprentice or children. . . . This power was confirmed in judicial decisions in England and North America, where the domestic chastisement of a wife went unpunished unless some permanent injury resulted from the husband's violence. Even where permanent injury or death resulted, the husband's actions were often justified on the grounds of, for example, provocation and any penalty he received was always light. The husband's right to chastise his wife received acceptance in popular culture by being known as the "rule of thumb,"

because it appeared that normal wife beating involved chastisement with a stick no bigger than a man's thumb. (United Nations, 1989, p. 11)

Both covertly and overtly, present-day institutions around the world continue practices that rationalize and support family violence. Almost universally, "The social impulse is to preserve the family at all costs, even if this compromises a woman's safety. As a male high court judge in Uganda said, 'it is better for one person to suffer rather than risk a complete breakdown of family life'" (Heise, 1989, p. 13). Furthermore, although an astonishingly high proportion of women applying for welfare benefits in the United States have been battered by their mates, public policymakers continue to attempt to pass legislation requiring them to marry as a condition of receiving assistance. In El Salvador, a man cannot be prosecuted for rape if he agrees to marry the woman he raped; to avoid public shame and to salvage family honor, many families coerce their young daughters into marrying their rapists (Cox, 1994).

Legal institutions support family-based female subordination in some cases through laws that prevent women from owning or renting residential property or taking out residential mortgages. Other societal institutions also perpetuate gender violence through their everyday practices. For example, by routinely undervaluing women's labor or by not documenting women's unpaid work, economic institutions render women's contributions invisible, undermine their value to the household, and maintain their dependence on men, thus making them more vulnerable to male violence (Jaquette, 1993). Some religious institutions promote male dominance and support physical "discipline" of wives and children by husbands and fathers, and educational institutions too often treat males and females inequitably and promote institutional norms of male dominance through modeling and practice. Also, societal institutions often collude in perpetrating violence: For example, religious, economic, and family institutions in India together form a configuration in which dowry abuse and dowry burnings of women result in families using the traditional dowry system to try to build a middle-class economic base in an increasingly consumerist society.

Repressive violence at the institutional level denies women their basic human and civil rights in most countries. This often takes the form of institutional discrimination; if laws against gender discrimination do exist, they are too often not enforced (Minnesota NASW Center, 1994). In some countries of the global South, denial of basic human and civil rights takes the more pernicious form of "legitimate" violence by the state. For example, many of the world's political prisoners are women activists from the global South who spoke out against gender-based violence. Women are tortured worldwide for their political beliefs. Military governments in Latin America have been particularly brutal: "Military regimes in Latin America have developed patterns of punishments specifically designed for women who are perceived as actively fighting against or in any way resisting the oppression and exploitation visited upon their peoples by dictatorial governments. . . . Gang rape, massive rape, becomes the standard torture mechanism for the social control of the imprisoned women" (Bunster-Burotto, 1986, pp. 297, 307).

Crimes at the individual level, such as rape, sexual assault, and sexual harassment, become violations of human rights when they are tolerated and not punished at the institutional level. For example, the U.S. military allegedly covers up sexual violations committed by officials ranging from local base commanders to top Pentagon officials: Perpetrators are allowed to resign, with an honorable discharge and no criminal record, in lieu of facing trial; women in the military who report rapes are often the ones who are punished, by being locked in psychiatric hospitals, forced to submit to lie detector tests, or even court-martialed. The response of the U.S. Congress to the military's Tailhook sexual harassment scandal provides another example of collusion between societal institutions: Following the highly publicized revelation of sexual malfeasance by military personnel, a bill was introduced in the U.S. Congress that would have required the Pentagon to properly investigate and track sex crimes; the bill got only three votes ("Rape's Defenders," 1996).

Another appalling form of violence is the sexual exploitation of children and women by tourists and international visitors to countries in Asia, Africa, and Latin America. Sexual exploitation in the sex tourism industry is institutionalized, carried out by organizations and corporations with the support or collusion of government authorities who permit or encourage it. In some countries, such as the Philippines and Thailand, growth of the local economy through local sex tourism was encouraged by the U.S. government and military as well. The perpetrators are almost always male; the children who are abused sexually may be either male or female, although girls constitute by far the greatest proportion of sexually exploited children (Ireland, 1993). In Sri Lanka, reports suggest that the perpetrators are almost exclusively Western men who exploit young boys. Young boys are similarly targeted in Thailand and the Philippines, but within a more organized and commercialized sex entertainment industry that emerged when U.S. forces used those countries for R&R (rest and recreation) during the Vietnam War (Ireland, 1993); female prostitution also is a profitable part of tourism development. Of course, sexual exploitation for profit is not limited to the global South. Child prostitutes are found in disturbingly large numbers in Western Europe and North America, and reports indicate a surge in sexual exploitation of children in the former communist countries of Eastern Europe (Ireland, 1993).

War is institutional violence carried out by government and military institutions. It is usually thought of as a legitimate form of violence that, although regrettable, is entirely justified and even necessary. Those who fight in war are given medals of honor and celebrated as heroes. However, from the perspective of war's victims, the essence of this form of institutionalized violence—its presumed legitimacy—is considerably different:

> The stories pour forth in an avalanche of horror. From Bosnia, young girls raped, gang-raped, raped again, mutilated, murdered. From Angola, Cambodia, Afghanistan, Mozambique, children literally torn to shreds by land-mines or, at best, dismembered, consigned to live entire lives as amputees. . . . From Somalia, Sudan, Rwanda, child refugees on the run, tears and terror intermingled, frantically fleeing civil war, cut down in their flight by mortars, bullets, machetes. (Lewis, 1994, p. 37)

Evidence of the harm done to women and children by the violence of war is overwhelming. In 1992 more people were killed in wars around the world than were killed for any year during the cold war, and 90 percent of them were women and children (Sivard, 1993). One and a half million children died in war zones in the past 10 years, and another 4 million have been permanently injured by weapons such as bombs, bullets, land mines, chemical weapons, and machetes (Global Child Health, 1995). Millions more children have been traumatized by the effects of war. Most of the millions of refugees fleeing from war or terrorism are women and children, and, after fleeing violent circumstances, women and girls are frequently confronted with violence of another sort, through rape, abduction, sexual abuse, and demands for sexual favors in return for protection and food. Rape is increasingly used as a weapon of war worldwide: 60 percent of Rwandan women and girls were raped in that country's war; rape was frequently used to degrade the regime's opponents during the final months of the Haitian dictatorship; Human Rights Watch reported that rapes by the military were routine in Kashmir, Peru, and Somalia in 1995 and complained that governments around the globe excuse sexual assault and fail to punish or prevent it when it is committed by those in uniform ("Rape's Defenders," 1996). On military bases in countries of the global South, in times of either peace or war, the U.S. military is implicated in high rates of prostitution. Another legacy of war is the estimated 105 million antipersonnel mines that lie in wait in the earth of 62 countries, killing and maiming thousands of people each year—and a disproportionate number of them are women and children (United Nations Development Programme [UNDP], 1994).

Violence at the Structural and Cultural Level

Gender violence and violence against children are deeply rooted in collective belief systems at the structural and cultural level. These beliefs include an ideology of white male superiority; an economy based on property and profit; and militaristic values that emphasize dominance, win–lose solutions, and the use of violence to maintain power and control. This worldview undergirds hierarchical family, economic, religious, educational, and governmental institutions. The result is that significant numbers of the world's population are routinely subjected to violence in all domains, simply because they are deemed to be subordinate.

The family is a societal institution with deep roots in a shared ideology that ensures male domination and control of women and children. In most cultures in which men are present in the family structure, it is they who hold primary power within the family; preserving such gender inequity often prompts violence against women and girl children. Deep-seated beliefs at the structural and cultural level provide the rationale for and normalize violence against women and children, so that

murder, assault, sexual abuse, coercion, and humiliation of women in
their own homes by their male partners are not considered unusual or
particularly blameworthy (United Nations, 1989). In fact, "Violence
against women is the function of the belief, fostered in all cultures, that
men are superior and that the women they live with are their possessions or chattels that they can treat as they wish and as they consider
appropriate" (United Nations, 1989, p. 33). Although this belief system
is often unacknowledged or denied, women throughout the world know
it exists and attest to its verity. One woman in the global South identified the universality of the problem when she blamed "centuries-old
cultural and religious traditions for institutionalizing and giving legitimacy to gender discrimination," which results in "a social and cultural
attitude where women are inferior—and discrimination tends to start
at birth" (Anderson & Moore, 1993, p. A1).

Interrelationship of the Levels of Violence

When sexual harassment, domestic homicide, rape, and so on are illegal
and culturally taboo, and the perpetrators of those acts are punished if
they are caught, then we have individual forms of violence. People are
not punished equally at this level, however, but according to hidden ideological and collective belief systems at the structural and cultural level.

When violent acts are not illegal or culturally forbidden, when they
are in fact the expected behavior of people acting as they think
they should in their institutional roles, then the violence is institutional
as well as individual. Thus, rape in the military is institutional violence,
whereas rape by a civilian is an individual crime. When violent behavior
in social institutions is so pervasive and ingrained that people in those
institutions do not perceive what is happening as harmful or violent—
corporal punishment of children in the United States, for example, or
parental encouragement of child prostitution in some parts of Thailand
and Myanmar—then institutional violence has reached its peak. The
perpetrators and victims of such violence are merely acting out their
institutional roles of patriarch and household dependent, master and
slave, superior and subordinate.

Structural and cultural violence is impersonal and completely invisible. At this level, people are marginalized, excluded, and neglected on

the basis of entrenched belief systems that determine the fundamental structure of institutional systems. An ideology of male superiority, property- and profit-based economic values, and militaristic values ensures gender and generation inequity and subordination.

Development and Violence against Women and Children: Making the Connections

> Female-focused violence undermines widely held goals for economic and social development in the Third World. The development community has come to realize that problems . . . cannot be solved without women's full participation. Yet women cannot lend their labor or creative ideas fully when they are burdened with the physical and psychological scars of violence. (Heise, 1989, p. 12)

A basic premise of this book is that real solutions to violence require real development strategies—such as sustainable human development—that are aimed at the eradication of powerlessness and poverty. But to promote people-centered and empowerment-oriented development—and to counteract the maldevelopment that often masquerades as genuine development—violence against women and children must first have a central place in the discussion. During the United Nations Decade for Women, for example, it became clear that no real development was possible unless the everyday concerns of women were addressed; these concerns include a life free from physical and mental violence, as well as provision of other essential needs. What was also clear was that women's rights were being eroded, frequently because planned development lacked a gender perspective. For their part, women realized that organizing against gender violence and promoting other women's issues would have little success unless "international and national priorities on military spending and nuclearisation, regional conflicts, debt, trade, etc. were also addressed" (Women's Feature Service, 1993, p. 5).

In this section, some connections between development processes and violence against women and children are discussed. The connections are undoubtedly complex and multifactorial. Thus, those that are presented here are offered for consideration and are not intended to be all inclusive nor the definitive analysis.

Militarism Impedes Development for Women and Children

The violence of war and the militarization of societies are treacherous impediments to healthy development of individuals and societies. Wars, political instability, and arms spending impede economic growth, poverty alleviation, and other aspects of development. Their effects are particularly detrimental for women and children. Global military spending in 1994, despite the end of the cold war, equaled the combined income of half of humanity. While military budgets swell, compelling social-development needs go unattended (Sivard, 1993).

Military spending affects development of women and children in the global South. The import of expensive weapons has undermined social development in many countries. More than 30 percent of countries of the global South spend more on their military budgets than on education, and almost 70 percent spend more on the military than on health care. For less than half the cost of their military expenditures, the global South could save 10 million lives a year by providing basic health care services (Sivard, 1993). These illustrations of the connection between spending on weapons and lack of social development come from UNDP (1994):

- India purchased 20 MIG-29 fighter jets from Russia; the price paid could have provided basic education for all of the country's 15 million girls who now get no schooling.
- The Republic of Korea ordered 28 missiles from the United States. For the same price, they could have immunized all of their 120,000 unimmunized children, plus provided safe water for three years to the 3.5 million people who are without it.
- Malaysia ordered two warships from the United Kingdom when they could have provided safe water for almost a quarter century to the 5 million people who do not have it.
- Pakistan placed an order with France for 40 Mirage 2000E fighters and three Tripartite aircraft. That same money could have provided safe water for two years to the 55 million people who are without it, family planning services for the 20 million couples seeking it, essential medicines for the nearly 13 million people who have no access to basic health care, and basic education for the 12 million children unable to attend primary school.

- For the $750 million spent on one Stealth bomber, the United States could have provided nutrition assistance to 75 million children in Asia, Africa, and Latin America (Midgley, 1991).

The United States is implicated in fueling violence in the global South—where most armed conflicts take place—for the sake of its own economic development. The United States is the top exporter of conventional weapons, and most of the arms are sold to countries in the global South, among which are some of the poorest countries in the world (Hartung, 1994).

Military spending affects social development of women and children in the United States.   Paralleling the trend in the global South, unprecedented spending in the United States for the military—a male-dominated sector—has resulted in reduced spending for health, education, and social services, those sectors in which women predominate as both workers and consumers. Because expenses for the military drain our nation's resources, militarism interferes with society's ability to address the problem of violence against women and children, an essential first step if development is to be possible. The Women's International League for Peace and Freedom (Midgley, 1991) gave these examples of connections between social spending and military spending:

- $1 billion spent by the United States for one day of the Persian Gulf War could provide nutritional supplements and prenatal care for 2,127,000 low-income families.
- $5 billion spent on 35 MX missiles on rails could provide AFDC benefits to 1,500,000 families.
- $3 billion spent on two Trident submarines could rehabilitate 150,000 units of low-income housing.
- $2 billion spent on two Army Reserve divisions could pay for comprehensive preschool for 769,000 disadvantaged children.
- $200 million (six hours of military spending) could support 1,600 rape crisis centers and shelters for battered women.

Wars undermine child development.   Around the world, the direct and devastating effects of wars, conflicts, and other forms of violence undermine children's development and that of their families, communities, and societies. Child soldiers in particular, who are recruited by force and made to fight in civil wars, have had their values distorted through military training and have been traumatized by war experiences. Demobilizing them and reintegrating them into society is essential both to their personal development and to the development of society (InterAction, 1994b), yet the resources to do so are limited by inordinate spending for military endeavors and wars.

Violence in U.S. cities undermines child development.   Militaristic attitudes are evident not only in the explosion of weapons and their use in the global South, but in the United States, too, weapons of all kinds can be had by just about anyone—including children. The escalation of violence among urban youths, in particular, has turned many communities into inner-city war zones. Children's exposure to such violence traumatizes them and threatens their normal development physically, intellectually, and emotionally. Distorted development of a society's children impedes development of society as a whole.

Domestic Violence Obstructs Development

Violence against women and children is in direct opposition to securing human-centered development goals. Women experience violence as a form of control that limits their ability to pursue options in almost every area of life, from the home to the schools, workplaces, and most public spaces. Development does not occur when domestic violence keeps a woman from participating in a development project or when fear of sexual assault or harassment prevents her from taking a job or going to school (Carrillo, 1991).

Development does not occur when violence is used to control women's labor in both productive and reproductive capacities. For example, case studies of victims of domestic violence in Peru and of garment workers in Mexican *maquiladoras* show that men frequently demand their wives' income by beating them (Wetzel, 1993). Indonesian female workers returning to their villages tell of harassment and sexual abuse in the workplace and of wages being withheld for months; in the Philippines, women workers in export-oriented industries claim that male managers make female employees choose whether to "lay down or lay off" (*AWRAN*

Report, 1985). A project of the Working Women's Forum in Madras almost collapsed when the most articulate and energetic women started to drop out because of increased incidents of domestic violence against them after they had joined (Carrillo, 1992). A women's employment training center in Chicago reports that domestic violence is one of the factors accounting for the large number of dropouts in literacy and job training programs involving public assistance participants (Raphael, 1995). The sexual harassment of hundreds of women workers in a U.S.-based Mitsubishi plant—their allegations made headline news in 1996—illustrates how women are impeded by violence even when they have jobs that pay well.

Violence has significant short- and long-term physical, emotional, and psychological effects with enormous social and economic costs that obstruct community and societal development. Violence against women disrupts their lives and denies them options. It destroys their health, denies their human rights, and hinders their full participation in society. Violence against women also affects the development of children and families; for example, a Canadian study reported posttraumatic stress, clinical dysfunction, and behavioral and emotional disorders in children from violent homes (Jaffe, Wilson, & Wolfe, 1986). Ultimately, violence against women deprives society of the full participation of women in all aspects of development, and violence against children deprives society of its potential.

Lack of Opportunities Can Lead to Violence

Violence increases with social disintegration.   Some have suggested that violence is the product of a system in which political and economic deprivation and oppression of individuals lead to social injustice. Traditional social norms and practices disintegrate, they maintain, in cities where populations have swollen because rural dwellers migrated to them in search of economic opportunities. When institutions are destroyed by global forces of markets, militarism and politics, or consumer culture and are not replaced with other, competent institutions, the inevitable result is inadequate basic resources and services, poor housing, and a precarious economic existence. Under such circumstances, violence becomes almost a way of life, which perhaps explains why some scholars see family violence as a by-product of underdevelopment. For example, researchers from Nigeria, Kenya, Egypt, and Bangladesh point to the subsistence existence and economic crises of many families as contributors to domestic abuse and tensions in society (Akanda & Shamin, 1984; Shamin, 1985; Wamalwa, 1987; Zaalouk, 1987).

However, violence that accompanies underdevelopment may not necessarily be caused by increased male stress, as some might conclude. Instead, it could arise from the interaction of two simultaneous developments: (1) the creation of new norms and cultures in which people feel deprived and desperate to attain things they had never before had or expected to get and (2) the breakdown of traditional means of preventing socially advantaged people from preying opportunistically on vulnerable people. Under the brutal conditions of "every man for himself," the vulnerable people are likely to be women, children, members of ethnic or religious out-groups, and poor people. The predators are likely to be men, members of ethnic or religious in-groups, and people who are not poor.

Lack of opportunity leads to youth violence. Conditions of poverty and lack of opportunity in overcrowded inner cities in the United States seem to be a primary cause of violence. Many see youth violence as the result of "the sullen rage of mostly boys and young men who live in poverty and squalor and are taunted by visions of affluence and ease which they have no hope of reaching" (*Washington Spectator*, 1990, p. 170). The Children's Defense Fund maintains that "it is the lack of loving care that turns children into savage teenagers and adults. . . . The number of youths held for alcohol and drug offenses increased by 56 percent between 1985 and 1987. . . . The rage and pain of these homeless, hopeless, abused, alienated children will continue to explode in our faces" (*Washington Spectator*, 1990, p. 173).

Lack of opportunity also seems to be a primary cause of violence in the lives of children in the global South. For example, nearly all of Latin America's street children—10 percent to 30 percent of whom are female—engage in some sort of economic activity on the streets to support themselves and to supplement family income; many report feeling proud of their contributions to their households (Rizzini & Lusk, 1994).

However, living on the streets makes children vulnerable to prostitution, drug abuse, violence, and death. On average, six street children in Colombia and four in Brazil are killed each day (Castilho, 1995).

Poverty forces rural people to move to urban areas, and poverty in urban areas often draws children into sexual exploitation by the sex tourism industry. Some children are lured or physically forced into sexual exploitation without their parents' knowledge; others are encouraged to become involved in the sex trade by their parents, who see it as a way to supplement family income to survive (Ireland, 1993).

Maldevelopment or Distorted Development
Can Lead to Violence

There are striking similarities in conditions of exploitation and increased burden on poor women in the global North and the global South. As Karen Nussbaum, head of the U.S. Women's Bureau, pointed out, current conditions faced by U.S. workers are similar to those usually associated with the global South: "The sweatshop has returned ... fire exits are locked ... contractors often disappear without paying their workers ... children play along narrow corridors littered with flammable plastic bags" (InterAction, 1994a, p. 1).

Too often, traditional development has increased the burden on women, who continue to do unpaid and uncounted reproductive work in the home and also contribute to the household through paid work in the economy. According to Esther Boserup (1970), pioneer economist who founded the field of gender and development studies, development sometimes results in even greater disempowerment of women—men's control over resources expands while women's traditional influence even in the home shrinks. Consequently, women become more vulnerable to male violence in two spheres, the home and the workplace. Thus, development programs that are not gender sensitive or committed to equity and empowerment produce increased violence and erosion of women's and children's rights.

Human deprivation is not alleviated by failed or restricted human development. To the contrary, when development fails, disparities between men and women persist and the violence of injustice is perpetuated. For example, the global South has made significant progress toward human development in terms of life expectancy, education, and health, but a gender-specific examination of indicators offers another perspective. Some indicators show that gaps between men and women have widened over the course of development, leading some to question whether attempts at development might not inevitably disadvantage women (Carrillo, 1992). In fact, some claim that most development policies and projects have had severe negative effects on the survival chances of poor women and their families (Rao, Anderson, & Overholt, 1991). International aid for development programs in Latin America, for example, has primarily enriched and protected the interests of the rich and international investors, as conditions for poor women and other marginalized people have deteriorated (Prigoff, 1992). The negative consequences of distorted development for women and children are illustrated by the example that follows, which explains how failure to account for gender-based division of labor and responsibilities resulted in unintended yet undeniably harmful results in Sri Lanka.

> The Mahaweli irrigation project in Sri Lanka was aimed at increasing rice production. The development project did in fact help rice production, but as the yield increased, family nutrition went down. What went wrong? The project failed to take into account women's roles as food producers and decision makers. It cut off women's traditional rights to land, and it failed to provide them with the technical information necessary for increasing their productivity under the new irrigation system. The plots assigned to families, but worked by women, were not adequate both for subsistence farming and for production of rice for sale. The cash from crop sales remained under the control of the men, who spent a good part of it on tobacco and liquor, while families had less to eat. (Jaquette, 1993, p. 50)

Given the reality of gender relations, the general invisibility of women's work, and the multiple and complex roles that women actually perform, market-only development policies predictably have adverse effects for women. This seems to have been particularly true of structural adjustment programs (SAPs), which are intended to transform economies of the global South into efficient, competitive producers for international markets; the World Bank and the International Monetary Fund (IMF) implemented SAPs widely in the 1980s (see chapter 4). SAPs have required many countries in the global South to decrease domestic consumption and shift scarce resources into production of cash crops for export. In addition, SAPs called for the imposition of harsh restraints on social spending for health care, education, and social services, the primary recipients of which have traditionally been women and children. To cut government spending, state-owned companies and state services have been privatized and civil services have been drastically downsized. In many countries of the global South, as well as in the United States, it is the public sector—not the private sector or the military establishment—that has provided most of the professional and managerial urban jobs for women. With SAPs, this is no longer the case. Under SAPs, the austerity measures that were imposed on social spending—funding primarily women's sectors—were rarely imposed on arms purchases or other military spending, which are the sectors dominated by men (MacEwan, 1990).

The effects on children have been particularly devastating: The United Nations estimates that millions of children worldwide died between 1982 and 1989 as a direct result of SAPs (UNICEF, 1994). Data from Sub-Saharan Africa, where SAPs were imposed on 36 countries, show that poverty is on the rise and that women, in particular, are worse off than they were a decade ago (McGowan, 1995). The U.S. version of SAPs begun in the 1980s—reduced social services, privatization of services, and increased military spending—has similarly adversely affected women and children. "The Effect of Structural Adjustment Programs on Women in Ghana" (McGowan, 1995) describes how SAPs have harmed women in Ghana; the story applies equally throughout the global South.

The Effect of Structural Adjustment Programs on Women in Ghana

The adverse consequences of the 1983 introduction of structural adjustment programs for the Ghanaian economy have been particularly difficult for the nation's poor; within that sector, gender inequities have grown as women shoulder a disproportionate amount of the burden.

Across several important categories, SAPs in Ghana have continued to decrease the living standards of women. In a decision-making process that is dominated by IMF and World Bank officials and a small minority of male political leaders and senior bureaucrats, policies have evolved that are detrimental to women in the areas of agricultural production, employment, health, and education. Higher prices for the export crop of cocoa mean increased revenues for the predominantly male cash-crop producers, yet women farmers do not share in this benefit. Rather, the removal of subsidies from crucial inputs has placed the means of production out of the reach of women farmers.

Employment levels among the women, like the rest of the population, shrank as state enterprises were privatized and the bureaucracy was reorganized. These trends also are detrimental to women, who in their role as managers of the household are forced to make difficult adjustments. Increased unemployment has also led to a breakdown in the family unit and driven women to prostitution as a means of income generation, and thereby hastened the spread of AIDS.

The introduction of user fees has reduced access for both men and women to basic health-care facilities. Women must therefore care for the ill within the household, labor that is unpaid and impinges on time that could be spent in paid endeavors. In addition, maternal mortality has risen because women experiencing difficult pregnancies are unable to afford the hospital costs of childbirth. UNICEF's 1993 figures place maternal mortality rates in Ghana as high as one death to 100 births, one of the highest rates in Sub-Saharan Africa.

User fees have been introduced also for educational services, which have not expanded to meet demand. Here, too, females are disproportionately affected by the changes. Drop-out rates are higher for girls than for boys, and the gap between the educational levels of boys and girls, especially in the higher grades, continues to widen.

Source: McGowan, 1995.

Moving toward Solution

This chapter provides evidence that many issues are the same for women in the United States and in the global South: violence in the home and the workplace, lack of public money for social spending, lack of affordable child care, low wages and poor working conditions, women's double workload and uncounted and unpaid labor, lack of access to economic resources, and the violence of war and militarism. The next chapter presents universal solutions: gender-centered development programming, women's rights, and women's self-organization. Common goals include reduced military spending, increased social spending, pay equity, and government-funded child care programs. Moreover, for solutions to be permanent, violence against women and children must be made illegal and punishable and, ultimately, patriarchy must be eliminated.

References

Akanda, L., & Shamin, I. (1984). Women and violence: A comparative study of rural and urban violence in Bangladesh. *Women's Issues, 1*(1), 3–11.

Anderson, J., & Moore, M. (1993, February 14–18). Born oppressed: Women in the developing world face cradle-to-grave discrimination, poverty. *Washington Post,* pp. A1–A6.

AWRAN Report. (1985). Manila, Philippines: Asian Women's Research and Action Network.

Boserup, E. (1970). *Women's role in economic development.* New York: St. Martin's Press.

Bunster-Burotto, X. (1986). Surviving beyond fear: Women and torture in Latin America. In J. Nash & H. Safa (Eds.), *Women and change in Latin America* (pp. 297–307). South Hadley, MA: Bergin & Garvey.

Carrillo, R. (1991). Violence against women: An obstacle to development. In Center for Women's Global Leadership (Ed.), *Gender violence: A development and human rights issue* (pp. 19–41). Highland Park, NJ: Plowshares Press.

Carrillo, R. (1992). *Battered dreams: Violence against women as an obstacle to development.* New York: United Nations Development Fund for Women.

Castilho, C. (1995, January). Children to the slaughter: Street life is deadly in Latin American countries. *WorldPaper,* p. 12.

Center for Protection of Children's Rights (CPCR). (1991). *Report on child rights violations: Annual report to 31 December 1991.* Bangkok, Thailand: Author.

Cox, E. S. (1994). Gender violence and women's health in Central America. In M. Davies (Ed.), *Women and violence: Realities and responses worldwide* (pp. 118–133). Atlantic Highlands, NJ: Zed Books.

Davies, M. (Ed.). (1994). *Women and violence: Realities and responses worldwide.* Atlantic Highlands, NJ: Zed Books.

Doek, J. E. (1991). Management of child abuse and neglect at the international level: Trends and perspectives. *Child Abuse and Neglect, 15*(1), 51–56.

Dziech, B. W., & Schudson, C. B. (1990). The legal system exacerbates child abuse. In J. Rohr (Ed.), *Violence in America: Opposing viewpoints* (pp. 123–130). San Diego: Greenhaven Press.

Global Child Health. (1995). *Global Child Health News and Review, 3*(1), 6.

Hartung, W. D. (1994). *And weapons for all.* New York: HarperCollins.

Heise, L. (1989, March–April). Crimes of gender. *World Watch,* pp. 12–21.

Herrmann, K. J., Jr. (1990, June 13). It's time to make kids people, too. *Chicago Tribune,* Sec. 1, p. 21.

InterAction. (1994a). *Local–global connections—Women thinking globally, acting locally: On the road to Beijing and the 21st century* (Report of an official U.S. government preparatory meeting for the Fourth United Nations World Conference on Women, Wilmington, DE). Washington, DC: Author.

InterAction (1994b, July 18). Strategies for families in war zones of Africa. *Monday Developments, 12,* 13.

Ireland, K. (1993, September). *Wish you weren't here: The sexual exploitation of children and the connection with tourism and international travel* (Working Paper No. 7). Save the Children Overseas Department. (Available from Save the Children, Mary Datchelor House, 17 Grove Lane, London SE5 8RD).

Jaffe, P., Wilson, S., & Wolfe, D. A. (1986). Promoting changes in attitudes and understanding of conflict resolution among child witnesses of family violence. *Canadian Journal of Behavioral Science, 18,* 356–366.

Jaquette, J. S. (1993). The family as a development issue. In G. Young, V. Samarasinghe, & K. Kusterer (Eds.), *Women at the center: Development issues and practices for the 1990s* (pp. 45–62). West Hartford, CT: Kumarian Press.

Koop, E. (1989). *Violence against women: A global problem.* Washington, DC: U. S. Government Printing Office.

Lewis, S. (1994). They will not get away with it forever. In P. Adamson (Ed.), *The Progress of Nations 1994* (p. 37). New York: UNICEF.

MacEwan, A. (1990). *Debt and disorder: International economic instability and U.S. imperial decline.* New York: Monthly Review Press.

Mann, J. (1994, April 20). A stand against domestic violence. *Washington Post,* p. D27.

McGowan, L. A. (1995, August). *The ignored cost of adjustment: Women under SAPs in Africa* (Paper prepared for the Fourth United Nations World Conference on Women). Washington, DC: Development Gap.

Midgley, J. (1991). *Women's budget* (4th ed.). Philadelphia: Women's International League for Peace and Freedom.

Minnesota NASW Center on Violence, Development, and Family Structure (1994). *Analysis of the linkages between violence and development/underdevelopment within the context of family structure* (report submitted to the Violence and Development Project, NASW, Washington, DC). St. Paul, MN: Author.

Omvedt, G. (1990). *Violence against women: New movements and new theories in India.* New Delhi: Kali for Women.

Portugal, A. M. (1988). Cronica de una violacion provocada? [Fempress especial]. *Contraviolencia* (Santiago, Chile).

Prigoff, A. (1992). Women, social development and the state in Latin America. *Social Development Issues, 14*(1), 56–70.

Rao, A., Anderson, M. B., & Overholt, C. A. (1991). *Gender analysis in development planning: A case book.* West Hartford, CT: Kumarian Press.

Rape's defenders. (1996, July 1). *Nation, 263,* 6–8.

Raphael, J. (1995). Domestic violence and welfare reform. *Poverty and Race, 4*(1), 19.

Rizzini, I., & Lusk, M. (1994). *Children in the streets: Latin America's lost generation.* Unpublished manuscript.

Rohr, J. (Ed.). (1990). *Violence in America: Opposing viewpoints.* San Diego: Greenhaven Press.

Sen, A. (1987). *Hunger and entitlements.* Helsinki, Finland: World Institute for Development Economics Research.

Shamin, I. (1985, December 2–5). *Kidnapped, raped, killed: Recent trends in Bangladesh families in the face of urbanization.* Paper prepared for the New Delhi Conference on Violence Against Women, New Delhi, India.

Sivard, R. L. (1993). *World military and social expenditures 1993.* Washington, DC: World Priorities.

United Nations. (1989). *Violence against women in the family.* New York: Author.

United Nations Children's Fund (UNICEF). (1994). *The progress of nations 1994.* New York: United Nations.

United Nations Development Programme (UNDP). (1994). *Human Development Report 1994.* New York: Oxford University Press.

Wamalwa, B. N. (1987). *Case study from Kenya.* Nairobi: Public Law Institute.

Washington Spectator. (1990). Poverty promotes teen violence. In J. Rohr (Ed.), *Violence in America: Opposing viewpoints* (pp. 170–175). San Diego: Greenhaven Press.

Wetzel, J. W. (1993). *The world of women: In pursuit of human rights.* New York: New York University Press.

Women's Feature Service. (1993). *The power to change: Women in the Third World redefine their environment.* Atlantic Highlands, NJ: Zed Books.

Zaalouk, M. El Husseiny. (1987). *Case study from Egypt.* Cairo: National Center for Social and Criminal Research.

Chapter 7

Sustainable Human Development as an Antidote to Violence against Women and Children

pg.160

> Genuine development improves the well-being and status of women. It recognizes long-overlooked economic contributions of women and the extra burdens that growing poverty places on them. It supports the struggles of women to survive and to achieve equality, dignity, and full human rights. (Oxfam America, n.d.)

A central idea among some international development workers in the 1970s was that development thinking and action needed to be expanded to include women. The message of the 1990s, according to Young, Samarasinghe, and Kusterer (1993), is that "the most fundamental development thinking and action—increasing productivity in meeting basic human needs, organizing for developmental social change, or solving the hardest new development problems—are already primarily women's activities" (p. 2). In other words, the current approach is not to include women in a gender-sensitive development process implemented primarily by men but to secure the participation of men and their resources in the gender-sensitive development process that is already underway and carried out mostly by women.

In country after country, women have demonstrated that they are becoming empowered to reject the oppression of patriarchal systems and to lift themselves, their families, and their communities out of poverty. Three themes emerge from the experiences of women working in the global North and in the global South, and together these themes constitute a powerful shared framework for using sustainable human development strategies as a vehicle for empowerment and an antidote to violence against women and children. First, the gender-specific daily roles and relationships of women and men must be transformed if methods for increasing the popular production of goods and services that

138

meet basic human needs are to meet with success. Second, women's experiences with their recent development initiatives place them "at the cutting edge of every path and every method of developmental social change: grassroots organizing, popular education, local and national nongovernmental organizations (NGOs), institution building by means of training and managed change in existing governmental and corporate organizations" (Young et al., 1993, p. 2). Third, women have taken the lead—both in their individual lives and in their collective social movements—in new areas of development work, including AIDS, democratization and civil society, and nationalist conflicts.

Clearly, the centrality, strengths, and leadership of women in development efforts in different fields in both the global North and the global South offer valuable lessons, which are the subject of this chapter.

Making Gender Violence a Central Issue in Development

Attempts to integrate women into development are doomed to failure if they do not make central two issues: (1) violence against women and (2) the militarism of societies. Development projects that deal with violence toward women are building blocks for more comprehensive, empowering, and therefore sustainable efforts that will enable women's full participation in the development process (Women's Feature Service, 1993).

In both the global South and in underdeveloped regions of the United States, development programs must be gender sensitive, which means looking first at issues of violence. Carrillo (1992) makes the case that the international development community should support projects that address various manifestations of gender violence as legitimate development projects in themselves. Development agencies can make an important contribution by highlighting the obstacles that gender violence puts in the path of the development process and identifying strategies for countering it.

Several countries have already begun to identify obstacles and strategies to overcome them. For example, "ladies only" cars were reserved in mass transit systems in Bombay to provide safe transportation to work for women; at the United Nations Development Fund for Women project in Tempoal, Mexico, staff understood that violence can occur when women become empowered, and they took the time to work with husbands and community members when violence did emerge as a result of women's changing roles (Carrillo, 1992).

Gender violence and strategies for reducing women's vulnerability should be documented in program reporting; reports that are disseminated should highlight the effect of violence on development and the ways in which development itself gives rise to new forms of gender-based violence (Carrillo, 1992). "The Chicago Experience" explains how development project staff in Chicago documented and addressed the issue of domestic violence and welfare reform.

The Chicago Experience: Domestic Violence and Welfare Reform

The Chicago Commons West Humboldt Employment Training Center (ETC) was started in February 1991 as a demonstration model to ascertain the level of skills and the range of problems presented by low-income people receiving public assistance and the programmatic effort and length of time needed to bring them into the labor market. ETC provides case management services as well as literacy, ESL, and GED classes; health care; child care; parenting and family literacy training; and self-help support groups, all at one site. Almost 500 participants have been helped since ETC's inception.

In addition to providing direct services, the ETC program staffers document what they learn about the needs of the welfare population in Chicago. They share their learning with other service providers, community groups, and academic researchers to begin a dialogue about poor people's needs and to affect the national debate in the United States about "welfare reform."

Statistics describing the characteristics of 91 women receiving Aid to Families with Dependent Children (AFDC) who entered ETC between July 1, 1993, and June 30, 1994, reveal a strong connection between domestic violence and long-term welfare receipt. Fifty-eight percent of the women were current victims of domestic violence, an additional 26 percent were past domestic violence victims, and 17 percent were past victims of sexual assault or incest survivors.

Domestic violence explains much about the difficulty of making the journey from welfare to work. ETC found that women do not come to basic skills classes regularly, because their attendance provokes violent behavior against them. Their decision to improve their skills and seek employment threatens their abusers, who prefer them to stay dependent. Coming to the ETC program is itself an act of resistance that most often exacerbates the violence. Staff see women with visible bruises, black eyes, and cigarette burns inflicted by abusers in the hope that their victims will be too embarrassed to come to school.

ETC believes that domestic violence is one of the factors accounting for the large number of drop-outs in literacy and job training programs. Some women fall asleep in class because they have not been able to get any sleep at home as a result of the conflict there. Often the conflict occurs the night before the GED test or a crucial entrance test for a job training program.

Because of the traumatization from domestic violence or incest, many women need professional therapy or medication to recover from the depression that has set in. ETC has demonstrated that once women extricate themselves from the violence and have some time to sufficiently recover from past trauma, great gains occur in literacy levels and employability. Training programs, however well-intentioned, that do not address this issue are doomed to failure.

ETC is making it known that welfare reform schemes, including those providing public service jobs, cannot succeed if female recipients remain in the grip of their abusers. The fact is that these women cannot successfully hold down jobs of any kind. AFDC women may get off welfare as a result of proposed new welfare plans, but they will become further trapped into remaining with their abuser, who does not want them to be economically independent.

ETC is advocating to change the fact that domestic violence remains dangerously disconnected from welfare reform. Most important, they declare that the relationship of domestic violence and sexual abuse and incest to teen pregnancy and welfare receipt mandates a strong domestic violence prevention effort aimed at young men and women. ETC insists that specialized services for domestic violence victims be an integral aspect of any welfare plan.

Source: Raphael, 1995.

Gender Analysis as a Central Development Methodology

Tisch and Wallace (1994) suggest that gender analysis be integrated into the planning, design, and implementation of all development projects. Moreover, women must participate in every project stage so that social, economic, and political inequalities or inequities between men and women can be identified and considered. As a methodological tool, gender analysis helps to identify "access to, and control over, productive resources, income sources, expenditures, and division of labor between men and women" (p. 161). Gender analysis also provides a new analytical framework for moving to an economic paradigm that includes women's productivity as a central economic principle.

Women's participation in every stage of planning and implementation should be required of all development projects so that the presence of social, economic, and political inequalities or inequities between men and women are considered.

Rao, Anderson, and Overholt (1991) developed a framework for gender analysis that aims to clarify general project objectives, assess how they relate to women's involvement with a project, and anticipate the effect of the project on women. The cornerstone of this framework is an adequate database that considers what women do and why. Gender analysis of this sort takes into account—and makes visible—household economic activities and measures them as part of total output of goods and services, in contrast to the treatment of household labor in the current economic paradigm (see "Economic Theory"). Ultimately, frameworks for gender analysis provide a way to develop power sharing both in the family and in the economy.

Economic Theory

A young girl in Zimbabwe starts her day at 4 A.M. when she walks barefoot, carrying a heavy tin about eleven kilometers from her home to fetch water. When she returns home at 9 A.M. she eats a little and then gathers firewood until midday. She cleans the utensils from the family's morning meal and prepares lunch for her family. She then walks in the hot sun until early evening, fetching vegetables for supper before making the evening trip for water. Her day ends at 9 P.M., after she has prepared supper and put her younger brothers and sisters to sleep.

A young, middle-class housewife in the United States spends her days obtaining, preparing, and serving food; cleaning up after meals; dressing and diapering her children; disciplining them; taking them to day care or to school; keeping an eye on or playing with them; putting away their toys, books, and clothes; putting them to bed; disposing of garbage; dusting; doing the laundry; going to the gas station and supermarket; repairing household items; ironing; making beds; paying bills; caring for pets and plants; sewing or mending or knitting; doing business with salespeople; answering the phone; vacuuming, sweeping, and washing floors; cutting the grass; weeding; shoveling snow; and cleaning the bathroom and kitchen.

> *A highly trained member of the U.S. military has the regular duty to descend to an underground facility where he waits with a colleague, for hours at a time, for an order to fire a nuclear missile. He is so skilled and effective that if his colleague were to attempt to subvert an order to fire, he would be expected to kill him if necessary to ensure a successful missile launch.*
>
> *A pimp and heroin addict in Rome regularly pays graft. Although his services, consumption, and production are illegal, they are, nonetheless, markets. Money changes hands. His activities are part of Italy's hidden economy. A government treasury measures the money supply and sees that more money is in circulation than has been reported in legitimate business activities; thus, a minimal value for the hidden economy is regularly imputed to Italy's national accounts. So part of the pimp's illegal services and production and consumption activities will be recognized and recorded.*
>
> *The two men in the case study work. The two women do not. You may believe that the women work full days, but according to the theory, science, profession, practice, and institutionalization of economics, you are wrong. The young girl in Zimbabwe is considered unproductive, unoccupied, and economically inactive. The young U.S. housewife has to face the fact that she fills her time in a totally unproductive manner—that she is economically inactive, and economists record her as unoccupied also. The U.S. military man is in paid work, work that has value and contributes, as part of the nuclear machine, to his nation's growth, wealth, and productivity (even though his primary activity is sitting and waiting). Even though the Italian pimp's activities are illegal and underground, they are recorded as contributing to his nation's productivity.*
>
> *Source:* Waring, 1988.

At every stage of the development process, gender analysis should include attention to connections between violence and development at the individual and institutional levels. Ultimately, people-centered development that redistributes resources in a just way, that involves meaningful participation, and that is environmentally sustainable can be achieved only if there is demilitarization of both societies and the deep-seated patriarchal belief systems that undergird them.

Strategies for Development and Social Change

Women undoubtedly face many problems and issues, but many creative solutions can be found. Once women believe in themselves and in their ability to work together, they become hopeful for the future, their aspirations evolve, and they begin to seek their own creative and constructive responses to their problems and develop into strong, self-reliant human beings (Chatterjee, 1993). Several alternatives to traditional development approaches are being tried around the world, from which many lessons can be distilled and applied across a range of specific development issues for women and children.

Grassroots Self-Help Projects

A decentralized and participatory model of development has appeared throughout the global South, cultivated by women's groups and ethnic communities. Such grassroots self-help projects offer an alternative to traditional development approaches and a real antidote for extreme poverty in communities of poor women and their families (Prigoff, 1992). Creative self-help projects that have been organized in the shantytowns of urban and rural Latin America cover a variety of community needs. Some produce services such as housecleaning and cooking collectives to free women's time for daily labor in production of services or commodities. Using a self-help model of development, these communities operate as extended families—people work in mutual support groups to manage the tasks of survival. An essential part of this empowerment model of development is the organization of a community of workers who participate in production and management decisions. Thus, features of the model include self-help, self-determination, and self-governance, as well as income generation.

For more than 20 years, a particularly successful grassroots project, the Self-Employed Women's Association (SEWA), has been organizing women workers in India, including small-scale vendors, home-based workers, and service providers (Chatterjee, 1993). SEWA's approach is to organize women so that they can attain full employment, work security, regular income, food, and social services. The key to SEWA's success is its combination of two strategies: (1) *struggle efforts,* which draw explicit attention to exploitative situations, bring visibility to workers' issues, create pressure on institutions to respond, and build unity and courage among the women and inculcate a spirit of sacrifice; and (2) *development efforts,* which create constructive alternatives to unacceptable situations, impart skills to the women and develop their capacity for self-sufficiency, and create asset ownership or control and autonomy for the workers. Struggle efforts have the potential to involve a multitude of women and to build a movement; development efforts help build an organizational base. Taken separately, neither struggle nor development efforts are likely to bring about change and create a new society. When the two approaches are combined, however, they have tremendous potential to effect change. SEWA's dual approach in confronting violence and injustice at individual, institutional, and structural and cultural levels is described in "SEWA."

SEWA

Through participatory involvement of the workers, SEWA uses struggle and development together to establish increased solidarity and increased concrete benefits for women at the grassroots. Through struggle efforts, women question the status quo and understand the nature of exploitation. From development efforts, women build their own alternatives. Successful development efforts always involve struggle at some point, and this capacity is inculcated in the women. Struggle efforts, on the other hand, establish concrete development activities to sustain involvement of its members. Struggle and development activities are carried out within the framework of two organizational forms, both of which are participatory and focused on worker identity of the members: the trade union form of organization is used for the struggle efforts and the cooperative form of organization is used for development efforts.

Union Structure and Struggle

SEWA is registered as a trade union under the Indian Trade Union Act of 1926. Through this structure, SEWA carries on its movement of struggle confronting injustice on three levels. The first is the injustice that women see directly—the immediate exploiter. This person may be a cruel policeman, employer, or contractor. The immediate exploiter, however, is supported by a second level of injustice—the government agencies and the legal structure. For example, the Labor Department—which is meant to protect workers— has been corrupted by and helps the employers; the municipality treats poor vendors as criminals; the courts seldom make judgments in favor of poor people, especially if they are women. All this exploitation can be sustained because of the injustice at the third and highest level—the level of policies and laws. To be effective, SEWA's struggle is carried out at all three levels of injustice through direct action (meetings, writing, demonstrations, Satyagrahas—acts of noncooperation—and strikes), through dealing with government departments (making complaints and filing legal cases in courts) and making attempts to bring about policy changes through campaigns, workshops, studies, and advocacy. Basic to all these strategies is further organizing of self-employed women workers.

Cooperative Development

Because a large majority of self-employed women do not own capital or the tools and equipment of their trade, they remain vulnerable to private moneylenders and remain indebted indefinitely at exorbitant interest rates. Thus, SEWA develops alternative economic organizations. The SEWA Bank is the oldest cooperative venture providing supportive services for self-employed women. It provides an integrated set of banking services and also provides its clientele with access to legal aid, productivity training and education, maternity protection, child care, and other social security services. It is participatory, with all the major trade groups from SEWA's union membership represented on the governing body—the board of directors—which makes all major bank decisions and sanctions all loans advanced. Any woman can open an account with SEWA Bank. Because the majority of account holders are illiterate, the Bank has evolved a unique system of identification: a card that has a photograph showing the woman holding a slate with her account number written on it.

Source: Chatterjee, 1993, pp. 81–93.

What SEWA has learned from organizing self-employed women over the years provides lessons for other women around the globe, including the United States. Chatterjee (1993) delineates six important points gleaned from SEWA's experience:

1. Organize for collective strength. When women begin to believe in the importance of coming together and acting collectively, they become strong, articulate, and full of hope. Organizing actions must be rooted in women's concerns. Organizing implies a participatory approach as women work closely as colleagues, sharing in one another's everyday joys and sorrows. Organizing not only unites women but also breaks down barriers of caste, community, religion, language, and geography.

2. Begin with the world of work. SEWA's consistent experience is that year-round work and regular income are the foremost priorities of self-employed women. Work transcends all other concerns—their very being, and that of their families, depends on their work.

Self-employed women are hardworking and resourceful; they be-lie the popular myth that poor people are lazy or wish to do only the bare minimum. SEWA found that women know only one thing: work, from dawn to dusk, with no time for rest or leisure, often at the cost of their health and well-being. Working poor women are an important resource; they are already economically active, but they require appropriate support systems and action to alleviate their continuing poverty and vulnerability to violence.

3. Take a holistic, integrated approach to organizing. People in India view their lives as an integrated whole, so programs cannot be com-partmentalized vertically or unidirectionally. For example, along with their overriding need for work and income, self-employed women need basic social security services—health care, child care, banking and credit services, housing, and insurance, for example—and these needs must be addressed by linking them to women's work. Also, SEWA's experience shows that women's involvement in regional de-velopment approaches strengthens local women, their economic activities, and their own organizations—and it also leads to success-ful overall development of a region.

4. Build on and strengthen women's potential. Women constitute a vast and promising resource—they have enormous potential and cre-ative abilities—and they should be treated as such at every stage of the development process. Over the years SEWA has witnessed the transformation of many individual women and groups of women—from despair to energetic leadership and hope—when this approach has been taken.

5. Build self-reliance. The Gandhian concept of *Swavalambanam* (self-reliance) implies the total development of a human being to the point where she can stand independently and with dignity from a position of strength. Through leadership training and action, ex-posure tours, and other methods, SEWA has helped women de-velop self-reliance not only in the world of work but in all aspects of their lives.

6. Combine grassroots organizing with policy-level interventions. A strong grassroots base is essential but not sufficient to influence policies, focus the direction of development, and deal with poverty

and inequality. Action is necessary also at national and international levels to influence, inform, and re-orient the direction for change that policymakers envisage.

Popular Education for Women's Transformation

Vella (1993) suggested that the knowledge gained through dialogues between women in the global South and in the global North can ultimately transform women's physical and social reality worldwide. She proposed several popular education principles that can help such dialogue be productive. The principles are equally applicable for helping women learn about development and violence prevention strategies in local, grassroots settings.

Popular education principles include ensuring the safety and inclusion of women as learners; honoring the importance of women's right to be engaged mentally, emotionally, and physically in their learning; preparing an appropriate, engaging learning design that respects the needs of the learners; integrating cognitive, affective, and psychomotor aspects of learning into all educational activities; engaging in respectful dialogue—that is, actively listening to women in development situations and responding—rather than monologue; sequencing and reinforcing learning from simple to complex; designing learning activities so that the resulting knowledge, skills, or attitudes are immediately useful to the learner; presenting learning that has relevance for women's lives; and helping learners to analyze (break down concepts, skills, and attitudes) and to synthesize (put ideas, skills, and attitudes together in a way that is congruent with the learner's culture and situation). The most important task is to incorporate all the principles of popular education and thereby become accountable to the learner.

Microenterprise Programs to Widen Economic Opportunities for Women

Microenterprise programs became popular economic development activities during the 1980s from Bangladesh to Zambia and Appalachia to Chicago. Such programs, which provide access to credit and other resources for self-employed workers in the informal sector, are important for widening economic opportunities for women (McDonnell, Himunyanga-Phiri, & Tembo, 1993). In 1976 Muhammad Yunis developed the model for microenterprise programs, which became the Grameen Bank in 1982; the project is described in "The Grameen Bank." The model has since been transferred successfully from the global South to the global North. Women participate at high levels because microenterprise activities can be performed within the home and thus are compatible with women's competing roles; furthermore, the programs are structured to meet women's needs, which are not met by established banks and credit unions (McDonnell et al., 1993).

The Grameen Bank

The Grameen Bank Project, launched in 1976 in the Bangladesh village of Jobra by Professor Muhammad Yunis, was set up to loan money to poor, landless, rural people who had no collateral for their loans. Women who applied for loans would not need the approval of their husbands or other family members to receive loans in their own names. The loans were small—averaging about $65 for first-time loans—and yet they provided flexibility and opportunity for starting small income-generating projects.

The first step in starting the Grameen Bank was to reach poor villagers and help them to understand the program. To reach women in a predominantly Muslim country such as Bangladesh was a difficult task. Because Dr. Yunis was known and respected in the village of Jobra, he was allowed to hold a meeting with village women at night. The women took their places at the meeting in a hut, however, while Dr. Yunis sat outside in the yard talking to them through female assistants. The women in the hut were neither seen nor heard. When it started to rain, Dr. Yunis was given shelter in another hut and the discussion continued. It soon became obvious that direct communication was needed to make the program clear to the women and the women finally came to understand that the idea of making bank loans available to them was in their interest. They moved to Dr. Yunis' hut, sitting behind a partition so they could hear but not see him. After a long session, the women were convinced of the benefit of taking out loans from the Grameen Bank so they could participate in small income-generating projects.

The banking system works in a unique way. Each Grameen Bank branch is headed by a manager who oversees field workers who are required to live and work in the villages in which they are assigned. Bank workers visit the villages and talk informally to villagers, explaining the rules and benefits of the bank. Any person who owns less than half an acre of farming land and has a very limited income is eligible for a loan for any income-generating activity. To get the loan, the person must form a group of five similarly situated people. Each group elects its own chair and secretary and holds weekly meetings. Several groups meet at the same time in a village; this group of meetings is called a Center. The Center elects a chief who conducts weekly meetings and is responsible for the observance of all rules prescribed by the bank. Loans are given to individuals or groups; only the person receiving the loan is responsible for his or her loan. All loans are for one year and are paid back in weekly installments. Each week every group member deposits one Taka (Bangladesh currency) as personal saving. This fund is operated by the group. In addition, each member pays a "tax" into a group fund. The group also must set up an emergency fund to which all group members contribute as insurance against default, death, or disability of a member.

The groups are a key to the Grameen Bank's success. A poor woman may feel vulnerable and powerless, but group membership helps her to feel protected and less alone. Peer pressure helps to ensure that the members will abide by bank rules and repay the loans. Discipline, unity, courage, and labor are the four principles of the Grameen Bank. The bank is more than an economic system for loans and credit; it is a social system.

The Grameen Bank Project has grown rapidly. By 1987, 300,000 loans had been given, 80 percent of them to women. With about half a million borrowers currently, the bank is growing at a rate of 10,000 to 15,000 new borrowers a month. It has reached 9,500 villages. The repayment rate is 98 percent. The focus has increasingly been to encourage women borrowers. Based on the Bank's experience, a loan to a woman results in more benefits to the family.

Source: Helmore, 1987, 1989; Saunders, 1988; United Nations Economic and Social Commission for Asia and the Pacific, 1984.

Microenterprise programs have helped women remove some of the larger barriers that constrain their economic opportunities and their dependence on often abusive husbands. Studies show that the strategy is viable and that it benefits women participants and their families, communities, and countries. However, a new model that offers a range of services beyond those provided in most microenterprise programs is now emerging. The H-P Women's Development Company in Zambia, begun in 1988, is one example of the new model. Besides providing access to resources such as credit, investment training, employment, and information, H-P gives support in such areas as legal services, child care, and housing. The program is operated by Zambian women for the benefit of Zambian women and is financed by capital realized by Zambian women. The significance of the program in the lives of women is proven by the account of a participant in the H-P project, Annie Tembo:

Annie Tembo's Story

Annie Tembo lives in Lusaka, Zambia. After being ordered by her husband to leave his house, Annie related her story:

My world was shattered as I was homeless and jobless, with two children and one on the way. I was forced to seek shelter with my sister until after I delivered our third child. Thereafter, I embarked on a search for a job and alternative accommodations. . . . When eventually I was employed . . . my employers refused to give me accommodation as they said that I was married and should be staying with my husband. They would give me accommodation only if my husband wrote a letter confirming that we were separated. I approached my husband for the letter, but he just laughed in my face. . . .

Once again, I was faced with very few options. I moved with my children into a former neighbor's two-room servant's quarters with no furniture. . . . In the next six months, I struggled to feed and clothe my children, plus pay their school fees. . . . I decided to start a small tailoring business and approached my bankers for a loan . . . [but] my application was rejected with no explanation.

I persevered with my life, and by sewing one item per night after all the children were asleep, I managed to rebuild my home. I bought a TV, fridge, and living room and bedroom furniture within the next and a half.

After I had been living apart from my husband for four years, he appeared one night at my doorstep, begging for forgiveness and asking for us to resume living together. He informed me that he had been transferred to Ndola and that his transfer would give us the chance to work things out between us.

Following advice from my parents and friends, and for the children's sake, I agreed to reconcile with my husband. I packed my newly acquired possessions and together we moved to Ndola.

Nine months later, while still unemployed, tragedy struck my life again. My husband was involved in a car accident and died instantly. The funeral lasted five days, and at the end of it all, not a single item of furniture was left, including the family car. My husband's relations had shared out, item by item, the furniture that I had painstakingly purchased.

My husband's employers told me . . . I could stay in their house for only three months. I found myself in the same predicament I had been in five years earlier. I had three children to clothe and feed, no husband, no home, and no job. It was on my return to Lusaka that I heard about the H-P Women's Development Company Limited. Through it I was able to revive my tailoring business. The company provided me with consultation and management services and advice on how to manage my business, maintain my books, and deal with stocks, sales, and profit.

Then the company gave me a loan . . . out of which I was able to buy a sewing machine and materials to make bedspreads to sell. My business prospered, and being unable to cope with the orders alone, I employed a full-time tailor whom I was able to pay from my sale proceeds.

Since I had no hope of acquiring a mortgage, I approached the H-P for a three-bedroom house in its housing project. The company made a house available to me through its mortgage scheme, which enabled me to pay for the house over a period of fifteen years. I am now waiting to move into my newly acquired property, which is due to be completed by the end of the year. It gives me a feeling of security to know that my children will be living in a house that no one can take away from them. Should I die before they grow up, H-P will ensure that my relatives do not grab it from them.

Through its legal services, H-P has also assisted me in repossessing all the property that had been grabbed from us after the death of my husband. It has struggled with the courts, and I probably would not have persevered or been able to afford the legal battle if I had had to pay a private lawyer.

Source: Reprinted with permission from McDonnell, S., Himunyanga-Phiri, T. V., & Tembo, A. (1993). Widening economic opportunities for women: Removing barriers one brick at a time. In G. Young, V. Samarasinghe, & K. Kusterer (Eds.), *Women at the center: Development issues and practices for the 1990s* (pp. 24–25). West Hartford, CT: Kumarian Press.

Empowerment of Women as a Way to Advance Sustainable Human Development Objectives

From the feminist writings and grassroots organizing experiences of women in the global South emerged an empowerment approach to development (Moser, 1986). Power, from this standpoint, is the right to determine choices in life and to influence the direction of change; it is not domination over others. The goal of this approach is the empowerment of women through the development of greater self-reliance and internal strengths. The approach acknowledges inequalities between men and women and the origins of women's subordination in the family; it also emphasizes that women's experiences of oppression differ according to their race, class, colonial history, and current position in the international economic order. Accordingly, women must challenge oppressive structures and situations simultaneously at different levels.

An excellent articulation of the empowerment approach has been made by Development Alternatives with Women for a New Era (DAWN). DAWN is a group of women organized before the 1985 World Conference on Women in Nairobi to analyze the conditions of the world's women and to formulate a vision of an alternative future society. That vision encompasses a world where inequality based on class, gender, and race is eliminated; where basic needs become basic rights and poverty and all forms of violence are erased; where each person has the opportunity to develop his or her full potential and creativity; where women's values of nurturance and solidarity characterize human relationships; and where women's reproductive role is redefined and child care is shared among men, women, and society as a whole (Moser, 1986).

Empowerment of women goes hand in hand with increased education and independent income through employment or self-employment. Other factors that contribute to women's empowerment are laws that ensure human rights equality for women, women's self-help groups, exposure to alternative gender roles through exposure to other cultures, and increased productivity of women's domestic work.

How Women's Empowerment Advances Development Objectives

Studies have demonstrated that increased education and income for women (that is, empowerment) further the objectives of people-centered development in several ways (Weaver, Rock, & Kusterer, 1994). First, increased income and education for women result in improved health and nutrition for them, their children, and their families; in other words, their quality of life is bettered. Studies show too that the combination of increased educational attainment, especially at the secondary level and beyond, and increased income opportunities leads to lower fertility rates, which also enhances the quality of life. Moreover, increased education and income have been shown to be linked to increased productivity in women's economic activities. Case studies in various cultures show that often women have a relatively high inclination to invest and save.

With increased education and income security, women are much more likely to participate in the organizational life of civil society, thus promoting the development goal of democratization. In addition, women's conduct of their day-to-day activities gives reason to believe that women's empowerment will also further the goal of environmental sustainability.

How Women Influence Economic Policies

Women around the world are becoming increasingly aware that the globalization of the economy and the agendas of economic powers such as the World Bank and the International Monetary Fund are not women's agendas. The overwhelming burden that women now carry because of structural adjustment programs (SAPs) and rapidly declining standards of living brings urgency to the need for women to enter the policy dialogue in full force, advocating for their own, their families', and their communities' interests.

This is precisely what women in Africa are doing. A growing number of African women's programs and organizations are working to address directly the effect of free markets, export-oriented policies, and other measures of structural adjustment; they are working also to find economic alternatives that serve the needs of most women and men. Some of the things they are calling for are the inclusion of women as full partners in all national and international decision-making processes; a shift in the objectives of SAPs and lending policies to place primary emphasis on equity concerns such as economic security and the health and well-being of women and poor people; the design of economic policies based on an accurate understanding of women and poor people, including gender and intrahousehold differences in production, consumption, access to resources, and responsibilities; an emphasis in economic policy reform programs on the role of women as producers and on their access to education, property rights, and financial credit; and accountable government, not less government (McGowan, 1995).

Implications for Social Workers

The social work profession has a clear commitment to social justice and gender equity, as articulated in the code of ethics and policy statements of the National Association of Social Workers. Schools of social work are mandated by the Council on Social Work Education to educate students about the oppression of women, people of color, and other vulnerable populations and to help them develop skills aimed at alleviating oppression and social injustice.

Social workers in the United States are well versed on issues related to family violence, but the connections between violence in the family and other forms of violence, as well as the effect of violence on human and social development, must be better understood. Social workers must fully understand how structures of power and domination at the societal level tend to be reproduced in structures of power and domination at all levels of social organization, including the family.

Strategies for social development and progress require the empowerment of women (Prigoff, 1992). "An International Training Institute for Women" describes a social work initiative that demonstrates one way women from the United States and the global South can learn together how to empower women to initiate and participate in the sustainable development of their communities.

An International Training Institute for Women

In May 1996, the University of North Carolina at Chapel Hill hosted a forum to initiate a long-term commitment to women working in sustainable development at the community level. The forum, sponsored by the School of Social Work, the Department of City and Regional Planning, and the university's Center for International Studies, brought together 200 women and men from Asia, Africa, North America, Latin America, and the Caribbean to discuss women's roles in sustainable development. The forum, entitled "Women, Community, and Sustainable Development: Collaborative Approaches to Skills, Theory, and Practice," explored the values, skills, and talents that women activists, practitioners, and academics bring to sustainable development efforts, as well as the strategies women need to become more active and effective agents of sustainable development. The face-to-face meeting enabled the sharing of information across group lines for the dynamic development of practical wisdom and promotion of policy improvements.

The focus of the forum was on the concrete ways women are currently involved in sustainable efforts and on the specific skills that women need to be full partners, at all levels, in sustainable development work. Participants heard from experienced leaders in sustainable development from Barbados, India, Latin America, Canada, and the United States, but most of all they heard from one another. The lessons they had learned in their own places, and understanding how those lessons related to the work of other women, became the heart of the forum. As one participant noted, "There're two parts to communicating: telling the truth and letting others tell the truth."

Speaking truths, or at least allowing each person to present his or her own reality, was the key to the forum's structure. Small group discussions were organized according to the participants' experience as grassroots leaders, academics, NGO [nongovernmental organization] representatives, or funding representatives. After discussing an issue in one of these groups, the same issue was discussed in groups organized by region (Asia, Africa, Latin America and the Caribbean, and North America). Topics could therefore be explored from both experiential and cultural perspectives. Volunteer interpreters were paired with each non-English speaker for the whole day, including breakfast, lunch, and dinner, so that both formal and informal communication could be shared.

Quotes from the evaluation forms helped us measure the usefulness of the forum structure to enable each one to teach and learn. "Use your internal sense of justice to survive," said a grassroots leader from Kentucky. A young academic from the United States said, "I questioned my work, my personality, and how I may contribute to some really bad systems out there. It was a weekend of self-pride and self-realization. . . . Maybe I'll just go home and cook up a revolution." "Yesterday was a typical woman's day," said a community leader from Antigua-Barbuda. "We did a lot of work, some networking, and a little bit a leisure." "I learned of the importance women have, and that I am not alone," said a grassroots leader from Honduras.

The unique nature of this inaugural forum—the ability to structure a dialogue and learning experience that incorporates issues of poverty, community, development, the environment, and the role women have in all of it—sets the tone for the annual meetings planned to follow. The connections among social and economic justice for women, family economies, local market economies, quality of life, and local environments—all aspects of sustainable development—will continue to be the focus of work directed toward building the capacity of grassroots women to do the things they do now even better.

The annual training institute will focus initially on grassroots women from the global South and on women from the southeast United States (with emphasis on Native American women and women of color engaged in development projects). The goal of the annual sessions is for participants to learn how to strengthen their own participation, leadership, and organizational skills in sustainable development practice and how to teach and train others in their communities the skills necessary to participate in such projects. A "lessons without borders" approach is inherent in the institute, with women from different parts of the world learning from one another's experiences. Following the training session, women will return to their development sites with support from cooperating NGOs and graduate students who assist with the institute. For two additional months the graduate students will assist participants in incorporating lessons learned at the institute in their community development efforts and evaluate the validity and cultural appropriateness of the institute experience. The cooperating NGOs will continue to supplement the training in their regional setting and will select participants for future institute sessions.

Source: Reprinted with permission from Dorothy Gamble, clinical assistant professor and assistant dean for student services, and Marie Weil, professor and director of the Community Social Work program, School of Social Work, co-leaders of the Women in Sustainable Development Project; and Helzi Noponen, assistant professor, Department of City and Regional Planning. All are at the University of North Carolina at Chapel Hill.

What You Can Do

The following suggestions are aimed at helping social workers learn from the experiences of women in both the global South and the United States. They should help you better understand violence against women and children within the context of development on a global scale.

- Learn what parallels exist between violence in the global South and in the United States; listen closely to the message of women who became empowered to stop violence in other countries. Read the life stories of women and social workers from countries of the global South who have learned—often through traumatic experiences and struggle—to analyze their own social reality and to be self-directing in life choices. Among the most extraordinary examples in a growing literature are works that relate the life journeys of articulate, indigenous women national leaders who dedicated their lives to community organization (Prigoff, 1992). Social workers can draw universal, inspirational, and useful lessons from the personal stories of these women. Publications about legendary heroines in Latin America include the following:

  Benjamin, Medea. (1987). *Don't be afraid, gringo. A Honduran woman speaks from the heart: The story of Elvia Alvarado.* San Francisco: Institute for Food and Development Policy.
  Bronstein, Audrey. (1983). *The triple struggle: Latin American peasant women.* Boston: South End Press.

de Chungara, Domitila, con Acebey, David. (1989). *Aqui tambien, Domitila!* (2nd ed.). Mexico, DF: Siglo Veintiuno Editores.

Menchu, Rigoberta. (1988). *I, Rigoberta Menchu: An Indian woman in Guatemala* (Elizabeth Burgos-Debray, Ed.). New York: Alpine Press.

Viezzer, Moema. (1977). *Si me permiten hablar: Testimonio de Domitila, una mujer de las minas de Bolivia.* Mexico, DF: Siglo Veintiuno Editores.

- Learn what women's groups and social workers are doing in countries of the global South to stop violence and promote development. Many case studies exist that relate personal stories from which universal lessons can be gleaned. Use the resources section at the end of this book as a start.

- Read about the Fourth World Conference on Women held in Beijing, China, in September 1995; learn what issues women from around the world joined together to address; find ways that you can join them.

- Learn about United Nations conventions that uphold the rights of women and children throughout the world. Come to understand that violence against children, gender violence, and lack of development opportunities for women are violations of fundamental human rights. Relevant United Nations declarations include the following: Convention and Declaration on the Rights of the Child; International Convention and Declaration on the Elimination of All Forms of Racial Discrimination; Convention and Declaration on the Elimination of Discrimination against Women; Convention on the Political Rights of Women; Declaration on the Protection of Women and Children in Emergency and Armed Conflict; and Declaration on the Promotion among Youth of the Ideals of Peace, Mutual Respect, and Understanding between Peoples.

- Join organizations that are committed to reducing gun violence and militarization; read their literature and respond to their calls for action in areas such as banning land mines, arms control legislation, trade restrictions on weapons, gun control in the United States, economic conversion, diverting military spending by the global North and the global South to the social needs of people, and so on.

- To ensure gender-sensitive programming at all levels, advocate that the numbers of women in leadership positions be increased in the

United Nations, international development organizations, NGOs, and community development projects in the United States.

- Use your knowledge of the effects of violence on women and children to educate the media and public institutions and to sensitize the general public, including women themselves, about the devastating personal and national consequences of continuing violence against women and children. Confront media portrayals (in music lyrics, movies, and books, for example) of women that perpetuate gender violence.

- Support community-based development projects in your area that involve women at all levels.

- Be an advocate for increased availability of child care and health insurance for workers, as well as for laws and regulations that prohibit gender and racial discrimination.

- If you are a school social worker, remember that schools are places where early attitudes about gender roles and gender violence are shaped, and thus they are ideal arenas for efforts to prevent violence. Ensure that children are taught that violence against women and children is unacceptable and that sexual harassment and abuse in the schools are not tolerated.

- Participate in cultural exchange programs, particularly those between women in the global South and women in the global North.

- Volunteer at your local rape crisis center. Participate in the annual Take Back the Night rally in your own community.

- If you have daughters or female children in your life, strive to help them become strong and empowered. Focus on their strengths; build up their self-esteem and foster self-acceptance; help them validate themselves by stressing education and financial independence; and teach them that they deserve to be treated with respect and that abuse is never something they deserve.

References

Carrillo, R. (1992). *Battered dreams: Violence against women as an obstacle to development.* New York: United Nations Development Fund for Women.

Chatterjee, M. (1993). Struggle and development: Changing the reality of self-employed workers. In G. Young, V. Samarasinghe, & K. Kusterer (Eds.), *Women at the center: Development issues and practices for the 1990s* (pp. 81–93). West Hartford, CT: Kumarian Press.

Helmore, K. (1987, September 30). Banking on the poor: Changing the face of foreign aid. *Christian Science Monitor,* p. 16.

Helmore, K. (1989, March 15). Banking on a better life. *Christian Science Monitor,* pp. 12–13.

McDonnell, N. S., Himunyanga-Phiri, T. V., & Tembo, A. (1993). Widening economic opportunities for women: Removing barriers one brick at a time. In G. Young, V. Samarasinghe, & K. Kusterer (Eds.), *Women at the center: Development issues and practices for the 1990s* (pp. 17–29). West Hartford, CT: Kumarian Press.

McGowan, L. A. (1995, August). *The ignored cost of adjustment: Women under SAPs in Africa* (paper prepared for the Fourth United Nations World Conference on Women). Washington, DC: Development Gap.

Moser, C.O.N. (1986). *Gender planning and development: Theory, practice and training.* London: Routledge.

Oxfam America. (n.d.). *Genuine development.* Boston: Author.

Prigoff, A. (1992). Women, social development and the state in Latin America. *Social Development Issues, 14*(1), 56–70.

Rao, A., Anderson, M. B., & Overholt, C. A. (1991). *Gender analysis in development planning: A case book.* West Hartford, CT: Kumarian Press.

Raphael, J. (1995). Domestic violence and welfare reform. *Poverty and Race, 4*(1), 19.

Saunders, R. (1988, January 5). Sound money for small farmers (memorandum to Dr. Muleya, MAWD). Unpublished.

Tisch, S. J., & Wallace, M. B. (1994). *Dilemmas of development assistance: The what, why, and who of foreign aid.* Boulder, CO: Westview Press.

United Nations Economic and Social Commission for Asia and the Pacific. (1984, November). *Bank credit for rural women: Report on study tour of Grameen Bank in Bangladesh.* New York: Author.

Vella, J. K. (1993). *Women and war.* Atlantic Highlands, NJ: Zed Books.

Waring, M. (1988). *If women counted: A new feminist economics.* New York: HarperCollins.

Weaver, J. H., Rock, M. T., & Kusterer, K. C. (1994). Women in development. Unpublished manuscript. (Available from Ken Kusterer, Development Studies Program, American University and Institute for International Research, 1815 North Fort Meyer Drive, #600, Arlington, VA 22209; (703) 527-5546).

Women's Feature Service. (1993). *The power to change: Women in the Third World redefine their environment.* Atlantic Highlands, NJ: Zed Books.

Young, G., Samarasinghe, V., & Kusterer, K. (Eds.). (1993). *Women at the center: Development issues and practices for the 1990s.* West Hartford, CT: Kumarian Press.

Part 4

Ethnoviolence and Development

Chapter 8

Connecting the Dots between Ethnoviolence and Development

> By peace we mean the absence of violence in any given society, both internal and external, direct and indirect. We further mean the nonviolent results of equality of rights, by which every member of that society, through nonviolent means, participates equally in decisional power which regulates it, and the distribution of resources which sustain it. (Garcia, 1981, p. 165)

We live in a multicultural world in which practically no country is ethnically homogenous, although some are more so than others. We are enriched by the diversity of our global village. Yet, too often, ethnic and racial tensions, conflicts, and wars mark strife among the world's diverse populations. In the United States, a society made up of a mixture of immigrants from all over the world, intergroup disagreements, conflicts, hate crimes, riots, and other forms of ethnic and racial violence occur on a daily basis (McLemore, 1994). Countless ethnic conflicts smolder in other parts of the world, including the Middle East, Central Asia, Africa, Eastern Europe, and Latin America (Jalali & Lipset, 1993; Levinson, 1993). About half of the world's nations have recently experienced some interethnic strife, often with brutal results (United Nations Development Programme [UNDP], 1994).

Violence based on ethnicity is a global problem. Although they are usually manifested first within states, ethnic conflicts almost invariably become international in scope for several reasons: the post–cold war world has produced a new ethnic consciousness; the world community has become more sympathetic to demands made by ethnic groups for self-determination and statehood; human rights have become an international concern; ethnic violence often creates refugees who flee across borders into other countries; and countries with close affectional links with ethnic groups in other countries are seldom indifferent to the fate of those groups. Moreover, a new wave of democratization around the world has served to strengthen the human rights and overall status of oppressed ethnic communities and, simultaneously, political liberalization has opened avenues for ethnic conflict.

Ethnic violence is of particular concern to the U.S. social work profession, which has a history of working to promote social justice for oppressed communities of color. Social workers can learn how to prevent and ameliorate ethnic violence by examining how countries in the global South have struggled with similar issues and problems; models and approaches used successfully in the South can be adapted for U.S. communities. Social workers can also come to view their professional role in an international context by understanding the connections between ethnic violence and development in the United States and in the global South.

To that end, this chapter examines current and historic ethnoviolence in the United States and in the global South from a multilevel perspective. It also discusses some of the complex problems that arise out of racial and ethnic conflicts, and it focuses on how conditions of underdevelopment and maldevelopment fuel ethnoviolence—which in turn impedes genuine development.

Key Concepts and Assumptions

This chapter is grounded in the value of cultural pluralism, which affirms racial and ethnic group identity as giving meaning and purpose to people's lives; diverse groups of people should be able to function competently within the norms, traditions, and values of their own cultures, as well as in the broader society in which they live; and everyone should not be forced into a single mold. Thus the existence of ethnic differences is not seen as a problem in itself. Rather, it is prejudice, discrimination, and the denial of equal opportunity based on ethnic difference that constitute the compelling problem.

A development-related problem addressed in this chapter is an imbalance in economic and social power between ethnic and cultural groups; consistently, one group prospers at the expense of others. In particular, people of color and indigenous people are systematically mistreated as a result of institutionalized inequality in social structures. At the extreme, the mistreatment can take the form of physical violence and genocide, but it occurs in many other forms as well.

Ethnic Groups and Ethnicity

Ethnic groups are seen as being socially constructed and defined; thus, what is and what is not an ethnic group can change over time and from place to place (Kivisto, 1995). The traditional sociological definition of ethnic group is any group of people distinguished by race, religion, nationality, or national origin (Gordon, 1964). In contemporary usage, ethnic groups are more broadly defined by shared beliefs, values, and cultural characteristics; a common identity; and a sense of solidarity (Richmond, 1988).

Ethnicity is broadly determined by features that may be present in varied combinations, including common geographical origin; migratory status; race; language or dialect; religious faith; ties that transcend kinship, neighborhood, and community boundaries; shared traditions, values, and symbols; literature, folklore, and music; food preferences; settlement and employment patterns; special interests concerning politics in the homeland and in the country of residence; institutions that serve and maintain the group specifically; an internal sense of distinctiveness; and an external perception of distinctiveness (Thernstrom, Orlov, & Handlin, 1980).

E. Pinderhughes (1989) defines ethnicity as

> connectedness based on commonalities (such as religion, nationality, region, etc.) where specific aspects of cultural patterns are shared and where transmission over time creates a common history. Race, while a biological term, takes on ethnic meaning when and if members of that biological group have evolved specific ways of living. . . . Ethnic values and practices foster the survival of the group and of the individuals within. They also contribute to the formation and cohesiveness of the group and to both group and individual identity. (p. 6)

Thus, ethnicity has many dimensions; it affects an individual's sense of identity and it affects the society's perceptions of—and responses to—groups of people (Kivisto, 1995).

Ethnicity's Deep Roots

Although ethnic diversity is a feature of all societies, how such diversity is perceived—and how much importance is attached to it—varies greatly because ethnicity is only one of many ways in which people identify themselves. Group identity, according to Horowitz (1992), is a powerful feature of social life based on a central principle of membership; people derive satisfaction from belonging to and identifying with groups that are regarded as worthy. It is therefore not surprising that most incidents of serious ethnic violence involve group members who have been invidiously judged and deemed unworthy (Horowitz, 1992).

Deeply rooted ethnic identity is usually associated with strong historical and geographic contexts that form powerful group boundaries. Under certain circumstances, ethnicity may displace other loyalties and become the sole basis of identity. In such cases, the likelihood of ethnic conflict increases (United Nations, 1995). For example, ethnic conflict is generally greater in Asia and Africa than elsewhere because Asian and African family ties, birth affiliations, and kinship are especially strong, and the importance of these bonds becomes linked with ethnic identity. Similarly, religious differences cause more intergroup conflicts in some parts of the world—where religion is not a matter of personal faith but an irrevocable identity—than they do in the West, where people generally recognize the right to choose one's religion.

A World of Multiple Ethnic Groups

Although varying definitions of ethnicity make precise figures impossible to establish, it is clear that the range of ethnic diversity is enormous. Estimates of the number of ethnic groups in the world range from 170, 233, or 575 to as many as 3,000 to 5,000 (when common language is the criterion) (Gurr, 1993; Nietschmann, 1987). About 40 percent of the countries of the world have more than five sizable ethnic populations, one or more of which faces discrimination and devaluation. Diversity in some countries is immense: There are about 450 different ethnic groups in Nigeria, about 350 in India, 90 in Ethiopia, and 80 in Brazil (United Nations, 1995). In some countries, as in Eastern Europe after the breakup of the Soviet Union and Yugoslavia, people from different ethnic groups struggle for self-determination or fight for dominance in their own nations.

Ethnoviolence: A Global Problem

Ethnoviolence is a general term that refers to violence perpetrated primarily on the basis of one's ethnicity. Such violence may be motivated by hate or prejudice, and it may also stem from economic and political competition. Ethnoviolence includes hate crimes or bias crimes, which are legally confined to offenses that stem from prejudice toward the victim and imply emotional involvement (Pacific Northwest NASW Center, 1994). Distinctions are usually drawn between physical violence and psychological violence, but this chapter's examination of ethnoviolence does not do so. Harassment and intimidation, which are intended to inflict psychological injury, may do more lasting harm to the victim than would a physical assault. Ethnoviolence thus covers the spectrum of violent acts: it includes harassment, personal insults, graffiti, physical assault, and so on (Ehrlich, 1990). Consistent with the broad definition of violence used throughout this book, ethnoviolence also includes institutional forms of discrimination.

Ethnoviolence is an integral and profoundly shameful part of world history. Witness the Holocaust in Nazi Germany, the 1994 campaign of genocide in Rwanda, and "ethnic cleansing" in former Yugoslavia. The history of the United States is fraught with ethnoviolence, beginning with the devastation of indigenous people by early European settlers (who were themselves fleeing from religious persecution) and the catastrophic violence done to Africans who were brought to this country as slaves. Wave after wave of immigrants coming to the United States— whether from Ireland, Eastern Europe, Asia, Southeast Asia, or Central America—have experienced harassment and discrimination (Weiss, 1990). Race relations are currently strained in many regions of the United States and becoming more so because of economic factors, reactions to affirmative action, and fears about immigration (Cozic, 1995; Tactaquin, 1995; Taylor, 1995). Racial confrontation is on the rise as well among some ethnic groups—African Americans, Hispanics, Koreans, and others—because of a combination of economic adversity and lack of knowledge of other oppressed communities of color (Taylor, 1995).

Ethnic conflict is generally defined as a violent conflict between or among groups who differ from each other in terms of culture, religion, physical features, or language (Levinson, 1993). In 1988, 111 violent conflicts took place around the world, most of which were called ethnic conflicts because they involved minority and majority groups within nations. In 1993 and 1994, 25 to 30 major wars involved regular use of violence—mass killings, executions, terrorist bombings, assassination, looting, rapes, forced expulsion, and other acts of violence—by one or more ethnic groups (Levinson, 1993; Panos Institute, 1994). Figure 8-1 shows selected ethnic conflicts that were underway in 1993 (Levinson, 1993).

According to Levinson (1993), there are distinctions among ethnic conflicts. One key distinction is between conflicts that occur in unranked situations (the ethnic groups are relatively equal in power or perceive themselves to be so) and those in ranked situations (the ethnic groups hold different positions in a hierarchy of power). Another distinction is between conflicts in the global South and those in the global North; the former often center on competition among ethnic groups for political dominance, and the latter often involve governmental repression and separatist movements by ethnic minorities. A third distinction can be made on the basis of the goals sought by the participants in the ethnic conflict, including conflicts spawned by separatist movements for political

Figure 8-1
Selected Ethnic Conflicts around the World, 1996

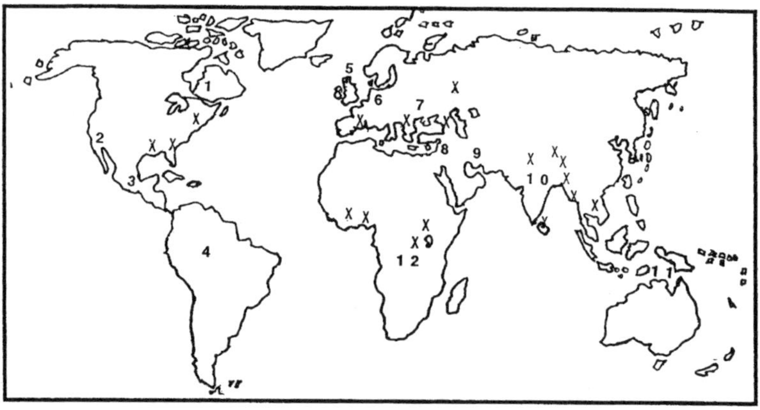

1. French Canadians
2. Blacks and Hispanic Immigrants in USA
3. Indigenous People in Mexico
4. Indigenous People in South America
5. Catholics and Protestants in Northern Ireland
6. Foreigners in Germany
7. Moldovans and Russians and Ukrainians
8. Palestinians and Israelis

9. Baha'i in Iran
10. Kashmiris, Sikhs, Nagas, Hindus, and Muslims in India
11. Timorese (Atoni) in Indonesia
12. Hutus and Tutsis in Burundi and Rwanda
X   Other Selected Conflicts

Source: Data from Levinson, D. (1993, August). Ethnic conflict and refugees. *Refugees, 93,* 4–9.

independence (for example, the Armenians in Azerbaijan, Palestinians in Israel and Israeli-occupied territories, Sikhs in India, Tibetans in China, Timorese in Indonesia, and Tamils in Sri Lanka); rivalry for autonomy, political power, or territorial control (Hungarians in Romania, Islamic fundamentalists in Algeria and Egypt, Hutus and Tutsis in Rwanda and Burundi); conquest or removal of a group from all or some of a territory (for example, Bosnian Muslims and Serbs, Croats and Serbs); or survival goals (Gypsies in Romania, Shiite Muslims in Iraq, Vietnamese in Cambodia, and Amazonian Indian groups in Brazil).

General causes of ethnoviolence and ethnic conflict include injustice and unequal distribution of economic resources and political power; competition over resources; revenge and territorial disputes, often based on a history of dominant and subordinate relationships among groups; repression and neglect of ethnic communities; and prejudice and ignorance (Pacific Northwest NASW Center, 1994).

Ethnoviolence and Ethnic Conflict at Different Levels

Ethnoviolence and ethnic conflict take many forms, from random individual actions involving physical or psychological injury and mob violence to organized war and campaigns of genocide. Ethnoviolence occurs on personal, institutional, and structural levels throughout the global North and the global South. For example, 300 indigenous people in 70 countries face widening spirals of violence (UNDP, 1994), and immigrants newly arrived in Europe and elsewhere in the global North face growing resentment, discrimination, and ethnic and racial violence (Frelick, 1994). The ubiquity of ethnoviolence is revealed in the following examples of its multilevel, multidimensional characteristics.

Individual Level of Ethnoviolence. At this level are individually oriented harmful actions against people or property. Perpetrators may be individuals or groups, either organized or unorganized, many of whom single out a person for attack because of the victim's ethnicity or perceived membership in an ethnic group. Individual acts of ethnoviolence occur in both the global North and the global South, but the United States can provide some particularly vivid examples.

U.S. history is replete with sordid incidents of ethnoviolence at the individual level. For centuries, communities of color in the United States were subject to lynchings, unsolved murders, beatings, and torture. Data from various sources suggest that random ethnoviolence continues to be extensive; it has increased since the 1980s, both in incidence and brutality; and it is considerably underreported (Sheffield, 1995). Studies of ethnoviolence on college and university campuses in the 1980s indicate that approximately 20 percent to 25 percent of students of color experienced some form of ethnoviolent attack during an academic year (Ehrlich, 1990). More than 100 black churches throughout the United States were burned or vandalized between 1990 and 1996. According to a report by the National Asian Pacific American Legal Consortium (Klanwatch Intelligence Report, 1995), violence against Asian Americans increased significantly in 1994. The Congressional Hispanic Caucus (1994) reported that a rise in hate crimes against Hispanics and Asian Americans accompanied an increase in immigrant-bashing rhetoric; in Los Angeles, for example, attacks on Hispanics and Asian Americans rose between 33 percent and 48 percent from 1991 to 1992. The passage below describes some incidents of anti-immigrant violence; similar examples can be found throughout the global North.

- Vandals ransacked the San Francisco office of the Coalition for Immigrant and Refugee Rights, covering the walls with anti-immigrant obscenities.
- A truckload of white teenagers shouted racial insults and then beat immigrant Alejandro Cuevas as he walked along a thoroughfare in Escondido, California.
- Immigrant activist Irma Munoz, 20, was assaulted twice on successive nights in Davis, California. In one of the attacks, her assailants scrawled "illegal" and "wetback" on her arm and leg with a ballpoint pen.
- A group of teens attacked immigrants at the border near San Diego. One of them shouted "white power!" as he was brought into a police substation after his arrest.
- A group called the Aryan Liberation Front claimed responsibility for five fire-bombings in Sacramento, California, between July and November 1993. The fire-bombings took place at a synagogue, the home of a Chinese-American city council member, a state agency

handling discrimination claims, and offices of the Japanese Americans Citizens League and the National Association for the Advancement of Colored People.

Some of the violence on the individual level is advocated and promulgated by organized hate groups. The Ku Klux Klan, in particular, has been responsible for some of the most brutal violence in U.S. history; between 1889 and 1941, the Klan lynched 3,811 black people. In recent years, the Klan has developed ties with several hate groups, such as white citizens' councils, skinhead groups, and the Aryan Nation and its various subsidiaries (see Figure 8-2). The Christian Identity Movement attempts to bring religious people into the white supremacy movement (Sheffield, 1995); Figure 8-3 shows the major Identity congregations throughout the country in 1995.

Violence and the threat of violence are not only physical. Psychological forms of ethnoviolence on the individual level include harassment, name-calling, verbal abuse, exclusion, and racial and ethnic insults. Ehrlich (1990) compiled this list of publicly reported incidents of ethnoviolence on college campuses in the 1980s:

- A Chinese-American student sits down at the end of a library table. A group of students sitting at the other end of the table begin telling ethnic jokes and directing anti-Asian slurs at her.
- A black clerk in the registrar's office is denied access to the promotional exam. Her supervisor tells her that she shouldn't bother taking it because it's too difficult for "you people."
- A faculty member finds a swastika painted on his door.
- A fraternity goes serenading in blackface.
- Racist letters are received by administrators and student activists.
- Two students shout racial insults at Asian students and spit tobacco juice on them during a bus ride to a dance.
- A group of sorority members dressed as mock Indians dance and whoop "Indian hollers" just outside the campus Native American Center.
- A Latina student returns to her dorm room to find an anonymous note under her door that says: "Hey, Spic. If you and your kind can't handle the work here at Bryn Mawr, don't blame it on this

Figure 8-2
Hate Groups in the United States in 1994

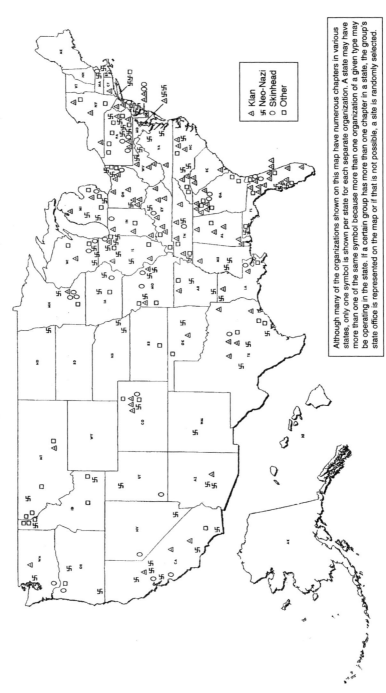

Klan
Neo-Nazi
Skinhead
Other

Although many of the organizations shown on this map have numerous chapters in various states, only one symbol is shown per state for each separate organization. A state may have more than one of the same symbol because more than one organization of a given type may be operating in the state. If a certain group has more than one chapter in a state, the group's state office is represented on the map or if that is not possible, a site is randomly selected.

Source: Klanwatch Intelligence Report, a project of the Southern Poverty Law Center, March 1995, pp. 16–17. Reprinted with permission of the Klanwatch Project, Southern Poverty Law Center, P.O. Box 548, Montgomery, AL 36101-0548.

Figure 8-3
Major Identity Congregations and Compounds

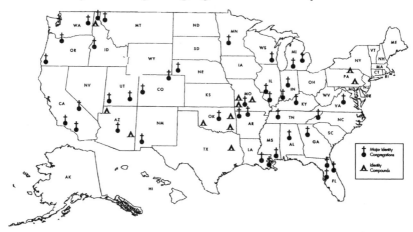

Source: Racist identity sect fuels nationwide extremist movement. *Klanwatch Intelligence Report*, a project of the Southern Poverty Law Center, August 1995, p. 4. Reprinted with permission.

racial thing. You are just making our school look bad to everyone else. If you can't handle it, why don't you just get out. We'd all be a lot happier."

- During Gay Pride Week, a group of men, believed to be fraternity members, interrupt a movie being watched by a gay group and block exits to the room. Later, a van providing shuttle service to women students is surrounded by men shouting antilesbian comments.

Institutional Level of Ethnoviolence. The individual level of ethnoviolence is not an autonomous phenomenon. Rather, it is made possible and undergirded by institutional practices that "allocate rights, privileges and prestige according to biological or social characteristics" (Sheffield, 1995, p. 435). At the institutional level, ethnoviolence is usually invisible, disguised by legal and other institutional mechanisms. Ethnoviolence at this level often takes nonphysical forms with psychological, long-term effects; yet even when the ethnoviolence is obvious and does involve physical violence, it can be rationalized as a necessary form of social control. For example, although some U.S. immigration officers mistreat Latinos—racial slurs, abusive language, harassment, and denial of human rights have been documented (Koulish, 1994)—such abuse is excused not only by officials but by the general public .

A covert, more subtle form of institutional ethnoviolence—the violence not seen as such, which is sometimes referred to as "passive oppression"—occurs around the world. A 1989 survey listed 261 minority groups in 99 of 126 countries as the victims of such ethnoviolence (Levinson, 1993). Ethnoviolence takes the form of "political, economic, or cultural repression of ethnic minorities that includes restrictions on voting, burdensome taxes, exclusion from certain professions, residential isolation, educational quotas, prohibitions on the use of the ethnic language, and restrictions on religious worship" (Levinson, 1993, p. 4). Ethnoviolence at the institutional level includes the criminalization of the African American male population of the United States, which was accomplished historically by a post-emancipation criminal code that resulted in thousands of ex-slaves being arrested, tried, and convicted for petty actions and more recently by the criminalization of minor drug offenses, along with unequal enforcement of laws and differential sentencing. Other examples include institutional failure to address the needs of marginalized groups for decent housing and access to medical care, for example, and the portrayal of ethnic and racial groups in a demeaning way in school curricula.

Ethnoviolence on the institutional level can involve police and military forces, who are seldom impartial actors in the face of ethnic conflicts. Usually, government forces are ethnically imbalanced as a result of "both historical socioeconomic maldistribution of opportunities and of deliberate recruitment strategies pursued by central governmentalities" (Enloe, 1977, p. 137). By way of illustration, Yugoslavia's army, whose officer corps is 85 percent Serbian, openly supported Serb guerrillas in the civil war in Croatia (Jalali and Lipset, 1993); in the United States, the police officers who beat Rodney King, a black man in Los Angeles, were predominantly white, as was the top echelon of the Los Angeles police force that supported the violence as a "necessary use of force."

Ultimately, ethnic conflict between groups within a country can lead to war. War itself is a pernicious form of ethnoviolence that involves both government military institutions as well as noninstitutionalized combatants. Most civil wars in the post–cold war world are ethnic, tribal, or religious conflicts that produce atrocities on nearly every continent. Among these atrocities are "Serbs practicing 'ethnic cleansing' of Muslims in Bosnia-Herzegovina, mass graves being unearthed in Guatemala and El Salvador, Somalian warlords laying waste to farms and leaving hundreds of thousands to starve, [and] Indonesian troops firing on unarmed protesters in East Timor" (Shuman & Harvey, 1993, p. 246). The brutal, systematic assaults on Muslim and Croatian women in Bosnia and Herzegovina in the early 1990s were an especially vicious part of a plan to destroy a society's cultural, traditional, and religious integrity—in effect, to destroy an entire Muslim population.

Structural and Cultural Level of Ethnoviolence. Ethnoviolence throughout the world is deeply rooted in a normative ideology of superiority at the structural and cultural level, which ensures the dominance of one group over another. Militaristic values at this level preserve that dominance: through violence and the threat of violence, individuals, groups, and institutions maintain the economic interests and other privileges of the group deemed superior.

The history of the United States is a case in point. Through conquest and exploitation, white European Americans became the dominant group in this country. The current ethnoviolence is thus rooted in racial violence, which began with the virtual destruction of Native American nations. White resistance to the inclusion of different groups in U.S. society, based on the widespread historical belief that those labeled as "nonwhite" are inferior and unacceptable as social equals, is still greater against those who are "nonwhite" than against those who are considered "white" (McLemore, 1994). The dominant U.S. culture values individuality, competition, and conquest and denigrates conflicting values of other ethnic groups, such as communalism and cooperation.

The colonial experience of countries of the global South also planted an ideology of superiority that is the root of much ethnic tension and violence. In the countries of Africa, for example, ethnic heterogeneity is often the result of national boundaries imposed by foreign powers, which for the most part ignored tribal cultural patterns in the subjugated societies. To institutionalize their dominance, the "superior" colonial powers counted people and sorted them into discrete and bounded groups, thus creating new categories of identity that replaced the interlocking, overlapping, and multiple cultural identities that existed before colonialism. Furthermore, colonial state policies actively promoted differential treatment of ethnic groups, which over time caused extensive economic and social disparities. After independence, systems of inequity continued and severe ethnic conflicts ensued (Jalali & Lipset, 1993).

Interrelatedness of the Levels of Ethnoviolence

Individual acts of ethnoviolence are integrally connected with violence at other levels. An individual act of ethnoviolence serves to demonstrate— and preserve—power over not only the victim but also the group to which the victim belongs. Individual ethnoviolence, together with institutional collusion and undergirded by norms embedded in the structural and cultural level, might be considered a kind of terrorism: Like other terrorist acts, it functions to limit the rights and privileges of individuals and groups and to maintain the superiority of the beliefs, values, and privileges of one group over another (Sheffield, 1995). Richard Wright (1937), in his brilliant autobiographical novel *Black Boy*, describes how his behavior was thoroughly controlled by a pervasive fear that wanton violence by whites could strike at any time:

> The things that influenced my conduct as a Negro did not have to happen to me directly; I needed but to hear of them to feel their full effects in the deepest layers of my consciousness. Indeed the white brutality that I had not seen was a more effective control of my behavior than that which I knew. . . . As long as it remained something terrible and yet remote, something whose horror and blood might descend upon me at any moment, I was compelled to give my entire imagination over to it, an act which blocked the springs of thought and feelings in me. (pp. 65, 150–151)

Individual, institutional, and structural levels of ethnoviolence form an intractable cycle of violence. Structural inequities based on an ideology of group superiority both give rise to and result in ethnoviolence on the institutional and individual levels. "Legitimate" ethnoviolence (police or military control of minority individuals or groups by force and violence or through other institutional mechanisms of social control) provokes illegitimate violence on the part of those harmed and marginalized; inevitably the state responds with more force, and the destructive cycle of violence escalates.

The result of this cycle of violence—war within or between nations—is characterized not only by state terrorism and human rights violations caused by military and police excesses (institutional level). Terrorism by so-called liberation groups can be equally brutal, and the continuation of the cycle of violence equally ensured. The Hamas in the Palestinian West Bank and Gaza and Tamil Tigers in Sri Lanka, for example, resort to assassinations and mass suicide bombings to advance their causes; they are also well known for smuggling drugs to collect funds.

Distinctions between individual and institutional levels of ethnoviolence can be intentionally obscured, so that what appears to be individual acts of ethnoviolence is actually hidden ethnoviolence at the institutional level, as when, to maintain its superiority, a dominant group exploits ethnic conflict between two subordinate groups. For example, a postapartheid inquiry into the causes of political violence in South Africa revealed that a "para-state apparatus" had furnished weapons and sent provocateurs to gangs in the townships, thus inciting ethnic hatred among dispossessed groups, and then reported on "black-on-black violence, which was obediently swallowed by many Western media outlets" (Hitchens, 1995).

Ethnoviolence and Development: Making the Connections

When war breaks out between nations (interstate conflict) or between different factions within a nation (intrastate conflict), there is rarely a single cause. Competition over land and other limited resources can heighten pre-existing ethnic and religious tensions. Factors such as unequal distribution of economic resources and political power, the repression or neglect of rural or minority populations, and environmental degradation can all contribute to a single conflict. Leaders may also encourage conflict to further their own agendas. For conflicts to be resolved rather than simply repressed, it is important that these multiple underlying causes be recognized and remedied. (Panos Institute, 1994, p. 2)

The escalating occurrence and severity of ethnoviolence around the world has led to efforts by analysts in the fields of economic development, peace and conflict studies, social development, and environmental studies to identify and assess causes and potential solutions. Key factors in the intensifying severity of ethnic conflict, they have found, include dominant patterns of global economic development, combined with the deteriorating condition of the physical environment. The complex causal factors involved in ethnic conflict are not linear in pattern. For example, ethnic rivalry may sometimes be the cause of ethnic conflict, but not always; in certain cases it may be the result of that conflict (Hoff, 1994). In other words, many interrelated factors are involved in situations of ethnic conflict, but several observations stand out:

- Ethnoviolence is connected to poverty and lack of development opportunities.
- Ethnoviolence is connected to unjust development or maldevelopment.
- Ethnoviolence obstructs development.
- Militarism fuels ethnoviolence.

Connections among Ethnoviolence and Poverty and Lack of Development Opportunities

Economic insecurity and ethnoviolence.   According to UNDP (1994), economic insecurity "is one of the main factors underlying political tensions and ethnic violence in several countries" (p. 25). However, only about one-fourth of the world's people are economically secure in the sense that they have an ensured basic income, either from productive and remunerative work or, if necessary, from some publicly financed safety net. Even in the United States and other rich nations, many people feel insecure: Jobs are increasingly difficult to find and keep because the number of jobs in industrial countries has failed to keep pace with the growth in the labor force in the past two decades. Young people, who are disproportionately involved in acts of ethnoviolence and ethnic conflicts, are more likely to be unemployed in both rich and poor countries. In the United States, for example, youth unemployment reached 14 percent in 1992; in Africa, the rate was above 20 percent in the 1980s. Furthermore, unemployment figures understate the scale of the crisis because many of those working are seriously underemployed. Without a social safety net, the poorest people cannot survive even a short period without an income (UNDP, 1994).

Economic stratification by race.   Even in countries characterized by racial and ethnic pluralism, economic stratification generally correlates with racial ancestry. In Latin America, for example, the privileged classes are largely of European background or have lighter skin than those who are less affluent (Jalali & Lipset, 1993). In the United States, race is highly correlated with socioeconomic status, a reflection of ethnoviolence at the institutional and structural and cultural levels. As the gap between the wealthiest and poorest Americans widened in the 1980s and 1990s, so too did the gap between people of color and whites (Gorey, 1995). Poverty rates are high for each of the major populations of color. The unemployment rate for African Americans is twice that for whites, and poverty rates among African Americans and Hispanics are nearly three times those of whites (UNDP, 1994; Weiss, 1990). Fifteen percent of children growing up in white homes in the United States are poor, whereas 38 percent of Hispanic, 44 percent of Asian and Pacific Island American, 45 percent of African American, and up to 90 percent of Native American children grow up in poverty (American Psychological Association [APA], 1993).

Connecting race or ethnicity, economic insecurity, and ethnoviolence.   There are two common notions about the cause of ethnic conflict: (1) conflict between groups is a problem of class and inequity, and (2) conflict between groups is a problem of race or ethnicity. These contradictory ideas exemplify a tendency to think in either–or terms rather than to see the interrelatedness of race, class, and ethnoviolence. Many social science disciplines have firmly established that poverty and its accompanying environmental conditions are major determinants of violence. It is the socioeconomic inequality of poor people—their sense of relative deprivation and lack of opportunity to improve their life circumstances—that facilitates higher rates of violence (APA, 1993). Because socioeconomic inequality and lack of opportunity are key characteristics of poverty for communities of color in the United States, it is no surprise that rates of violence are higher in those communities.

Ethnicity alone is a risk factor for victimization by hate crimes. However, when lack of development opportunities and socioeconomic inequality are added to the equation, the possibility of hate crimes escalates. When institutional structures and political policies support intolerance and racism, the possibility of ethnic conflict escalates even more. For example, H. Pinderhughes (1993) found that deteriorating economic prospects for 88 white delinquents in New York City raised anxiety, fear, and competition; their heightened uneasiness, when combined with community sentiment and peer-group activity against other ethnic and racial groups, facilitated bias-related violent crime.

The situation of refugees and immigrants around the world provides further evidence of connections between lack of development opportunities and ethnoviolence. In Western Europe, large-scale migration of guest-workers from countries not sharing the predominant culture or language has created new ethnic tensions, particularly in France, Switzerland, and western Germany. Rising unemployment and lack of development opportunities in the host countries heightens ethnic tensions between local and foreign workers. In Germany, racist attacks on foreign workers have reached explosive levels, with more than 600 attacks reported in 1989 alone (Jalali & Lipset, 1993). In the United States, which receives not even 1 percent of the world's migrants annually, racism has dominated and continues to dominate immigration policies; around the country, hate crimes are committed against immigrants and those perceived to be immigrants (Tactaquin, 1995).

As the population of some parts of the United States—California, for example—has changed from primarily white people to mostly African American, Latino, and Asian people, the blame for declining economic conditions has been placed on immigrants and, by extension, all people of color (Ong & Valenzuela, 1995). Ethnic groups, pitted against one another, adopt a divide-and-conquer strategy that stresses competition over opportunities and resources. The combination of economic deprivation and political anti-immigrant rhetoric creates conditions that are ripe for the kind of violence that erupted in Los Angeles in 1992 between Korean American storekeepers and long-deprived African American and Latino residents (Cho, 1995).

Unjust Development or Maldevelopment and Ethnoviolence

The development process itself can be a form of ethnoviolence. It can also become a source of ethnic conflict between groups when development projects serve the interests of wealthier social groups and exclude groups that have been traditionally marginalized, such as ethnic minorities, indigenous people, and women (Panos Institute, 1994). The maldevelopment that characterized colonialism—peoples of one nation were subjected to horrendous injustice by people of another nation for economic gain, regardless of the costs to indigenous people—is the root of many current ethnic conflicts. Colonial powers of the global North drew arbitrary boundaries between countries with no regard for ethnic and religious group identity, thus creating conditions for territorial and resource disputes between intranational ethnic groups after independence. The Eritrean struggle to secede from Ethiopia and the dispute between Ethiopia and Somalia over the Ogaden are examples of conflicts that grew out of the legacy of colonialism, with devastating consequences (Panos Institute, 1994).

The United States also was developed at the expense of ethnic and racial minorities. Exploitation of indigenous people and genocide were the methods by which colonial frontiers expanded. Slavery was the route to economic development of the South, and the U.S. railroad system was built largely by the backbreaking and poorly paid labor of Chinese immigrants (Zinn, 1980). Other examples abound.

Unjust development and indigenous people.   Indigenous people around the world often must struggle to maintain control over their traditional resources when development projects are undertaken; they must struggle also to receive their share of the benefits accruing from the projects' exploitation of those resources. For example, the extraction of petroleum has made Nigeria one of the richest countries in Africa, but very little of the wealth has gone to the Ogoni, the indigenous people who live in the main oil-producing regions; their demands for improved living conditions have been violently suppressed by the Nigerian government (Panos Institute, 1994).

In the United States, the traditional lands of Native American people were exploited for vast, damaging mining operations; Native Americans suffered the adverse effects of the mining, but they never reaped their fair share of the wealth accrued from that mining (Hoff & Polack, 1993). During the cold war, Native American workers toiled in the mines and mills of the Colorado Plateau under abysmal, deadly conditions for as little as $1 to $2 a day to provide the uranium for the U.S. nuclear arsenal. Many of the workers were later diagnosed with cancer and respiratory ailments linked to that work; of 3,317 miners who had been examined by 1960, 108 had died by 1967. The workers were 11 times—17.8 times for those who had worked the mines for three or more years—more likely than unexposed populations to develop heart disease (Eichstaedt, 1995; Hudgens, 1995). More recently, the lands of reservation people were polluted through illegal dumping of toxic wastes, the industrial byproducts of development (Chehak & Harjo, 1990).

Another example comes from Chiapas, Mexico, where the indigenous peasants have suffered abuse and neglect since the time of the Spanish conquest, with predictable results. More than half of the people have no access to medical services; the mortality rate is among the highest in the country; and more than 70 percent of the children quit school after their first year because they must work to survive. Chiapas is a major producer of petroleum and generates 55 percent of Mexico's hydroelectric power, but only 30 percent of Chiapan houses have access to electricity. On January 1, 1994, groups of armed indigenous and *mestizo* people occupied four towns in the state of Chiapas in an uprising aimed at gaining their rights (Panos Institute, 1994). Unfortunately, the Mexican government, after an initial period of negotiation, escalated government repression of the peasants instead of heeding the call for change.

Unjust development, maldevelopment, environmental destruction, and ethnoviolence.   When development does not value environmental sustainability, the adverse effects often fall disproportionately on poor ethnic minorities and rural communities (Hoff & Polack, 1993; Lusk & Hoff, 1995). When the distribution of pollution is analyzed by both income and race, race has consistently been found in most cases to be more strongly related to incidence of pollution than to income (Bryant, 1996). The following examples depict the links between environmental risks and poverty and racism:

- Hispanic farmworkers in the west and southwest United States are continuously exposed to particularly toxic pesticides that are used in the production of grapes (Hoff & Polack, 1993; World Watch Institute, 1987).

- An estimated 44 percent of urban black children in the United States are at risk for lead poisoning (Truax, 1990).
- There are more toxic waste and other garbage disposal facilities in low-income and minority communities—including traditional Native American land and urban centers—than elsewhere (Bullard, 1990; Chehak & Harjo, 1990; Truax, 1990; United Church of Christ, 1987).
- Faced with financial incentives and other pressure, depressed rural areas of the United States and impoverished nations of the global South become garbage dumps and hazardous waste disposal sites (Berlet, 1990; Hoff, 1990).
- Herbicides and pesticides banned in the United States are exported for use in production of fruit, vegetables, and meat in Latin American countries and other countries of the global South (Krebs, 1990). Ten thousand people in the global South die each year from pesticide poisoning, and another 400,000 suffer acute toxic effects (Hoff & Polack, 1993).

Although poor and marginalized people of color suffer disproportionate consequences of environmental hazards, the harm cannot be contained within the boundaries of their communities in our increasingly interdependent world. For example, banned substances that are sold in the global South may return to the United States in imported foods, and the pesticides sprayed on California grapes are ingested by children across the country. In addition, nonsustainable development has raised the danger that, for the first time in human history, the requisites of every nation's security—air, water, land, and life itself—may be permanently destroyed.

The mismanagement of natural resources not only threatens every nation's life support systems; it also increases the potential for interstate war and ethnic conflict. Direct competition for resources such as oil or water can pit nation against nation or one group against another within a nation (Shuman & Harvey 1993). Violence often results when competition for scarce resources is superimposed on preexisting social or ethnic divisions. For example, one of the obstacles that had to be overcome before the historic peace agreement between Israel and Jordan could be finalized was a dispute over how to share water resources (Panos Institute,

1994), and fishing rights have long been a source of conflict between Americans and Canadians and between Native American and white people within the United States, often resulting in incidences of violence (Shuman & Harvey, 1993).

Ethnoviolence Impedes Development

The costs to society of intolerance and ethnic conflict are enormous: denial of human rights, breakdown of political order, and decline of economic performance. The escalation of ethnic conflict into civil and regional wars has ravaged many regions of the global South.

Ethnoviolence obstructs individual and social development.   The Panos Institute (1994) describes how ethnic conflicts that become wars obstruct the development of individuals in countless ways. Women and children are often the major victims. Sometimes civilians are the intentional targets, either as random victims of the conflict or as victims of organized genocide and "ethnic cleansing." People also die when food and water supplies and medical services are cut off. Survivors lose their homes, families, and communities. Women are often targeted for sexual and other violence.

Many people, particularly women and children, become refugees, either fleeing to another country or to another region within their own country. One report cited by Jalali and Lipset (1993) maintained that more than half of the world's 30 million refugees at the beginning of 1990 were fleeing from civil wars and repression that began as communally based conflict. The pressure of large numbers of refugees competing with local people for limited resources can itself become a source of conflict. Both civilians and soldiers are traumatized by war, and survival can become an everyday struggle.

Ethnoviolence can have a profound psychological impact on society, particularly through the blocking of the normal development of its children.   A society that has been brutalized and desensitized to violence is apt to accept a gun culture in which people believe that settling disputes by violent means is natural and acceptable.

Ethnoviolence obstructs economic development.   The economic costs of war to societies are equally horrendous. Resources are depleted, productivity in agriculture and other industries declines as the military absorbs labor resources, countries incur tremendous debt, infrastructures are often destroyed, and economic development is discouraged. When conflict is prolonged, every aspect of normal life is disrupted. Southern Sudan serves as an example: Damage to roads and fear of armed attack along major routes have disrupted commerce and the delivery of food, fuel, and other essential items; schools, hospitals, homes, and businesses have been destroyed or fallen into disrepair for lack of funds, materials, and maintenance; government services on the most basic level have deteriorated or ceased; few people have access to safe water or waste disposal; rates of disease and death among children are high because of largely preventable ailments such as diarrhea and malnutrition (Panos Institute, 1994).

The long-term development effects of intergroup war are felt in other regions of the global South as well. For example, the poor performance of the Sri Lankan economy since the mid-1980s can be traced to ethnically driven conflicts, as can famine conditions in African countries such as Ethiopia and Sudan, where interethnic warfare has prevented farmers from growing food and millions have faced starvation (Jalali & Lipset, 1993). Richardson and Samarasinghe (1991) put the issue of the costs of the Sri Lankan ethnic conflict this way:

> Over a six-year period (1983–1988) the country has lost US $4.2 billion—the equivalent of 68 percent of Sri Lanka's 1988 GDP—as a result of the conflict. The magnitude of the loss raises an important policy issue, especially for governments—that is, the need to consider carefully the medium-to long-term economic implications of the alternative responses available to them when facing a violent political challenge from a disaffected minority, or for that matter, any other politically disaffected group. (p. 209)

The devastating effects of war on the environment diminish the land's capability for production and the environment's capacity to sustain life. Scorched-earth tactics deplete topsoil; bombed factories, refineries, and power plants release toxic chemicals into the atmosphere, land, and water; and defoliants destroy trees and shrubs. Later, hidden land mines inhibit tilling of the land; and fleeing refugees, desperate for firewood, shelter, and food, may destroy forests or overcultivate marginal land. The phenomenon of "environmental refugees"—people who are forced to leave home regions that have been decimated by war and are thus unable to sustain them—illustrates the relationship among poverty, degradation of the environment, and disintegration of culture through intergroup war (Jacobson, 1988; Lusk & Hoff, 1995). "Ethnic Conflict in Rwanda" describes the effect of the ethnic conflict on 30 years of development progress in Rwanda.

Ethnic Conflict in Rwanda

Before the Rwandan conflict, this small, isolated country in Africa with limited economic resources was considered to be a place where development aid would bear fruit. In 1990, the outbreak of war dimmed such hope. When war erupted in the northern part of the country—known as the "granary of Rwanda"—most of the people there fled. Production at the biggest tea factory in the Mulindi region was curtailed for three years and the factory became headquarters of the Rwandan Patriotic Front. One of the biggest pastoral projects in another region was destroyed. Thousands of animals were slaughtered, and malnutrition levels climbed. Several development projects in the northern part of the country—including schools, hospitals, and small- and medium-scale enterprises—were destroyed.

The war had a devastating effect on the environment. Twenty years of reforestation efforts were wiped out: In some areas, refugees cut down thousands of acres of forest for firewood and shelter; in other areas, local authorities encouraged people to clear trees to expose hiding places of members of the Rwandan Patriotic Front. Rwandan agriculture will continue its decline as heavy rains, unimpeded by trees and bushes, wash fertile topsoil down the steep hillsides.

The death of Rwanda's president in April 1994 propelled the country into a murderous and destructive madness. Hundreds of thousands of people were killed and millions displaced. The capital city—which was the heart of the economy—became a ghost city. It was bled dry. All the infrastructure was destroyed; there was no running water, electricity, or telephone service. Members of the former government fled with all the government's money, leaving behind debts incurred from heavy arms purchases abroad. The foreign aid targeted to Rwanda by countries of the global North and nongovernmental organizations for long-term development was redirected to assist the thousands of refugees created by the war.

Four years of war thus completely destroyed more than 30 years of painstakingly gained achievements.

Source: Jean-Marie Muhiewa (Rwandan journalist). (1994). *Conflict and development* (p. 6). Washington, DC: Panos Institute. Used with permission of the Panos Institute.

Militarism Fuels Ethnoviolence

The causes of ethnic conflict are usually domestic or regional disputes, but external sources enable the escalation of such conflict into armed confrontation by supplying weapons or the financial means to purchase them (Deng & Zartman, 1991). The United States is one of the top producers of weapons, and nations of the global South are the major purchasers (Hartung, 1994). Enormous military arsenals put political leaders from a particular group in the position to repress people from another group.

Powerful government and military leaders, armed with sophisticated and deadly weapons, often seek to consolidate their power and elite status by inflaming historic ethnic and religious tensions. For example, tensions between the Hutu and Tutsi ethnic groups in Rwanda were systematically heightened by a relatively small but powerful group of government and military leaders, with the devastating results described previously. The environmental destruction wreaked by such wars causes people to struggle for increasingly limited resources, which may contribute to more conflicts in the future (Hoff & Polack, 1993).

U.S. dependence on arms production and sales for economic development also imposes tremendous burdens on development in our own country. Some argue, convincingly, that excessive military spending has harmed the economic health of our society and that it diverts spending for social welfare needs such as health and education, which endangers the future welfare of society (Barnet, 1981; Bluestone & Harrison, 1982; Dumas, 1986; Galbraith, 1981; Iatridis, 1988; Korotkin, 1985; Mahony, 1982; Russett, 1970; Sivard, 1991). "Ethnoviolence against Native Americans" poignantly describes how Native American people have been victimized by an environmental form of ethnoviolence carried out to further the goals of the military.

Ethnoviolence against Native Americans

More than half of all the uranium in the United States lies beneath or immediately adjacent to Native American reservations; most of the uranium used in U.S. nuclear weapons comes from mines on the reservations.

Like many other of our country's achievements, the dawn of the American nuclear age began with a betrayal of indigenous people's rights. In 1919 the U.S. Congress opened Native American lands, previously protected by treaty, to any prospector with a pick and shovel. Prospectors could stake claims to any land they wished for a small payment to the Department of the Interior. At that time, uranium was the primary source of radium, which was used to treat cancer and to make luminescent dials and watches. Because there was rich uranium in the Belgian Congo, however, mining on Native American lands was curtailed at first.

Then came World War II and the rush to develop the atomic bomb. Uranium mining returned to the reservations with a vengeance that haunts the lives of Native American people to this day. The race to arm the U.S. with atomic weapons during the 1940s and 1950s led to a mining frenzy that threw to the wind any concerns about safety and health, particularly when the miners were Native Americans. The miners dug the uranium ore with picks and shovels in small mines called dog holes and blasted rocks with dynamite. They breathed radon gas and silica-laden dust. They ate food tainted with uranium oxide and drank the water that dripped from the mine walls. They carried the uranium home to their wives and children on their bodies and clothing. Later, they died painful, prolonged deaths from radiation exposure.

There were many accidents. In June 1962, 200 tons of radioactive waste washed into the Cheyenne River near the Pine Ridge reservation in South Dakota. The biggest accident—and possibly the worst nuclear accident in U.S. history—occurred in July 1979 when a dam holding 100 million gallons of radioactive water and 1,100 tons of radioactive waste burst, spilling into the Rio Puerco on the Navajo reservation. (Owners of the dam had known two months before the collapse that the dam was cracked, but they did not repair it.) Within three hours, the radioactive water had reached the city of Gallup, New Mexico, nearly 50 miles away, and the radiation level exceeded safe boundaries by more than 6,000 times. The spill killed more than 1,000 sheep, horses, and other livestock that drank from the river and forced the evacuation of 1,700 Navajos.

By the early 1980s, after the end of the mining boom, more than 1,200 uranium mines had been abandoned and remained uncovered. Highly radioactive waste alongside the mines was left to blow in the wind and seep into the groundwater. For example, the largest open-pit uranium mine in the world, the Jackpile mine, left a 3,000-acre crater and radioactive slag piles for the Native Americans of Laguna Pueblo when it was abruptly abandoned in 1981. The tribe had been informed in 1978 by the Environmental Protection Agency that all of their water sources had been dangerously contaminated by radioactivity and that the tribal council building, community center, and newly constructed housing were radioactive as well.

Source: Ewen, 1996.

Toward Resolution

Ethnoviolence and ethnic conflict are the inevitable products of an inequitable and unjust distribution of power and resources. Sustainable human development—which, among other things, seeks to remedy inequity, promote democratic participation, and expand economic opportunity to those who have gone without it—offers a route to peace. The next chapter explores sustainable human development as an antidote to ethnoviolence and discusses its implications for the social work profession.

References

American Psychological Association (APA). (1993). *Violence and youth: Psychology's response: Vol. I. Summary report of the American Psychological Association Commission on Violence and Youth.* Washington, DC: Author.

Barnet, R. (1981). *Real security: Restoring American power in a dangerous decade.* New York: Simon & Shuster.

Berlet, C. (1990, September–October). Taking off the gloves. *Greenpeace, 15,* 18–21.

Bluestone, B., & Harrison, B. (1982). *The deindustrialization of America.* New York: Basic Books.

Bryant, B. (1996). Key research and policy issues facing environmental justice. *Poverty and Race, 5*(4), 5–6.

Bullard, R. D. (1990). *Dumping in Dixie: Race, class and environmental quality.* Boulder, CO: Westview Press.

Chehak, G. E., & Harjo, S. S. (1990, January–February). Protection quandary in Indian country. *Environmental Action,* pp. 21–22.

Cho, S. K. (1995). Korean Americans vs. African Americans: Conflict and construction. In M. L. Anderson & P. H. Collins (Eds.), *Race, class and gender* (pp. 461–470). Belmont, CA: Wadsworth.

Congressional Hispanic Caucus. (1994, October 7). *Fact & Fiction: Immigrants in the U.S.* Washington, DC: U.S. Congressional Hispanic Caucus Report.

Cozic, D. P. (1995). *Ethnic conflict.* San Diego: Greenhaven Press.

Deng, F. M., & Zartman, I. W. (Eds.). (1991). *Conflict resolution in Africa.* Washington, DC: Brookings Institution.

Dumas, L. J. (1986). The military albatross: How arms spending is destroying the economy. In J. Wallace (Ed.), *Waging peace: A handbook for the struggle to abolish nuclear weapons* (pp. 100–105). New York: Harper & Row.

Ehrlich, H. J. (1990, March). *Campus ethnoviolence and the policy options* (Institute Report no. 4). Baltimore: National Institute against Prejudice and Violence.

Eichstaedt, P. H. (1995). *If you poison us: Uranium and Native Americans.* Santa Fe, NM: Red Crane Books.

Enloe, C. (1977). Police and military in the resolution of ethnic conflict. *Annals of the American Academy of Political and Social Science, 433,* 137.

Ewen, A. (1996). A plague on a people. *Peace and Freedom, 56*(1), 8–10.

Frelick, B. (1994). The year in review. In U.S. Committee for Refugees (USCR), *World Refugee Survey — 1994* (pp. 2–9). Washington, DC: USCR.

Galbraith, J. K. (1981, June–July). The economics of the arms race—and after. *Bulletin of Atomic Scientists,* pp. 13–16.

Garcia, C. (1981). Androgyny and peace education. *Bulletin of Peace Proposals, 2,* 163–178.

Gordon, M. M. (1964). *Assimilation in American life.* New York: Oxford University Press.

Gorey, K. M. (1995). Environmental health: Race and socioeconomic factors. In R. L. Edwards (Ed.-in-Chief), *Encyclopedia of social work* (19th ed., Vol. 1, pp. 868–872). Washington, DC: National Association of Social Workers.

Gurr, T. R. (1993). *Minorities at risk: A global view of ethnopolitical conflicts.* Washington, DC: U.S. Institute of Peace.

Hartung, W. D. (1994). *And weapons for all.* New York: HarperCollins.

Hitchens, C. (1995). Minority report. *Nation, 260*(5), 191.

Hoff, M. D. (1990). *Impact of the farm crisis on rural women: Implications for social action and policy.* (Available from the North American Farm Alliance, P.O. Box 102, Covert, MI 49043)

Hoff, M. D. (1994). *Economic development, environment and violent conflict* (research abstract submitted to the Pacific Northwest NASW Center on Violence, Development, and Ethnicity, Portland, OR).

Hoff, M. D., & Polack, R. J. (1993). Social dimensions of the environmental crisis: Challenges for social work. *Social Work, 38,* 204–211.

Horowitz, D. L. (1992, March). *The helping professions and the hurting conflicts* (CASID Distinguished Speaker Series no. 10). East Lansing: Michigan State University, Center for Advanced Study of International Development.

Hudgens, A. G. (1995, February 13). Bury my heart at Los Alamos. *Nation,* pp. 210–213.

Iatridis, D. S. (1988). New social deficit: Neoconservatism's policy of social underdevelopment. *Social Work, 33,* 11–15.

Jacobson, J. L. (1988). *Environmental refugees: A yardstick of habitability.* Washington, DC: World Watch Institute.

Jalali, R., & Lipset, S. M. (1993). Racial and ethnic conflicts: A global perspective. In D. Caraley (Ed.), *New world politics: Power, ethnicity, and democracy* (pp. 55–76). Montpelier, VT: Capital City Press.

Kivisto, P. (1995). *Americans all: Race and ethnic relations in historical, structural, and comparative perspectives.* Belmont, CA: Wadsworth.

Klanwatch Intelligence Report (pp. 16–17). (1995, March). Montgomery, AL: Southern Poverty Law Center.

Korotkin, A. (1985). Impact of military spending on the nation's quality of life. *Social Work, 30,* 369–372.

Koulish, R. E. (1994). Human and civil rights abuses by immigration authorities at the U.S.–Mexico border. *Poverty and Race, 3*(5), 9–12.

Krebs, A. V. (1990, May–June). Monsanto strategy pushes chemical/biotech dependency. *North American Farmer,* pp. 2–3. (Available from the North American Farm Alliance, P.O. Box 102, Covert, MI 49043)

Levinson, D. (1993, August). Ethnic conflict and refugees. *Refugees, 93,* 4–9. (Published by the Public Information Service of the United Nations High Commissioner for Refugees, Geneva)

Lusk, M. W., & Hoff, M. D. (1995). Sustainable social development: A model for pragmatic social change. *Social Development Issues, 16*(3), 20–31.

Mahony, Bishop R. (1982). The case for nuclear pacifism. In E. W. Lefever & E. S. Hunt (Eds.), *The apocalyptic premise* (pp. 279–293). Washington, DC: Ethics and Public Policy Center.

McLemore, S. D. (1994). *Racial and ethnic relations in America.* Needham Heights, MA: Allyn & Bacon.

Muhiewa, J-M. (1994). *Conflict and development.* Washington, DC: Panos Institute.

Nietschmann, B. (1987). The Third World War. *Cultural Survival Quarterly, 11*(3), 1–16.

Ong, P., & Valenzuela, A., Jr. (1995). Job competition between immigrants and African Americans. *Poverty and Race, 4*(2), 9–12.

Pacific Northwest NASW Center on Violence, Development, and Ethnicity. (1994). [Research Brief Summary Report submitted to the Violence and Development Project, Portland, OR]

Panos Institute. (1994). *Conflict and development.* Washington, DC: Author.

Pinderhughes, E. (1989). *Understanding race, ethnicity, and power.* New York: Free Press.

Pinderhughes, H. (1993). The anatomy of racially motivated violence in New York City: A case study of youth in southern Brooklyn. *Social Problems, 40*(4), 478–492.

Racist identity sect fuels nationwide extremist movement. (1995, August). *Klanwatch Intelligence Report* (pp. 1, 3–5). Montgomery, AL: Southern Poverty Law Center.

Richardson, J. M., & Samarasinghe, S.W.R. de A. (1991). Measuring the economic dimensions of Sri Lanka's ethnic conflict. In S.W.R. de A. Samarasinghe & R. Coughlan (Eds.), *Economic dimensions of ethnic conflict* (pp. 194–223). London: Pinter Publishers.

Richmond, A. H. (1988). *Immigration and ethnic conflict.* Hong Kong: MacMillan Press.

Russett, B. M. (1970). *What price vigilance? The burdens of national defense.* New Haven, CT: Yale University Press.

Sheffield, C. (1995). Hate-violence. In P. S. Rothenberg (Ed.), *Race, class, and gender in the United States: An integrated study* (pp. 432–441). New York: St. Martin's Press.

Shuman, M., & Harvey, H. (1993). *Security without war: A post-cold war foreign policy.* Boulder, CO: Westview Press.

Sivard, R. L. (1991). *World military and social expenditures.* Washington, DC: World Priorities.

Tactaquin, C. (1995). An international perspective on migration. *Poverty and Race, 4*(2), 1–6.

Taylor, R. A. (1995). America's ethnic conflicts: An overview. In C. P. Cozic (Ed.), *Ethnic conflict* (pp. 10–13). San Diego: Greenhaven Press.

Thernstrom, S., Orlov, A., & Handlin, O. (Eds.). (1980). *Harvard encyclopedia of American ethnic groups.* Cambridge, MA: Harvard University Press, Belknap Press.

Truax, H. (1990, January–February). Minorities at risk. *Environmental Action,* pp. 19–21.

United Church of Christ. (1987). *Toxic wastes and race in the United States.* New York: Commission for Racial Justice, United Church of Christ.

United Nations. (1995, March 6–12). *Ethnic violence.* Paper prepared for the World Summit for Social Development, Copenhagen, Denmark.

United Nations Development Programme (UNDP). (1994). *Human development report 1994.* New York: Oxford University Press.

Weiss, J. C. (1990). Violence motivated by bigotry: Ethnoviolence. In L. Ginsberg et al. (Eds.), *Encyclopedia of social work* (18th ed., 1990 suppl., pp. 307–319). Silver Spring, MD: NASW Press.

World Watch Institute. (1987). *State of the world report.* New York: W. W. Norton.

Wright, R. (1937). *Black boy.* New York: Harper & Row.

Zinn, H. (1980). *A people's history of the United States.* New York: Harper & Row.

Chapter 9

Sustainable Human Development as an Antidote to Ethnoviolence

> Ultimately, prevention of conflict will require that the underlying inequity, injustice, and poverty which often sow the seeds of war be remedied. (Panos Institute, 1994, p. 13)

The discrimination and lack of opportunity—in other words, the passive ethnoviolence—besetting subordinated groups lead to the emergence of movements in societies around the world that strive to bring about social change. Some movements use nonviolent strategies and some use violent strategies. Some movements demand secession, some aim for cultural autonomy, some pursue equal rights within the prevailing political system, and some seek a more pluralistic society. Whatever strategy or goal they espouse, all movements express a group identity and a desire for more equitable distribution of power and resources (Jalali & Lipset, 1993).

The frequent use of military or police forces to intervene in ethnic conflicts and other ethnoviolence reflects a fundamental belief in violence as the solution to conflict. The argument in this chapter is that prevention strategies—based on principles of sustainable human development—are much more effective than force as an instrument for peace. To create a world in which diverse people live together in peace, dignity, and security, we must narrow the gap between the wealthy elite and the impoverished masses by encouraging the redistribution of resources, particularly income and land; promote strong, participatory democracies that ensure ethnic and racial minority groups' rights with constitutional protections; uphold vibrant civil societies; strengthen communities while protecting and preserving diverse cultures; foster greater understanding among racial and ethnic groups; and adopt nonviolent methods of conflict resolution.

Promote Sustainable Development and Efficient Resource Use

One of the principles of sustainable development is equity, which calls for redistribution of resources so that the poorest people have expanded economic opportunities and increase their quality of life in ways that are environmentally, economically, and socially viable over the long term. Development assistance has the potential to reduce ethnic conflict both in the global South and in impoverished communities in the United States. To realize that potential, however, the rationale for development assistance must be to help poor people, not to curry favor with a strategically important government or particular politicians. Development assistance must also promote self-reliance rather than increased dependence; encourage redistribution of land, resources, and income to narrow the gap between wealthy and poor people; help nations become self-sufficient providers of food, water, shelter, clothing, and health care; and minimize environmental degradation (Shuman & Harvey, 1993).

Sustainable development occurs when nations and communities meet current needs without compromising the ability of future generations to meet their own needs. Proponents of sustainable development recognize the fundamental interdependency between humans and the natural environment, and they understand that human society will very likely collapse if natural systems continue to be depleted beyond replaceable levels (Lusk & Hoff, 1995). Alternative ideas for promoting sustainable development can be found within cultures that have been subordinated and persecuted. For example, Hoff and Polack (1993) described four ideas of traditional Native American cultures that provide the foundation for sustainable development: (1) the preeminence of spiritual reality; (2) the essential relatedness of all beings on earth, from which flows respect for all living things; (3) the living nature and sacred character of the earth; and (4) an alternative definition of power, one that includes the concept of reciprocity, or the obligation to give back for what is taken (Brown, 1982; Neihardt, 1972).

As a first step toward promoting sustainable development in poor communities in the United States, the environmental justice movement works to eliminate environmental racism. *Environmental justice* refers to

> those cultural norms, values, rules, regulations, behaviors, policies and de-cisions that support sustainable communities, where people can interact with confidence that their environment is safe, nurturing and productive. Environmental justice is served when people can realize their highest po-tential without experiencing "isms." Environmental justice is supported by decent-paying and safe jobs, quality schools and recreation, decent housing and adequate health care, democratic decision-making, personal empower-ment, and communities free of violence, drugs, and poverty. These are com-munities where both cultural and biological diversity are respected and highly revered and where distributive justice prevails. (Bryant, 1996, p. 5)

The environmental justice movement is based on the principle that community members can and must be intimately involved in shaping environmental policies. This includes participatory research, whereby community people become an integral part of studies aimed at detect-ing exposure to environmental toxins and determining the potential health effects of economic development in their own communities.

Sustainable development is an antidote to ethnoviolence. Some main-tain that if communities were "self-sufficient in energy, water, food, and other essential resources, fewer ethnic conflicts and wars would be trig-gered than in the current world of conflict-producing dependencies, externalities, vulnerabilities, and inefficiencies" caused by overconsump-tion and competition over resources (Shuman & Harvey 1993, pp. 119–120). Bioregionalism in the United States is an example of a social move-ment that is working to apply the principles of sustainability—as well as those of democracy—to development models. The bioregionalism move-ment emphasizes conservation and local self-sufficiency, community and decentralized political structures, and cultural pluralism and coopera-tion (Sale, 1985).

Promote Participatory Democracy

Democracy can help reduce ethnic conflict. However, the development of truly democratic systems is not an easy task. In countries that are in transition to democracy, for example, new institutional structures and traditions may not be strong enough to constrain conflict: Witness the resurgence of a plethora of old ethnic conflicts in the countries of the former Soviet Union. Another complication of democracy building arises when democratic politics pave the way for forces that are considered undemocratic. For example, in 1992 the Islamic fundamentalists in Algeria—who, many believe, are not committed to democracy—nearly gained power through free and fair elections. Such dilemmas occur not only within the context of countries; they are also part of democracy building in local communities.

If investment in democracy is to prevent ethnic conflict from escalating into civil war, it must amount to more than periodic voting and majority rule. Many people live in democratic systems throughout the world, but in many of these political systems people are not empowered because they are not involved in decisions that affect their lives. In cases where the majority can rule without limit, members of racial and ethnic minority groups are persecuted and often seek protection through autonomy. In addition, the foreign policy establishment of almost every democracy—including the United States—is characterized by secrecy, hierarchy, and authoritarianism, all of which weaken participatory decision making about issues that profoundly affect people's lives. Shuman and Harvey (1993) propose the development of "strong" democracies that make use of three basic political tools to help inoculate a country against ethnic unrest and civil war: (1) constitutional protections for racial and ethnic minority groups; (2) the principle of subsidiarity; and (3) a vibrant civil society.

Constitutional protections for racial and ethnic minority groups make a pluralistic society possible. For example, communities of color are legally protected in the United States under the Fourteenth Amendment to the Constitution. As a result, most civil rights movements in our country have fought for pluralism and fairness rather than secession and separatism.

The principle of subsidiarity encourages participation and empowerment. The essence of subsidiarity is that governance should always proceed from the level closest to the people so that decisions are made by those who are affected. Decisions made at too low a level may not give due consideration to all of the effects of an action. For example, an upstream community may decide to dump solid waste into a river, without regard for communities that are downstream. Conversely, decisions made at too high a level may circumvent public input, thereby creating resentment and stifling local creativity; for example, the federal government may issue thousands of regulations for local trash disposal and decide that an incinerator should be built in a poor urban neighborhood.

A comparative study of the democratic experience in 26 nations of the global South points to the potential of the principle of subsidiarity in reducing ethnic violence. The study concluded that when the state responds to ethnic mobilization with exclusion and repression, violence festers; when ethnic leaders are allowed to share power, however, they generally act according to the rules of the game (Jalali & Lipset, 1993). Political arrangements reached in South Africa after apartheid and in Malaysia are examples of how conflict can be mitigated through power sharing. Power sharing can also be key to preventing ethnic conflict caused by economic disputes.

A vibrant civil society—the web of nongovernmental groups, organizations, and movements that empower citizens to solve their own problems—can help resolve ethnoviolence. Without such organizations, citizens' only recourse is the government. If the government is unable or unwilling to help, which often is the case, citizens inevitably turn against the government. Civil society provides a critical mechanism for releasing steam from potentially explosive social problems and for resolving problems through grassroots inventiveness. In the United States, groups such as the National Association for the Advancement of Colored People, the National Organization for Women, labor unions, and the United Way have been important in fighting racial injustice, seeking fair treatment and better working conditions, and helping people in need.

Nongovernmental organizations (NGOs) around the world are breaking new ground in resolving ethnic conflicts. For example, the Neve Shalom Kibbutz, located between Jerusalem and Tel Aviv, has set up the only Jewish–Arab bilingual school system in Israel as a means of promoting reconciliation. In South Africa, labor unions have been important proponents of equal protection in the workplace.

Shuman and Harvey (1993) cautioned that promoting democracy through force or threat of force does not work and in fact results in even less democracy; nevertheless, they wrote that the promotion of strong democracy everywhere, including our own backyard, has many benefits:

> Just as strong democracy reins in the excesses of national leaders, it also checks group conflict. If the rules of the game are fair, people are willing to play and occasionally lose. By creating protections for minorities, moving more decision-making power to communities, and helping nongovernmental organizations to flourish, strong democracy offers a hope—perhaps the only hope—for resolving internal strife through politics instead of bullets. (pp. 88–90)

Strengthen Communities

Lack of a sense of connectedness among people is at the root of many issues related to ethnic conflict and racial strife. Although immigration and birth patterns have made the world more ethnically diverse, neighborhoods and schools—particularly in the United States—continue to be segregated. The more physically isolated ethnic groups are from one another, the easier it is to support public policies that benefit one's own group over other groups. A sense of division and powerlessness in communities, which is fed by popular culture, polarizes citizens; they feel cut off from one another and from their leaders. Ethnic tension tears at the fabric of community.

Solutions to ethnoviolence lie in seeing our destinies as intertwined and striving to work with one another despite our differences. One way to do that is for institutions to move from providing services to collaborating with communities, so that citizens gain more authority for public affairs and work together for common ends. Harry Boyte, who directs the Center for Democracy and Citizenship at the Hubert H. Humphrey Institute for Public Affairs at the University of Minnesota, believes that a sense of community can be reestablished through "the principle of unintended consequences." In other words, by getting people working together on a project that they care about, links among them can be forged. Because people often come to respect those they work with on projects of mutual concern, Boyte maintained that "public work is the only deeply successful way to deal with diversity" (Schier, 1995, p. 16).

Protect Ethnic Culture

Only the preservation of ethnic identity—not assimilation—will allow development of the flexibility and tolerance needed for moving beyond the tendency toward ethnic polarization. It is when ethnic or cultural identity is threatened that it becomes most important to people. When they do not feel free to express their ethnicity through language, traditions, and rituals, people are less likely to develop a sense of connectedness and shared goals with the larger society (United Nations, 1995). Cultural values of ethnic communities also can serve to enhance resilience and protect individuals against harsh and stressful life conditions; negative messages about ethnic cultures within the mainstream culture, on the other hand, undermine those cultures' ability to protect. Values such as communalism, familism, and group harmony are important deterrents to violence.

Thus, an essential ingredient for successful management of ethnic conflict is sensitivity to protecting the language rights, religion, and culture of ethnic communities. Without this sensitivity, and without political devices and mechanisms for power sharing, "not even the most carefully crafted and generous affirmative action policies designed to protect a minority and foster its economic interests can resolve the tensions inherent in a multi-ethnic society or bring them down to tolerable levels of stability" (De Silva, 1992, p. 9).

Sustainable development projects are developed with respect for local cultures. Development assistance does not work when it is based on the predominant values of industrialized countries or on European or Euro-American value systems. Rather, it works best when givers and receivers respect each other's cultures and interact as equals. Oxfam America learned this lesson about the cultural dimension of development from desperately poor refugees who had been displaced by war in Southern Sudan. The refugees were barely surviving in huts made of sticks and rags. Oxfam America workers expected that the refugees needed emergency food, better shelter, or land. However, when asked what they needed most, the refugees said they needed help to reestablish their traditional village schools. For them, education was a bridge to the future and to the past; the schools could be run by the people themselves in their temporary location and taken with them when they returned home. If Oxfam America had not consulted the refugees, it might have made the culturally biased assumption that material needs were paramount for people who clearly possessed almost nothing. Making such an assumption might have inadvertently weakened the refugees' will to go home and kept them from rebuilding their strongest resource for survival (McAfee, 1992).

Improve Race Relations

Efforts at improving race relations in the United States traditionally involve people from the dominant (white) culture working with groups that have been victimized by discrimination. Recently, however, white people have joined together in groups to examine their own attitudes and actions and to expunge racism within themselves, without the constraints and well-meaning pretenses that racially mixed situations can elicit. For example, a group in Austin, Texas, called "White Allies: Healing the Wounds of Racism," is designed for white people who want to learn more about racism within themselves. People who participate in such groups find the work exhausting as they struggle to come to terms with their fears and shame about colluding with injustice and racism. Some think the temporary separatism of these groups is a necessary first phase in healing and improving race relations.

Various multiracial discussion groups dedicated to eliminating racism and promoting improved race relations have been formed in communities across the United States. Talking about racial and ethnic differences in a way that reduces ethnic tensions is not easy, but fear and uncomfortable feelings must be faced if useful dialogue is to take place. Communication aimed at improving multicultural relationships must be carried out in an open, respectful environment in which people of all races and ethnic groups can express their thoughts and feelings. People have done just that in the groups that are described in "The Study Circles Resource Center" (Study Circles Resource Center, 1992).

The Study Circles Resource Center

The Study Circles Resource Center (1992) is a program that helps communities use small-group, democratic discussion to talk to one another about race relations. SCRC points out that two ingredients are necessary to make this dialogue happen at the local community level: (1) leadership that has connections to diverse segments of the community and that takes a strong role in bringing them together for dialogue; and (2) the ability to assist those who are participating in the dialogue to have honest and respectful conversations.

- A neighborhood discussion group in Memphis, Tennessee, wanted to bridge the huge communication gap between blacks and whites in their community and learn from people with different backgrounds. They therefore formed an intentionally integrated discussion group called "The Wednesday Night Club," which meets once a month in group members' homes to discuss current social issues.
- Some women members of an African American–Jewish coalition in New York decided to form a women's dialogue group. As leaders in various large organizations, they had worked together on social issues, but they realized that there were few opportunities to learn about each other's unique perspectives and experiences gained from their racial and ethnic backgrounds.
- "Church pairing," in which predominantly white and predominantly black churches join together to learn from each other and work together, is promoted and practiced by many churches around the country.
- In some communities, volunteers monitor incidents of racist violence and then help develop community responses to them.
- In some cities, there are community service or peer-tutoring programs that bring together students from diverse backgrounds. Common Ground, a youth leadership program launched in Hartford, Connecticut, exemplifies this approach. It brings together sophomores and juniors from public high schools in Hartford and surrounding towns for leadership training, community service, and a better understanding of how people from varying racial and ethnic backgrounds can work together to address common concerns.
- Informal and formal student groups across the United States organize to fight racism on their campuses. They hold teach-ins, vigils, rallies, and discussions. Some of them organize to lobby for or against specific campus or governmental policies.
- Some college and university administrators sponsor racism and race relations workshops as part of their freshman orientation programs or for faculty members who will be working with racial or ethnic minority students in the classroom.
- Around the country, teachers at all levels bring discussion of race relations into their classrooms.
- The Women's International League for Peace and Freedom launched a Racial Justice campaign. They decided that the best place to begin

was within their own organization by re-educating their own board,
staff, and members about racism.

Source: Study Circles Resource Center. (1992). *Can't we all just get along? A Manual*
for discussion programs on racism and race relations (pp. 13–14). Pomfret, CT:
Author. Used with permission of Study Circles Resource Center.

Counter Hate Groups

People who accept responsibility for guarding their communities
from the divisive influence of hate groups are at the same time working to promote improved race relations. There are many examples of
how communities have taken actions against white supremacist groups
in the United States (Bullard, 1991). When the Ku Klux Klan arrived in
a Maine town to burn a ceremonial cross and recruit new members,
town inhabitants—many of whom had recently been laid off and might
have been expected to be receptive to hate mongering—greeted the
Klan rally with a massive peaceful protest against racism. A 1987 Klan
march in Greensboro, North Carolina, drew 125 people, but the effect
was diminished by a celebration of racial harmony held the day before, in which six times that many people participated—city officials,
ministers of various churches, police officers, and hundreds of citizens
of all ages and colors. More and more communities are realizing that
if white supremacist groups are allowed to march and recruit without
any vocal community opposition, their chances of winning converts
and stirring up trouble are increased.

Another way of countering hate crimes by white supremacist groups
is to bring civil suit against them (Bullard, 1991). The Klanwatch project
of the Southern Poverty Law Center in Montgomery, Alabama, has successfully taken the Ku Klux Klan to court in several parts of the country.
For example, in Texas in 1981, a U.S. district court judge ordered the
Klan to stop harassing Vietnamese fishermen, who had been subjected
to threats, cross burnings, and boat arson in Galveston Bay. In another
case, the mother of a black youth lynched by the United Klans of America
was awarded $7 million in damages by an all-white jury in Mobile, Ala-
bama in 1987; the jury found the Klan organization liable for the violent
acts of its members. Members of the Invisible Empire and the Southern

White Knights also were found liable in 1987 by an Atlanta jury for an attack on civil rights marchers; the groups were ordered to pay nearly $1 million in damages.

Promote Nonviolent Conflict Resolution Efforts

Even if strong democratic systems and sustainable human development strategies quite successfully tackle the sources of conflict, ethnic groups will still have disagreements with one another. In these instances, the objective is to resolve conflict peacefully before those involved resort to violence. The United States has many tools for resolving conflicts between nations without violence. "It can work with other nations bilaterally or multilaterally. Or it can strengthen norms, regimes, and institutions. Far from being a dull enterprise, the peaceful resolution of conflicts will call on [our] fullest faculties of daring, courage, imagination and idealism" (Shuman & Harvey, 1993, p. 161).

Conflict resolution specialists talk about "two-track" diplomacy. The first track involves regular state-to-state diplomacy. The second track involves others, namely, NGOs, universities, citizens groups, ordinary citizens, and so on. On the first track, intergovernmental organizations such as the United Nations play a lead role in resolving conflicts around the world (see "Conflict Resolution Process Developed by United Nations").

Conflict Resolution Process Developed by United Nations

According to the United Nations, the eruption of ethnic conflict is almost always a result of social exclusion and disintegration that has paved the way by weakening the social fabric. There are often clear transitional stages between the initial escalation of tensions, the first incidence of violence, and the proliferation of warning signals that precede full-scale conflict. It is at these points in time that interventions need to be first considered. Although the following stages and interventions are related to large-scale conflicts within or between countries, they may have relevance for ethnic conflicts within and between communities in the United States as well.

Counteracting propaganda: Violence requires psychological preparation. Genocide must begin with a stage in which one group begins to define another in terms that make its elimination desirable. For example, years of considerable psychological preparation in Germany, in which great care and detail was given to identifying different "superior" and "inferior" racial types, preceded the Holocaust. Because propaganda plays a crucial role in this psychological preparation for violence, it can be at least monitored and countered with a more balanced presentation of the facts about ethnic groups and their aims.

Monitoring mobilization: Violence also needs material and institutional preparation. Weapons have to be obtained and, in many cases, armed forces and command structures created and training given. These preparatory stages can also be monitored, countered, and sometimes prevented, for instance with strict control of arms sales and military mobilization.

Third-party intervention: Once ethnic conflict has broken out, third-party intervention is sometimes imperative, although chances of success are quite limited at this stage. The international isolation of the South African regime was essential in forcing it into negotiations, whereas external initiatives played both positive and negative roles in the Palestinian settlement.

In most cases, it is crucial that space be provided for negotiation at the beginning of conflict resolution. The resolution process is helped when third parties are either neutral to the conflict or united in their approach to it. External intervention is usually not successful, however, when it attempts to define and enforce solutions rather than to serve in the role of facilitator between the combatants. If peace is forcibly imposed, it will break down once the force is removed, as happened in Somalia.

Source: United Nations, 1995.

NGOs can play a critical role in conflict resolution on the second track, particularly during intrastate conflicts. By working at the grassroots level, NGOs can help develop a broader consensus, thus making peace more sustainable and rebuilding possible (Panos Institute, 1994).

Kahn (1994), reporting on a study involving members of conflicting groups from diverse cultures or backgrounds, came to some tentative conclusions about conflict resolution. Kahn pointed out that, historically, mild-mannered negotiators appear to fare better than hard-liners, whose approach says, in effect, that "might makes right." The successful negotiators tend to be individuals such as Nelson Mandela and F. W. de Klerk, who facilitated conflict resolution in South Africa. This new, negotiator prototype for conflict resolution and mediation is being used increasingly both domestically and internationally.

Dialogue groups, in which people from groups in conflict meet to speak their truths and to listen to one another, came into vogue in the mid-1970s and flourished until the mid-1980s. For example, a dialogue group in Beersheva, Israel, between Israeli Arabs and Jews, called Partnership, was directed by a social worker from the United States (Kahn & Bender, 1985). Dialogue groups made up of members of diverse ethnic groups have considerable potential for reducing conflict and promoting multicultural understanding. "Dialogue in Southern California" describes some creative efforts at conflict resolution in southern California in the 1990s.

Dialogue in Southern California

Peace Action Network (formerly SANE/FREEZE) sponsored a series of dialogues in 1992 among Bosnian Muslims, Croats, and Serbs who live in southern California. Group members were recruited from three agencies that reflected their strong emotional loyalties: the Serbian American Community Coalition, the Croatian National Association, and the Islamic Center. The group met once a month for 10 months. Each meeting lasted three hours. Intense hostility among the groups was expressed at the meetings and a bomb threat led to the group's termination. Nonetheless, the group reached consensus on a document they produced—"Proposal for Peace in the Balkans"— which continued to circulate for years after the group disbanded. A public television station produced a documentary about the project, which aired in February 1993 and has been repeated several times since.

In the wake of the 1992 civil unrest in south-central Los Angeles, several initiatives were undertaken to resolve conflicts among diverse groups. The Congregational Church of Christian Fellowship, which had already been active in multicultural dialogue, conducted weekly "Community Conversations" in 1994 on topics such as "Creating a Just Peace in Los Angeles," "Rebuilding Los Angeles," and "Race Relations." "Conversations" drew multicultural audiences: African Americans, Latinos, Koreans, and whites.

The Martin Luther King Dispute Resolution Center (MLKDRC) resolves civil disputes between south-central residents through mediation and conciliation. Types of disputes include those between landlord and tenant, neighbor and neighbor, consumer and merchant, and employer and employee. Project Mediation is a nonviolent conflict resolution training program for at-risk youth. The program introduces youth to practical nonviolent coping skills. The Asian Pacific American Dispute Resolution Center joined with the MLKDRC in a venture called the Joint Mediation Project, which has been operating as a bilingual mediation service to communities speaking Korean, Japanese, Chinese, and Tagalog. The initial focus of the project in the aftermath of the 1992 uprising was to assist Angelenos with conflict resolution and to address the tension between

African Americans and Korean Americans. The project team consists of a member of each group working as a mediator representing his or her respective group, for the purpose of managing cross-cultural disputes and to raise awareness of nonviolent alternatives to conflict.

Process Work Seminars promote dialogue between groups based on the thesis that changes in individuals lead to changes in society. Developed by Arnold Mindell and based on the philosophy and psychology of the late psychoanalyst Karl Jung, these experiential seminars are occurring in both the United States and in other countries. The focus of the seminars is on modeling how one can heal oneself (or a group) from prejudice. After the 1992 uprising in Los Angeles, a style of process seminars, called "Interracial Dialogue Process," used trained facilitators to help individuals focus on understanding their own prejudices as well as institutional racism.

Conflicts between African American and African immigrant groups have been a new reality in Los Angeles in the past several years. In 1990, the U.S. Census Bureau revealed that 28,850 African immigrants lived in Los Angeles and more than half of them emigrated between 1980 and 1990. The African American community and the newly arrived African immigrants are divided by vastly different cultures, history, values, and persistent misconceptions and stereotypes about each other. Many of the new immigrants feel that their American counterparts place too much emphasis on material things and image and have misperceptions about them as a result of geographical and historical ignorance; for example, too many African American people see Africa as one country rather than the world's largest continent containing 52 nations and thousands of ethnic groups and languages. African immigrants, on the other hand, denigrate African Americans for what they see as a lack of ambition and often fail to see or understand African Americans' feelings of disenfranchisement and powerlessness stemming from institutionalized racism that has affected their lives.

Conflicts between the two groups have been addressed by several organizations, including the African American Cultural Center, the Museum in Black, the UCLA African Study Center, the African International Village, and Leimert Park's Comedy Act Theater. As a result, increased awareness and communication have significantly improved relationships between the two groups. Also, they have begun to realize that they could both profit culturally and economically by joining forces.

Source: Kahn, A. (1994). *Violence and social development between conflicting groups.* (Unpublished paper written for the California NASW Center on Violence, Development, and Trauma and submitted to NASW's Violence and Development Project, Washington, DC.) Used with permission of the author.

Alternative Self-Defense Strategies

Once a conflict erupts, extraordinary skills, political and otherwise, are required to manage if not resolve it. Although this chapter stresses the prevention and resolution of ethnic conflicts and ethnoviolence, alternatives are needed for occasions when adversaries resort to force. Shuman and Harvey (1993) proposed two basic principles to be followed when military and police force is used to respond to riots and intergroup wars: (1) consistent with tenets of conflict prevention and resolution, force should be employed truly as a last resort; and (2) force should be structured and used exclusively in defensive, nonprovocative ways.

Alternative self-defense strategies that do not use force are also worthy of consideration. *Nonviolent resistance* is an approach that requires active pacifism, which prohibits the shedding of any person's blood except one's own; disobedience to unjust laws; and refusal to collaborate with unjust authorities. Proponents of pacifism point to its long and honorable history with renowned accomplishments—the abolition of slavery and the success of the civil rights movement of the 1960s in the United States, for example, and the independence of India from British rule (Dyson, 1984).

Civilian-based defense is a national defense against internal usurpations and foreign invasions by prepared nonviolent noncooperation and defiance by the society's population and institutions (Sharp, 1985). Its aim is to deny attackers their objectives, to become politically ungovernable by would-be tyrants, and to subvert the attackers' troops and functionaries to unreliability and even mutiny. Successful use of this strategy requires enormous organization and cooperation.

Economic conversion is a strategy of turning "swords into plowshares." It proposes dismantling a large portion of the world's war-making capabilities and transferring resources from military to civilian purposes through a planned process that would not cause social and economic dislocation. In the United States, five economic conversion bills have been introduced since 1963, four in the House of Representatives and one in the Senate. The most comprehensive of these was the Defense Economic Adjustment Act (H.R. 101), introduced in 1977, which became a model for conversion proponents and attracted growing legislative support during the early 1990s. Since 1980 there has been considerable grassroots conversion activity in the United States, Britain, Germany, Sweden, and Italy (Renner, 1990). Major issues related to economic conversion include the need to adapt research, production, and management practices in arms-producing factories to civilian needs and criteria; and the need to retrain employees, refashion production equipment, and find civilian uses for military bases and personnel (Renner, 1990).

Implications for Social Work: What You Can Do

The social work profession has a long history of seeking ways to promote social justice for oppressed populations and a long-standing commitment to people and groups that have been marginalized and persecuted. Social workers of the Settlement House era expressed moral indignation about the violence of war and understood that people who are poor and powerless are victims of a violent world. The collective work of early social workers with immigrants led to a distinctive understanding about the interrelatedness of war, ethnic violence, and an unjust social order.

Social workers' constellation of skills and attitudes—genuineness, caring or unconditional positive regard, empathic understanding—are the same characteristics that are required of peacemakers. A framework for promoting peace consists of practice approaches that support caring and that heal relationships. Social work skills such as empathic communication and active listening are antidotes to violence and essential ingredients for successful, nonviolent resolution of conflicts.

The fundamental principle of equality of all human beings is a crucial concept for social workers. It is also the cornerstone for social justice, and it requires serious consideration of what is just and unjust, what is equality and inequality. Although some social workers are involved in promoting social justice and equality on a societal level, most practice is at the individual level, where social workers help people by touching them, by direct contact, one person at a time (Horowitz, 1992). The experience of social workers with ethnic conflict is also drawn from life itself and from conflict itself, rather than from constitutions and electoral systems.

Horowitz (1992) discusses the need for social workers to alter their professional orientation so they can confront the attitudinal, institutional, and legal obstacles to a just society. Without taking on the role of advocacy for social reform and policy-centered approaches to their work, social workers can treat the social and political issues that their clients face only as personal problems.

Although work at the societal level is essential for the prevention of ethnic conflict, much can be accomplished at other levels to reduce ethnic conflict. Work at the individual level can have truly important effects. The social work profession can play a pivotal role in preventing even severe ethnic rioting, in which members of one group attack, kill, and mutilate members of another group. Because it is possible to anticipate such events, it is possible also to intervene early at the local level, where social workers practice. The social work profession can play a role in "countering rumors, in forcing or embarrassing authorities to do their jobs, in generally countering the pall of hostility and condonation that comes over localities about to experience such violence" (Horowitz, 1992, p. 11). Two tasks are especially important: (1) identify the pressure points of conflict and violence where a local, service-oriented approach will be fruitful; and (2) provide the kind of powerful, professional education that makes service to the client, regardless of ethnic identification, the paramount value—services must not end at ethnic boundaries even in times of conflict. In other words, social workers must be socialized to "transcend their ascriptive loyalties" and develop "a resilient, even impervious, professional ethic" (Horowitz, 1992, p. 12).

Through their work with both victims and perpetrators, social workers see firsthand the tragic consequences of ethnoviolence. A rich history of practice experience has yielded knowledge and collective understanding of economic, political, and social issues that make the profession uniquely equipped to prevent and resolve ethnoviolence and to promote peace and social justice. An example from Israel shows how social workers can use this accrued knowledge and skill to address ethnic conflict in their communities directly (Korazim & Sheffer, 1994). Ossim Shalom— meaning both "social workers for peace" and "to act for peace"—is the name of a community demonstration project that was formed in 1990 by a group of eight Jewish and Arab social workers; their purpose was to curb interethnic violence and to advance the cause of peaceful coexistence in Jerusalem. The goals of the group are to promote change in the way public resources are allocated and to better social services for the more disadvantaged groups in society, regardless of ethnicity. Attention to these development issues was critical: The experiences of Ossim Shalom suggest that Jewish–Arab conflicts in Israel often occur between two deprived groups, both victims of unjust social service distribution policies. That reality, coupled with each group's ignorance about the other's characteristics and norms, is a formula for ethnoviolence. A description of the beliefs underlying Ossim Shalom is contained in the following case study.

Ossim Shalom

Ossim Shalom was established by Jewish and Arab social workers from a wide range of social services and faculty from all five schools of social work in Israel. The founders hold differing world views and political orientations.

Ossim Shalom is a recognized professional organization, asserting its responsibility to work to enhance the peace process. It believes that the struggle for peace and the struggle for social welfare are one. A cessation of intergroup hostility and violence in Israel will lead to an improvement in the quality of life for all citizens. Ossim Shalom believes that sincere attempts to reach peace agreements would allow the Israeli government to redirect monies to enhance social services and address such social problems as high unemployment, the absorption of immigrants, and the deteriorating educational, health, and social welfare systems.

Ossim Shalom therefore calls for continuing negotiations with the representatives of the Palestinians and the Arab states in order to create new relationships among the peoples of the region; it calls upon the political parties in Israel and upon the government to pursue peace actively. Only peace will lead to a narrowing of the deep social gaps and to the creation of a society based on concern for the individual and his or her welfare.

Source: Korazim & Sheffer, 1994.

Social workers can act in various ways to promote peaceful relationships between ethnic groups and to reduce ethnoviolence. The following suggested actions are aimed at addressing problems and causes of ethnoviolence within the context of sustainable, people-centered development and strong democratic institutions.

- Find out how you can become involved in the International Decade of the World's Indigenous People, which began in December 1994. The program of action includes regional meetings, information exchange, assistance to indigenous people through training courses, fellowships, technical support, research and documentation, and partnership projects. A draft short-term program of activities for the decade has been issued, with the themes of promoting social development and strengthening the role of indigenous women and improving living conditions and health of indigenous peoples. Contact Julian Burger, Centre for Human Rights, Palais des Nations, CH-1211 Geneva 10, Switzerland. Tel: +41-22/907 3413; fax: +41-22/917 0212.

- Oppose anti-immigrant sentiment by organizing grassroots-level education, such as cultural awareness days, and help recent immigrants who are leaders of their communities use the media to promote assistance efforts for their conflict-ridden countries; write to your political representatives to propose more progressive immigration policies.

- If you work with immigrants in your social work practice, be aware of the fundamental struggle for them to hold on to their cultural identity without feeling ashamed of their differences while they try to establish themselves in a new culture. Find ways to help them stay connected or reconnect with their cultural heritage. Help them tap into their culture as a resource and as the source of their fundamental sense of belonging.

- Promote greater respect for cultures by helping to increase understanding about ethnic groups, by encouraging acceptance of cultural diversity, and by respecting ethnic values and norms and incorporating them into programs for violence prevention and social and economic development. Publicize, admire, and explicitly preserve the cultural traditions and achievements of underprivileged groups. Encourage schools of social work to promote a multicultural curriculum.

- Conduct self-assessments of your own prejudices and stereotypes. Be willing to engage in the difficult work of facing your own fears and shame in relation to racism. Join with others for support in expunging your own racist thoughts and actions.

- Learn about grassroots organizing, intervention, and advocacy with racial and ethnic communities. Study nonviolent social change movements such as the United Farm Workers Union and La Causa, which were mobilized by Cesar Chavez in the western and southwestern United States, and the nonviolent philosophy of Dr. Martin Luther King, Jr.
- Promote strong democracy both in the United States and abroad. In the United States, advocate for more and better access by the American people to foreign policy information. Find out about weapons deployments, intelligence activities, and the strategic doctrines of U.S. leaders. With more information, the American people can assess the magnitude of threats to their national security, help prevent serious foreign policy blunders, and improve the accountability of U.S. leaders. A specific action toward increasing public access to information would be to support efforts to narrow national security exceptions to the Freedom of Information Act (Shuman & Harvey, 1993).
- Become an advocate for the principle of nonprovocation in ethnic conflicts in other countries—that is, speak out against the rationalization that U.S. military interventions, covert actions, and weapons shipments are efforts to promote freedom and democracy. Promote U.S. policies that seek instead to help people abroad reform their governments according to their own values and visions—that is, promote policies that help them exercise more fully the same democratic rights that Americans seek to exercise themselves. Stand ready to accept the result of democratic processes even when they seem ideologically disappointing (for example, such tolerance would have led U.S. leaders to approve of the Chilean presidential election of 1970, even though it brought to power Salvador Allende, a parliamentary Marxist). Specifically, you might advocate the complete abolition of covert actions by the Central Intelligence Agency; if, during well-defined national security emergencies, covert actions are warranted, they should be under the control of the Department of Defense, where better-established procedures for congressional oversight exist (Shuman & Harvey, 1993).

- Critically analyze the economic and social effects of militarism and violence on employment rates, welfare of children and families, and homelessness, all of which have a disproportionately negative effect on communities of color. With a clear understanding of the effect of militarism on the economy and the impact of budget priorities on oppressed populations, social workers are in a position to advocate for legislation aimed at economic conversion, transfer of funds from military to human services programs, and nuclear disarmament and other weapons reductions. Engage in strategies such as lobbying, educating, organizing, forming coalitions, and policy advocacy.
- Clinical social workers can conduct assessments and interventions that concern the psychological and cultural aspects of ethnoviolence, the common roots of personal and political violence, and nonviolent change strategies. Identify how social work colludes with structural injustice through the use of social control practice strategies that aim to modify the feelings or behavior of those who have been oppressed rather than to change the oppressive situation. Promote peace and social justice in all practice settings by using nonviolent skills and strategies. For example, school social workers can use strategies of nonviolent conflict resolution to resolve disputes between students; family therapists can use the same skills to promote nonviolent communication among family members; occupational social workers can help resolve disputes about work and between employee and employer; and community organizers can use nonviolent conflict resolution methods to resolve conflicts between groups.
- Because discrimination and injustice must be confronted if ethnoviolence is to be prevented, work to change institutions: Lobby for legislation that seeks to eliminate inequities in the various systems with which social workers interact; file friend-of-court briefs in legal suits brought against lending, housing, and other institutions for violations of individual and group rights; lobby for gun control legislation; and work to reduce violence and negative stereotyping based on race and gender in the media (Van Soest & Bryant, 1995).

- Find out how views on affirmative action differ and help focus the debate on expanding opportunities for everyone—divide-and-conquer politics based on race and scarcity will not lead to peace.

References

Brown, J. E. (1982). *The spiritual legacy of the American Indian.* New York: Crossroad.

Bryant, B. (1996). Key research and policy issues facing environmental justice. *Poverty and Race, 5*(4), 5–6.

Bullard, S. (Ed.). (1991). *The Ku Klux Klan: A history of racism and violence.* Montgomery, AL: Klanwatch.

De Silva, K. M. (1992, August). *Ethnic conflict, the search for peace, and the development process* (CASID Distinguished Speaker Series no. 11). East Lansing: Michigan State University, Center for Advanced Study of International Development.

Dyson, F. (1984). *Weapons and hope.* New York: Harper & Row.

Hoff, M. D., & Polack, R. J. (1993). Social dimensions of the environmental crisis: Challenges for social work. *Social Work, 38,* 204–211.

Horowitz, D. L. (1992, March). *The helping professions and the hurting conflicts* (CASID Distinguished Speaker Series no. 10). East Lansing: Michigan State University, Center for Advanced Study of International Development.

Jalali, R., & Lipset, S. M. (1993). Racial and ethnic conflicts: A global perspective. In D. Caraley (Ed.), *New world politics: Power, ethnicity, and democracy* (pp. 55–76). Montpelier, VT: Capital City Press.

Kahn, A. (1994, August 22). *Violence and social development between conflicting groups.* (Unpublished paper written for the California NASW Center on Violence, Development, and Trauma and submitted to NASW's Violence and Development Project, Washington, DC.)

Kahn, A., & Bender, E. (1985). Self-help groups as a crucible for people empowerment in the context of social development. *Social Development Issues, 9*(2), 4–14.

Korazim, Y., & Sheffer, N. (1994). Ossim Shalom: A community demonstration project of social workers in Israel. In B. Chetkow-Yanoov & Y. Korazim (Eds.), *Conflict resolution by social workers in Israel: A reader* (pp. 83–100). Tel Aviv: Israel Association of Social Workers.

Lusk, M. W., & Hoff, M. D. (1995). Sustainable social development: A model for pragmatic social change. *Social Development Issues, 16*(3).

McAfee, K. (1992, summer). What is development? The varieties of wisdom. *Oxfam America News*, p. 8.

Neihardt, J. G. (1972). *Black Elk speaks: Being the life story of a holy man of the Oglala Sioux*. Lincoln: University of Nebraska Press.

Panos Institute. (1994). *Conflict and development*. Washington, DC: Author.

Renner, M. (1990, June). *Swords into plowshares: Converting to a peace economy* (World Watch Paper 96). Washington, DC: World Watch Institute.

Sale, K. (1985). *Dwellers in the land: The bioregional vision*. San Francisco: Sierra Club Books.

Schier, M. L. (1995, spring). Community and diversity: Americans struggle with how to promote both. *Humphrey Institute News*, pp. 4–6, 16.

Sharp, G. (1985). *National security through civilian-based defense*. Omaha, NE: Association for Transarmament Studies.

Shuman, M., & Harvey, H. (1993). *Security without war: A post–cold war foreign policy*. Boulder, CO: Westview Press.

Study Circles Resource Center (SCRC). (1992). *Can't we all just get along? A manual for discussion programs on racism and race relations*. Pomfret, CT: Author.

United Nations. (1995, March 6–12). *Ethnic violence*. Paper presented at the World Summit for Social Development, Copenhagen, Denmark.

Van Soest, D., & Bryant, S. (1995). Violence reconceptualized for social work: The urban dilemma. *Social Work, 40*, 549–557.

Part 5

Drug-Related Violence and Development

Chapter 10

The Relationship of Drug-Related Violence to Development

> Drug abuse and attempts to control the flow of illicit narcotics have come to pervade U.S. relations with the Third World in recent years. The drug issue carries substantial potential for conflict and mutual recrimination between [the global] North and [the global] South. The main drug-consuming countries are rich and industrialized; the main drug-producing countries are poor and predominantly agricultural. . . . Producing countries and consuming countries blame each other for the accelerating drug traffic and advocate, respectively, demand-side and supply-side solutions. (Lee, 1988, p. 87)

The growing international commerce in drugs has flooded the United States with narcotics that have transformed too many of our cities into war zones, created untold human distress, destroyed communities, and incurred costs that exceed $60 billion (Shuman & Harvey, 1993). The drug problem is not confined to our country, however. The misery caused by narcotic drugs travels the world without respect for national borders. The illegal production and distribution of drugs is spawning worldwide crime and violence, and drug consumption is destroying individuals and communities around the globe. The drug problem is one of the most corrosive of all threats to human societies (United Nations Development Programme [UNDP], 1994).

This chapter documents how the main narcotic drug–producing countries (Afghanistan, Bolivia, Colombia, Iran, Pakistan, Peru, and Thailand) and the main consuming nations (the United States and Canada) are locked together in a cycle of drug abuse and violence. It also shows the connections between drug-related violence and maldevelopment along the continuum of drug production, distribution, and consumption. The chapter that follows demonstrates that strategies for sustainable human development employed in both the global South and the global North offer a way to address the root causes of the drug problem.

Assumptions and Key Concepts

This chapter is based on the following assumptions: (1) the problem of drug-related violence cannot be solved within any one nation, but requires instead coherent and cooperative international and local solutions that address the causes of drug production, distribution, and consumption; (2) social workers, who struggle daily with the consequences of substance abuse, must do so with an understanding of the multidimensional nature of the problem—including its root causes—and find ways to take action on several fronts from a global perspective; and (3) real solutions lie in eradicating poverty—one root cause of the drug problem—through strategies for sustainable human development.

Drugs and Addiction

Drug abuse, including alcoholism, is a major social problem in the United States; it affects every social system in which social workers function. The array of drugs is astounding; Table 10-1 shows some of them, both legal and illegal, as well as those that may or may not have legitimate medical uses. The list includes stimulants, depressants, narcotics, cannabis, hallucinogens, and inhalants. Several of the drugs have their own long and unique histories of remedial or traditional ceremonial use. For example, morphine was first used as a cure for opium addiction and later found to produce addiction itself, and heroin was intended to be a harmless cure for coughs. Although there are regional differences in drugs of choice, patterns of use, and community and societal responses, there can be little doubt that drug abuse and addiction problems "significantly threaten the well-being of individuals and families; the workplace and other organizations; all age, gender, and socioeconomic groups; communities of all types; and the overall health and well-being of the nation" (Center for Substance Abuse and Mental Health Services Administration, 1995, p. 7).

Whatever the drug of choice, drug abuse is a progressive condition or disease—not a failure of individual will power—from which many individuals can recover. Even though drug addicts commit more crimes than nonaddicts, a premise of this chapter is that treatment, not punishment, is a solution to addiction (Schmoke, 1990).

Table 10-1
Psychoactive Drugs Identification Chart

Drugs	Medical uses	Medical names	Slang names	Forms	Usual administration	Effects sought	Possible effects	Overdose	Long-term effects
Stimulants									
Nicotine	None	Nicotine	Butt, chew, smoke, cig	Pipe, tobacco, cigarettes, snuff	Sniff, chew, smoke	Relaxation	Respiratory difficulties, fatigue, high blood pressure	None	Dependency, lung cancer, heart attack, respiratory ailments
Caffeine	Hyperkinesis, stimulant	Caffeine	None	Chocolates, tea, soft drinks, coffee	Swallow	Alertness	Increased alertness, pulse rate, and blood pressure; excitation, insomnia, loss of appetite	Irritability	Dependency may aggravate organic actions
Amphetamines	Hyperkinesis, narcolepsy, weight control, mental disorders	Dexedrine, Benzedrine	Speed, bennies, dexies, pep pills	Capsules, liquid, tablets, powder	Inject, swallow	Alertness, activeness	Increased alertness, pulse rate, and blood pressure; excitation, insomnia, loss of appetite	Agitation, increase in body temperature, hallucinations, convulsions, possible death	Severe withdrawal, possible convulsions, toxic psychosis
Cocaine	Local anesthetic	Cocaine	Coke, rock, crack, blow, toot, white, blast, snow, flake	Powder, rock	Inject, smoke, inhale	Excitation, euphoria	Increased alertness, pulse rate, and blood pressure; excitation, insomnia, loss of appetite	Agitation, increase in body temperature, hallucinations, convulsions, possible death	Dependency, depression, paranoia, convulsions

Table continues

Table 10-1
Psychoactive Drugs Identification Chart (*continued*)

Drugs	Medical uses	Medical names	Slang names	Forms	Usual administration	Effects sought	Possible effects	Overdose	Long-term effects
Depressants									
Alcohol	None	Ethyl alcohol	Booze	Liquid	Swallow	Sense alteration, anxiety reduction	Loss of coordination, sluggishness, slurred speech, disorientation, depression	Total loss of coordination, nausea, unconsciousness, possible death	Dependency, toxic psychosis, neurologic damage
Sedatives	Anesthetic, sedative hypnotic, anticonvulsant	Secobarbital, Phenobarbital, Seconal	Barbs, reds, downers, sopors	Capsules, tablets, powder	Inject, swallow	Anxiety reduction, euphoria, sleep	Loss of coordination, sluggishness, slurred speech, disorientation, depression	Cold and clammy skin, dilated pupils, shallow respiration, weak and rapid pulse, coma, possible death	Dependency, severe withdrawal, possible convulsions, toxic psychosis
Tranquilizers	Anti-anxiety, sedative hypnotic	Valium, Miltown, Librium	Downers	Capsules, tablets	Swallow	Anxiety reduction, euphoria, sleep	Loss of coordination, sluggishness, slurred speech, disorientation, depression	Cold and clammy skin, dilated pupils, shallow respiration, weak and rapid pulse, coma, possible death	Dependency, severe withdrawal, possible convulsions, toxic psychosis

	Medical Uses	Trade or Other Names	Other Names	Form	Usual Method	Effects Sought	Possible Effects	Effects of Overdose	Withdrawal Syndrome
Narcotics Opium	Analgesic, antidiarrheal	Paregoric	None	Powder	Smoke, swallow	Euphoria, prevent withdrawal, sleep	Euphoria, drowsiness, respiratory depression, constricted pupils, sleep, nausea	Clammy skin, slow and shallow breathing, convulsions, coma, possible death	Dependency, constipation, loss of appetite, severe withdrawal
Morphine	Analgesic, antitussive	Morphine, pectoral syrup	None	Powder, tablet, liquid	Inject, smoke, swallow	Euphoria, prevent withdrawal, sleep	Euphoria, drowsiness, respiratory depression, constricted pupils, sleep, nausea	Clammy skin, slow and shallow breathing, convulsions, coma, possible death	Dependency, constipation, loss of appetite, severe withdrawal
Heroin	Research	Diacetylmorphine	China white, smack, junk, H, horse	Powder	Inject, swallow	Euphoria, prevent withdrawal, sleep	Euphoria, drowsiness, respiratory depression, constricted pupils, sleep, nausea	Clammy skin, slow and shallow breathing, convulsions, coma, possible death	Dependency, constipation, loss of appetite, severe withdrawal
Codeine	Analgesic, antitussive	Codeine, Empirin compound with codeine, Robitussin AC	None	Capsules, tablets, liquid	Inject, swallow	Euphoria, prevent withdrawal, sleep	Euphoria, drowsiness, respiratory depression, constricted pupils, sleep, nausea	Clammy skin, slow and shallow breathing, convulsions, coma, possible death	Dependency, constipation, loss of appetite, severe withdrawal
Cannabis THC	Research, cancer chemotherapy antinauseant	Tetrahydrocannabinol	THC	Tablets, liquid	Swallow	Relaxation, euphoria, increased perception	Relaxed inhibitions, euphoria, increased appetite, distorted perceptions, disoriented behavior	Fatigue, paranoia, possible psychosis	Amotivational syndrome, respiratory difficulties, lung cancer, interference with physical and emotional development

Table continues

Table 10-1
Psychoactive Drugs Identification Chart (continued)

Drugs	Medical uses	Medical names	Slang names	Forms	Usual administration	Effects sought	Possible effects	Overdose	Long-term effects
Hashish	None	Tetrahydro-cannabinol	Hash	Solid resin	Smoke	Relaxation, euphoria, increased perception	Relaxed inhibitions, euphoria, increased appetite, distorted perceptions, disoriented behavior	Fatigue, paranoia, possible psychosis	Amotivational syndrome, respiratory difficulties, lung cancer, interference with physical and emotional development
Marijuana	Research	Tetrahydro-cannabinol	Pot, grass, sinsemilla, dobie, ganja, dope, gold, herb, weed, reefer	Plant particles	Smoke, swallow	Relaxation, euphoria, increased perception	Relaxed inhibitions, euphoria, increased appetite, distorted perceptions, disoriented behavior	Fatigue, paranoia, possible psychosis	Amotivational syndrome, respiratory difficulties, lung cancer, interference with physical and emotional development
Hallucinogens PCP	None	Phencyclidine	Angel dust, zoot, peace pill, hog	Tablets, powder	Smoke, swallow	Distortion of senses, insight, exhilaration	Illusions and hallucinations, distorted perception of time and distance	Longer and more intense "trips" or episodes, psychosis, convulsions, possible death	May intensify existing psychosis, flashbacks, panic reactions

LSD	Research	Lysergic acid diethylamide	Acid, sugar	Capsules, tablets, liquid	Swallow	Distortion of senses, insight, exhilaration	Illusions and hallucinations, distorted perception of time and distance	Longer and more intense "trips" or episodes, psychosis, convulsions, possible death	May intensify existing psychosis, flashbacks, panic reactions
Organics	None	Mescaline, psilocybin	Mesc, mushrooms	Crude preparations, tablets, powder	Swallow	Distortion of senses, insight, exhilaration	Illusions and hallucinations, distorted perception of time and distance	Longer and more intense "trips" or episodes, psychosis, convulsions, possible death	May intensify existing psychosis, flashbacks, panic reactions
Inhalants Aerosols and Solvents	None	None	Glue, benzene, toluene, freon	Solvents, aerosols	Inhale	Intoxication	Exhilaration, confusion, poor concentration	Heart faiure, unconsciousness, asphyxiation, possible death	Impaired perception, coordination, and judgment; neurologic damage

Source: Center for Substance Abuse Prevention and Mental Health Services Administration. (1995). *Curriculum modules on alcohol and other drug problems for schools of social work* (pp. 21–22). Washington, DC: National Clearinghouse for Alcohol and Drug Information.

Drugs and Global Interdependence

The production and distribution of drugs hinge on global interdependence, which is a product of the globalization of the economy and international trade. In fact, narcotic drugs are one of the biggest items of international trade: Over the past two decades, the narcotics industry has become a highly organized multinational business that employs hundreds of thousands of people and generates billions of dollars in profits. Drug trafficking generates about $500 billion a year; about $85 billion in drug profits are laundered through financial markets each year (UNDP, 1994). The retail value of drugs in the 1990s exceeds the international trade in oil, and the total value of the drug trade worldwide is greater than that of the oil industry; in fact, only the arms trade surpasses the drug trade in total value (King & Schneider, 1991).

Countries are linked by drugs in many ways: Efforts to control dependence-producing drugs are international in scope; U.S. tobacco is targeted at the global South because U.S. domestic restrictions are likely to decrease consumption in the United States; and the environmental harm done by narcotics production and processing know no borders.

Illegal Narcotics as the Focus of Analysis

Although even a product that has legitimate uses can be abused, this chapter will focus on illegal narcotics, particularly heroin and cocaine. There are several reasons for narrowing the focus: The connections between violence and development can be examined in more depth by limiting the scope of the discussion; the trade in illegal narcotics destabilizes relationships among countries, thus posing a serious threat to the international community; and heroin and cocaine are the two narcotics with the clearest links between the consuming countries of the global North and the producing countries of the global South.

Heroin is a product of the opium poppy, a hardy plant grown mostly in Asia. After the plant flowers, its egg-shaped seedpod produces opium latex. Farmers cut the seedpod with a curved knife and then scrape off the congealed sap (opium) after it hardens. Refining converts the opium into morphine, heroin, and other narcotic drugs. Opium was a prominent commodity—along with coffee, tea, and spices—during European colonialism in Asia in the 17th and 18th centuries. Opium is now produced in the "golden triangle" of Laos, Myanmar (formerly Burma, and the world's largest producer), and Thailand (see Figure 10-1). It is also produced in the "golden crescent" (Figure 10-2), which includes Afghanistan, Iran, and Pakistan (Panos Institute, 1993).

Heroin is a sedative that first produces a quick "rush," followed by oblivion, drowsiness, sleepiness, and depression (Wilson & DiIulio, 1990). In the United States, it is most often injected, and needles are often shared (which, of course, increases the risk of contracting human immunodeficiency virus [HIV], the virus that causes acquired immune deficiency syndrome [AIDS]). Historically, African Americans have been overrepresented in the heroin-using population, which might account for the stigmatization of heroin users by drug control officials as a "class beyond social redemption" (Walker, 1992, p. 203). However, heroin use among adults over 35 years of age in the general U.S. population showed a significant increase in the early 1990s (Gray, 1995).

Figure 10-1
Opium Production: The Golden Triangle

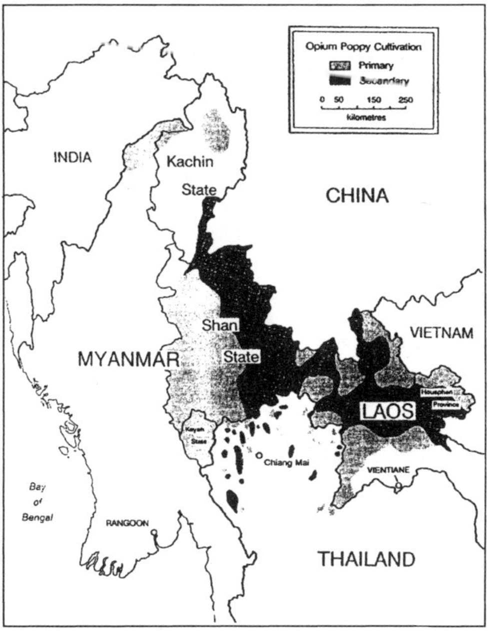

Source: Thingtham, C. N. (1992). Fruitful harvest from alternative crops. In M. L. Smith (Ed.), *Why people grow drugs: Narcotics and development in the Third World* (p. 41). Washington, DC: Panos Institute. Used with permission of The Panos Institute.

Figure 10-2
Opium Production: The Golden Crescent

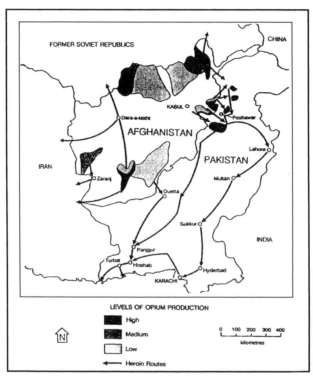

Source: Thingtham, C. N. (1992). Fruitful harvest from alternative crops. In M. L. Smith (Ed.), *Why people grow drugs: Narcotics and development in the Third World* (p. 51). Washington, DC: Panos Institute. Used with permission of The Panos Institute.

Some countries in the global South have also experienced a dramatic rise in consumption of heroin. Heroin is the preferred drug in Pakistan, Thailand, Myanmar, and Malaysia, where it is cheap and readily available (M. L. Smith, 1992b). Officials acknowledge that there are 50,000 heroin users in Sri Lanka, 145,000 in Malaysia, and 1.1 million in Pakistan, 43 percent of whom are between 16 and 20 years of age (M. L. Smith, 1992b). In some countries, such as Myanmar and Thailand, people are increasingly injecting heroin instead of smoking it—the traditional method of consumption—thus, again, increasing the risk for HIV and AIDS (King & Schneider, 1991; M. L. Smith, 1992b).

Cocaine is a narcotic substance derived from the coca plant, a bushy shrub grown in South America (see Figure 10-3). Peru produces 60 percent of the coca leaves for the international market, Bolivia produces

Figure 10-3
Coca Production in South America

Source: Smith, M. L. (1992a). The Gordian knot: The connection between narcotics and development. In M. L. Smith (Ed.), *Why people grow drugs: Narcotics and development in the Third World* (p. 13). Washington, DC: Panos Institute. Used with permission of The Panos Institute.

30 percent, and Colombia produces 8 percent; the remainder comes from Ecuador and Brazil (Panos Institute, 1993).

The coca plant has been sacred to the indigenous populations of the Andes since pre-Inca times because of its durability and its medicinal qualities. Cocaine is only one of the 14 alkaloids found in the coca leaf, which contains more than 28 nutrients that supplement the daily diet of many Andean people (Panos Institute, 1993). Coca has been used by indigenous people for thousands of years to minimize the pains associated with hunger and to increase the endurance of workers (Benjamin & Miller, 1991):

> The leaves of the coca bush had been chewed by Andean peasants for at least 4,000 years before the early Spanish explorers arrived in South America. Coca leaves have nutritional value as food, and the cocaine alkaloid in them acts as a powerful appetite suppressant, an effective antidote for altitude sickness,

a potent local anesthetic, and a central nervous system stimulant. It is little wonder that the Incas revered coca leaves as a gift of the gods. (p. 255)

In the 1980s, coca became a profitable export crop because of the international demand for coca-derived drugs. Cocaine, a stimulant, produces euphoria and increased alertness; crack cocaine produces exceptional euphoria and often stimulates addicts to acts of violence and daring that make them dangerous to themselves as well as to others (Wilson & DiIulio, 1990). Approximately 6 million people in the United States abuse cocaine or crack (Koch, 1990).

Currently, in the Andean regions, coca is a serious threat. A mixture of coca paste and tobacco—*pitillo* in Peru and Bolivia and *basuco* in Colombia—causes quick addiction and permanent brain damage when it is smoked. Colombia has as many as 500,000 *basuco* smokers, primarily unemployed youths and other marginalized people (M. L. Smith, 1992b). In Panama, cocaine and crack are increasingly available and very cheap—a dose of crack sells for $1. Little is known about drug consumption in Africa, although the reported incidence is rising in Nigeria, Kenya, and South Africa and there is some evidence of increasing heroin and cocaine use (Flynn, 1993).

Drug-Related Violence: A Multilevel Global Affliction

The overall perspective emphasized throughout this book applies to the global problem of drug-related violence: There are individual, institutional, and structural and cultural levels of drug-related violence; individual and institutional forms are intimately connected and both are rooted in deep, structural and cultural belief systems; drug-related violence takes many more forms than is usually acknowledged (overt and covert, legal and illegal, active and passive, organized and unorganized, and so on); and legitimate violence (that exerted by established authorities seeking to control by force and violence) provokes illegitimate violence on the part of those harmed and marginalized.

Drug-Related Violence at the Individual Level

Drug-related killings over the past decade have plagued several large cities in the United States. Although overall crime and homicide rates actually decreased between 1980 and 1987, in specific enclaves the horror stories are all too true. In south central Los Angeles, in much of Newark, in and around the housing projects of Chicago, in the South Bronx and Bedford-Stuyvesant sections of New York, and in parts of Washington, DC, conditions are not much better than they are in Beirut on a bad day. Drugs, especially crack, are sold openly on street corners; rival gangs shoot at each other from moving automobiles; automatic weapons are carried by teenagers onto school playgrounds; innocent people hide behind double-locked doors and shuttered windows. In Los Angeles there is at least one gang murder every day, Sundays included. A ten-foot-high concrete wall is being built around the junior high school one of us attended, in order, the principal explained, to keep stray bullets from hitting children on the playground. (Wilson & DiIulio, 1990, p. 53)

Violence associated with illegal narcotics at the individual level takes myriad forms. Daily newspapers around the world document murders, assaults, robberies, and gang activities, many of which are drug related. Less-publicized forms of drug-related violence harm untold numbers of people daily: child abuse and neglect, wife battery, drug overdose, and family and community disintegration. A particularly hideous act of violence is done to more than 300,000 U.S. babies each year, according to a 1991 report of the Inter-American Commission on Drug Policy: these infants are born exposed to illicit drugs, including cocaine and crack (M. L. Smith, 1992b).

Intrapersonal violence.   The harm that a drug addict does to self is another form of violence at the individual level, one that leads ultimately to death. A critical international concern is drug use among the estimated 100 million street children who are using drugs at younger and younger ages; in Colombia and Bolivia, for example, eight-year-old children deal in and smoke *basuco* cigarettes (United Nations High Commissioner for Refugees press release, April 22, 1994, Geneva). During the initial stages, street children use drugs as a functional coping mechanism—it helps them to stay awake for work, to be alert to possible violence, to get to sleep, to dull physical or emotional pain, and to go without food. However, the long-term effects—lung damage, irreversible brain and kidney damage, malnourishment, HIV and AIDS—often result in death (United Nations High Commissioners for Refugees press release, April 22, 1994, Geneva).

Common criminality.   Drug abusers are responsible for much of the violent crime in the United States (Koch, 1990), just as they are in countries in the global South with rising rates of consumption of hard drugs, particularly among young urban men (M. L. Smith, 1992b). Studies of connections between drugs and violence in the United States reveal that, in 1989, "sixty percent of arrestees for violent offenses tested positive for at least one illegal drug . . . and violent crime frequency increases with drug frequency" (Reiss & Roth, 1993, p. 185). Specific studies confirm the correlation: Among a sample of 279 male heroin addicts in southern California, there were 6,251 arrests; 573 narcotics users in Miami, during a 12-month period, were responsible for 6,000 robberies and assaults, almost 6,700 burglaries, and more than 46,000 other events of larceny and fraud; and a 1983 study showed that high rates of criminality among heroin addicts in Baltimore coincided with those periods when they were using—rates were markedly lower during times of recovery from addiction (Schmoke, 1990).

Organized crime.   Gangs and more highly organized crime syndicates, which play crucial roles in the consumption and distribution of illegal narcotics, also are responsible for much drug-related violence. For example, vendettas—settling accounts by murdering rivals, debtors, double-crossers, and informers, and sometimes their relatives—are one form of violence carried out by organized crime (Leon, 1987). Organized crime and violence thrive especially well at the distribution networks along the drug routes of the global South; Kalashnikov assault rifles are the weapon of choice (M. L. Smith, 1992b).

Another tactic is to murder prominent citizens or authorities who refuse to cooperate with organized crime in the illicit drug business (Leon, 1987). In Colombia, for example, dozens of judges and journalists were assassinated in the 1980s by the Medellin cartel, a group of about 20 families that deals in cocaine by the ton and claims to supply 80 percent of all cocaine consumed in the United States (Leon, 1987). In Mexico between 1992 and 1995, victims of drug-related shootings included the Roman Catholic Cardinal of Guadalajara, dozens of police officers, and former state prosecutors (Golden, 1995). People in authority are not the only ones who confront violence for noncooperation: In some regions of the global South, organized traffickers (and sometimes guerrillas and warlords) use the threat of force to persuade peasant farmers to grow drugs (M. L. Smith, 1992b).

Drug-Related Violence at the Institutional Level

Links between crime organizations and legitimate institutions.   Crime organizations often have the help—sometimes inadvertent, sometimes motivated by profit—of legitimate people and organizations at the institutional level. E. F. Hutton, Merrill Lynch, and the Bank of Boston are among U.S. companies that, through carelessness, shoddy record keeping, or other unfortunate business practices, have been involved in the illicit drug trade; some banks have faced criminal indictments (Andelman, 1994). Corruption is rampant in many drug-producing and drug-trafficking countries. From news accounts we learn that the president of Zambia was accused of putting money from drug trafficking into a trust fund and three Zambian government officials were persuaded to resign ("Zambia," 1994); in Thailand 17 current and former members of parliament, including at least one cabinet member, were alleged to have connections with the drug trade (Boyd, 1994); all ranks of military officers in Guatemala have been implicated by the Drug Enforcement Administration in drug trafficking (Smyth, 1994); and in 1995 the president of Colombia was accused of deciding to accept drug money to finance his political campaign (Haven, 1996). There is a common belief in Mexico that drug traffickers find it easy to acquire accomplices within the government, even at the highest levels of law enforcement (Robberson, 1993).

Political violence.   Drug trafficking is also linked with political violence on the institutional level, carried out by both subversive political groups and repressive state police and military institutions. Political violence includes such actions as terrorism, torture, murder, and other methods of inflicting pain, physical damage, or death in the context of a political confrontation or in pursuit of political ends. Leon (1987) cites several allegations of links between drug traffic and subversive political activities; for example, during the Nicaraguan civil war in the 1980s, a revolutionary guerrilla group in Colombia reportedly worked out a deal with Nicaraguan government officials whereby Nicaragua would be a waystation for Colombian shipments of cocaine going to the United States. Another claim was that the U.S. Central Intelligence Agency sponsored the smuggling of marijuana and cocaine from Honduras to the United States in exchange for weapons for the Nicaraguan contras.

Whatever the truth of such allegations, it is clear that the top echelon of the illegal narcotics industry shares many interests with established economic and political institutions and elites. In Colombia, for example, cocaine traffickers have aligned themselves with conservative groups of rural landowners, right-wing businessmen, and certain factions of the military in a common struggle against revolutionary guerrilla groups and poverty-stricken civilian advocates for social justice (Lee, 1988). At the same time, there is evidence that leftist guerrillas align themselves and their struggle with that of poor peasant farmers who grow drugs for survival. For example, in a region of Peru where more than 90 percent of farm income is from coca cultivation, it has been claimed that growers express their interests through moderate leftist leaders and perhaps even with the help of the more radical Sendero Luminoso (Shining Path) guerrillas (Lee, 1988).

War on drugs and institutional violence.   In their efforts to combat illegal drug production, distribution, and consumption, the U.S. legal system and governmental agencies engage in legitimate forms of violence—or, as characterized in previous chapters, "the violence not seen as such." Some examples: Police SWAT teams and paramilitary task forces carry out sweeps in housing projects and mass evictions of drug suspects and their families, without regard for the human rights and personal safety of residents; city officials, politicians, and fearful citizens call for the National Guard and federal troops to patrol ghetto "war zones"; and in producer countries, police and military try to curtail narcotic crop cultivation by carrying out slash-and-burn raids and other surprise assaults on peasant farmers (Panos Institute, 1993).

In the United States, the war on drugs during the 1980s and 1990s produced longer federal and state prison sentences, mandatory minimum terms, and tighter parole policies for drug offenses and violent crimes. The result has been a threefold increase in the number of inmates imprisoned in the United States; because of differential apprehension, prosecution, and sentencing treatment under the legal system, a disproportionate number of them are members of racial and ethnic minority groups. The startling disparities between reported drug use by whites and racial and ethnic minority groups, and between drug arrest rates for African American and white people, suggest that the war on drugs is a racist war. For example, whites who regularly use cocaine outnumber blacks four to one, yet African American youths account for 71 percent of all juveniles arrested for cocaine and opium-derivative charges (Coalition for Juvenile Justice, 1993). Representative Robert Scott of Virginia made the point succinctly in testimony before the U.S. Congress in 1995: "Mr. Chairman, 5 grams of crack, 10 doses, a couple hundred dollars worth, five years mandatory minimum; 500 grams of powder, 5000 doses, tens of thousands of dollars to get the same penalty.... Ninety-five percent of those convicted of crack offenses are black and Hispanic. Seventy-five percent of those convicted of powder offenses are white" (Cockburn, 1995, p. 656).

Drug-Related Violence at the Structural and Cultural Level

Such disparate laws and treatment at the institutional level are grounded in collective beliefs at the structural and cultural level, among which is an ideology of superiority based on race. Another part of the structural and cultural level—the economic structures, which are based on profits and property—also helps ensure the dominance of some over others. As Salazar (1993) points out, "All drugs ... have been transformed by the capitalist mode of production into commodities. These produce substantial profits for the entrepreneurial organizations that produce and sell them as well as those that move the capital and profits derived from them" (p. 85). Furthermore, "It might be said that for the United States ... the production and sale of illegal drugs constitute just one more productive branch ... of the Latin American and Caribbean economy, ... contributing in some degree to the expanded reproduction of capitalism on a world scale, despite the contradictions in the economic movement that are generated" (p. 86).

Militaristic values at the structural and cultural level emphasize dominance, win–lose solutions, and the ready use of force to solve problems. Such is the basis for institutional strategies in the U.S. war on drugs—sending the National Guard and military troops into poor neighborhoods, border towns, and agricultural areas of the global South. Drug trafficking and militarism go hand in hand in other ways as well, as demonstrated by military involvement at the highest levels in drug trafficking and violence. For example, in Myanmar, the world's largest producer of opium, guerrillas, ethnic insurgents, and the military all participate in the trafficking of narcotics and are all armed (Panos Institute, 1993). Another example comes from Afghanistan, where warfare and drugs became inextricably intertwined: War led to the breakdown of traditional agricultural systems, thus encouraging tribal people—especially those who had left their homelands during war but later returned—to take up opium production; by the 1980s, Afghanistan had established itself as one of the largest poppy producers in the world and Mujahadeen commanders had consolidated their control over the trade. Drug dealers in the area also have access to sophisticated weapons left over from the Afghan War (Panos Institute, 1993).

Connections among the Levels of Drug-Related Violence

Individual forms of drug-related violence—homicide, muggings, suicide, drug abuse, and so on—often seem irrational and senseless if studied as separate incidents. However, when viewed in the context of oppressive history, such individual acts of violence might be considered the outcome of efforts to escape from institutional and structural and cultural violence by producing, distributing, or consuming illicit drugs (Midwest NASW Center, 1994). The interrelatedness of drug-related violence within the context of global interdependence is illustrated in the following case study.

The Interelatedness of Drug-Related Violence within the Context of Global Interdependence

Psycho, a broad-nosed youth with flat-cut hair, lives on a tough street corner in the town of Santa Tecla, El Salvador. Psycho's life mirrors the turmoil of his troubled country. He was raised during El Salvador's 12-year civil war and served two years in the army, fighting Marxist insurgents. Then, like many of his countrymen, he went to the United States in hopes of a better life. Three years after the war ended, he is back in El Salvador. But Psycho did not return to his slowly recovering country with hard-earned cash or skills.

Instead, he is a hardened criminal, a convicted armed robber who readily takes off his shirt to reveal a torso covered with the tattoos of his Los Angeles gang. At 24 years of age, after having served three and a half years in a U.S. prison, Psycho was deported to El Salvador.

> *All around the poor neighborhoods of Santa Tecla, the debris of war has been replaced by the graffiti of gangs. Over the past several years, U.S. gangs have gone international, setting up branches in countries such as El Salvador and recruiting new foot soldiers from among poor people and the veterans of the region's recently ended civil wars.*
>
> *Once a focal point of the U.S. struggle against communism, Central America is now the locus of a new threat: transnational crime. Multinational gangs are part of a growing array of organized crime rings that specialize in cross-border trafficking and that have turned Central America and Mexico into hemispheric clearinghouses for drugs, contraband, and stolen property. U.S.-manufactured weapons, smuggled south and traded for drugs or cash, are rerouted to gangs and guerrilla bands in Colombia, Central America, and Mexico, or re-exported to gangs.*
>
> *For U.S. gangs seeking to expand into international smuggling, El Salvador has been particularly fertile ground since its civil war ended in 1992. The war left thousands of combat veterans from both the government and rebel sides who, in many cases, had spent most of their lives as soldiers and knew no other profession. Often their military unit was the closest thing they had to a family. Faced with high unemployment and little education, the transition to gangs—which offer the same sense of camaraderie—was easy.*
>
> *Most of the more than 50 gangs in El Salvador were founded by returning Salvadorans, who made them affiliates of gangs they had joined in the United States. Gang members returning from the United States bring back knowledge of gang life and ritual. And they bring contacts with their homies, or confederates in U.S. gangs, giving them ready access to a drug distribution network.*
>
> *Once established, the gangs find a ready source of personnel—and weapons— in demobilized, often demoralized soldiers and other disillusioned youths. Partisan history seems to make little difference: Psycho, a leader of the Mara Salvatrucha, served in the Salvadoran army; he shares power in the gang with Crazy Face, a former urban commando of the Marxist insurgents.*
>
> *Mafia organizations that move narcotics and traffic in children pay the gangs to provide the "muscle" for their activities and do whatever killing is necessary.*

Source: Farah & Robberson, 1995.

The distribution and consumption of drugs creates its own perpetrators and victims. For example, children can be born physically damaged and prone to both substance abuse and violence because of physiological factors related to their parents' substance abuse. Living in a violent environment created by the sale and use of narcotics can further predispose children to become victims or perpetrators of violence, or both

(Borrill, 1993; Calicchia, Moncata, & Santostefano, 1993; Chassin, Rogosch, & Barrera, 1991; Virkkuner & Linnoila, 1993; Yudofsky, Silver, & Hales, 1993).

When the sale and use of narcotics eventually lead to societal turmoil and violence, the institutional response is often increased repressive violence instead of efforts at prevention or rehabilitation—and thus the cycle of violence is completed (Van Soest & Bryant, 1995). In the 1980s and 1990s, the U.S.-declared "war on crime" and its attendant spate of prison construction constituted a new order of militarization. In highly repressive situations—as exist under military-dominated governments of the global South, for example—the distinction between the police and the military disappears; militaristic values dominate at the structural level, and the cycle of violence is perpetuated (Giddens, 1985).

Globally, the 1980s were a decade of intensified injustices and poverty caused by unrestrained resource consumption on the part of rich countries in the global North. The result was a "sense of alienation and loss of hope [that] fueled the problem of drugs and violence" (Korten, 1990, p. 16). It should not be surprising that people without access to power and resources, frustrated and discouraged by unequal and unjust treatment, sometimes turn to drug production, distribution, or consumption. The next section further explores connections between the drug problem and maldevelopment (social and economic injustice).

Making Connections between Drug-Related Violence and Maldevelopment

There are many connections that can be made between drug-related violence and maldevelopment. As stated before, lack of development opportunities can influence people to grow, sell, or consume drugs to survive, make money, or escape life's realities. At the same time, drugs block the healthy development of individuals, families, communities, and societies and create nightmarish public health and social problems. Drug-related violence on personal and institutional levels often makes the barriers to individual and societal development insurmountable.

Links between drug-related violence and maldevelopment are indisputably complex. Nevertheless, exploration of the political, economic, and social contexts in which drug production, distribution, and consumption take place can yield some understanding of the nature of the global drug problem.

Drug Production and Development or Maldevelopment

> Farming peasants gain their livelihood either willingly or through coercion in the growing and processing of crops for production of psychoactive drugs. While such enterprises are often seen as necessary for survival and even make some sense in terms of economic development, the result is often a thwarting of more productive human development possibilities. (Midwest NASW Center, 1994)

Peasant farmers in the global South, primary producers of crops that are turned into illegal drugs, often cultivate opium poppies and coca shrubs simply to survive and to feed their families (M. L. Smith, 1992b). They receive only a tiny fraction of global drug revenues, but even that minuscule amount may be motivation enough when they are beset by powerful forces related to maldevelopment: lack of viable economic alternatives; failed economic policies; and civil conflicts and international wars that increase local poverty, disrupt agricultural and irrigation systems, and dislocate millions of people (Panos Institute, 1993). "Drug Production in Bolivia" illustrates some of the development issues surrounding this lack of economic alternatives.

Drug Production in Bolivia

At a coca market in a remote jungle village in Bolivia, farmers haul 50-pound bags of coca leaves for miles on their backs and bicycles. A 42-year-old mother is helped by her children to carry five bags of coca four miles to the market. She says she has no way to support her family except by growing coca; she tried to grow other crops such as pineapples and oranges only to find that no one would buy them.

In 1995 the U.S. government gave Bolivia an ultimatum: Either destroy several thousand acres of coca plants or face the end of millions of dollars in economic aid and a boycott of international loans. As the farmers lug their heavy bags of coca leaves to market in this remote village, they talk about little else but these demands that Bolivia cut its coca production. The common sentiment among the growers is that no matter how much pressure is put on them to stop growing coca, they will never give it up because they have no other means to survive. They see coca production as a necessity,

even though they receive only a pittance of the money made from coca pro-
duction and even though they lead hard, subsistence-level lives.

   The Bolivian government has been unwilling to enforce laws that pro-
hibit the planting of new coca crops for several reasons: (1) Coca is an en-
trenched part of the country's culture—the use of coca leaf is an Andean
tradition dating back thousands of years, and it is still used for cultural,
religious, and medicinal purposes. (2) Coca is also an entrenched part of
Bolivia's economy. Although there is a legal market in the country for tradi-
tional uses, most of the coca grown in the region goes to make cocaine, which
is often refined in crude jungle labs by organized drug cartels. An estimated
10 percent of Bolivia's work force receive their income from drug-related
activities, which bring hundreds of millions of dollars into the country's
economy. (3) Growers have broad public support—the general feeling is that
the growers are scapegoats for a drug-abusive United States.

   Farmers continue to replant coca even though doing so is illegal. In this
remote jungle village where they have brought their crops to market, they con-
cur that they will grow coca until markets, infrastructure, and processing plants
are in place to make other crops worthwhile. Until then, they will grow the one
crop—coca—that will enable them to take care of their families.

Source: Sims, 1995.

A confluence of forces in the 1980s contributed to an increase in coca
and opium poppy production. At the same time that the global South
was experiencing falling prices for many of its typical exports, international demand for illegal drugs was increasing. Moreover, national debts
and poverty rose in the global South while services decreased, partly
because of the structural adjustment programs that were discussed in
chapter 4 (Panos Institute, 1993). Poor farmers, hard hit by declining
national economies and services, stepped up production of the crops that
they could sell. Because the source countries for drugs have a centuries-
long tradition of drug use, the individual "grower may not even be fully
aware of the future uses to which his harvest will be put" (M. L. Smith,
1992b, p. 1); and when growers are aware, they may feel that "foreign
drug 'abuse' is an inappropriate use of narcotics for which they are not
responsible" (Panos Institute, 1993, p. 4).

   Drug production for international export has produced a cycle of violence and further maldevelopment on an unimaginable scale. What happened in the Andes in the 1980s provides a vivid illustration (M. L. Smith,
1992b). After many mainstream agricultural development initiatives for
growing rubber, tobacco, tea, coffee, cacao, rice, maize, and so on had

failed because of inadequate resources and support, Colombian drug traffickers began to appear in the region with ample resources: coca seeds, demonstration plots, venture capital, and guaranteed purchase of the harvest. Thus, the 1980s became "the cocaine decade" for Colombia, Peru, and Bolivia. The social, economic, and political impact on South America and the rest of the world was enormous: in Brazil, cocaine-selling gangs caused street crime to spiral; Ecuador and Venezuela, which could not control the financial operations of Colombian traffickers, became preferred centers for money laundering; Argentina, at the other end of the continent, saw a marked increase in traffickers who exploited its diverse trade links with Europe; Caribbean island nations became waystations for drugs en route to consumer markets; Mexico became a major transshipment country; Central American countries were used as refueling and transshipment points on midnight routes to U.S. consumers; and the United States became the main consumer market for cocaine.

Connections between Maldevelopment and Drug Distribution and Trafficking

Illegal drug distribution and trafficking is a prime example of socioeconomic maldevelopment. It is characterized by violence and complex, interconnected relationships at personal, institutional, and structural levels (Midwest NASW Center, 1994). Maldevelopment—whether manifested as underdevelopment, lack of development opportunities, or unjust development—encourages trafficking in narcotics; a career in illegal drug distribution may appear to be an attractive and lucrative alternative to joblessness and poverty. It also distorts economic systems and creates a culture of violence that undermines healthy development in the United States, in the global South, and around the globe.

The cycle of drug-related violence and maldevelopment cannot be fully understood or adequately addressed without comprehending the extent and operations of the global drug trade. Free trade and high-speed telecommunications facilitate smuggling of illicit drugs and laundering of the resulting "dirty" money around the world. It has been estimated that "one billion dollars in crime profits [most of it drug-related] is wire-transferred through world financial markets every day" (Watson et al., 1993, p. 20). This is particularly true in ex-communist nations, whose weakened governments lack the resources to combat the well-funded, heavily armed, and ruthless tactics of organizations such as the mafias of the United States, Mexico, Italy, and Russia, as well as the Chinese triads, Colombian cartels, Japanese Yakuza, Jamaican posses, Aryan Brotherhood, Texas syndicate, and the drug-lord–controlled armies and rebel insurgent bands in Myanmar, Peru, and Afghanistan, among other places (M. L. Smith, 1992b; Watson et al., 1993).

Cooperation among international crime organizations is growing on an unprecedented scale. The map in Figure 10-4 shows the outstretched tentacles of organized crime groups in an intricate network of drug shipment routes and money-laundering bases around the globe (Watson et al., 1993). The map also identifies several nations that could become nuclear traders, evoking the chilling prospect of nuclear arms entering the circle of drug crime, terrorism, and violence.

Links along the illegal drug network are many and complex. Beginning in Burma, for example, "a broker . . . might be approached by another broker representing Hong Kong businessmen who want to invest in a shipment of heroin. . . . The investors strike a deal with a group of ethnic Chinese in the United States. . . . The heroin may change hands several more times between these U.S. importers and street retailers, who for the most part are not Chinese but Italian-American, African-American or Dominican" (Witkin & Griffin, 1994, p. 44).

Drug trafficking, violence, and maldevelopment in the United States.   Drug dealing and gangs are most prevalent in our underdeveloped inner cities, which are characterized by high unemployment and job scarcity, substandard educational systems, and social services budget cuts, among other indicators. In such environments of underdevelopment, the drug trade distorts the economic system: It creates an illegal source of revenue and simultaneously constrains legitimate forms of economic development through its exacerbation of violent crime rates. The consequences of these conditions fall disproportionately on people of color. According to an update of the Kerner Report, one reason the economic status of African American people has failed to improve relative to whites over the past 20 years is that so many African Americans are "trapped in drug-crime-infested inner cities, where economic progress is slow" (Ostrowski, 1990, p. 74).

Figure 10-4
Drug Shipment Routes and Principal Money Laundering Bases

DRUGS - VIOLENCE - MALDEVELOPMENT

We have watched many of our young kids turn to dope to cope because they are without hope. Young Black children who have the capacity to become doctors and lawyers and engineers and scientists have given up working at summer jobs of flipping burgers and ringing cash registers in exchange for the street corner hustling of cocaine and crack and marijuana. . . . Black America has watched and wept as many lives have become twisted and have been snuffed out by the powerful lure of drug addiction. (Rangel, 1988, p. 82)

In our underdeveloped cities, money from distributing drugs is highly attractive. Dealers pay about $12,000 for a kilo of cocaine and sell it in small packets on the streets for about $250,000. The drug trade provides jobs to children of all ages: nine-year-olds employed as lookouts may earn $100 a day; slightly older children who take the drugs from place to place may earn $300 (Rohr, 1990). Los Angeles is estimated to have has the largest number of drug-dealing gangs—between 500 to 600 different gangs, according to some estimates, with memberships of 50,000 to 70,000 people, mainly teenagers (Rohr, 1990).

Drug trafficking, violence, and maldevelopment in the global South.   Although studies show that drug traffickers leave only a small share of their profits in source countries, even that small amount can distort economic systems. In the global South, revenue from drug sales has actually helped some countries to endure severe financial crises caused by high debt burdens and structural adjustment programs. For example, Colombia came through the Latin American debt crisis essentially unharmed as a result of "conservative financial management and a blind eye to the money flowing into its international reserves from trafficking"; Peru and Bolivia also have avoided economic collapse because of "the hard currency that they have from the drug trade as a last resort" (M. L. Smith, 1992b, p. 25). A closer look at the economic dimension of the cocaine trade reveals the economic benefits of the cocaine industry for poor countries: It is a relatively important source of foreign exchange for the Andean countries; it provides jobs in various phases of the industry (cultivation, processing and refining, transportation, and smuggling); cocaine traffickers invest some of their profits in legal businesses; and the industry is an economic safety valve that provides jobs, incomes, and foreign exchange when the formal economy fails to deliver (Lee, 1988).

However, the negative results of the drug traffic's distortion of economic systems are equally consequential: It overvalues local currencies by 10 percent to 20 percent, which makes it hard for legitimate exporters to recover their costs; it makes a country less attractive for foreign investment; it deprives a country of legitimate revenues—drug traffickers do not file tax reports; and it stacks the deck against legitimate development by outbidding other businesses in wage payments (M. L. Smith, 1992b).

The close relationships between drug merchants and politicians and business people in some countries have further contributed to maldevelopment. Traffickers around the world have used their tremendous drug profits to invest directly in legitimate businesses, such as banking, real estate, industry, and communications. A new elite coalition has thus been forged in parts of the global South. For example, a coalition of drug traffickers and local cattlemen in the Middle Magdalena Valley, one of Colombia's major agricultural areas, allegedly organized militias to battle guerrillas and to eradicate union organizers and community activists; their aim was to deprive peasants of access to land and control over their own labor (Jimenez, 1994). Such new upper-class alliances rely on the cooperation of the armed forces, police, and other institutional players. Given the extraordinary mobility of wealth and the declining capacity of poorer people to make claims, elites around the world have been emboldened to further consolidate their wealth and power, thus increasing the gap between rich and poor (Jimenez, 1994).

Drug Consumption and Maldevelopment

> Users, misusers, and abusers of drugs at all socioeconomic levels—particularly in rich industrialized countries—wittingly or unwittingly contribute to conditions of violence and maldevelopment that are often produced by hazardous encounters and activities that take place in illegal markets and that result from consuming drugs. (Midwest NASW Center, 1994)

At the other end of the drug production chain is drug consumption. Most consumers of illegal narcotics live in industrialized countries of the global North, particularly the United States, where yearly consumer spending on narcotics reportedly exceeds the combined gross domestic product of more than 80 countries in the global South (UNDP, 1994). Although people of all social classes use and abuse illegal narcotics, studies have revealed correlations between maldevelopment and poverty and drug use. For example, a study of drug use among U.S. teenagers showed that "adolescents raised in impoverished urban communities continue to be at high risk for involvement in drug use and drug sales and for serious delinquency" (Greenwood, 1992, p. 448). Another study of 6,002 U.S. households found that the highest rates of abusive violence occurred in families whose annual incomes were below the poverty line, whose fathers were unemployed, and whose child caretakers had some history of drug use (Wolfner & Gelles, 1993). M. L. Smith (1992b) maintained that the huge growth of the cocaine market in the United States in the 1980s "came from a social acceptance of recreational drug use *and the intensification of poverty in inner cities*" (p. 17). Conditions in urban areas in the global South resemble those found in our inner cities—high unemployment, lack of services, inadequate or no education, and so on; those characteristics of underdevelopment make the risk of drug use high in both places, but particularly so in urban areas of producer countries because of easy access to cheap, dangerous drugs.

Consumption of drugs destroys the development of the productive capacity of individuals and families, which further impedes the legitimate development of communities. Developmental problems—the legacy of infants and children exposed to drugs—influence broader development processes. Such problems vary according to the type and frequency of the mother's drug use while the embryo is being formed, but short-term effects include delayed psychomotor development (Chasnoff, Burns, Burns, & Schnoll, 1986); maladaptive behavior related to temperament, sleep, and attachment processes (Wachsman, Schuetz, Chan, & Wingert, 1989); as well as delayed physical development (Kaye, Elkind, Goldberg, & Tytun, 1989; R. I. Smith, Coles, Lancaters, & Fernfoff, 1986). Long-term studies indicate that some drug-exposed children exhibit problems such as poor motor skills, speech and language delays, short attention span, extreme apathy or aggressiveness, and difficulty in forming bonds with others (Zuckerman, 1993).

The effect of trauma incurred by drug-related violence, when introduced early in life, is literally, physically, built into the individual. Severe neglect by parents who abuse drugs is a condition that produces ongoing trauma for infants and young children. Studies show that the brain mass of those traumatized in early life is smaller than normal and that brain structures responsible for higher reasoning, learning ability, and decision making are too small to control the larger limbic brain structures that register overwhelming emotions. When old enough to abuse drugs, these individuals often self-medicate their overwhelming emotions or act on them in violent, destructive ways, and they lack the cognitive ability to change their behavior (Van der Kolk & Saporata, 1993).

However, the effects of drug abuse do not stand alone—they interact with the effects of maldevelopment in an intricate dance of destruction. The widely publicized problem of intrauterine exposure to crack cocaine illustrates the point. At least one study suggests that the developmental outcomes for children whose mothers abused crack while pregnant depend on the multiple risk factors to which they are exposed—including in many cases the effects of poverty. Thus, for children living in poverty, prenatal drug exposure is only one of several treatable or preventable biological and social stressors that cause unfavorable outcomes. Focusing on cocaine without paying corresponding attention to inadequate nutrition, health care, and education allows the blame to be placed solely on the mothers and not also on the conditions of poverty (Sherman, 1994).

Maladaptive behavior caused by drug use is too often a legacy of poverty and childhood exposure to drugs. The social, economic, and even political consequences are enormous not only for users and their families but also for their communities and for entire societies. Not the least of the concerns is the threat to civil order. The billions of dollars spent on drug-related crime, law enforcement, and treatment—about $20,000 per person per year—drain resources that could be used for social and economic development programs (Deschenes, Anglin, & Speckart, 1991). Moreover, all those billions of dollars have not eradicated—or even much ameliorated—the drug problem. Sustainable human development, however, may be able to succeed where money alone has failed. The next chapter explains how.

References

Andelman, D. A. (1994). The drug money maze. *Foreign Affairs, 73*(4), 94–108.

Benjamin, D. K., & Miller, R. L. (1991). *Undoing drugs: Beyond legalization.* New York: Basic Books.

Borrill, J. (1993). Understanding human violence: The implications of social structure, gender, social perception, and alcohol. *Criminal Behavior and Mental Health, 3*(3), 129–141.

Boyd, A. (1994). Thailand's political drug culture. *World Press Review, 41*(8), 35.

Calicchia, J. A., Moncata, S. J., & Santostefano, S. (1993). Cognitive control differences in violent juvenile inpatients. *Clinical Psychology, 49*(5), 731–740.

Center for Substance Abuse Prevention and Mental Health Services Administration. (1995). *Curriculum modules on alcohol and other drug problems for schools of social work.* Washington, DC: National Clearinghouse for Alcohol and Drug Information.

Chasnoff, I. F., Burns, K. A., Burns, W. J., & Schnoll, S. H. (1986). Prenatal drug exposure: Effects on neonatal and infant growth and development. *Journal of Neurobehavioral Toxicology and Teratology, 8*(4), 357–362.

Chassin, L., Rogosch, F., & Barrera, M. (1991, November). Substance use and symptomatology among adolescent children of alcoholics. *Journal of Abnormal Psychology, 100,* 449–463.

Coalition for Juvenile Justice. (1993). *Pursuing the promise: Equal justice for all juveniles* (1993 Annual Report to the President, the Congress, and the Administrator of the Office of Juvenile Justice and Delinquency Prevention). Washington, DC: Author.

Cockburn, A. (1995, November 27). Beat the devil: The white man's answer. *Nation, 261,* 656–657.

Crime goes international. (1993, December 13). *Newsweek,* pp. 20–21.

Deschenes, E. P., Anglin, M. D., & Speckart, G. (1991, spring). Narcotics addiction: Related criminal careers, social and economic costs. *Journal of Drug Issues, 21,* 383–411.

Farah, D., & Robberson, T. (1995, August 28). U.S.-style gangs build free trade in crime. *Washington Post,* pp. A1, A17.

Flynn, S. (1993, winter). Worldwide drug scourge: The expanding trade in illicit drugs. *Brookings Review,* 6–11.

Giddens, A. (1985). *The nation-state and violence.* Los Angeles: University of California Press.

Golden, T. (1995, July 30). Mexican connection grows as cocaine supplier to U.S. *New York Times,* pp. 1, 6.

Gray, M. (1995). African Americans. In J. Philleo & F. L. Brisbane (Eds.), *Cultural competence for social workers: A guide for alcohol and other drug abuse prevention professionals working with ethnic/racial communities* (pp. 71–101). Washington, DC: Center for Substance Abuse Prevention, National Clearinghouse for Alcohol and Drug Information.

Greenwood, P. (1992). Substance abuse problems among high-risk youth and potential interventions. *Crime and Delinquency, 38*(4), 444–458.

Haven, P. (1996, August 31). Accusers jailed, but Colombia's president free. *Austin American Statesman*, p. A28.

Jimenez, M. F. (1994, September 5–12). Tragic realism. *Nation, 260*, 246–249.

Kaye, K., Elkind, L., Goldberg, D., & Tytun, A. (1989). Birth outcomes of infants of drug abusing mothers. *New York State Journal of Medicine, 89*(5), 256–261.

King, A., & Schneider, B. (1991). *The first global revolution*. New York: Pantheon Books.

Koch, E. I. (1990). Upholding drug laws can reduce drug violence. In J. Rohr (Ed.), *Violence in America: Opposing viewpoints* (pp. 67–72). San Diego: Greenhaven Press.

Korten, D. (1990). *Getting to the 21st century: Voluntary actions and the global agenda*. West Hartford, CT: Kumarian Press.

Lee, R., III. (1988, fall). Dimensions of the South American cocaine industry. *Journal of InterAmerican Studies and World Affairs, 30*, 87–103.

Leon, C. A. (1987, May 13). *Observing violence*. Paper presented at the 140th Annual Meeting of the American Psychiatric Association, Chicago.

Midwest NASW Center on Violence, Development, and Substance Abuse. (1994). *Conceptualized linkages* (Report submitted to the Violence and Development Project). Columbus, OH: Author.

Ostrowski, J. (1990). Repealing drug laws can reduce drug violence. In J. Rohr (Ed.), *Violence in America: Opposing viewpoints* (pp. 73–79). San Diego: Greenhaven Press.

Panos Institute. (1993). *Narcotics and development*. Washington, DC: Author.

Rangel, C. B. (1988, September 16). Statement presented before the House Select Committee on Narcotics Abuse and Control as cited in Rohr, J. (1990). *Violence in America: Opposing viewpoints*. San Diego: Greenhaven Press.

Reiss, A. J., & Roth, J. A. (Eds.). (1993). *Understanding and preventing violence*. Washington, DC: National Academy Press.

Robberson, T. (1993, May 31). Mexican drug dealers cut pervasive path: Nation is top supplier to U.S. *Washington Post*, pp. A21, A25.

Rohr, J. (Ed.). (1990). *Violence in America: Opposing viewpoints*. San Diego: Greenhaven Press.

Salazar, L. S. (1993). "Drug trafficking" and social and political conflicts in Latin America: Some hypotheses. *Latin American Perspectives, 20*(1), 83–98.

Schmoke, K. L. (1990). More law enforcement cannot reduce drug violence. In J. Rohr (Ed.), *Violence in America: Opposing viewpoints* (pp. 59–66). San Diego: Greenhaven Press.

Sherman, A. (1994). *Wasting America's future.* Boston: Beacon Press.

Shuman, M. H., & Harvey, H. (1993). *Security without war: A post-cold war foreign policy.* Boulder, CO: Westview Press.

Sims, C. (1995, July 11). Defying U.S. threat, Bolivians plant more coca. *New York Times,* p. A3.

Smith, M. L. (1992a). The Gordian knot: The connection between narcotics and development. In M. L. Smith (Ed.), *Why people grow drugs: Narcotics and development in the Third World* (p. 13). Washington, DC: Panos Institute.

Smith, M. L. (Ed.). (1992b). *Why people grow drugs: Narcotics and development in the Third World.* Washington, DC: Panos Institute.

Smith, R. I., Coles, C. D., Lancaters, J., & Fernfoff, P. N. (1986). The effect of volume and duration of prenatal ethanol exposure on neonatal physical and behavioral development. *Journal of Neurobehavioral Toxicology and Teratology, 8*(4), 375–381.

Smyth, F. (1994, August 2). Justify my war: Why Clinton eyes Haiti's drug trade and ignores Guatemala's. *Village Voice,* pp. 15–16.

Thingtham, C. N. (1992). Fruitful harvest from alternative crops. In M. L. Smith (Ed.), *Why people grow drugs: Narcotics and development in the Third World.* Washington, DC: Panos Institute.

United Nations Development Programme (UNDP). (1994). *Human development report 1994.* New York: Oxford University Press.

Van der Kolk, B., & Saporata, J. (1993). Biological response to psychic trauma. In J. Wilson & S. Raphael (Eds.), *The international handbook of traumatic stress syndromes* (pp. 25–33). New York: Plenum Press.

Van Soest, D., & Bryant, S. (1995). Violence reconceptualized for social work: The urban dilemma. *Social Work, 40,* 549–557.

Virkkuner, M., & Linnoila, M. (1993, September). Brain serotonin, type II alcoholism, and impulsive violence. *Journal of Studies on Alcohol, 11,* 163–169.

Wachsman, L., Schuetz, S., Chan, L. S., & Wingert, W. A. (1989). What happens to babies exposed to phencyclidine (PCP) in utero. *American Journal of Drug and Alcohol Abuse, 15*(1), 31–39.

Walker, W. O., III. (1992, fall). Review essay: Drug trafficking in Asia. *Journal of InterAmerican Studies and World Affairs, 34,* 201–216.

Watson, R., Katel, P., Gutkin, S., Waller, D., Liu, M., & Spencer, R. (1993, December 13). Death on the spot: The end of a drug king. *Newsweek,* pp. 19–21.

Wilson, J. Q., & DiIulio, J. J. (1990). More law enforcement can reduce drug violence. In J. Rohr (Ed.), *Violence in America: Opposing viewpoints* (pp. 52–58). San Diego: Greenhaven Press.

Witkin, G., & Griffin, J. (1994). The new opium wars: The administration plans to attack the lords of heroin. *U.S. News and World Report, 117*(14), 39–44.

Wolfner, G. D., & Gelles, R. J. (1993). A profile of violence toward children: A national study. *Child Abuse and Neglect, 17*(2), 197–212.

Yudofsky, S. C., Silver, J. M., & Hales, R. E. (1993, spring). Cocaine and aggressive behavior: Neurobiological and clinical perspectives. *Bulletin of the Menninger Clinic, 57,* 218–226.

Zambia: Drug skirmishes. (1994). *Economist, 332*(7872), 38.

Zuckerman, B. (1993). Developmental considerations for drug- and AIDS-affected infants. In R. Barth, J. Pietrzak, & M. Ramler (Eds.), *Families living with drugs and HIV* (pp. 37–58). New York: Guilford Press.

Chapter 11

Reducing Drug-Related Violence through Sustainable Human Development Strategies

> Responses to the challenges posed by narcotics cropping and trafficking [and consuming] and their related problems [such as violence] must also be matched by a concerted international effort to resolve the underlying links of poverty and underdevelopment. Rather than approach the narcotics issue as a problem exclusive to the Third World, it must be linked with the broader question of development. Development alone will not be the solution to the narcotics problem, but it does provide a more adequate platform for dealing with the underlying causes. (Smith, 1992, p. 114)

The growth, distribution, and consumption of illegal narcotics have created a systemic cycle of violence and maldevelopment that cannot be broken without a thorough understanding of the interplay between supply and demand in the global North and global South. That understanding leads to the conclusion that strategies for sustainable human development might help reduce drug-related violence. The arguments supporting this conclusion are based on the following convictions:

- Focusing on only one strategy to solve the problem—the law enforcement approach favored in the U.S. "war on drugs," for example—is ineffective because it fails to recognize the different motives of growers, traffickers, and consumers.
- Solutions will be found in a combination of strategies, not in only one idea or program.
- "Quick-fix" strategies are futile and often create more problems.
- The problem must be addressed in the context of development, including an understanding of addiction as a disease requiring treatment rather than punishment.
- Sustainable human development strategies provide a promising approach for addressing one of the root causes of the drug problem—poverty—in all three of its phases (Smith, 1992).

252

Strategies for sustainable human development emphasize meeting basic human needs; expanding economic opportunities, especially for poor people; protecting the environment; promoting meaningful democratic participation, particularly by poor people, in economic and political decisions; adherence to human rights standards; and demilitarization of resources and solutions. There are no easy prescriptions or magic formulas for using principles of sustainable development to address the problem of drug-related violence, but the suggestions that follow can at least open the dialogue.

Curbing the Production of Narcotics

To reduce the supply of illegal narcotics at its source, U.S. foreign policy must focus on poverty in the global South, for that is the chief reason farmers turn to growing drug crops. Shuman and Harvey (1993) logically pointed out that, as long as the average coca farmer can earn more for a pest-resistant crop that fetches a relatively stable price, the incentives for such agriculture will remain irresistible. The problems of the peasants who grow coca, poppies, and marijuana as export cash crops must be addressed in the context of development rather than from the viewpoint of the police and the military (Smith, 1992).

Farmers need viable alternatives to earning their living by narcotics crop production. Viability means more than replacing narcotics crops with other agricultural products. Several other ingredients go into successful crop substitution, such as local marketing systems that protect perishable crops, provide transport to market, and good prices; support for the farmers while their new crops take hold enough to guarantee an income; and national and international policies that provide favorable trade, credit, infrastructure, training, price, and resource conditions (Panos Institute, 1993). Without these supports in place to ensure viable alternatives, policies of crop eradication should be prevented from eliminating the only source of income and survival left to many people (Salazar, 1993).

Countries of the global South that seek to reduce drug production should first define and address their own economic, social, and safety needs. Only then can they begin to employ strategies that successfully address the drug problem. In 1991, for example, an agreement for countering drug production and trafficking was concluded between Peru and the United States; at the insistence of the Peruvian president, the agreement dealt also with economic and social issues in Peru (Palmer, 1992).

However, generating strategies that address social and economic variables is complex and costly, and most countries of the global South that produce narcotics do not have sufficient resources for the task (Panos Institute, 1993).[1] Moreover, because the narcotics trade is fueled by consumption as well as production, the United Nations Development Programme (UNDP, 1994) asserted that it is unreasonable to expect the global South to bear the entire cost of clamping down on production and export. So how much should the global North pay to support efforts to reduce drug production? A pragmatic approach would be for the global North to be generous in supporting vital sustainable development programs (UNDP, 1994).

Shuman and Harvey (1993) suggested ways in which local communities in the United States can engage directly in the grassroots development strategies of communities in the global South. For example, they proposed that North American cities "consider adopting a town or village in Peru, Bolivia, or Colombia, so that U.S. citizens may work side by side with Latin American citizens to promote economic alternatives to growing coca. . . . Americans should send sister communities farming equipment, provide small-scale loans, and help build roads, bridges, water systems, and schools" (p. 249). An additional way to get resources and programs to grassroots communities is to support and protect nongovernmental organizations (NGOs).

In situations of government neglect and underdevelopment in Latin America—in which the state does not provide services and public works such as roads, health posts and schools, or other needed services—coca farmers have developed a system of mutual aid through which they operate their own community development programs. Coca producers have thus shown that, even in dire circumstances, they possess a strong sense

---

[1]Most efforts to date have not adequately considered such matters, and they have met with only limited success—eradicating crops in one place merely shifts production to another place. For example, when Thailand managed to reduce opium production, producers moved to Myanmar and to the Lao People's Democratic Republic (UNDP, 1994).

of community and political organization; their example illustrates the willingness, ability, and potential of poor people to engage in alternative development programs. In Colombia, for example, farmers join *sindicatos* (coca-producer unions of peasant workers). The *sindicatos* are de facto forms of government. At least once a week, members of the unions join together to work on community tasks; they repair roads, remodel schools, and maintain the soccer fields. The *sindicatos* also distribute land, organize the people, and regulate the economic and social life of the community (Davila, 1992).

Curbing Drug Trafficking

People traffic in drugs for different reasons. For example, the motivations of legitimate individuals and organizations (businesspeople and representatives of governments) may be different from those of illegitimate crime organizations, which in turn are different from those of inner-city youths who see no other viable alternatives. These different motivations must be taken into account to find effective ways to curb drug trafficking.

In underdeveloped U.S. cities, sustainable human development is needed so that drug traffickers can earn a decent living without selling drugs. As long as marginalized youths in society can make 100 times more by selling drugs than by working at a fast-food restaurant that pays minimum wage and offers no health benefits and no future, the inducement to sell drugs will be irresistible. Furthermore, even that fast-food job might not be available—unemployment rates are high in inner cities. A development approach calls for adequate educational opportunity, jobs that pay a decent wage and provide health care coverage, economic development programs that bring business and industry back into inner-city communities, and adequate community resources and infrastructure to support the healthy development of individuals and neighborhoods.

Many grassroots organizations in the United States are attempting to provide alternatives to the drug trade. For example, several entrepreneurial groups were started in Washington, DC, in the 1990s, one of which is Multi-Cultural Youth Education, Inc. Such programs offer realistic reasons to stay in school by showing how business can tap into the strengths and interests of youths. As one 18-year-old boy commented, "Most kids on the street are business-minded. . . . They know how to make money. They use the resources they have. And that's drugs" (De Silva, 1994, p. DC8). These programs propose that there are ways to use the business savvy and resources of youths that do not involve drugs.

These approaches address an important aspect of the problem, but membership in drug-related gangs is motivated also by other needs: for belonging and community, for psychological as well as financial security. In an urban environment of economic scarcity, the gang serves as a mutual aid system to meet such needs. Reacting to gang violence only from a criminal perspective does not address this motivation or need. If they are to be successful, youth intervention programs must address and work toward mitigating the social inequality that causes these youths to turn to drugs and gangs. This means enhancing the socioeconomic status of high-risk youths by providing opportunities for quality schooling, skills building, and meaningful job placement that is sustainable beyond their participation in the program. "The Contra Costa County Prevention Program" profiles a violence prevention program with a multifaceted approach that addresses the multiple dimensions of the problem (Cohen & Swift, 1993).

The Contra Costa County Prevention Program

The Contra Costa County Prevention Program in northern California focuses its violence prevention initiative in the western part of the county, which includes densely populated urban centers where unemployment is high, the educational system is underfunded, and the population is ethnically diverse with a high percentage of new immigrants.

The principle on which the program is based is that violence emerges from multiple causes—personal, social, and economic—and thus violence reduction requires multifaceted efforts. It is based also on the understanding that the health of a community depends on many variables in many systems—the family, education, health, work, criminal justice, and social services; effective responses to violence, then, must marshal resources on both local and national levels.

Prevention Program takes a systematic approach to its work. It acts as a catalyst for bringing key people and organizations together and thus is able to galvanize support for broad-based and long-lasting change. Three tools maximize collaboration: Coalition Building (an eight-step procedure designed to bring people and organizations together); the Spectrum of Prevention (which outlines effective strategies); and Partnerships for Institutional Change (a method for shifting policies and resources within established organizations).

Coalition Building

Local violence prevention initiatives are developed in conjunction with community-based organizations already focused on particular aspects of the problem. This strategy brings together people in organizations that concentrate on a form of violence (battered women's programs, for example) or that serve a particular population at risk (youth services bureaus, for example). Such existing community-based organizations join with Prevention Program to form a single coalition that coordinates comprehensive prevention services. A list of the agencies involved in the coalition demonstrates the breadth of issues and the diversity of organizations that are committed to working collaboratively on violence prevention: Familias Unidas, Lao Family Community Development, Opportunity West, Police Activities League, Youth Services Bureau, Rape Crisis Center, Battered Women's Alternatives.

The Spectrum of Prevention

The benefits of diverse coalition membership can be realized when the coalition identifies and implements a broad range of strategies. Prevention Program delineates six levels of activity, all of which reflect the views that environmental factors are the largest determinant of health status, that individual education aimed at changing behavior is not sufficient, that changing institutional priorities—as well as laws and organizational policies—is essential for creating safe communities, and that a prevention-oriented approach can reduce violence only by transforming the environmental and community contributors to violence. The six levels include (1) strengthening youths' individual knowledge and skills (including instruction about the root causes of violence, cultural differences, and nonviolent conflict-resolution methods); (2) educating the community; (3) training providers; (4) building coalitions; (5) changing organizational practices; and (6) influencing policy and legislation.

Partnerships for Institutional Change

Because institutions determine the priorities of a community, control much of its resources, and affect its culture, they must play a central role in creating solutions to problems of violence. First of all, they must change their own practices to be effective agents of violence prevention. At one level, institutions may become active partners in Prevention Program by having an active representative in the coalition and contributing money, volunteers, or other resources. A second level of institutional involvement is for those organizations that do not recognize violence prevention as relevant to their mission, or whose operations may actually impede violence prevention efforts. Institutions that are reluctant to become active in violence prevention efforts are encouraged to make specific changes that have been defined as critical by the violence prevention coalition. Organizations whose activities actually contribute to the problem of violence (for example, television networks and other media that perpetuate stereotypes and glorify violence) may require pressure or regulation to force institutional change. Government might also collaborate with the coalition on projects to reduce violence: for example, a public works department might be persuaded to install better lighting in a high-crime neighborhood or policymakers might be persuaded to adopt gun and ammunition control and rational drug policies.

Source: Cohen & Swift, 1993.

In international trafficking in narcotics, too, different motivations—greed, profit, or power, for instance—call for different approaches. International trafficking thrives in part because serious international drug enforcement does not exist. Nations rely on primitive law enforcement networks to eradicate poppy and coca crops, to prevent large-scale laundering of drug profits, and to prosecute drug lords. Criminals therefore move to countries with the weakest antidrug policies, and there are no enforceable international laws to stop them from doing so. International organizations and laws that can deal effectively with drug trafficking must be put in place to "help nations put globetrotting drug lords behind bars" (Shuman & Harvey, 1993, p. 248). Law enforcement officials believe that internationally enforced rules against money laundering are needed to counteract the global links of organized crime (Elliott et al., 1993). Some suggest that the legalization of drugs might eliminate the swaggering power and undeserved wealth of drug traffickers, but there is not much public support for that approach.

A particular challenge is the problem of military involvement in drug trafficking in some countries. Rosenberg (1988), who maintained that efforts to reduce the Honduran role in drug trafficking needed to begin with the military, made this proposal: The United States should support democratization in Honduras, because elected leaders—who must be accountable to their country's people and sensitive to international concerns—would be less willing to tolerate military complicity in trafficking.

Reducing Consumption of Narcotics

Solutions to drug-related violence do not lie just with the source countries. In fact, experience shows that curbing demand for narcotics is more important than curbing supply (UNDP, 1994). Ultimately, the solution to the problem of drug consumption in the United States lies in wiping out the demand, which means alerting people to the lethally addictive properties of narcotics and providing treatment for those already addicted. Around the mid-1970s—when cocaine became popular among some well-to-do groups in the United States—the global North began to pay more attention to drug use prevention, public education, and rehabilitation. The public awareness campaign worked—in part. The number of people in the United States using cocaine has dropped by 50 percent since 1985, but this represents change only among middle- and upper-class users. A hard core of users remains concentrated in underdeveloped urban areas, especially among young and unemployed people (Smith, 1992).

Addiction is a disease, and drug-related crime often results from the need to feed that addiction (Schmoke, 1990). When policymakers understand those facts, they can turn their focus from law enforcement efforts to drug abuse prevention and treatment. Moreover, evidence seems to support the effectiveness of treatment for cutting demand and cutting costs: A federally funded study conducted by the RAND Corporation found that treatment is seven times more cost-effective than local enforcement in cutting cocaine demand, 11 times more effective than border interdiction, and 22 times more effective than trying to control foreign production (Rydell & Everingham, 1994). Evidence also reveals that heavy users cost society in numerous ways: increased crime and health care needs, urban decay, and lack of productiveness. Shifting funds from expensive, largely ineffective drug interdiction efforts to treatment programs for hard-core users would therefore seem to be a sensible policy for addressing crime and other problematic economic, health, and urban issues.

Drug prevention programs aimed at young children can reduce the demand for drugs by teaching children how to resist them. Cooperative community programs, in which police and therapists work together to debrief youngsters who have been traumatized by drug-related forms of violence, have proved effective with youngsters who are at particular risk of violence and drug use (Marans & Cohen, 1993). Other programs, such as violence-prevention programs in schools, have been found to promote children's ability to solve problems nonviolently, even youngsters who are predisposed to act violently because of drug-related trauma; the highest rates of long-term effectiveness are achieved with the youngest children (National Association for the Eductaion of Young Children, 1995).

Some say that by the time children become teenagers, it may be too late for drug abuse and violence prevention and education programs to be effective, but some intervention approaches are proving them wrong. In cities around the country, the 1995 rate of violent crimes—including murder, robbery, rape, and assault—fell to its lowest level since 1989 (Shapiro, 1996). Some of the credit for such change may go to community development approaches such as the one described in "Community Policing in New Haven." The New Haven experience illustrates how community safety can be improved not through "law and order" and vigilantism but through grassroots activism. The construction of democratic institutions in neighborhoods and cities can make a genuine difference in keeping young people from drugs and crime.

Community Policing in New Haven

In New Haven, as in a handful of other communities, the phrase "community policing" has taken on new meaning. In New Haven, when a new police chief—Nicholas Pastore—was appointed in 1990, he "turned standard police practice on its head, demilitarizing and decentralizing" the department and remaking it into a multipurpose vehicle for advancing civil society (Shapiro, 1996, p. 19). This new approach was grounded in the theory that crime can most effectively be combated by organizing people to identify exactly what makes their neighborhoods unsafe.

At the same time that social welfare programs were being dismantled, Pastore turned New Haven's police into a frontline community intervention agency, especially for teenagers. The approach involved identifying the youths who are in greatest danger and then throwing at them everything the system has to offer. At the request of residents, homework centers were established in neighborhood precinct houses. A counseling program for children who witness violence was initiated. A domestic violence specialist was put in charge of all police training.

The New Haven approach is based on the idea that neighborhood residents can make meaningful contributions to police policy—even teenagers, who sit on a Board of Youth Police Commissioners that interviews every prospective officer. At the same time, the evaluation of police performance went from quantity of street-level arrests to how well detectives coped with "corrupt organizations that systematically make citizens' lives more dangerous or difficult—whether that happened to be gun-wielding drug gangs, pyramid-scheming fraternal clubs or crooked city hall politicos" (Shapiro, 1996, p. 20).

Has this new approach worked? Perhaps it is too soon to tell, but there are compelling signs of success. For example, the 1995 murder rate was down 44 percent from 1994; New Haven went from one SWAT team raid every two weeks to two a year in 1994 and 1995. Although the city is hardly crime-free, young people in New Haven are substantially less likely to be shot than they were in the past. Even people who dislike Pastore's approach credit his policies with turning the city around.

Pastore, for one, believes that his approach will have more long-term effectiveness than "quick fix" approaches such as prison expansion and mandatory minimum sentences that, he maintains, make the streets less safe. His reasoning is persuasive: "Eventually most of the 1.5 million—and growing— Americans incarcerated today are going to come out uneducated, unemployable, politically disfranchised and angry. If we continue to quick-fix by expanding our prisons, this drop [in crime] is just the lull before the storm. You will within a few years have a significant segment of society who are prison-influenced and prison-behaved" (Shapiro, 1996, p. 19).

Reducing the consumption of illegal drugs requires long-term, sustainable approaches to development. Many wealthy and educated people use illegal drugs, of course, but too many heavy "drug users are poor and desperate—seeking some kind of anesthesia for the hopelessness of their lives. For them, drugs may be dangerous, but they have little left to lose" (UNDP, 1994, p. 37). Obviously, relieving the distress that feeds drug addiction is a goal that should be pursued and a solution that can strengthen families and communities in both the global South and in underdeveloped regions of the global North (UNDP, 1994). The first and foremost need is for jobs, jobs that might offer young people hope and bring in enough income to sustain a family. The choice between unemployment and a high-paying job in the underground economy is hardly a choice at all—if there are no other alternatives, we are virtually ensured an endless supply of young criminals.

Funding Strategies for Sustainable Human Development

The solution to the drug epidemic requires long-term, multifaceted, concerted, and comprehensive approaches that get at its root causes. Such an approach calls for bold policy initiatives that are very expensive. The paradox is that the United States and the entire international community end up paying in any case—and they pay a lot more downstream than they would have had they paid upstream (UNDP, 1994). For example, for $25 billion—half the cost American cities are now paying in terms of crime, sickness, and other damages from the drug war, and a fraction of the total cost of the Persian Gulf War—the United States could pay every rural family in Latin America $1,000—the typical annual income for a coca farmer—not to grow coca (Shuman & Harvey, 1993). An impressive, effective public works program for the underdeveloped regions of the United States could be financed by the annual cost of drug-related crime and incarceration.

Priorities have to change to free money for development in the source countries of the global South and in underdeveloped areas in the primary consumer countries of the global North. Shuman and Harvey (1993) maintained that, if the United States were "freed of the expense of the arms race and unilateral interventions, [it could] invest in genuine debt relief, sustainable development, and family planning. Today it spends only about $300 million each year on assistance to population, energy, and environmental programs abroad—about one-thousandth of its total military expenditures, or two-thirds of the cost of a single B-2 bomber" (pp. 248–249). Reordering of priorities is possible, despite pessimism to the contrary. UNDP (1994) proposed, for example, a 3 percent reduction in global military spending from 1995 to 2000, which would produce $85 billion in new money for sustainable human development throughout the world.

To summarize, development interventions that are sustainable and that reduce drug-related violence must include meaningful participation (citizen-led empowerment), environmental sustainability (regeneration rather than destruction of the environment), equitable redistribution of resources (priority to poor people), and demilitarization to free up resources for development (Shuman & Harvey, 1993; UNDP, 1994). Although it now seems a far-off possibility, an ultimate goal would be "for all of the nations of the world to develop a viable plan of international cooperation directed toward solving all of the economic, social, political, and cultural problems that underlie both the production and overconsumption of all the drugs that are currently on the market, recognizing the legitimate interests of both the producing and the consuming countries" (Salazar, 1993, pp. 95–96).

Implications for Social Workers: What You Can Do

> Social work is local, mainly person-to-person. How can social workers even begin to address the issue of globalization? By first understanding what they are dealing with. Understanding of the connections between private troubles and global changes will not in itself lead to action. But it can provide a foundation for more relevant intervention. (Richan, 1995, p. 3)

People cannot be considered apart from their environment, which this chapter has attempted to show. Although most social work practice occurs on a person-to-person level, social workers need to understand that individual problems might—and most often do—have their roots in larger systems. They must understand also how those macro-level systems operate so they can intervene effectively. As for the problem of drug-related violence, the challenges are great.

Typical social work interventions include drug prevention and treatment models, which must be approached within a cultural context. In other words, they must be guided by the cultural norms and uniqueness of individual clients as well as by the development capacity of communities. As if all of these demands were not enough, social workers must take a global perspective if the social work profession is to have any relevance in addressing the cycle of drug-related violence and maldevelopment.

Key to these endeavors is that social workers understand that their clients are part of a system that perpetuates itself and therefore must be targeted from all angles. "Diagnosing Drug Problems" helps explain how knowledge of global interdependence can aid diagnosis of drug problems.

Diagnosing Drug Problems

After a drug deal gone bad, an African American youth lies dead on a north Philadelphia street corner. We dig into his background and find that he dropped out of high school in the 10th grade, never held a job for more than a few months, and was raised by his grandmother because crack had taken over his mother's life.

The diagnosis will include all the important points: the crack trade, family breakdown, poor schools, neighborhood blight. All, that is, except perhaps the most crucial one: the demise of the apparel industry in north Philadelphia.

Until the 1950s, this part of Philadelphia was the center of a thriving garment and textile industry, which accounted for a fourth of all industrial jobs in the city. Now those jobs have moved to Central America and Southeast Asia, where some of the same companies that used to operate in north Philadelphia now hire children to work for a few cents an hour. They have left behind a litter of abandoned factories and a community in which the most lucrative careers are in pushing drugs.

Last summer the Leslie Fay Company, a manufacturer of women's wear, announced that it was laying off 1,000 workers at its Wilkes-Barre, Pennsylvania, plant. Most of these were middle-aged women who had been with the company for more than a decade. Leslie Fay moved the work to its Honduran operations, where 12- and 13-year-old girls worked 54 hours a week in 100-degree heat for less than 40 cents an hour. The garments made there sell for the same high prices in U.S. stores.

The New Global Technology

In her book, The Global Factory, *Rachel Kamel tells how the computer and the satellite have transformed the manufacture of clothing. Now it is possible to integrate production worldwide, seeking out the cheapest labor costs and weakest workplace and environmental laws. So one part of the garment can be made in one country, another part in a second country, and assembly take place in still a third. Time was when cheap labor meant cheap goods, but no more. You can no longer tell where that dress or coat with the high price tag was made.*

Return of the Sweatshop

Sociologist Elizabeth Petras used to have her students look at the labels of their jackets to see where they were made. She wanted them to make the connection between those Hong Kong and Singapore labels and the demise of garment workers in this country.

But then she began getting a different kind of answer. Many students said "Made in the USA." That launched her on an investigation that led her into the seamy side of American industry: the return of sweatshops.

In Philadelphia's Chinatown, a second-story loft looks abandoned. Inside, however, as many as 60 Asian immigrants are toiling away in virtual servitude, producing clothing that will be sold in a suburban mall a few miles away. The workers, many without documentation, are at the mercy of their employers. The scene is duplicated dozens of times here and in New York City. So it is that these two cities again become centers of the garment industry in the United States. But there is an added note: the entry of organized crime.

Interstate 95 is the corridor connecting parts of the operation in New York and Philadelphia, with truckers as the linchpin. Recognizing the potential profits in this traffic in human misery, the Mafia has moved in and now plays a key role.

Coming Full Circle: The Drug Traffic

It would be silly to suggest that every youth's death on the streets of north Philadelphia can be attributed to the decline of the clothing industry. The mayhem that is robbing this and other urban centers of a generation of young people is the result of a combination of factors, not the least of which is the availability of crack. But here again, we must look at the larger picture.

It was the drive for profits that gutted north Philadelphia's industrial base, creating a sense of hopelessness. Hopelessness is the perfect breeding ground for the drug trade, which offers a temporary escape from reality to the buyer and the lure of big money to the seller.

It was also the drive for profits that led U.S. financial institutions to encourage developing countries to build up a staggering debt burden and, now, to pressure them to pay off their debts. One way of doing that is to abandon traditional subsistence farming and go to cash crops, displacing peasants from the land in the process.

In some countries the peasants have found a way to survive the resulting upheaval: Grow coca leaves. These in turn end up on the streets of north Philadelphia in the form of crack.

Source: Richan, W. (1995, spring). "Social problems" go global: The case of the garment trade. *Peace and Justice* [a newsletter of NASW's National Peace and Justice Committee], pp. 3–4. Used with permission of the author, who is professor emeritus, Temple University.

This diagnosis of one youth's death poignantly illustrates the links between private troubles and social problems caused by maldevelopment. The following suggestions are aimed at helping social workers develop a foundation—from the perspective of global interdependence—for relevant responses to the problem of drug-related violence.

- Learn more about the interdependent causes and consequences of the cycle between drug-related violence and maldevelopment; use the resources listed at the end of this book as a start.
- Learn about alternative solutions to the problem that go beyond national borders and that include cooperative international solutions to reduce both supply and demand; reject the "blame game" by striving to understand how both the global North and the global South are hurt by the drug epidemic and acknowledge our own responsibility.
- Learn as much as you can about international development issues and use that learning to advocate for solutions that address the root causes of the drug problem—poverty and maldevelopment. Reject quick-fix, simplistic, law-and-order solutions that are expensive and ineffective, and reject any solutions that do not include development as a primary focus.
- Advocate for a reduction in military expenditures worldwide to free up resources for development.
- Support NGOs that promote grassroots development in the global South and in the United States.
- Learn more about culturally sensitive approaches to addressing drug-related violence, such as the use of naturally existing helping networks—the church, extended family, community elders, and community healers. Respect family and community norms.

References

Cohen, L., & Swift, S. (1993, October). *A public health approach to the violence epidemic in the United States.* Unpublished manuscript. (Available from Larry Cohen, MSW, Center for Injury and Violence Prevention, Education Development Center, 55 Chapel Street, Newton, MA 02158-1060)

Davila, A. (1992). Participation, not eradication. In M. L. Smith (Ed.), *Why people grow drugs: Narcotics and development in the Third World* (pp. 93–104). Washington, DC: Panos Institute.

De Silva, D. R. (1994, September 22). "At risk" youths get the business, and a chance. *Washington Post,* pp. DC1, DC8.

Elliott, M., Waller, D., Liu, M., Elliott, D., Nagorski, A., Sullivan, S., Vivarelli, N., Padgett, T., Strasser, S., & Huus, K. (1993). Global mafia: A *Newsweek* investigation. *Newsweek, 122*(24), 22–31.

Marans, S., & Cohen, D. (1993). Children and inner-city violence: Strategies for intervention. In L. Leavitt & N. Fox (Eds.), *The psychological effects of war and violence on children* (pp. 281–301). Hillsdale, NJ: Lawrence Erlbaum.

National Association for the Education of Young Children. (1995). *Early violence prevention: Tools for teaching of young children*. Washington, DC: Author.

Palmer, D. S. (1992, fall). Peru, the drug business and Shining Path: Between Scylla and Charybdis? *Journal of InterAmerican Studies and World Affairs, 34,* 65–88.

Panos Institute. (1993). *Narcotics and development*. Washington, DC: Author.

Richan, W. (1995, spring). Social problems go global: The case of the garment trade. *Peace and Justice* [a newsletter of NASW's National Peace and Justice Committee], pp. 3–4.

Rosenberg, M. B. (1988, summer–fall). Narcos and politicos: The politics of drug trafficking in Honduras. *Journal of InterAmerican Studies and World Affairs, 30,* 143–165.

Rydell, C. P., & Everingham, S. S. (1994). *Controlling cocaine: Supply versus demand programs*. Santa Monica, CA: RAND Corporation.

Salazar, L. S. (1993). "Drug trafficking" and social and political conflicts in Latin America: Some hypotheses. *Latin American Perspectives, 20*(1), 83–98.

Schmoke, K. L. (1990). More law enforcement cannot reduce drug violence. In J. Rohr (Ed.), *Violence in America: Opposing viewpoints* (pp. 59–66). San Diego: Greenhaven Press.

Shapiro, B. (1996). How the war on crime imprisons America. *Nation, 262*(16), 14–21.

Shuman, M. H., & Harvey, H. (1993). *Security without war: A post-cold war foreign policy*. Boulder, CO: Westview Press.

Smith, M. L. (Ed.). (1992). *Why people grow drugs: Narcotics and development in the Third World*. Washington, DC: Panos Institute.

United Nations Development Programme (UNDP). (1994). *Human development report 1994*. New York: Oxford University Press.

Part 6

Healing

Chapter 12

From Violence and Trauma to Processes of Healing

Coauthored by Arline Prigoff, PhD

> Psychological trauma is an affliction of the powerless. At the moment of trauma, the victim is rendered helpless by overwhelming force. . . . Traumatic events overwhelm the ordinary systems of care that give people a sense of control, connection, and meaning. It was once believed that such events were uncommon. In 1980, when posttraumatic stress disorder was first included in the diagnostic manual, the American Psychiatric Association described traumatic events as "outside the range of usual human experience." Sadly, this definition has proved to be inaccurate. Rape, battery, and other forms of sexual and domestic violence are so common a part of women's lives that they can hardly be described as outside the range of ordinary experience. And in view of the number of people killed in war over the past century, military trauma, too, must be considered a common part of human experience; only the fortunate find it unusual. Traumatic events are extraordinary, not because they occur rarely, but rather because they overwhelm the ordinary human adaptations to life. (Herman, 1992, p. 33)

This book has documented global conditions of violence and attempted to connect the dots between violence and development processes within the contexts of poverty, gender violence, violence against children, ethnoviolence, and illegal narcotics. The violent acts or situations that have been addressed are traumatizing to the extent that they shatter assumptions about basic security and safety in the world, about the availability of protection for self and others, and about the ability to protect oneself. Violent acts or situations are traumatizing not only for the victim but also for witnesses, related family members, the community, and people who help those who are traumatized.

This chapter focuses on the traumatizing consequences of violence, whether rape and battery of women; sexual or physical abuse of children;

Arline Prigoff, PhD, is professor and coordinator of community government relations, Division of Social Work, California State University, Sacramento.

robbery, assault, or murder; hate crimes; brutal acts of war; torture of political prisoners; or chronic hunger, lack of adequate shelter, and other conditions of absolute poverty or systemic forms of oppression. The chapter (1) delineates key assumptions and beliefs and defines key concepts; (2) discusses the violence-related trauma of institutional and structural and cultural forms of violence—poverty, oppression, war, refugee situations, and state-sponsored torture; and (3) shows how unresolved trauma impedes development and perpetuates a cycle of violence.

Assumptions and Key Concepts

The following beliefs and assumptions provide the framework for this chapter:

- Wherever class stratification and political or military strife are intense—whether in low-income areas and oppressed communities of color or among refugees and immigrant populations in the United States and the global South—high percentages of the population may be survivors of traumatic events (California NASW Center, 1994).
- The effects of trauma at any level of violence—individual, institutional, or structural and cultural—are pervasive and impair the attainment of one's full potential as a human being.
- Manifestations of psychic trauma are fairly consistent whether the victims are from the United States or from countries of the global South (Florida NASW Center, 1994).
- Trauma is an obstacle to human, social, and economic development.
- Unresolved emotional trauma plays a role in creating and maintaining an intractable cycle of violence.

Trauma Defined

Trauma is defined as an emotional state of discomfort or stress resulting from memories of an extraordinary, catastrophic experience that shattered the survivor's sense of invulnerability to harm (Figley, 1986). The American Psychiatric Association (APA, 1994) defined a traumatic event as one that poses a serious threat to one's life or physical integrity. Trauma also results from witnessing a threat to the life or physical integrity of another person and from learning about unexpected or violent death, serious harm, or threat of harm experienced by a family member or other close associate (APA, 1994). A traumatic event can be an individual experience or one involving many people. Primary victims experience the trauma directly, and secondary victims experience the trauma indirectly through others (Bedics, Rappe, & Rappe, 1991).

Whenever someone is powerless to protect self or others from a life-threatening assault or terrifying condition, that person is likely to be traumatized (California NASW Center, 1994). Studies of people's responses in such situations and the normal recovery process were launched by Erick Lindemann's examination (1944) of bereaved disaster victims of the Coconut Grove Nightclub fire in 1943. Crisis theorists initially focused on intervention with individuals immediately following traumatic events in an attempt to mitigate long-term psychological, social, and psychosomatic consequences.

Posttraumatic Stress Disorder Defined

Posttraumatic stress disorder (PTSD), as defined by the APA (1994), is exposure to a traumatic event involving actual or threatened death or serious injury; threat to the physical integrity of self or others; and intense fear, helplessness, or horror. It is characterized by recurrent episodes of reexperiencing the event; avoidance of stimuli associated with the trauma and numbing of general responsiveness; and persistent, dysphoric hyperarousal.

PTSD results when a traumatic experience threatens and exceeds a person's ability to maintain safety and self-respect. Reactive and self-protective defenses of denial and avoidance, evoked by fears and feelings of powerlessness, become characterological and dysfunctional if underlying issues are unresolved over time. Chronic use of denial and avoidance, as characteristic defenses, is likely to produce dysfunctional behavior in different aspects of the person's life. Development of PTSD is influenced by factors such as the characteristics of the trauma itself (intensity, duration, number of deaths, and so on), social support, personality and life history, and health (Society for Traumatic Stress Studies, 1989).

PTSD strikes all cultural, socioeconomic, racial, and religious groups, with several populations identified as being at risk, including political refugees; torture victims; disaster survivors; combat veterans; and the survivors of rape, incest, alcoholic homes, assault, homicide, crime, domestic violence, the Holocaust, war, and terrorist attacks. Persons at risk for secondary traumatic stress disorder include service personnel and helping professionals who respond to traumatic events and who treat those who are traumatized (Bedics et al., 1991; Figley, 1995).

Ramsay (1990) pointed out that, although many people experience some symptoms of PTSD after exposure to extreme stress, the full posttraumatic stress syndrome may be less common. There are also inherent difficulties in diagnosing PTSD because the symptoms cut across diagnostic groups (for example, alcoholism, drug dependence, somatization disorders, psychosis, affective disorders, phobic disorders, antisocial personality disorder, or organic mental syndrome). The coexistence of PTSD and alcoholism is particularly complicated, because many PTSD symptoms can be effectively self-medicated with alcohol—at least initially; repeated alcohol use results in increased tolerance and consumption, and attempts to decrease consumption or to abstain may lead to alcohol withdrawal symptoms that are similar to and exacerbate the original stress symptoms (Ramsay, 1990).

Consequences of Violence-Related Trauma

Psychological trauma—emotional wounding that results from sudden, prolonged, or repeated experiences of a life-threatening nature—gained public recognition as a mental health problem after the First and Second World Wars (Kardiner & Spiegel, 1947). The therapeutic needs of traumatized veterans laid bare the vulnerability of human beings when exposed to life-threatening events. War-related psychiatric disabilities and their links to other psychiatric conditions revealed that "people who have endured horrible events suffer predictable psychological harm" (Herman, 1992, p. 3). The Vietnam War—in which U.S. servicemen carried out not only military battles but also actions against unarmed civilian populations—resulted in the further identification and classification of posttraumatic stress as a diagnostic category (Figley, 1978; Figley & Leventman, 1980; Sonnenberg, Blank, & Talbott, 1985). Life narratives confirm the depth of psychological damage—subordination, shame, and self-blame, among others—experienced by survivors of other forms of violence as well (see, for example, Angelou, 1970, 1978).

Neurophysiological studies (Grof, 1992; Penfield, 1975; Pribam, 1971, 1986) reveal that violence-related trauma produces intense feelings of rage, powerlessness, and associated mental imagery. When neither escape nor resistance—ordinary human responses to threat—are possible, human self-defenses may be overwhelmed and disorganized, thus producing traumatic reactions (Selye, 1956). Scenes and images of acts of violence are permanently imprinted in the psyche, along with associated feelings of terror and anguish. Reactive depression—loss of sense of self and self-worth by people who found themselves unable to protect themselves and others in situations of abuse or other trauma—has long been noted in the field of mental health (S. Freud, Ferenczi, Abraham, Simmel, & Jones, 1921). Dissociation, a process by which awareness of a current or past life event is cut off and not integrated in conscious memory, also was observed early (Janet, 1891/1970) and continues to be observed (Lynn and Rhue, 1994).

Traumatic experiences evoke three main categories of reactive defenses, namely, hyperarousal, intrusion, and constriction:

> Traumatic events produce profound and lasting changes in physiological arousal, emotion, cognition, and memory. . . . After a traumatic experience, the human system of self-preservation seems to go onto permanent alert, as if the danger might return at any moment. . . . In this state of hyperarousal . . . the traumatized person startles easily, reacts irritably to small provocations, and sleeps poorly. . . . Traumatized people relive the moment of trauma not only in their thoughts and dreams but also in their actions. . . . The helpless person escapes from her situation not by action in the real world but rather by altering her state of consciousness. . . . These alterations of consciousness are at the heart of constriction or numbing, the third cardinal symptom of posttraumatic stress disorder. (Herman, 1992, pp. 35–42)

Violence-Related Trauma: A Multilevel Phenomenon

Violence has been defined throughout this book as any act or situation that causes physical or psychological injury, both direct attacks and destructive actions that do not involve a direct relationship between victims and perpetrators (Van Soest & Bryant, 1995). Different forms of violence occur on individual, institutional, and structural and cultural levels. Violence between individuals has been presented as a manifestation of unresolved conflicts and systematic oppression on the institutional and structural levels of society.

This conceptual framework recognizes that interpretation of and response to a violent act or situation vary, depending on the type and level of violence. The same is true of trauma's consequences. Thus, trauma and PTSD are more readily comprehended when they result from violence at the individual level than when they are a consequence of the often unseen violence at the institutional level. Violence at the individual level includes harmful actions against people or property, and the victim (and injuries), perpetrator (and motivation), and immediate consequences are visible. At the institutional level, however, harmful actions are carried out as seemingly necessary acts of social control that may not even be seen as forms of violence at all. Traumatic consequences of violence at the structural and cultural level are invisible to people who view life through the lens of the dominant culture. Victims also often remain silent, rendered impotent by insult as well as injury, by social stigma, and by blame for personal weakness.

Institutional and structural and cultural forms of violence, which are rarely considered crimes, are likely to remain hidden and denied until revealed by resistant survivors. Although usually not seen as such, acts of violence at these levels are destructive because they cut off the access of certain populations to life support resources and provoke traumatic reactions that may include self-destructive behaviors and interpersonal violence. This chapter examines several forms of violence, including violence at institutional and structural and cultural levels, that produce trauma.

Children Are Traumatized Every Day in the United States

Children, as well as people who are poor, are particularly vulnerable to traumatization because they are relatively powerless. Every day in the United States children are traumatized by homelessness and the intensifying political assaults against single-parent families; by domestic violence followed by divorce; by growing up in families where there is addiction; by the sale of lethal weapons; and so on. Moreover, the increasing stratification of economic and political power now occurring in the United States and around the world, which comes from the globalization of the market economy, is shattering the security of families and communities everywhere. When communities and families become economically marginalized, violence and trauma are very likely to escalate.

Although the United States is not now engaged in warfare, the prevalence of handguns in society places all citizens at risk of becoming victims or witnesses of violence. Scenes involving the use of lethal weapons are traumatizing. A culture in which images of lethal weapons and their use are everyday occurrences—through films, television, and video games—is a culture that places vulnerable children at risk of traumatization and impaired cognitive development.

Poverty, Class Stratification, and Chronic Community Violence as Trauma

Basic security is shattered under conditions of poverty and deprivation. When human beings are unable to provide for their own basic needs and those of dependent family members, such conditions are physically and psychologically damaging and life-threatening. Homelessness, for example, is a predicament that by definition lacks basic security and therefore is traumatizing, especially for children. In the United States and the global South, the numbers of such traumatized children are growing; their homelessness and poverty leave them potentially scarred and at risk of lifelong emotional impairment.

During the past two decades, economic, technological, and political events have exponentially increased the gap between rich and poor people within the United States and between countries of the global North and countries of the global South (Beeghley, 1989; Braun, 1991; Grutsky, 1994; Reiman, 1984). Consequently, many low-income communities have become further depleted and defeated; power and resources to generate recovery are lacking, and past efforts at community recovery often have failed. Traumatizing conditions of poverty and deprivation often give rise to high levels of interpersonal violence which, in turn, cause further trauma. In his analysis of violence in Algeria, Fanon (1968) vividly described the cycle of trauma-related violence:

During the colonial period in Algeria and elsewhere many things may be done for a couple of pounds of semolina. Several people may be killed over it. You need to use your imagination to understand that; your imagination, or your memory. In the concentration camps men killed each other for a bit of bread. I remember one horrible scene. It was in Oran in 1944. From the camp where we were waiting to embark, soldiers were throwing bits of bread to little Algerian children who fought for them among themselves with anger and hate. (pp. 307–308)

Chronic violence among poor, socially stigmatized people in U.S. cities, often described as inner-city war zones, is producing social disaster and destroying community infrastructures. Children who are exposed to chronic violence in their own neighborhoods—where they know neighbors who are gang members or addicted to drugs or alcohol and where the violence is ongoing and often random—may experience particularly high stress. This social disaster occurs at precisely the time when children need reliable social structures to reassure them and to offer moral interpretation of their world (Garbarino, 1993). Studies of children and parents exposed to chronic community violence show that both parents and children are often traumatized. When parents are traumatized and their ability to provide a safe environment undermined, they can lose confidence and become emotionally unresponsive to their children (Carnegie Corporation, 1994).

Oppressive Social Systems as Trauma

Inequality in economic and political power—fundamental features of social stratification—are manifestations of social relations of dominance and subordination embedded in the structural and cultural level. Because social systems are holographic, patterns in the structure of power relations at the structural and cultural level are likely to be replicated in status and role relationships in institutional and smaller subsystems at the individual level (Schaef, 1987). Thus, the traumatizing consequences of oppression—characterized by dominance, abuse of power, and related powerlessness—apply to all levels of social formation: between individuals; within families, communities, and nations; and between countries (Freire, 1970; Laing, 1965; Laing & Esterson, 1970; Memmi, 1965; Miller, 1984, 1986).

Oppressive systems deny—except to those at the center of the circle of power—the right to exercise fundamental human capabilities: the right to perceive, to think and interpret, to feel, to want and choose, and to imagine (the five freedoms defined by Satir, 1976). Covert rules of oppressive systems also prohibit the right to talk, to make mistakes, and, even more constricting, to trust. A system that operates with these rules is abusive and traumatizing, whether it is the family of origin of a recovering alcoholic or a government that sends tanks to fight unarmed students in Tiananmen Square.

The Violence of War Traumatizes

War—violence that is an institutional manifestation of deeply embedded militaristic values at the structural and cultural level—produces social disaster in the form of dramatic and overwhelming destruction of the infrastructure of daily life. War traumatizes everyone in its wake, but children may be especially affected. Children who witness indescribable actions during war—the violent killing or maiming of their parents, siblings, friends, or others by land mines, horrific beatings, and rape—are haunted for years by those images. Save the Children (1994) estimated that such emotional distress affects 10 million children—one in every 200—caught up in conflicts around the globe: "Some children are consumed by guilt that they were powerless to help, . . . angry that the villains got away with it, . . . [and they harbor] grief and bitterness which can result in aggressive behaviour" (p. 20). Traumatized children may stop speaking, become closed and reserved, have thoughts of revenge, feel bitter and distraught, and exhibit other symptoms of PTSD. For example,

> A five year old girl who witnessed a bomb explosion in Northern Ireland which killed a policeman, suffered two years of broken sleep; another child who was separated from her family and taken to an orphanage when she was five years old spoke to no one for five months; a two year old girl from Rwanda—who was found alive among the 4,000 corpses near the scene of a bloody massacre by militia—doesn't speak, is always alone, does not play with other children or move voluntarily, has not formed any attachments with the workers, suffers from diarrhea, and her body often shakes. (Save the Children, 1994)

The results of systematic, scientifically based research focusing on the symptomatology of child victims of violence point to a variety of responses to the trauma. For example, studies of the Israeli–Palestinian conflict reveal increased aggressiveness, fear, and anxiety in children (Punamaki, 1982); a preliminary study of Kuwaiti children after the 1990–91 Gulf War confirms the significant effect of exposure to war atrocities on children, including posttraumatic stress reactions (with the highest PTSD scores among children who reported hurting someone else) (Nader & Pynoos, 1993); and a study of 492 Israeli schoolchildren—who had to enter shelters or sealed rooms and carry gas masks continuously during repeated SCUD missile attacks—demonstrates that high-technology warfare and the threat of conventional, chemical, or biological missiles have marked psychological effects on children (Schwarzwald, Weisenberg, Waysman, Solomon, & Klingman, 1993).

The particular conditions of warfare may affect the level of stress that children experience. Masser (1992), reporting on Central American refugee children, maintained that guerrilla warfare is more stressful for children than conventional warfare: "The blurred distinction between friend and enemy, civilian and combatant, together with the ongoing, long-term nature of the fighting, engenders greater difficulty" (p. 442). A study of the emotional reaction of 480 children exposed to different levels of war stress in Croatia revealed that both refugees and local children showed more depressive symptoms than did children of the same age who were assessed before the war (Zivcic, 1993). The Croatian conflict was particularly stressful to children because it was unexpected and unpredictable.

Traumatization of Refugees

Posttraumatic stress disorders are endemic among refugee populations. Forced migration in particular causes serious trauma for individuals and families because "it removes from one's life all that is important and familiar: family, friends, language, culture" (Kahn, 1994, p. 21). Despite vast differences in their backgrounds and cultures, such refugees encounter similar traumatic experiences before and during escape, and they all suffer the stress of waiting for relocation: Women are often raped, and families are torn apart and often stranded without food or shelter

(National Association of Social Workers, 1990a). Resettlement stress has been labeled a form of chronic strain because its conditions are long term (Turner & Avison, 1990). Interviews conducted in 1984 with immigrants who moved to Los Angeles from Ethiopia, Eritrea, Cambodia, Vietnam, Iran, El Salvador, Guatemala, Armenia, and Russia—including Holocaust survivors—revealed that all had experienced various degrees of trauma and somatization. The result is often a rupture of ego cohesiveness that may express itself in various debilitating ways (Kahn, 1994).

Studies confirm a multitude of symptoms and high rates of PTSD among refugees, whether Central American children in Los Angeles (Masser, 1992), Cambodian adolescents who survived massive trauma as children (Realmuto et al., 1992), or refugee women in El Salvador (Bowan, Carscadden, Beighle, & Fleming, 1992). Although the nature of the trauma, the age of the victim, the individual's personality, and the community's response all play a role in the severity of symptoms, certain features are common to all sufferers of PTSD: reexperiencing the traumatic event, anxiety, flashbacks, psychic numbing, depression, isolation, hyperarousal, hyperalertness, and impairment of memory and concentration (National Association of Social Workers, 1990b).

Half of the world's refugees are children, many of whom suffered the trauma of war before becoming refugees. Research studies document the cumulative effect of war on children. For example, a study of Cambodian adolescents and young adults found that those who reported greater war trauma as children demonstrated a greater rate of PTSD diagnoses and symptoms as adolescents or young adults; they also were more vulnerable to the strains of resettlement in the United States and to depressive symptoms related to recent stressful events (Clark, Sack, and Goff, 1993). Other studies similarly show that adolescent and adult refugees from Cambodia have considerable PTSD symptoms and depression (Kinzie & Sack, 1991; Kroll et al., 1989).

High rates of psychological trauma in targeted groups within nations controlled by repressive regimes have also been reported by mental health practitioners in Latin America and in refugee communities in the United States and Canada (Carmack, 1992; Kordon, Edelman, & Equipo de Asistencia Psicol Ugica de Madres de Plaza de Mayo, 1987; Lira & Castillo, 1991; Reszczynski, Rojas, & Barcelo, 1991). For example, a study

of 203 Chilean children younger than 12 years of age whose fathers had
been detained or disappeared revealed traumatic family crises of more
than four years' duration:

> A cycle of hope and despair was repeated endlessly, draining and exhaust-
> ing the emotional reserves of everyone in the family. The normal psycho-
> logical process of mourning was arrested, and the reparation for the loss
> they had suffered was not possible. . . . The symptoms reported and ob-
> served were those of withdrawal (78 percent), depression (70 percent),
> intense generalized fear and fear triggered by specific environmental stimuli
> such as sirens, uniformed people, the sounds of automobile engines at
> night (78 percent), and loss of appetite and weight, sleep disturbances,
> regression in behavior and school performance, dependency and clinging
> behaviors toward their mothers in about half of the cases. The factors as-
> sociated with the severity of symptoms were younger age, long duration
> of exposure to trauma, family and social isolation (due to fear of friends'
> relatives and of stigma), and to inadequate or untrue explanations for the
> parental absence. (Allodi, 1980, p. 229)

Trauma is often the result of ethnic conflicts (see chapters 8 and 9).
The experiences of a social worker in Israel from 1976 to 1981, related in
"Trauma in Israel," illustrate several ramifications of ethnic-related
trauma.

Trauma in Israel

*In Israel I was first exposed to large populations of people—many of them
entering the country shortly before or during the time of my arrival—who
had experienced severe psychic trauma resulting from group conflict in their
countries of origin. There were several waves of immigration. For the most
part, Jews left the former Soviet Union, Arab lands, Ethiopia, and various
other trouble spots of Central Europe because of actual or feared persecution
for being Jewish. Many Argentineans fled their country either because of
persecution for being Jewish or for their political beliefs and actions. Jews
from South Africa and the former Southern Rhodesia emigrated to Israel
out of fear for their lives because of their involvement in antiapartheid political action or, conversely, because of threats against whites during a period of racial turmoil. There were also at this time about 25 people from
Vietnam who were rescued at sea in the 1970s by an Israeli ship. Making up
a large part of the population were former Holocaust survivors of the late
1940s migration as well as dislocated Palestinians who were feeling not only
grief and loss but also discrimination and disadvantage as members of an
"out group" in the society.*

I treated and supervised the treatment of those immigrants and refugees who were referred for social services by primary care physicians because of physical symptoms that exhibited no obvious physical basis. PTSD had not yet been identified. Primarily these ailments could be considered as conversion symptoms—i.e., psychic trauma residue converted into physical manifestations—and secondarily, the symptoms could provide the survivor with continuous proof of his or her very existence (Kinsler, 1984).

Among the Jews, there seemed to be more physical and psychological symptomatology (body aches, heart palpitations, gastrointestinal disorders, migraine headaches, depression, sleep disorders, and anxiety) in contrast to the Palestinians and Vietnamese. I speculated that this occurred because the Jewish immigrants were not permitted to mourn. They were told they were home, it was all okay now, and to forget about the past. They were frequently given new names, professions, and identities in addition to absorbing a new language, culture, and environment.

In addition, Holocaust survivors were presenting themselves at the clinics with a series of physical and emotional complaints 40 years after their trauma. This condition has been called Post Traumatic Stress Disorder Delayed. In retrospect, they felt that the mental health profession had let them down decades ago when they needed to talk it out. A common grievance was "I don't think they were able to handle the horrors I needed to describe."

Heightened contentions and paranoia emerged among the various Jewish subgroups who lived in close proximity to one another. In their frustration about not being familiar with or having mastery over their new environment, one group blamed the other for their respective anguish and the other group blamed the newcomers for "ruining the country." Although violence between groups was minimal, domestic violence increased. At the time I left Israel, there were two shelters for battered women. Perhaps—because historically Jews have been loath to fight one another—the violence was acted out in the family and the military or turned inward, causing somatization.

Source: Kahn, A. B. (1994). *Violence and social development between conflicting groups* (paper prepared for the California NASW Center on Violence, Development, and Trauma and submitted to the NASW Violence and Development Project, Washington, DC), pp. 18–20. Malibu, CA: Author. Adapted and used with permission of author.

Trauma and Victims of Torture

It is clear from the foregoing discussion that many refugees have been traumatized by war. Many also flee from countries where torture is a widespread practice. Torture is "the deliberate, intentional, and systematic infliction of pain and suffering, either physical or mental, at the hands or the instigation of public officials or others in positions of authority, with the purpose of extracting a confession, punishing, or intimidating the person or others" (Garcia-Peltoniemi & Jaranson, 1989, p. 5). The practice of torture is a particularly sinister form of violence at the institutional level. Regardless of age, gender, or culture, torture always involves the corrupt, abominable—and systematic and strategic—use of power aimed at rendering the victim defenseless and destroying human capacity to take meaningful action (Garcia-Peltoniemi & Jaranson, 1989).

Unfortunately, torture is not an aberration—it has been documented in more than 90 countries (Roth, Lunde, Boysen, & Genefke, 1987). More and more, refugees endure torture before leaving their homelands (Goldfeld, Mollica, Pesavento, & Faraone, 1988). For example, refugees fleeing Indochina in the 1980s often endured torture, as well as starvation and forced separation; Americas Watch and Amnesty International, among other groups, have condemned the Salvadoran government for its human rights abuses—including torture—during and following the 1989 civil war (National Association of Social Workers, 1990a).

Children who are tortured early in life are profoundly traumatized. A study of the effects of torture on Chilean children, for example, revealed anxiety, sensitivity to loud noises, insomnia, nightmares, enuresis, introversion, aggressiveness, behavior problems, and somatic complaints (Cohn, Holzer, Koch, & Severin, 1980).

Sexual violence is often associated with the torture and detention of women and female adolescents (Goldfeld et al., 1988). Torture of women invariably includes an attempt to destroy their female identity, and the victims are made to feel ashamed of their womanhood in every possible way. The magnitude of this problem is likely to be underappreciated because women often do not seek treatment—doing so is tantamount to admitting to having been raped, which results in ostracism and further isolation from their own communities (Garcia-Peltoniemi & Jaranson, 1989).

In addition to suffering psychological trauma, torture victims may also have suffered head injuries and severe malnutrition, both of which can produce later neurological and psychiatric difficulties (Holtan, 1986).

Culture is also a significant dimension in understanding torture-related trauma. The cultural context in which torture occurs, the political situation in the country of origin, and the refugee's political beliefs influence the victim's interpretation of the experience. Garcia-Peltoniemi and Jaranson (1989) described three distinct groups. The first, best exemplified by Cambodian refugees, come from areas in which torture and organized violence were so frequent that they attained ethnocidal proportions reminiscent of the Holocaust. People in this group typically are unable to find the words to describe the experience of torture; they are unable also to define themselves as victims in need of or deserving treatment; moreover, karmic or fatalistic beliefs prevent the community from offering much support to those afflicted with psychological symptoms. The second group, best exemplified by South African and Latin American refugees, consists of people who are articulate and outspoken about the political or religious values that led to their arrest and subsequent torture by an oppressive government. They tend to see themselves as both needing and deserving treatment, and they often conceptualize treatment in political terms. The third group includes ethnic minorities from countries in the grip of a civil war, such as Ethiopia and El Salvador. For many in this group, it is not only the torture experience itself but their current state of exile that is most painful (Garcia-Peltoniemi & Jaranson, 1989).

Incidents of torture in countries under repressive regimes are fairly well publicized, but it is less well known that torture is not unheard of in the United States, particularly in the prison system. In fact, a Human Rights Watch investigation of more than 20 prisons and jails in New York, California, Florida, and Tennessee showed extensive abuses of the minimum standards for the treatment of prisoners established by the United Nations. Despite countless lawsuits, inhumane treatment amounting to torture continues at both state and federal facilities (Burkhalter, 1995). A nurse's account of an incident at a prison in northern California provided an illustration:

A mentally ill inmate named ___ had his hands cuffed behind his back by a group of corrections officers and was forced into a tub of 145-degree water. [The nurse] heard an officer say of the [inmate], who is African American, "It looks like we're going to have a white boy before this is through; his skin is so dirty and rotten it's all fallen off." She saw that _____'s skin had indeed peeled off and was hanging in clumps around his legs. When officers attempted to return the prisoner to his cell, over the protests of the medical staff, he collapsed and was taken to the emergency room. (Burkhalter, 1995, p. 17)

Unresolved Trauma Perpetuates a Cycle of Violence

The cycle of violence has now been well established in studies and treatment of family violence, spouse abuse, elder abuse, and child abuse (Florida NASW Center, 1994). Considered in the context of a cycle of violence, apparently irrational violent acts are often revealed to be the symptoms of painful, embarrassing, and shameful experiences and secrets caused by unresolved, violence-related trauma (Kordon & Edelman, 1986).

The cycle of violence repeats itself endlessly, as may the behavior of perpetrators and victims of trauma. Almost without exception, the life histories of perpetrators show evidence of earlier incidents of victimization. Human beings intuitively try to overcome devastating assaults to self-esteem, which are among the psychological consequences of an inability to protect self and vulnerable others. Unless trust is restored through social processes of psychological healing, striving to overcome powerlessness may impel a victim to test out similar situations again, either by provoking repeated abuse or by reversing the roles so that the victim becomes a victimizer. This is particularly true when the person encounters new stress, which is intensified by the existing stress of the unresolved trauma. It is then that repressed events are likely to reappear through a reenactment of the scene, but this time with the victim becoming the perpetrator of the violent act. Such role reversal is a critical dynamic in the cycle of violence.

Those who are familiar with the dynamics of family violence and child abuse understand that the seeds of violence are sown during childhood. Children who grow up in families and neighborhoods where chaos and aggression are part of everyday interactions are more likely than others to find violence acceptable and to become abusive spouses and parents. It has been maintained that physical punishment of children by their parents is the greatest single risk factor for the victim of this abuse later becoming a perpetrator of violence (National Committee to Prevent Child Abuse, 1994).

There is considerable support for the notion that violent parents— whether child abusers or advocates of corporal punishment—produce violent children and violent teachers produce violent students (Morales, 1994). This is particularly significant information in that physical punishment of children by their parents is legal in all 50 states and corporal punishment in schools is legal in all but 11 states. A random sample of families in the United States revealed that 97 percent of parents of three- and four-year-old children used corporal punishment; a replication study done 10 years later found that 20 percent of parents began hitting their children before the age of one (Morales, 1994). Every state in the country attempts to protect children from child abuse, but the fact is that children two to five years old are unable to distinguish between child abuse and corporal punishment—both are traumatic for the child, and both fix the child in the cycle of violence (Morales, 1994).

Violence-Related Trauma and Development: Making the Connections

The effect of violence-related trauma on human, social, and economic development cannot be overestimated. Unresolved trauma—whether the result of exposure to the trauma of war, high-crime neighborhoods, political or ethnic conflict, racism, sexism, or poverty—often leads to the developmental impairment of individuals (Garbarino, 1993). When many primary and secondary trauma victims are developmentally impaired, impeded in providing support to family and friends, or engaged in self-destructive and other destructive behaviors, the adverse effects on society are inevitable and overwhelming. The contributions that people impaired by unresolved trauma might have made in many arenas—the family, the community, the workforce, and so on—are lost to society. The costs to society are measured not only in lost contributions but also in the price paid for construction and maintenance of jails, hospitals, detention centers, and so on. The rest of this chapter deals with the ways in which unresolved trauma from violence impedes development.

Violence-Related Trauma Impedes Human Development

Although trauma symptoms may be manifested differently according to developmental stage, gender, culture, and other factors, the long-term effect on individuals and families is the same: The survivors are left with less fulfilling lives and their potentiality and productivity are impeded. Maldeveloped or underdeveloped—that is, damaged—individuals do not have the resources to participate in positive, effective ways in the development of their communities.

Trauma impedes individual development.   From birth to death, human beings develop and fulfill their potential by accomplishing a series of age-related tasks or challenges. Therefore it is not surprising to find evidence that reactions to trauma differ according to a person's developmental stage at the time of the trauma (Bedics et al., 1991). When adults are exposed to trauma—assuming that they were in a steady state before the disruption—their functioning may decline but, once the trauma has subsided, they may return to their previous level of functioning.

The process differs for children, however. Trauma in a child does not interrupt a steady state; rather, it interrupts a growth process and interferes with the acquisition of new developmental skills. Thus, during a period of trauma, children do not simply decline in functioning as adults do; they also fail to acquire skills they might have gained during that period. After the trauma subsides, they need not only to return to their previous functioning level but also to make up for lost time and acquire the skills they did not acquire because of the trauma (Masser, 1992).

PTSD work with veterans of the Vietnam War has yielded some valuable insights about the effect of trauma on adolescents (the average age of soldiers of that war was 19.6 years). Developmentally, teenagers' task is to solidify values and stabilize personality. When adolescents are exposed to or are participants in violence—whether in war or in violent inner-city environments—the conflicting roles of combatant and survivor, and the conflicting values associated with such roles, cause a distinct disruption of their development at this stage of life (Bedics et al., 1991). Research evidence suggests that unresolved guilt appears among the characteristics of some Vietnam veterans with PTSD; soldiers who were younger and in lower ranks were more vulnerable to PTSD (Bedics et al., 1991; Murray, 1992).

Trauma impedes the development of families.   Just as violence-related trauma impedes the development of individuals throughout the life cycle, it also affects the family life cycle (Scaturo & Hayman, 1992). When individuals and entire families are exposed to external traumas—such as war, civil strife, oppression, poverty, forced migration, and political torture—there are long-term reverberating psychological effects on the family that impede successful completion of tasks at each stage of the family life cycle (Scaturo & Hayman, 1992). The first stage of the family life cycle—courtship and mate selection—usually takes place in late adolescence and young adulthood, a time that typically coincides with the age of military conscription. The traumatic experiences of the person in combat and their emotional consequences "are a genuine disruption of the couple's primary emotional attachment and bond" (Scaturo & Hayman, 1992, p. 275). At each subsequent stage of the family life cycle—marriage, childbirth and child rearing, midlife, children leaving home, and retirement—the effects of trauma are felt. Scaturo and Hayman believe that the emotional numbing of PTSD as a psychological defense against traumatic recollection is felt more acutely in the struggle to bond and remain attached to one's children than in any other area of family life. "Despite a strong need for intimacy with their children, witnessing the brutality of war upon children and refugees in a combat zone, regardless of the particular war or era of military services, seems to have left a certain type of emotional scar upon and distance among many former combatants which may include a range of reactions" (p. 279) to their children that serve as barriers to normal child development processes.

Violence within the family itself is traumatizing and impedes normal family development. Women who are victims of domestic violence are significantly at risk for developing PTSD, which impedes the accomplishment of family developmental tasks (Astin, Lawrence, & Foy, 1993). PTSD symptoms in children who are victims of abuse, incest, and family dysfunction have been widely documented by researchers (Eth & Pynoos, 1985; Frederick, 1985; Wolfe, Gentile, & Wolfe,

1989). Children who were very young and preverbal at the time of the trauma may show PTSD symptoms years later, even into adulthood—thus affecting their future family life as well (Bedics et al., 1991).

Unresolved Trauma Impedes Moral Development

Even the many possible developmental impairments resulting from unresolved trauma do not constitute the whole story. Studies of traumatized children also point to the role of social crisis in either impeding or stimulating moral development.

Children can overcome traumatic situations in healthy ways.   Children do survive the danger of war and violence and overcome its challenges, particularly if they get security from a primary adult in their lives. For example, Anna Freud's reports on children exposed to trauma during World War II show that children in the care of their own mothers or a familiar mother substitute were not psychologically devastated by wartime experiences, principally because their caregivers maintained day-to-day care routines and projected high morale (A. Freud & Burlingham, 1943). A similar theme emerges from a study of children exposed to violence in a public housing project in Chicago (Dubrow & Garbarino, 1988); although mothers identified shootings as their major worry about their children's safety, they also sought to use a variety of coping mechanisms to protect them from immediate harm. However, none of this suggests that children escape unscathed; in fact, there is considerable evidence of chronic and profound problems even for children who receive compensatory care.

Violence-related trauma can socialize children into a culture of violence.   Being a child in a highly stressful environment—including economically stressful situations of chronic, even if not acute, danger—can lead to long-term mental health concerns, even when the child has parental protection (Garbarino, 1993). In their efforts to protect their children from the negative influences and dangers of high-crime neighborhoods, parents may adopt child-rearing strategies that impede normal development in children. For example, fear felt by parents in high-crime environments may manifest itself as a restrictive, punitive style of discipline (including physical assault), which may well produce heightened aggression and acceptance of violence as the "modus operandi for social control" (Garbarino, 1993, p. 109). In turn, a young person can rationalize his or her gang's use of force as an effective tactic for gaining power and influence. Although parents' attempts to protect their children from the consequences of self-destructive behaviors are well intentioned—and may appear to be eminently sensible as well—the side effects may be detrimental to a child's moral development in the long run. In other words, traumatized children who are socialized into a culture of violence may accept violence as part of their moral foundation.

Identification with the aggressor and truncated moral development. Another way children adapt to traumatic situations is to identify with the aggressors and model themselves after those powerful, aggressive individuals and groups in their environment that cause the danger in the first place. Chronic violence—coupled with a political ideology favoring violence—may be associated with truncated moral development characterized by a vendetta mentality. Research in Northern Ireland and the Middle East, for example, reveals that children who lived in violently conflictual communities remained stuck at more primitive stages of moral development than that of children whose communities were not so conflictual (Fields, 1987). When adults in the community do not model higher-order moral reasoning or are intimidated if they try to do so, then the process of moral truncation that is common to situations of violent conflict can proceed unimpeded. Fields (1987) concluded that when children are exposed to danger deriving from political conflict in the context of antidemocratic and authoritarian institutions (including the family), the result is likely to be truncated moral reasoning, particularly among boys. Garbarino (1993) pointed out by way of illustration that this appears to have happened in Northern Ireland, where both Protestant and Catholic teachers learned that attempts to engage their students in dialogue that could promote higher-order moral reasoning would be squashed by extremist elements.

Adapting to violence by identifying with the aggressor has also been cited in case studies of people who have been taken hostage and who subsequently show positive regard for their captors, abused children who have strong attachments to their abusive parents, and former cult members who are loyal to malevolent cult leaders (Dutton & Painter, 1993). The concept of identification with the aggressor "predicts that in situations of extreme power imbalance, where a person of high power is intermittently punitive, subjugated persons might adopt the dominator's assumed perspective of themselves, and internalize or redirect aggression toward others similar to themselves" (Dutton & Painter, 1993, p. 107). Dutton and Painter (1993) described the "traumatic bonding" of battered women with their batterers thus: "As the power imbalance magnifies, the subjugated person feels more negative in their self-appraisal, more incapable of fending for themselves, and is, thus, increasingly more in need of the dominator. This cycle of relationship-produced dependency and lowered self-esteem is repeated, eventually creating a strong affective bond from the low to high power person" (p. 107).

Unresolved Trauma and Violence against Self

The long-term, destructive effects of unresolved emotional trauma on psychosocial and cognitive development are such that former victims of violence may victimize themselves further. All kinds of trauma, regardless of the precipitating event or situation, evoke self-protective responses. Fight-or-flight responses may work initially for self-protection but, unless accompanied by a process of emotional healing, they are likely to become ingrained and produce self-defeating patterns of behavior.

The flight response to extreme stress means avoiding painful memories, and when avoidance is used as a defense against the reactive shame of self-blame, trauma is frequently hidden and denied (Figley, 1978, 1985; Gil, 1983; Herman, 1992; Schaef, 1987; Van der Kolk, 1987; Waites, 1993). When the truth about a traumatic event and its associated emotions are not communicated to others, both event and feelings may become buried and inaccessible to consciousness. However, even when there is no conscious awareness and recall, the frightening experience is recorded in long-term memory and remains there with all the feelings and fears of the original recording (Penfield, 1975; Pribam, 1971, 1986). The denial mechanism replaces actions that would mobilize support, address the painful realities, and promote healing.

Toward Healing

When survivors of trauma try to avoid the pain embedded in their memories—involuntarily or on purpose—they may also lose the ability to observe and cope with current reality. Long-term destructive effects on psychosocial and cognitive development of an individual or family may include a high risk for addiction to mood-altering substances or behaviors that may alleviate a sense of inner emptiness and provide relief from tension (Nakken, 1988; Williams, 1992).

Whenever someone who has been a victim of violence maintains silence and does not respond emotionally or verbalize feelings of fear, fright, sadness or desperation, that person is at risk of developing emotional defenses that tend to become rigid and chronic. That person is therefore likely to have—perhaps for a lifetime—serious emotional or psychological problems, or both. The next chapter explores approaches that go beyond potentially damaging attempts to avoid the effects of trauma—approaches that in fact help people heal from trauma and its consequences.

References

Allodi, F. (1980). The psychiatric effects in children and families of victims of political persecution and torture. *Danish Medical Bulletin, 27*(5), 229–232.

American Psychiatric Association (APA). (1994). *Diagnostic and statistical manual of mental disorders* (4th ed.). Washington, DC: Author.

Angelou, M. (1970). *I know why the caged bird sings.* New York: Random House.

Angelou, M. (1978). *And still I rise.* New York: Random House.

Astin, M. C., Lawrence, K. J., & Foy, D. W. (1993). Posttraumatic stress disorder among battered women: Risk and resiliency factors. *Violence and Victims, 8*(1), 17–28.

Bedics, B. C., Rappe, P. T., & Rappe, L. O. (1991). Preparing BSW professionals for identifying and salvaging victims of post traumatic stress disorder. In B. Shank (Ed.), *B.S.W. education for practice: Reality and fantasy* (pp. 94–100). St. Paul, MN: University of St. Thomas.

Beeghley, L. (1989). *The structure of social stratification in the United States.* Needham Heights, MA: Allyn & Bacon.

Bowan, D., Carscadden, L., Beighle, K., & Fleming, I. (1992). Post-traumatic stress disorder among Salvadoran women: Empirical evidence and description of treatment. *Women and Therapy, 13*(1–2), 267–279.

Braun, D. (1991). *The rich get richer: The rise of income inequality in the United States and the world.* Chicago: Nelson-Hall.

Burkhalter, H. J. (1995). Torture in U.S. prisons. *Nation, 261*(1), 17–18.

California NASW Center on Violence, Development, and Trauma. (1994). *Healing a traumatized community: Lessons from the Atlantic Coast of Nicaragua* (report submitted to the NASW Violence and Development Project, Washington, DC). Sacramento, CA: Author.

Carmack, R. M. (Ed.). (1992). *Harvest of violence: The Maya Indians and the Guatemalan crisis.* Norman: University of Oklahoma Press.

Carnegie Corporation. (1994, April). *Starting points: Meeting the needs of our youngest children* (report of the Carnegie Task Force on Meeting the Needs of Young Children). New York: Author.

Clark, G., Sack, W., & Goff, B. (1993). Three forms of stress in Cambodian adolescent refugees. *Journal of Abnormal Child Psychology, 21*(1), 65–77.

Cohn, J., Holzer, K.I., Koch, L., & Severin, B. (1980, November). Children and torture. *Danish Medical Bulletin, 27,* 238–239.

Dubrow, N., & Garbarino, J. (1988). Living in the war zone: Mothers and young children in a public housing project. *Child Welfare, 68*(1), 3–20.

Dutton, D. G., & Painter, S. (1993). Emotional attachments in abusive relationships: A test of traumatic bonding theory. *Violence and Victims, 8*(2), 105–120.

Eth, S., & Pynoos, R. (Eds.). (1985). *Post traumatic stress disorder in children.* Washington, DC: American Psychiatric Press.

Fanon, F. (1968). *The wretched of the earth.* New York: Grove.

Fields, R. (1987, October 25). *Terrorized into terrorist: Sequelae of PTSD in young victims.* Paper presented at the Meeting of the Society for Traumatic Stress Studies, New York.

Figley, C. R. (1978). *Stress disorders among Vietnam veterans.* New York: Brunner/ Mazel.

Figley, C. R. (Ed.). (1985). *Trauma and its wake: The study and treatment of post-traumatic stress disorder.* New York: Brunner/Mazel.

Figley, C. R. (1986). *Trauma and its wake* (Vol. 2). New York: Brunner/Mazel.

Figley, C. R. (1995). *Compassion fatigue: Secondary traumatic stress disorder—Theory, research, and treatment.* New York: Brunner/Mazel.

Figley, C. R., & Leventman, S. (Eds.). (1980). *Stranger at home: Vietnam veterans since the war.* New York: Brunner/Mazel.

Florida NASW Center on Violence, Development, and Trauma. (1994). [Report submitted to the NASW Violence and Development Project, Washington, DC.] Tallahassee, FL: Author.

Frederick, C. (1985). Children traumatized by physical abuse. In S. Eth & R. Pynoos (Eds.), *Post traumatic stress disorder in children* (pp. 73–99). Washington, DC: American Psychiatric Press.

Freire, P. (1970). *Pedagogy of the oppressed* (M. B. Ramos, Trans.). New York: Herder & Herder.

Freud, A., & Burlingham, D. (1943). *War and children.* New York: Ernest Willard.

Freud, S., Ferenczi, S., Abraham, K., Simmel, E., & Jones, E. (1921). *Psycho-analysis and the war neurosis.* New York: International Psychoanalytic.

Garbarino, J. (1993). Children's response to community violence: What do we know? *Infant Mental Health Journal, 14*(2), 103–114.

Garcia-Peltoniemi, R. E., & Jaranson, J. (1989, December 1). *A multidisciplinary approach to the treatment of torture victims.* Paper presented at the Second International Conference of Centres, Institutions and Individuals Concerned with the Care of Victims of Organized Violence, San Jose, Costa Rica.

Gil, E. (1983). *Outgrowing the pain: A book for and about adults abused as children.* New York: Dell Publishers.

Goldfeld, A. E., Mollica, R. F., Pesavento, B. H., & Faraone, S. V. (1988). The physical and psychological sequelae of torture: Symptomatology and diagnosis. *Journal of the American Medical Association, 259*(18), 2725–2729.

Grof, S. (with Bennett, H. Z.). (1992). *The holotropic mind.* New York: HarperCollins.

Grutsky, D. B. (Ed.). (1994). *Social stratification in sociological perspective: Class, race & gender.* Boulder, CO: Westview Press.

Herman, J. L. (1992). *Trauma and recovery.* New York: Basic Books.

Holtan, N. R. (1986). *When refugees are victims of torture.* Washington, DC: U.S. Committee for Refugees.

Janet, P. (1891). Étude sur un cas d'aboulie et d'idées fixes. *Revue Philosophique, 31.* Translated and cited in H. Ellenberger (1970), *The discovery of the unconscious.* New York: Basic Books.

Kahn, A. B. (1994, August 22). *Violence and social development between conflicting groups* (paper prepared for the California NASW Center on Violence, Development, and Trauma). Malibu, CA: Author.

Kardiner, A., & Spiegel, H. (1947). *The traumatic neuroses of war.* New York: Hoeber.

Kinsler, F. (1984, November 8). *Surviving and overcoming trauma.* Paper presented at the Serving Survivors Conference, Los Angeles, November 8, 1984.

Kinzie, J. D., & Sack, W. (1991). Severely traumatized Cambodian children: Research findings and clinical implications. In F. L. Ahearn, Jr., and J. Athey (Eds.), *Refugee children: Theory, research, and services* (pp. 92–106). Baltimore: Johns Hopkins University Press.

Kordon, D. R., & Edelman, L. I. (1986). *Efectos psicologicos de la represion politica.* Buenos Aires, Argentina: Sudamericana/Planeta.

Kordon, D. R., Edelman, L. I., & Equipo de Asistencia PsicolUgica de Madres de Plaza de Mayo. (1987). *Efectos psicologicos de la represion politica* (2nd ed.). Buenos Aires, Argentina: Sudamericana/Planeta.

Kroll, J., Habenicht, M., MacKenzie, T., Yang, M., Chan, S., Nguyen, T., Ly, M., Phommasonvanh, B., Nguyen, H., Vang, Y., Souvannasoth, L., & Cabrugao, R. (1989). Depression and post traumatic stress disorder in Southeast Asian refugees. *American Journal of Psychiatry, 146,* 1592–1597.

Laing, R. D. (1965). *The divided self.* Baltimore: Penguin.

Laing, R. D., & Esterson, A. (1970). *Sanity, madness and the family.* London: Tavistock.

Lindemann, E. (1944, September). Symptomatology and management of acute grief. *American Journal of Psychiatry, 101,* 141–148.

Lira, E., & Castillo, M. (1991). *Psicologia de la Amenaza Politica y del Miedo.* Santiago, Chile: Instituto Latinoamericano de Salud Mental y Derechos Humanos.

Lynn, S. J., & Rhue, J. W. (Eds.). (1994). *Dissociation: Clinical and theoretical perspectives.* New York: Guilford Press.

Masser, D. (1992). Psychosocial functioning of Central American refugee children. *Child Welfare, 71*(5), 439–456.

Memmi, A. (1965). *The colonizer and the colonized.* New York: Orion.

Miller, A. (1984). *For your own good: Hidden cruelty in child-rearing and the roots of violence* (H. Hannum & H. Hannum, Trans.). New York: Farrar, Straus & Giroux.

Miller, A. (1986). *Thou shalt not be aware: Society's betrayal of the child.* New York: Meridian.

Morales, A. T. (1994). *Homicide prevention and social work* (paper submitted with the Report from the California NASW Center on Violence, Development, and Trauma to the NASW Violence and Development Project, Washington, DC). Los Angeles: Author.

Murray, J. (1992). Post-traumatic stress disorder: A review. *Genetic, Social, and General Psychology Monographs, 118*(3), 313–330.

Nader, K., & Pynoos, R. (1993). A preliminary study of PTSD and grief among the children of Kuwait following the Gulf crisis. *British Journal of Clinical Psychology, 32,* 407–416.

Nakken, C. (1988). *The addictive personality: Understanding compulsion in our lives.* New York: HarperCollins.

National Association of Social Workers. (1990a, March). *Fact sheet on refugees.* Silver Spring, MD: Author.

National Association of Social Workers. (1990b, March). *Fact sheet on trauma.* Silver Spring, MD: Author.

National Committee to Prevent Child Abuse. (1994). Addressing the issue of violence. *Memorandum, 1*(3), p. 1.

Penfield, W. (1975). *The mystery of the mind: A critical study of consciousness and the human brain.* Princeton, NJ: Princeton University Press.

Pribam, K. H. (1971). *Languages of the brain: Experimental paradoxes and principles in neuropsychology.* Englewood Cliffs, NJ: Prentice Hall.

Pribam, K. (1986). The cognitive revolution and mind/brain issues. *American Psychologist, 41*(5), 507–520.

Punamaki, R.-L. (1982). Childhood in the shadow of war: A psychosocial study on attitudes and emotional life of Israeli and Palestinian children. *Current Research on Peace and Violence, 1,* 26–40.

Ramsay, R. (1990). Post-traumatic stress disorder: A new clinical entity? *Journal of Psychosomatic Research, 34*(4), 355–365.

Realmuto, G. M., Masten, A., Carole, L. F., Hubbard, J., Groteluschen, A., & Chun, B. (1992). Adolescent survivors of massive childhood trauma in Cambodia: Life events and current symptoms. *Journal of Traumatic Stress, 5*(4), 589–598.

Reiman, J. H. (1984). *The rich get richer and the poor get prison* (2nd ed.). New York: Macmillan.

Reszczynski, K., Rojas, P., & Barcelo, P. (1991). *Tortura y resistencia en Chile: Estudio medico-politico.* Santiago, Chile: Editorial Emision.

Roth, E. F., Lunde, I., Boysen, G., & Genefke, I. K. (1987). Torture and its treatment. *American Journal of Public Health, 77*(11), 1404–1406.

Satir, V. (1976). *Conjoint family therapy: A guide to theory and technique* (Rev. ed.). Palo Alto, CA: Science & Behavior Books.

Save the Children. (1994, November). *Children at war.* London: Author.

Scaturo, D., & Hayman, P. (1992). The impact of combat trauma across the family life cycle: Clinical considerations. *Journal of Traumatic Stress, 5*(2), 273–288.

Schaef, A. W. (1987). *When society becomes an addict.* New York: Harper & Row.

Schwarzwald, J., Weisenberg, M., Waysman, M., Solomon, Z., & Klingman, A. (1993). Stress reaction of school-age children to the bombardment by SCUD missiles. *Journal of Abnormal Psychology, 102*(3), 404–410.

Selye, H. (1956). *The stress of life.* New York: McGraw-Hill.

Society for Traumatic Stress Studies. (1989). *The initial report of the Presidential Task Force on Curriculum, Education and Training.* Dubuque, IA: Kendall/Hunt Publishing.

Sonnenberg, S., Blank, A. S., Jr., & Talbott, J. A. (Eds.). (1985). *The trauma of war: Stress and recovery in Vietnam veterans*. Washington, DC: American Psychiatric Press.

Turner, R. J., & Avison, W. R. (1990). Sources of attenuation in the stress-distress relationship: An evaluation of modest innovations in the application of event checklists. In J. Greeley & P. Leaf (Eds.), *Research in community mental health* (Vol. 7, pp. 265–300). Greenwich, CT: JAI Press.

Van der Kolk, B. A. (Ed.). (1987). *Psychological trauma*. Washington, DC: American Psychiatric Association.

Van Soest, D., and Bryant, S. (1995). Violence reconceptualized for social work: The urban dilemma. *Social Work, 40*, 549–557.

Waites, E. A. (1993). *Trauma and survival: Post-traumatic and dissociative disorders in women*. New York: W. W. Norton.

Williams, C. (with Laird, R.). (1992). *No hiding place: Empowerment and recovery for our troubled communities*. New York: HarperCollins.

Wolfe, V., Gentile, C., & Wolfe, D. (1989). The impact of sexual abuse on children: A PTSD formulation. *Behavior Therapy, 20*, 215–228.

Zivcic, I. (1993). Emotional reactions of children to war stress in Croatia. *Journal of the American Academy of Child and Adolescent Psychiatry, 32*(4), 709–713.

Chapter 13

Toward Solution: Approaches to Healing from Violence-Related Trauma

Coauthored by Arline Prigoff, PhD

O nly healing can interrupt the cycle of violence, whether domestic violence in a family or intergroup warfare in a nation. This chapter examines ways that communities in the global South and the global North are healing from violence-related trauma, and it outlines steps people worldwide can take for healing and recovery. These beliefs are inherent:

- We have much to learn from strategies of people and communities in the global South who are working toward healing and achieving justice and equity as an antidote to violence-related trauma.
- All levels of prevention and intervention are required to counter and alleviate the residual, long-term effects of violence-related trauma.
- The most effective way to intervene is to ameliorate the factors causing violence through the promotion of sustainable human development, with an emphasis on eliminating oppression and inequity. This requires empowerment and advancement of individuals, families, and communities, particularly among sectors of the population that have been politically, economically, culturally, or socially marginalized and stigmatized.

Much understanding about how to facilitate healing has been gained from community work with trauma victims in both the United States and countries in the global South. In the United States, self-help groups and community-based service organizations that work with people who have been traumatized have given us new perspectives on the treatment of emotional problems. In the global South, ethnic communities have found unique ways to heal from loss and trauma through rituals and

---

Arline Prigoff, PhD, is professor and coordinator of community government relations, Division of Social Work, California State University, Sacramento.

traditions (California NASW Center, 1994). This chapter presents findings from some of these approaches to healing from violence-related trauma.

Healing through Personal and Community Empowerment

Productive methods of healing involve both personal and community empowerment, with restoration of pride and dignity and of self-validation and self-help as the basis of healing at both levels. Community empowerment approaches enable individuals, families, and communities to make peace with the past, regain control of their lives, and rebuild. Through community ritual, ceremonies, and methods of healing that build rapport and trust and promote supportiveness and communication skills, the destructive consequences of violence-related trauma can begin to be erased. The context within which individuals; families; and religious, national, or ethnic groups can maintain or regain vitality and health is self-affirmation of a community, the power and strength of its people revealed in their survival as they confront the truth of historic suffering.

Five steps are important to rebuilding a safe, caring context for living: (1) becoming aware of anger in response to violation of personal or group boundaries; (2) pursuing full disclosure of the truth in regard to past violent and abusive events; (3) expressing grief at irredeemable losses; (4) making an empowering and spiritual decision to assume responsibility—by self or community—through self-help, self-control, and self-expression; and (5) taking personal or community action for self-determination, with self-disciplined advocacy and assertiveness (California NASW Center, 1994). What follows is discussion of critical aspects of the process: speaking the truth, developing trust, grieving, and community development actions.

The Importance of Speaking the Truth

An empowerment-based approach to healing from violence-related trauma requires that the truth about historic experiences be revealed. The true history of events, which is essential for healthy revitalization, is based on the perceptions and emotional memories of survivors whose human rights have been violated. To be conscious of one's experiences—

without hiding the facts from others—and to tell the truth constitute the best answer to pathology and the preventive way to maintain mental health.

Thinking and speaking about traumatic experiences are important in the empowerment process. When painful or frightening memories and the feelings associated with them are shared with other people in communicative dialogue, conscious awareness and reality testing are set in motion. Through disclosure and sharing, feelings of anxiety and powerlessness in response to those events are likely to be defused and diminished over time; they then become part of conscious life history and contribute to the development of identity. Feelings of grief over losses can be expressed and fears overcome.

Survival is a victory, and it is necessary to remember well those things that are dangerous in life's path. There are very important lessons to be learned in a confrontation with death or mortality, which add to the maturity and strength of survivors. Cognitive development and the capacity to analyze world problems grow through conscious examination of painful and destructive realities of life just as much as through the recognition of positive experiences.

The Need to Develop Trust

To search for forgotten and unhappy memories, confidentiality and trust are critical because trust of others has been destroyed for traumatized people. The inability to protect oneself, and the absence of protection by others, is likely to make one lose both trust in oneself and the sense of connection with one's own power. This pain and sadness of self and spirit must be faced. Traumatized people sometimes find it easier to share their feelings in a self-help group in which all other members were equally unable to protect themselves. The Institute of Noetic Sciences (1993) noted the benefits of therapeutic engagement in self-help groups:

> The growing evidence that health is directly related to social support and connectedness to others has led, in recent years, to the establishment of therapy groups for people with everything from drug dependency to cancer. Most such groups serve multiple purposes for their participants. . . . Members often reinforce behavioral change by offering praise, understanding, and encouragement. . . . The primary benefit of groups may be that they

allow people to share feelings and emotions, reducing social isolation and increasing the sense of connectedness that research has so clearly tied to health. . . . Groups often offer a way of establishing honest and open bonds with others. (p. 128)

The Necessity of Grieving

Grief work involves soul-searching issues related to life's meaning and goals that have been shattered by humiliation, abuse, and injustice and by laws that grant impunity to brutal people in positions of power (California NASW Center, 1995). "The Power of Mutual Support" illustrates this concept.

The Power of Mutual Support

Nancy Baron, a clinical psychologist based in Boston, has spent the last two years exploring ways in which psychology can be used to help war widows and children displaced by civil strife in Sri Lanka. She began by helping a small nongovernmental organization that was working with war widows, most of whom were under 30 years old, and some of whom had up to eight children. Many of the displaced families had been in camps for up to four years. "The [organization] knew they had to do skill development in order for these women to earn a living. What they didn't realize is that you can't do that when someone is not ready. These women have to change the way they think. They need to accept the fact that they need to become independent women," which for many was a sad turn of events in a culture that raised women to be dependent not only on a husband but on his extended family if something happened to him. "But in a war situation, the extended family is in as much difficulty as she is."

Baron realized that in Sri Lanka she was working with a society that does not give people an opportunity to express sadness. "The society tries to make people forget. We gave them an opportunity to explore their feelings." She started with a large group of perhaps 30 war widows from the four ethnic factions affected by the fighting. She used art to overcome language barriers. "They drew an early childhood that was happy, a young adulthood that was happy and then the beginning of trouble after the death of the husband." She broke the big group into smaller groups of four, one from each ethnic unit. "The women would be able to sit together and say that each group was responsible for killing each other's husbands. Everyone was crying, and they were able to hug each other."

One woman did not cry. She pointed to the scar on her face and said that her husband had stabbed her. She was relieved when he was killed. "The women empathized with her. They could talk about the experience."

"Sometimes when we look at the pictures of refugee camps, we look at the people and they look like poor, illiterate people. We lose sight of who they are. But when you sit in a room and let them speak, you realize they are intelligent women . . . incredibly perceptive and insightful in helping each other."

Baron, who is a consultant with the International Federation of Red Cross and Red Crescent Societies, says her goal is to help these women find ways to organize and help each other. They continue to meet for group self-help, creating links across ethnic divisions that someday could translate into political power once civil strife ends. She also has trained hundreds of preschool teachers in how to run play programs for children and how to teach parents to talk to children about loss. "The war widows were not telling the children their fathers were dead," because they were reluctant to give the children any more pain. "I suggested the children already knew, and the mothers said, 'You're probably right.'" Baron created a storybook and discussion guide for adults to read to children to open the way for talking about death and the courage it takes to go on with life. She told a group of war widows, "In this society, the mother cries in one room, the father in another and the child in another room. I said I think we need to cry in the same room." They agreed with her.

The U.S. Agency for International Development has funded a program to train social workers to go into displacement camps to work with groups of 30 parents at a time and teach the concepts in Baron's book. "We teach them why you talk to children, why you tell the truth, why you need communication." She hopes this training program will be taken to Rwanda, where she says there may be as many as 40,000 children who have lost both parents and who have been exposed to traumas beyond the imagination of most Americans.

Relief efforts that fail to address the loss these children have suffered and the anger that is bound to be in them will be dangerously shortsighted. The U.S. Agency for International Development, along with the Defense Department, spent $78.3 million on relief efforts in Rwanda between April 6 and July 17. This first wave of help has gone to the basics such as medical supplies, food, and safety. "But after that," says Baron, "you have to look at the psycho-social needs. When children grow up in situations where they have suffered terrible trauma and stress and the future looks very bleak, if you're not careful, those children become angry enough to become the future revolutionaries."

Source: Mann, J. (1994, August 10). Learning to cry in the same room. *Washington Post*, p. E15. ©The Washington Post. Reprinted with permission.

For healing to occur, several emotional states in the grieving process must be encountered and expressed: (1) denial of the reality of permanent loss; (2) anger that accompanies growing awareness; (3) hope to reverse loss by magical bargaining; (4) depression that accompanies recognition of permanent loss; and, finally, (5) acceptance of loss that is resolved in a new identity (California NASW Center, 1995; Kubler-Ross, 1969, 1974).

Grief work with refugees and victims of violence in the global South involves methods different from those that helping professionals in the United States typically understand as posttraumatic stress disorder (PTSD) counseling. Metaphorical stories and cultural legends are instrumental in healing the wounds of traumatic experiences or other losses. Group activities—drama, dance, storytelling, artwork, music, and sand play—help rebuild community and repair losses of safety and trust. Community-based interventions are based on cultural rituals, community ceremonies, and communal spiritual experiences that confront death yet achieve survival—even rebirth—through identification with the spirit of the deceased and unity with a higher cosmic power.

Community Development Actions for Healing and Empowerment

When communities break down because of war, effective psychosocial intervention into war traumas begins (and may end) with community development in its fullest sense. Women in particular have experienced empowerment through the formation of new communities in which they share leadership and fill essential roles. Conscientization—wherein women both analyze and take action against political and economic oppression and gender subordination—is an important element in the empowerment process (Roe, 1992). Even social systems that are reestablished with known boundaries, social norms, and expectations often do not reflect the traditional power relationships of the past. When community development evolves thus, women, instead of being relegated to support positions, share with men in the generation of ideas, programs, and leadership.

The new communities take on various forms: they may be nuclear communities formed among internally displaced people in sprawling and impersonal barrios outside urban centers, refugee camps administered and maintained through self-governing work cooperatives, or entire villages of displaced people formed into base Christian communities where faith and community organizing go hand in hand. Displaced women in these communities create new definitions of mothering and care that in turn lead to collective actions to confront injustice. Examples include groups such as the Mothers and Grandmothers of the Plaza de Mayo in Argentina; the Association of Families of the Detained or Disappeared in Chile; the Mutual Support Group for Relatives of the Disappeared in Guatemala; and the Committee of Mothers and Relatives of Political Prisoners, the Disappeared, and the Assassinated in El Salvador (Roe, 1992).

Cooperative approaches in the global South that address the self-identified needs and priorities of those who have been violently displaced have also been quite successful. Psychologists working in a refugee camp in El Salvador, for example, reported positive psychosocial results from implementing such an approach (Roe, 1992). Cooperative arrangements covered such areas as child care, agriculture, food preparation, sewing, and carpentry. Responsibilities were distributed so that all contributed to the survival and well-being of the settlement. New arrivals were assimilated by providing them with integral roles in the community and an immediate peer group of cooperative members.

In some urban war zones in the United States—wracked by crime, violence, and underdevelopment—other forms of cooperative projects are being initiated to rebuild neighborhood communities. A Kansas City project illustrates such empowerment-based approaches to healing and rebuilding community. Neighbors in five underserved neighborhoods are engaged in a project funded by local people, organizations, and government that is putting neighbors back on the streets, at the windows, on the phones, and in the schools. Forty-two block leaders are "neighboring" young people who live nearby through offers of homework help, safe houses, sleepovers, dances, field trips, cooking classes, wake-up services, home visits, parent education, transportation, school advocacy, referrals, snacks, and guidance—a list of services that rivals many comprehensive social services programs. The block leaders are not staff (although they get 40 hours of training and $8 an hour for 12 hours a week)—they are neighbors, offering natural supports to other neighbors, being visible, acting as friends and guides to parents, reweaving the fabric of their communities. The lesson of rebuilding traumatized communities that they are learning is that, given recognition and resources, committed neighbors can reduce crime and rebuild community block by block (Pittman, 1995).

Healing Traumatized Children and Promoting Child Development

Children whose development is impaired by the traumatization of war and community violence begin anew the cycle of violence. Thus, it is imperative that we effectively address violence-related trauma in children. Acute danger and chronic danger require different interventions (Garbarino, 1993). When children face acute danger, the process of adjustment often requires only that reassurance be offered: "You are safe again; things are back to normal" (p. 106). This intervention works for normal children who had been leading normal lives.

However, children who are exposed to chronic danger that affects their daily social reality—danger such as war or unending community violence—are likely to make long-term accommodations that include persistent PTSD, alterations of personality, major changes in patterns of behavior, or ideological interpretations of the world that capitulate to ongoing danger. These developmentally impaired children need help so that they can heal. An interactive climate created by adults and endorsed—or at least not stifled—by the larger society through its political, educational, and religious institutions can stimulate a necessary process of moral development, if the child is free of debilitating psychopathology (Garbarino, 1993). Families can provide the emotional environment necessary for helping children make positive moral sense of danger and trauma; communities can carry the process to the next step of stimulating higher-order moral development by presenting a democratic milieu, such as in schools. If children are to be resilient in a climate of chronic violence, what is needed is a balance of social supports for parents and parental capacity to buffer social stress in their children's lives.

Games, visual images, and symbols have been effective in helping children speak without words about their trauma. Save the Children (1994) supports workshops in Angola, Mozambique, the West Bank and Gaza, Central America, Rwanda, and Bosnia to help teachers, social workers, and community workers develop skills in listening to and communicating with children who are victims of war and disaster. Unskilled volunteers are taught the principles and processes needed to care for traumatized children, including gaining their trust and helping them express their experiences through acting out games and stories, dance, drawing, and religious ceremony (Save the Children, 1994).

In some displaced communities, child development is an essential part of intervention. For example, in a refugee camp in El Salvador, parent education included child development and day care for children from birth to seven years; in another Salvadoran camp, a day care center for approximately 200 children from three months to five years of age was run by 17 mothers who had been trained in child education and child health. In the Philippines, parents are trained to be paraprofessionals and program designers for children who were traumatized by armed conflict; these parents not only intervene effectively in their children's lives but also are empowered by their knowledge that they are not helpless (Roe, 1992).

Community Organizing for Mental Health in Traumatized Communities

In traumatized communities—particularly during wartime—community-level interventions for broad and potentially mild problems may be more appropriate than individually oriented, Western-based mental health practices. Group-level interventions in such communities may be appropriate for some severe problems, whereas individual-level interventions may be appropriate for the most severe war-related difficulties. "Community level interventions draw on the premise that the breakdown of social structure may be a critical factor in determining the overall impact of war traumas on children and families. Because the social structure provides the norms and context for interpreting and understanding traumatic events and circumstances, interventions at the level of these community structures may provide a highly relevant, potentially effective vehicle for intervention" (Jensen & Shaw, 1993, p. 705).

Consciousness raising is an integral part of community building that awakens people to their capacity to actualize their own power and understanding. Communities can do a great deal to prevent the destructive consequences of trauma through campaigns of public education and truth speaking by community leaders (Prigoff, 1993). In planning and implementing programs for collective healing from emotional trauma through community mental health services, full disclosure of available facts about the traumatizing event and associated feelings is a crucial element for recovery.

As emphasized earlier, women play an important role in healing because of their investment in family and community life. A treatment program in El Salvador that emphasized women's roles serves as an illustration (Bowan, Carscadden, Beighle, & Fleming, 1992). The program was developed by a mental health team that recognized that individual talk-style therapies were beyond the means and realities of peasant women who struggle to maintain daily life in a war-torn country. The program had five specific goals: (1) to clearly associate symptoms to the traumatic event so that the women could understand that their PTSD symptoms were, in fact, a fairly normal reaction to an abnormal event—this understanding was facilitated by encouraging close, mutually supportive relationships in which women could talk to each other about their shared experiences, their lives before the trauma, and their current feelings; (2) to help women overcome the feelings of helplessness and loss of control over their lives that are common experiences with PTSD—the ability to help someone else was used as an effective way to reduce feelings of helplessness; (3) to reduce "survivor guilt" through helping others, so that the guilt experienced by those who survived events that killed others was lessened; (4) to lessen the anxiety and arousal that are common to PTSD—relaxation techniques such as massage and movement therapy were used in addition to the approaches already described; and (5) to help the women realize that, although their lives had changed dramatically, they were still the same people they were before the trauma.

Based on those five goals, several steps for community organizing were developed and put into a treatment manual. These steps include (1) identifying existing networks—family, workplace, schools, churches, informal gatherings—that could serve as sources of support; (2) identifying people in each of the networks to provide information on needs and problems within the network; (3) if the identified leaders seem agreeable, proposing group activities to them—for example, information groups about the various reactions to trauma and group sessions to help reduce feelings of shame or guilt about their problems; (4) encouraging women who had been through a common trauma to become united around a common goal, such as building a church or school, harvesting crops, or setting up a kitchen; and (5) offering nonverbal healing techniques, such as art therapy, to women who were experiencing trauma-related difficulties.

In "Trauma in El Salvador," Martha Bragin, a social worker with the New York City NASW Center on Violence, Development, and Trauma, describes what she learned from another community approach to trauma in El Salvador.

Trauma in El Salvador

In 1987, the Women's Association in El Salvador realized that children were being traumatized by witnessing their parents being killed or tortured and exposed to constant shelling in the night. The first thing they worried about was the future of the country. "We're building a new world and if we have children who have been raised since babies having their parents taken from them, seeing people tortured and killed, they are being brutalized." They worried that, with these things happening to them and with no intervention, these children could not take on the task of making a humane society as adults. And, of course, they worried about the communities. They began to see the mental health symptoms among children in particularly bad circumstances. . . . They wanted some simple technique to help them. So they invited a representative of MADRE to a Peace Camp and I went.

From the work we did at the Peace Camp, we developed a two-pronged program. One of the things we wanted to do was to integrate the world of mental health into the everyday lives of people. We arranged for a "health promoter" in every repopulated zone or in every organized section of the city to take social histories of people and find out some of the root causes of symptoms that were secondary to the original trauma. This was very hard. We had to teach people to take such a social history without carrying around information that would be useful to the government. You cannot sit down and write a nice social history and risk the government coming in and confiscating your notebook and everything about your life.

So, people had to learn what information they had to know and to memorize it. These health promoters were very valuable because they were repositories of people's lives. So it became natural to take women who were ordinarily traditional healers or wise women, people in the community who knew about people already, and then to teach them how to alleviate basic trauma symptoms. We smuggled into the country the United Nations manual on Helping Workshops for Children. The UN was physically present, but the government of El Salvador would not have UN materials distributed properly to the workers, who also could not read. We had to find a level of women who could read and help them to train those who could not read from the manuals. They would then use the manuals to help the teachers deal with basic stress events. The manuals gave us a vehicle through which we could teach people to talk. The behavior was that you never talk about your troubles, your pains, your suffering. If you don't talk about it, you don't have to worry. So we taught people to talk. And we taught them to listen. And we taught them to do a simple psychosocial diagnosis from memory as community helpers.

Since talking was not so popular, for the second part of our program, we decided to do group work and got some of the younger women together and asked them to educate us about their community and the problems of their community. We played games and then taught them how to use the game to get at their fears and concerns and those of the young people. They began to work with us to set up groups for the youth.

The youth would act out, responding to their fears, worries, and the bleakness of their future. So we had youth groups for them to help them to express together not only their hopes for the country but also their hopes for themselves.

The real potential for social work took hold for me in such a way that got me thinking about the work that I do in the United States. In these groups, the young people would become less depressed and it would be easy for them to take action as small collective groups. They started out as youth groups . . . [and became] activist centers . . . not because someone guided them to do that but because, in the developmental process, adolescents need hope and want to change the world. You free them of the depression which has come down on them—fears of the government, fears from the death of their families and the devastation they found all around them, and the hopelessness. These kids began to develop on their own. When they no longer had to make decisions on their own and in fear, then they could make decisions as a collective and begin to do work in ways that were most useful. They began to help each other, collectively. I had taken my social work skills to El Salvador and returned with a model developed there that I could use with children at risk in the United States.

Source: Martha Bragin, LCSW, New York City NASW Center on Violence, Development, and Poverty, 1994. Printed with permission of the author.

Healing from Ethnically Based Trauma

When individuals and communities have been traumatized by ethnic conflicts, hate crimes, and other forms of ethnically based violence, the injustice and deep hurt that they experience often gets played out in revenge scenarios. The cycle of violence continues and inevitably results in new eruptions of ethnic conflicts, even over a period of many years and multiple generations. What follows is a discussion of some promising approaches to processes of healing that involve both victims and perpetrators as vital components of prevention and rehabilitation.

The Power of Apology

Apologizing is based on the notion that when a wrong has been committed, the first step in righting it is acknowledging that a wrong was done. Only then can those involved move on to heal the effects of the injury. This applies to both individuals and groups (Shaw, 1994). Based on her preliminary investigation of survivors of ethnically based trauma, Kahn (1994) emphasizes the "power of apology" from one group to another, both as part of the healing process and as a precursor for negotiation:

> The need to receive an apology or an acknowledgement from the perpetrators is an important factor in the healing process for individual victims of rape or other forms of physical and sexual abuse. In the same vein, between nations that have been at war or otherwise in conflict with one another, even though the war or conflict has supposedly been resolved or ended, an apology is still longed for by the oppressed one (for example, China from Japan). Whether between individuals, groups, or nations, apologies for former wrongs (in tandem with a conciliatory forgiver) tend to soften the memory of former conflict and promote an atmosphere from which mending and progress can emerge. Only then, I suggest, is it possible in the language of the day to "put it behind you and get on with it." (p. 24)

Apologies from perpetrators of violence—and their descendants—can take place in different ways. In dialogue groups, such as those discussed in chapter 9, for example, representatives of a group who are either currently being, or have historically been, mistreated by another group may meet with representatives from the perpetrator group to engage in a process of healing. Such a process calls for representatives from the injured group to speak the truth about how their group has been harmed; after listening to the grievances, representatives of the group that perpetrated the injury let the speakers know what they heard and understood of that truth, and they apologize for the harm done by their group.

Apologies can also be made by political leaders in government-sponsored settings. For example, apartheid South Africa's former president, Frederik de Klerk, was reported by the media in 1996 to have apologized to that country's truth commission for the pain and suffering caused by the system of racial separation. The Truth and Reconciliation Commission was convened to help South Africans come to terms with their country's past and to heal by compensating victims of political violence and granting amnesty (that is, forgiveness) to those who acknowledge and apologize for their part in apartheid atrocities. In the United States in 1996, George Wallace apologized to Vivian Malone Jones for physically blocking her entry to the University of Alabama in 1963 when he was governor of the state and she was the first young black woman to enroll in the university; the apology was followed by his presentation of an award to Jones—who said she forgave him long ago for what he had done to her—in honor of her courage in integrating the university and becoming its first black graduate.

Public apologies can also be made through organizations representing those who have done harm to another group. For example, in 1996 the General Conference of the United Methodist Church adopted a resolution of apology (the "Sand Creek apology") for the actions of a lay preacher who led a 1864 massacre of Native American people at Sand Creek in eastern Colorado; more than 200 members of the Cheyenne and Arapaho tribes—mostly women and children—were killed. The apology included a call for church leaders to meet with tribal elders to pray together in a healing service of reconciliation.

Another form of apology includes making reparation. For example, Germany compensated Jewish survivors after the Holocaust, and the U.S. Congress enacted a law in 1988 that granted restitution payments for civilians who had been interned during World War II. Section 2 of that act acknowledged that

> a grave injustice was done to both citizens and permanent resident aliens of
> Japanese ancestry by the evacuation, relocation, and internment of civilians

during World War II. . . . These actions were carried out without adequate security reasons and without any acts of espionage or sabotage documented . . . and were motivated largely by racial prejudice, wartime hysteria, and a failure of political leadership. The excluded individuals of Japanese ancestry suffered enormous damages, both material and intangible, and there were incalculable losses in education and job training, all of which resulted in significant human suffering for which appropriate compensation has not been made. For these fundamental violations of the basic civil liberties and constitutional rights of these individuals of Japanese ancestry, *the Congress apologizes on behalf of the Nation.* (Carnes, 1995, p. 54; emphasis added)

An acknowledgment of wrong and formal apology that is yet to be forthcoming is one from the U.S. government and the state governments that sanctioned slavery. Although the Thirteenth, Fourteenth, and Fifteenth Amendments to the U.S. Constitution were enacted to remedy inequalities between African American and white citizens, nowhere do these amendments acknowledge the wrongs and sufferings of slavery. Similarly, the U.S. Supreme Court has never issued an opinion overruling the theory of racial inferiority contained in the *Dred Scott v. Sanford* decision; not even in the *Brown v. Board of Education* opinion did the justices directly state that "we explicitly overrule the statements of racial inferiority we articulated in Dred Scott because that theory is wrong; no race is superior or inferior to any other" (Mirer, 1994, p. 4). With no official recognition of or apology for the evils of slavery in the United States, a great psychological wound remains unhealed, haunting our national psyche (Shaw, 1994).

The Role of Forgiveness

Forgiving people who have suffered deep hurt is being explored as part of healing from trauma. For example, Father L. Martin Jenco, the keynote speaker at the First National Conference on Forgiveness (an interdisciplinary conference held in spring 1995 at the University of Wisconsin–Madison), spoke of how he overcame the traumatic experience of imprisonment by terrorists in Lebanon in the mid-1980s by forgiving his captors. Peace researchers consider interpersonal forgiveness to be the smallest unit of peacemaking, one that is beginning to be viewed as a legitimate method of international conflict resolution as well (B. Flanigan, personal communication, 1995). The approach is consistent with

Gandhian thought that counterhatred only increases the depth of hatred, that the only way to get out of violence is through nonviolence, and that the only way to overcome hatred is through love (Merton, 1965).

Feminists caution, however, that forgiveness without repentance on the part of the perpetrator—without acknowledgment of the harm done to another and apology that involves real change and reparation—may be meaningless and even harmful to those who have been violated. Forgiveness without accountability is a well-known and important part of the problem in the cycle of domestic violence. A basic principle based on work with women recovering from battering relationships is that an apology merits forgiveness only after full disclosure and acknowledgment of past abuse by a perpetrator. Fortune (1991) pointed out that forgiveness is not forgetting but rather "letting go of the immediacy of the trauma, the memory of which continues to terrorize the victim and limit possibilities," and that forgiveness does not mean "trusting or returning to the offender" (pp. 175–176).

Another important word of caution comes from Hunt (1994), who warns against confusing the need for repentance with forgiveness. To do so "masks the fact that some sins are so deeply intertwined in unjust structures that they cannot be separated out and forgiven without substantive changes taking place in those structures" (p. 14). In other words, apology and forgiveness of violence at the individual level cannot be a substitute for apology and forgiveness of violence at the institutional and structural and cultural levels.

Ethnic Identity as Source of Healing

Garbarino (1993) presented the concept of a people's determined struggle to persist as an approach to healing from ethnic conflict and trauma. Research, such as that documenting the resilience of Palestinian children living with their families under siege in Lebanese refugee camps, supports the thesis (Cutting, 1988). Garbarino (1993) suggested that success in retaining psychological integrity in the face of war trauma is related to adults' political and ideological commitment to national or ethnic struggles. For example, he saw a parallel between Zionism—the sustaining ideology for Jews seeking to create the State of Israel—and nationalist ideological movements among African

Americans in the United States, such as the Black Panther Party and the Black Muslims. Ideology and ethnic identity are resources that may have important consequences for the care that traumatized children receive as well as the interpretation offered to them of the meaning of events. Although a determined struggle to persist has the potential for resulting in enhanced moral development, it also has the potential for resulting in impaired moral development in which a desire for revenge predominates, as discussed in an earlier section of this chapter (Garbarino, 1993).

Culture and Spirituality in Healing

> Ethnocultural factors . . . shape common and unique human responses to psychological traumatization. (M. B. Williams & Sommers, 1994. p. 221)

Sensitivity to cultural issues is important for the healing of posttraumatic stress conditions. Much can be learned from the ethical and spiritual traditions of communities that have discovered the capacity of spiritual power, rather than the power of brute force and weaponry, to heal trauma. Within ethnic cultural communities in many parts of the world, particularly among indigenous, non-Western peoples, traditional rituals and ceremonies provide healing communion. Spiritual traditions recognize the sources of power within nature, in the human soul, and in nurturing circles of community (California NASW Center, 1994). "An Indian Sweat Lodge" describes a healing ritual that includes spiritual aspects of redemption and rebirth.

An Indian Sweat Lodge

During the four rounds of the sweat lodge ceremony, each participant has the opportunity to speak honestly and openly about himself, although there is no coercion to do so and a minimum of group pressure. Typically, the environment is conducive to self-disclosure, which serves to create a sense of cohesion and bonding among the members. In the lodge, each person experiences self-confrontation and listens to others in the security provided by the darkness. Furthermore, the darkness eliminates external stimuli, particularly facial and other nonverbal cues from the other members; it demands an inner self-focus in order to find one's own light and vision of the self-in-the-present. The darkness comes to symbolize many things, including ignorance, uncertainty in life, pain, aloneness, fear, and death. The reduction of external stimuli also facilitates powerful unconscious processes, including primary process thinking and repressed affect, so that the individual can speak of these terrors and images more freely in the darkness of the lodge.

It is important to recognize that the womblike quality of the lodge directly concerns a psychological inner space. First, the lodge can be regarded as maternal in nature because the small, dark space encapsulates the members in a manner that makes it difficult to move and change positions. Second, the business of the lodge is purification, healing, and strengthening of character through emotional release. The ritual forces awareness of one's psychological state. . . . This maternal reattachment is typically described as feelings of being connected in deeper ways to mother earth. . . . It is clearly possible to speculate that the lodge contains multiple symbolic, sensory, and neuropsychological effects. In terms of maternal inner space, the lodge symbolizes the possibility of the self being created in a new form, one that emerged from the process of the ceremony and envisions a new life beyond.

Source: Wilson, 1989.

Research shows how traditional ethnic beliefs and rituals help people heal from violence-related trauma. For example, one study concerned Cambodian adolescent refugees who had been detached from their families and were living in group foster care in Australia and in foster families in the United States (Eisenbruch, 1991); the children reported that they thought their painful feelings of loss could be alleviated by traditional religious beliefs and rituals. When they had access to Buddhist monks and to Cambodian traditional healers, the study found, they indeed were helped to make sense of their feelings. The children who had been placed in Cambodian group care in Australia attended an annual ritual held to venerate the souls of the dead and incorporate the survivors into their community. Afterward, they reported that they felt relieved to have understood more clearly who they were. Such ceremonies help survivors of the trauma and separation of war come to terms with their losses, reduce the tensions between life in their new world and in their cultural world, and consolidate their sense of self. By addressing their subjective picture of what the trauma meant to them and by following their cultural ways of expressing distress and their cultural strategies for overcoming it, survivors find antidotes to cultural bereavement.

Healing from Violence-Related Trauma and Democracy Building

The empowerment and community-based approach to healing that has been emphasized in this chapter is similar to the perspective of Paulo Freire, Brazilian founder of the pedagogy of the oppressed and of consciousness-raising groups. Freire (1969, 1970) taught that people who have been oppressed—those who have suffered from social stratification, subordination, low social status, and lack of resources and those who have survived economic, political, and cultural domination—have the greatest potential for achieving world changes without violence. This they can do by learning to see themselves not as victims of forces beyond their control but as people in a unique position to make sense of and improve the world. Through consciousness-raising groups, people who have been oppressed learn to see with their own eyes rather than society's; observe their social conditions; analyze what they see in an unjust world; and decide to change their own way of being, from reactor to actor, to end inequality.

Repressive governments often aim to frighten people into submission and destroy grassroots leadership through the use of torture. Thus, healing victims of torture—the humane thing to do in any case—is a particularly important strategic step toward cultivating democracy. The Center for Victims of Torture (CVT) sees torture as "a long term, intentional wounding of the community, where repressive elements attempt to mold society over generations" (CVT, 1994, p. 2). "The Center for Victims of Torture" describes the work of the CVT.

The Center for Victims of Torture

In the spacious living room of a bulky three-story house on a bluff above the Mississippi River, an Ethiopian man and woman sat across from each other on sofas. They spoke, but not much. I would have interviewed them, except here at the Center for Victims of Torture a house rule holds that the patients are to be left alone by the news media.

This right to anonymity is sensible and necessary. The reasons include confidentiality, personal security and protection from newspeople who might aggress with our customary in-your-face pryings: How did you feel when the secret police applied electric shocks to your genitals, or what kind of nightmares did you have during your two years in a dungeon and are you still having them?

Answers to those questions aren't needed to learn that the center is a sanctuary of peace and mending for survivors of politically motivated torture. Since May 1985, nearly 500 torture victims from 32 countries have been served as outpatients by a staff that includes physicians, nurses, psychiatrists, and social workers. A third of the patients are Ethiopians.

Minnesota is home to 2,000 Ethiopian refugees; an estimated 80 percent were tortured by one of Africa's most brutal regimes. Amnesty International reports that in the 1980s, the torture methods used against Ethiopians included: beating on the soles of the feet, with the victims tied to an inverted chair or hung upside down by the knees and wrists from a horizontal pole; electric shocks; sexual torture, including rape of female prisoners or tying a heavy weight to the testicles; burning parts of the body with hot water or oil; and crushing the hands or feet.

Helping survivors come back physically and emotionally from that trauma is the work of Douglas Johnson, director of the center. . . . "Torture is widespread," Johnson said while standing before a tapestry in the foyer of the center. "We think there are at least 200,000 survivors in the United States. People who are torture victims were usually leaders of their community. The government had decided to disable them as part of a political strategy."

The full-treatment center, which is nonprofit and pays $1 a year rent to the University of Minnesota on its East Bank campus, is the only one of its kind in the United States. Other sites include Copenhagen, London, and Toronto. The idea for the program originated in 1985 with former governor Rudy Perpich, a liberal Democrat who conjectured—rightly, it turned out— that in politically progressive Minnesota volunteers would rally behind the center. Many have. More than 100 volunteers, in addition to the professional staff of 25, are part of the program.

Until recently, ministering to torture victims has been a side interest, if that, among human rights groups. Their missions have ranged from exposing governments that torture to rounding up the oppressors for prosecution. While that has been going on, professionals dealing with tortured refugees and asylum seekers suffering posttraumatic stress disorders have been largely on their own.

The comparative neglect of the treatment side of the human rights movement shows up in the international lack of financial support. In 1981, the United Nations created the Voluntary Fund for Victims of Torture. A decade later, few governments were showing interest. In 1992, the fund dispensed only $1.6 million, which was half the amount requested from centers around the world.

> *During the Reagan and Bush years, the United States, which sells arms*
> *to large numbers of torturing governments—Saudi Arabia, Israel, Turkey,*
> *Guatemala and Indonesia, among others—kicked in $100,000 a year, and*
> *some years nothing. The assessment of Douglas Johnson was accurate: "Rela-*
> *tive to the size of our economy and our population, the U.S. contribution*
> *was callous."*
>   *That may be changing. . . . The Comprehensive Torture Victims Relief*
> *Act is to be introduced in the Senate, legislation that will request $45 mil-*
> *lion for domestic and international programs. Considering the huge amount*
> *of torturing going on every day nearly everywhere, the small sum should be*
> *seen only as start-up money.*
>
> Source: McCarthy, C. (1994, July 19). Finally, balm for the wounds of torture.
> *Washington Post,* p. D10. ©The Washington Post. Reprinted with permission.

Although immediate care and healing are critical to stopping the cycle
of violence, the use of force and systematic exploitation by the powerful
must be exposed and confronted before the world can heal from the
violence that is engulfing human societies. Any long-term solution requires that the causes of violence be extinguished, which includes promoting sustainable human development with an emphasis on social justice, equity, and empowerment.

Implications for Social Workers

The social work profession is particularly suited for understanding the impact and treatment of violence-related trauma for three reasons: (1) social
workers examine the effect of events on individuals throughout the life span;
(2) social workers recognize the importance of cultural diversity and the
need to base any intervention on cultural responses to trauma; and (3) social work's unique theoretical frameworks recognize the person–environment continuum. The profession's history of community organizing and
action, organizational and systems change, and advocacy and empowerment provides the essential perspective to intervene on the macrolevel.

The role and tasks of social workers in many community-based agencies now differ from the traditional role of mental health clinician; they
now act as, among other things, educators, facilitators, and technical con-
sultants for resource development. In whatever role they assume, however, they must plan interventions that stimulate processes of healing so

people can overcome the psychological trauma that is so severely crippling to psychosocial and cognitive development. Regardless of program structure, client population, or social work role, the steps in processes of healing and recovery have some common elements.

The following steps in the healing process are a synopsis of healing approaches discussed in the previous section. The steps given in "Seven Steps toward Healing" may be undertaken by people in clinical settings within health services, in therapeutic sessions with licensed therapists, in community self-help programs that pursue spiritual paths to indigenous healing, through community group projects that incorporate mental health concepts, or within partnerships between oppressed communities and mental health professionals.

Seven Steps toward Healing

1. *A decision, out of desperation, is made to try to change one's life through involvement in a therapeutic program of personal transformation. There is desperate hope, and a small measure of trust, that something can be done to make a difference for the better. Twelve-step programs celebrate and commemorate this critical first step.*

2. *The foremost therapeutic task is full disclosure of the history of traumatic events, achieved through a patient, step-by-step process in which past threats and fears are reexamined realistically in a relatively safe and supportive environment. Activities use projective materials and instruments, including art and art therapy, story telling, sand trays, doll play, music and dance, guided imagery, or direct narrative interviews, which may be combined with hypnosis.*

3. *The history of trauma is continually reviewed to retain the recall of painful experience; thereby awareness is maintained as conscious memory and not repressed and hyperarousal is defused. Dissociated, split-off aspects of the self may be reintegrated in a reborn or reconstructed self.*

4. *Losses must be mourned and recognized as irreversible and irrevocable. The steps on a path to recovery traverse barriers of denial, anger, magical thinking, and the depths of depression to arrive at a full expression of grief.*

5. *Healing and recovery require small, daily, risk-taking steps toward growth and self-actualization. On the way to healing, the trip of a survivor may lead to a place of empowerment where a new identity may be constructed within a circle of new friends who merit trust (Everstine & Everstine, 1993).*

6. *To address problems of addiction, it is necessary to confront painful memories rather than avoid or deny them, and then to seek out—and establish*

contact and conscious communication with—the survivor who is still alive within the self.

7. *Rebuilding of community takes place through personal, political, and spiritual processes of social transformation and transcendence (Dobash & Dobash, 1992; Maslow, 1970; Moyers, 1993; Phillips & Frederick, 1995). Intuitive sense of connectedness between energy in the universe, in the social circle, and within the self is experienced as spiritual healing. Group meditation and relaxation exercises may be used.*

Source: Institute of Noetic Sciences, 1993.

Suggestions for Successful Social Work Intervention

The following suggestions for social workers are based on issues addressed in this chapter:

- *Macro-level interventions are required in dealing with violence-related trauma.* Social workers must understand the sociology and historical context of violence to address environmental factors that have not only permitted the violence but may have institutionally promoted it. Commitment to social justice is basic in community practice with victims of trauma. Action for change at institutional and structural levels is the responsibility of all social workers.

- *Cross-cultural sensitivities are basic prerequisites for working with anyone who has been traumatized.* A comprehensive approach to mental health diagnosis that is culturally relevant allows for people's cultural constructions of mental health. Cultural bereavement—discussed earlier as a concept that emphasizes the cultural meaning of loss and trauma—can bring relativist and universalist approaches to trauma into balance, particularly when working with refugees. It can minimize the chances that refugees are misdiagnosed with psychiatric disorders when their symptoms actually represent a significant communal suffering, the expression and meaning of which are culturally determined (Eisenbruch, 1991).

- *Social workers must acquire basic information about the diagnosis and treatment of PTSD.* Early intervention can prevent PTSD, and early diagnosis of PTSD can shorten the duration of treatment for those traumatized by violence. Thus, social workers must be able to recognize PTSD symptoms and intervene appropriately and effectively. Social work education should include PTSD in the curriculum and practitioners should get information from continuing education seminars and reading (Bedics, Rappe, & Rappe, 1991).

- *Social workers should assume that refugees have experienced some sort of trauma.* Furthermore, they must communicate a sense of understanding about the pain and suffering that refugees may be going through. Social workers can encourage refugees to talk by providing a safe environment.

Background inquiry is important in working with refugees because of the high frequency of trauma and stress among them. Based on her research with Central American refugees, Masser (1992) recommends that child welfare workers seeking to improve the psychosocial functioning of refugee children develop interventions that include the parents or caregivers, teachers, and other members of the child's community. The social worker's role needs to extend beyond the individual to the community and includes educating the community that comes into contact with refugee children also— law enforcement officers, educators, public assistance and child abuse workers, and medical professionals—so that they come to understand the distress experienced by the children and its manifestations and learn how to reduce some of the postmigration stressors.

When working with all refugees, social workers must address the multiple issues of PTSD, grief, and depression; cross-cultural conflicts in values and behaviors, particularly age, gender, and family roles; and intergenerational acculturation. Yee (1992) emphasized the importance of understanding the losses particular to elderly refugees: their homeland in which most of their lives were lived, a familiar, comfortable culture, many social relationships, and their esteemed place in the family and community that they thought was their privilege during the last stage of the life cycle.

- *Social workers must ask troubled refugees directly whether they have been tortured.* Direct inquiry is important not only to detect the underlying cause of their problems; it is also important because, similar to others who have been physically abused in other circumstances, few victims of torture will spontaneously disclose that experience. However, social workers must first face their own feelings about torture. Because the idea of torture is so repugnant, the initial reaction of social workers may be shock, denial, and disbelief, and "even if unstated, the denial may be communicated to the torture victim through subtle behaviors and facial expressions" (Holtan, 1986, p. 2). Survivors of torture are further devastated when others do not seem to believe their stories.

Although telling the truth about their experiences is essential to the healing process, it is important to shield victims from having to retell the story constantly to a series of helping professionals. To that end, Holtan (1986) suggested that a case manager coordinate information among all those involved with a torture survivor.

Social workers should keep in mind four issues during the treatment of torture victims: (1) the torture survivor needs to have a secure and trusting feeling toward the social worker and institution; (2) initial interviews may evoke a catharsis and a regression into a seemingly more troubled state; (3) there may be strong feelings of survivor guilt, which is an anger directed inward, that treatment can help relieve and dispel; and (4) the torture victim must eventually establish a new sense of integration with society (Holtan, 1986). On the policy level, social workers can support legislation in the U.S. Congress for programs for treating victims of torture, such as the Comprehensive Torture Victims Relief Act that was introduced in the Senate in 1994 (see "The Center for Victims of Torture," p. 321).

- *Social workers must be aware that they themselves are at risk of being traumatized.* Social workers who deal with violence-related trauma can themselves be traumatized or suffer secondary traumatization through compassion fatigue (Figley, 1995). If the environment in which social workers intervene remains hostile and victims are repeatedly traumatized, social workers are at particularly high risk (Straker & Moosa, 1994). For example, social workers and psychologists working with trauma victims in South Africa responded to the environment of civil conflict and political repres-

sion in the same way that other therapists respond to trauma such
as domestic violence and child abuse: Their feelings included powerlessness, anger and outrage, fear, anxiety, and vulnerability
(Straker & Moosa, 1994).

Certain factors in situations of political repression and civil conflict, however, complicate the resolution of such reactions. One is
the risk of direct traumatization of the social worker whose work
constitutes a challenge to the state. For example, Shirley Gunn,
a South African trade union social worker, was imprisoned and
put in solitary confinement with her nursing infant for 64 days in
1990, because she was politically active in the Mass Democratic
Movement, a group aligned with the African National Congress.
Similarly, some social services workers with Casa Alianza in Guatemala City have been abducted and arrested for defending street
children against police abuse (Committee for International Human Rights Inquiry, personal communication, New York, 1991).

Social workers in the United States can intervene in such situations by joining the Committee for International Human Rights
Inquiry and participating in its letter-writing campaigns to governments that persecute and traumatize social service workers and
their clients (see the resource section at the end of the book for
more information).

• *Learn about the role of acknowledgment, apology, and reparations
and forgiveness in healing from trauma.* This is a new area of intervention that seems consistent with social work professional values
and has the potential for increasing our understanding of the healing process. Contact the International Forgiveness Institute, which
conducts research, scholarly inquiry, education, and problem solving on the intrapersonal, interpersonal, community, societal, and
global levels, for information about conferences and resources for
learning (see the resource section for more information). Become
familiar with the vibrant literature on healing and recovery (Eth
& Pynoos, 1985; Gil, 1983; James, 1989; Janoff-Bulman, 1992;
Malchiodi, 1990; Ochberg, 1988; Pilisuk & Parks, 1986; Van der
Kolk, 1987; Waites, 1993; Whitfield, 1989; Wilson, 1989).

- *Become politically involved in shaping policy decisions and making leaders accountable.* Findings of studies on socioeconomic and ethnic stratification in the United States and comparative human development studies conducted by research centers—including the United Nations—make it clear that policy decisions by leadership groups have profound effects on the status of physical and mental health, general quality of living, and levels of violence in a society (Andersen & Collins, 1995; Kerbo, 1991; Mies, 1986; Rothenberg, 1995; United Nations Development Program, 1994). Administrative leaders in corporate and governmental institutions control and are responsible for decision-making power, access to resources, and channels of communication, which affect both the quality of life in society as a whole and the well-being of different sectors of that society. To be healthy and secure, communities need leadership by responsible adults who are willing to acknowledge and learn from their own mistakes or careless, destructive acts; to make restitution for abuse of power; and to demonstrate integrity, with commitment to humanistic and spiritual values, in the building of a caring society. Prevention of violence requires that kind of quality in local and national leadership. Social workers can play an active role in bringing about sound policies and accountable leadership.
- *Organize and support self-help efforts.* Self-help programs, which emphasize empowerment of a community of survivors and the importance of mutual support in the recovery process (Schuler, 1992; C. Williams, 1992), and support groups are potent antidotes to rising levels of violence and social disintegration throughout the world. Social workers can be effective organizers for self-help groups and other nongovernmental and social action organizations.

References

Andersen, M. L., & Collins, P. H. (Eds). (1995). *Race, class and gender: An anthology* (2nd ed.). Belmont, CA: Wadsworth.

Bedics, B. C., Rappe, P. T., & Rappe, L. O. (1991). Preparing BSW professionals for identifying and salvaging victims of post traumatic stress disorder. In B. Shank (Ed.), *B.S.W. education for practice: Reality and fantasy* (pp. 94–100). St. Paul, MN: University of St. Thomas.

Bowan, D., Carscadden, L., Beighle, K., & Fleming, I. (1992). Post-traumatic stress disorder among Salvadoran women: Empirical evidence and description of treatment. *Women and Therapy, 13*(1–2), 267–279.

California NASW Center on Violence, Development, and Trauma. (1994). *Healing a traumatized community: Lessons from the Atlantic Coast of Nicaragua* (report submitted to the NASW Violence and Development Project, Washington, DC). Sacramento, CA: Author.

California NASW Center on Violence, Development, and Trauma. (1995, April). *The conceptual framework of the project on violence and development* (paper presented at a workshop of the California Chapter Committee for the NASW Violence and Development Project, Washington, DC). Sacramento, CA: Author.

Carnes, J. (1995). Home was a horse stall. *Teaching Tolerance, 4*(1), 50–57.

Center for Victims of Torture (CVT). (1994). Developing new strategies against torture. *Storycloth, 2*(1), 2.

Cutting, P. (1988). *Children of the siege.* London: Heinemann.

Dobash, R. E., & Dobash, R. P. (1992). *Women, violence and social change.* London: Routledge & Kegan Paul.

Eisenbruch, M. (1991). From post-traumatic stress disorder to cultural bereavement: A diagnosis of Southeast Asian refugees. *Social Science Medicine, 33*(6), 673–690.

Eth, S., & Pynoos, R. (Eds.) (1985). *Post traumatic stress disorder in children.* Washington, DC: American Psychiatric Press.

Everstine, D., & Everstine, L. (1993). *The trauma response: Treatment for emotional injury.* New York: W. W. Norton.

Figley, C. R. (1995). *Compassion fatigue: Secondary traumatic stress disorder—Theory, research, and treatment.* New York: Brunner/Mazel.

Fortune, M. F. (1991). *Violence in the family: A workshop curriculum for clergy and other helpers.* Cleveland: Pilgrim Press.

Freire, P. (1969). *La educacion como practica de la libertad.* Montevideo, Uruguay: Tierra Nueva.

Freire, P. (1970). *Pedagogy of the oppressed* (M. B. Ramos, Trans.). New York: Herder & Herder.

Garbarino, J. (1993). Children's response to community violence: What do we know? *Infant Mental Health Journal, 14*(2), 103–114.

Gil, E. (1983). *Outgrowing the pain: A book for and about adults abused as children.* New York: Dell Publishers.

Holtan, N. R. (1986). *When refugees are victims of torture.* Washington, DC: U.S. Committee for Refugees.

Hunt, M. E. (1994). To forgive or not to forgive? *Living Pulpit, 3*(2), 14–15.

Institute of Noetic Sciences (with Poole, W.). (1993). *The heart of healing.* Atlanta: Turner.

James, B. (1989). *Treating traumatized children: New insights and creative interventions.* Lexington, MA: Lexington Books.

Janoff-Bulman, R. (1992). *Shattered assumptions: Towards a new psychology of trauma.* New York: Free Press.

Jensen, P., & Shaw, J. (1993). Children as victims of war: Current knowledge and future research needs. *Journal of the American Academy of Child and Adolescent Psychiatry, 32*(4), 697–708.

Kahn, A. B. (1994, August 22). *Violence and social development between conflicting groups* (paper prepared for the California NASW Center on Violence, Development, and Trauma). Malibu, CA: Author.

Kerbo, H. (1991). *Social stratification and inequality: Class conflict in historical and comparative perspective.* New York: McGraw-Hill.

Kubler-Ross, E. (1969). *On death and dying.* New York: Macmillan.

Kubler-Ross, E. (1974). *Questions and answers on death and dying.* New York: Macmillan.

Malchiodi, C. (1990). *Breaking the silence: Art therapy with children from violent homes.* New York: Brunner/Mazel.

Mann, J. (1994, August 10). Learning to cry in the same room. *The Washington Post,* p. E15.

Maslow, A. H. (1970). *Religions, values and peak experiences.* New York: Penguin Books.

Masser, D. (1992). Psychosocial functioning of Central American refugee children. *Child Welfare, 71*(5), 439–456.

McCarthy, C. (1994, July 19). Finally, balm for the wounds of torture. *The Washington Post,* p. D10.

Merton, T. (Ed.). (1965). *Gandhi on non-violence.* New York: New Directions.

Mies, M. (1986). *Patriarchy and accumulation on a world scale: Women in the international division of labour.* London: Zed Books.

Mirer, J. (1994). H.R. 40: If not now, when? *Poverty and Race, 3*(6), 4–5.

Moyers, B. (1993). *Healing and the mind.* Garden City, NY: Doubleday.

Ochberg, F. M. (Ed.). (1988). *Post-traumatic therapy and victims of violence.* New York: Brunner/Mazel.

Phillips, M., & Frederick, C. (1995). *Healing the divided self: Clinical and Ericksonian hypnotherapy for post-traumatic and dissociative conditions.* New York: W. W. Norton.

Pilisuk, M., & Parks, S. H. (1986). *The healing web: Social networks and human survival.* Hanover, NH: University Press of New England.

Pittman, K. (1995, May–June). Rebuilding community, block by block. *Youth Today,* p. 46.

Prigoff, A. (1993, August). *Violence, trauma, loss and deprivation: Psychological wounds and processes of healing.* Paper presented at the 10th Annual North America–Nicaragua Health Colloquium, Managua, Nicaragua.

Roe, M. (1992). Displaced women in settings of continuing armed conflict. *Women and Therapy, 13*(1–2), 89–102.

Rothenberg, P. S. (Ed.). (1995). *Race, class and gender in the United States: An integrated study* (3rd ed.). New York: St. Martin's Press.

Save the Children. (1994, November). *Children at war.* London: Author.

Schuler, M. (Ed.). (1992). *Freedom from violence: Women's strategies from around the world.* New York: OEF International.

Shaw, T. M. (1994). Apology/acknowledgement is imperative. *Poverty & Race, 3*(6), 3–4.

Straker, G., & Moosa, F. (1994). Interacting with trauma survivors in contexts of continuing trauma. *Journal of Traumatic Stress, 7*(3), 457–468.

United Nations Development Programme. (1994). *Human development report 1994.* New York: Oxford University Press.

Van der Kolk, B. A. (Ed.). (1987). *Psychological trauma.* Washington, DC: American Psychiatric Association.

Waites, E. A. (1993). *Trauma and survival: Post-traumatic and dissociative disorders in women.* New York: W. W. Norton.

Whitfield, C. L. (1989). *Healing the child within: Discovery and recovery for adult children of dysfunctional families.* Deerfield Beach, FL: Health Communications.

Williams, C. (with Laird, R.). (1992). *No hiding place: Empowerment and recovery for our troubled communities.* New York: HarperCollins.

Williams, M. B., & Sommers, J. F., Jr. (Eds.). (1994). *Handbook of post-traumatic therapy.* Westport, CT: Greenwood Press.

Wilson, J. P. (1989). *Trauma, transformation and healing: An integrative approach to theory, research, and post-traumatic therapy.* New York: Brunner/Mazel.

Yee, B. (1992). Markers of successful aging among Vietnamese refugee women. *Women and Therapy, 13*(1–2), 221–237.

Part 7

Epilogue

Chapter 14

Developing a Global Professional Perspective on Violence

> Everyone wishes to live in peace, but it is not achieved by merely talking or thinking about it, nor by waiting for someone else to do something about it. We each have to take responsibility as best we can within our own sphere of activity. (Dalai Lama, 1994, p. x)

The purpose of this book has been to expand the frame of professional social work discourse within which violence is defined, its contexts analyzed, and its prevention and amelioration explored. To that end, the definition of violence has been broadened and links drawn among violence and individual, social, and economic development. Parallel conditions and causes of violence in the United States and in countries of the global South have been examined in relation to poverty, gender violence, violence against children, ethnoviolence, and drug-related violence. Just as common problems and universal causes of violence have been explored, shared solutions have been proposed. Throughout the book, stories were showcased that reveal how people around the globe are finding an antidote to violence in the development of their communities by using strategies of sustainable human development. Part 6 examines and summarizes processes of healing from violence-related trauma that are underway around the world.

Some of the ideas have admittedly been bold and have exceeded the boundaries of traditional social work considerations. Skeptics may be quick to point out the limitations of thinking in such comprehensive, global terms. Rethinking our conception of violence to include what is unseen on institutional and structural levels could leave social workers feeling even more powerless than they already do. Critics might say that the concept of sustainable human development—although everyone might quickly agree with its tenets—is too broad and nebulous to be of any practical use in social work practice. They might also say that problems of violence—as well as poverty—will always be a reality no matter what idealistic standards we might embrace. They also might say that addressing issues of violence from a global perspective is far beyond the scope of the social worker's role.

It is indeed tempting to be pessimistic after wading through the many examples of different types of violence documented in this book. However, the good news—also documented in the stories shared throughout each chapter—is that grassroots community groups throughout the world are finding their voices and solutions to violence by resisting top-down models of development. Thus, the question is not whether the book's perspective on violence is too broad but whether the book's proposals, considered *as a system,* have any potential to produce better results than we have been able to achieve so far.

This final chapter summarizes the book's central theme about the global interdependence of violence and about the lessons offered by communities using sustainable human development strategies. It then discusses the need for the social work profession to develop a global perspective on violence and proposes a paradigmatic shift in the profession's consciousness about violence and our place in the global order. Such a shift implies that when social workers address violence prevention and reduction, they do so with an understanding of the relationship between violence and oppression inherent in social and economic injustice and a recognition of the need for community responses.

Lessons without Borders: Global Links and Comparative Insights

> By studying social problems in other countries, social workers can learn how these countries identify and define needs, and this knowledge can increase their awareness of social problems in their own societies. . . . American social workers have gained greater insights into their society's social problems by studying similar problems elsewhere. (Midgley, 1992, p. 14)

Violence as conceptualized in this book occurs on three distinct yet interrelated levels—individual, institutional, and structural and cultural—and takes different forms. The violence we see on the individual level is usually illegitimate, overt, and physical. The violence at the institutional and structural and cultural levels is often legitimate, covert, and may take nonphysical forms and thus is less readily seen. Included in this concept of violence, then, is poverty as a form of violence that does not destroy life with a single blow as does direct physical violence, but which blocks the full development of the life potential of millions of people. Also included are patterns of exploitation and inequity, a form of institutional violence based on racist, sexist, and other oppressive ideologies not usually recognized or acknowledged.

Such broadly conceived patterns of violence are displayed worldwide and are often accompanied by maldevelopment, chronic poverty, and unfulfilled potential. As this book makes clear, neither violence prevention nor amelioration is likely to be achieved or sustained without understanding that maldevelopment is a major part of the problem and that sustainable human development is a necessary ingredient for solution. Making connections between violence in the United States and in the global South within the context of development is an approach to shared solutions that derives from "lessons without borders." The reality of global interdependence means that we are so closely tied to events overseas that virtually every decision, however local it may seem, has an international facet. Social workers are particularly linked to the global South—where the vast majority of the world's people live—by common manifestations of violence, specifically oppression and poverty. Three questions concerning links between violence and development in the United States and the global South were addressed throughout this book: (1) How do violence-related problems in the global South affect the United States and vice versa? (2) How are social problems in the United States similar to those in the global South, and how do they differ? and (3) What lessons can we learn from efforts of other countries to solve problems similar to ours? Table 14-1 illustrates some of the connections among poverty, violence against women and children, ethnoviolence, drug-related violence, and trauma that were discussed throughout the book in response to those questions.

Challenges for the Social Work Profession

Many social work authors have written clearly and eloquently about ways in which social work practitioners and academicians can reorient

Table 14-1
Summary of Observations Concerning Violence

Form of Violence	Global Linkages[a]	Comparative Insights[b]	Best Practices[c]
Poverty-related violence	Poverty-related diseases in the global South spread to United States and vice versa (e.g., vaccination against smallpox in global South saves United States hundreds of millions of dollars)	Poverty stacks the odds against normal development of children in United States and global South; poor children more likely to die from infectious diseases, suffer from all physical maladies; vaccination rates in United States compared with some countries in global South	Grassroots level strategies increase vaccination rate in global South; oral rehydration therapy used in global South is a practical, low-cost and painless alternative to treating hundreds of children hospitalized by diarrhea each year in United States
	U.S. industry jobs decrease because production is moved to global South	Worker exploitation compared; "sweat-shop" working conditions of garment workers—mostly young women and girls—in maquiladoras (factories built in part with U.S. funds in free-trade zones that receive breaks on taxes and tariffs) similar to "sweat-shop" conditions of garment workers in United States	Grassroots micro-enterprise, credit, and self-employment projects worldwide; trade union solidarity across borders; fair trade organizations
	International search for better opportunities, migration and hyper-urbanization	Family homelessness and street children, squatter settlements and floating populations	Self-help housing, Habitat for Humanity approaches, cooperatives; participatory projects
	Export of U.S. weapons to the global South fuels violence and drains resources for meeting human needs	Military expenditures are disproportionate to expenditures for social needs in both United States and the global South	Forums for disarmament, regulating the arms trade, UN mediation in conflicts, reducing military spending

Form of Violence	Global Linkages[a]	Comparative Insights[b]	Best Practices[c]
Gender violence and violence against children	Globalized media images of family norms and values reinforce subordination of females and children; increasingly insecure household ties; wars and militaristic values promote ideology of superiority	Comparative impacts of economic pressures and women's incomes in different types of traditional family structures; sex tourism industry exploits women and children in global South compared with sexual violation in United States	Women's self-help projects emphasizing struggle efforts and development efforts (e.g., SEWA, Grameen Bank); women's community-based education and pressure campaigns; empowerment approaches to development
Ethno-violence	Dominant patterns of global economic development leads to unequal distribution of resources and power, repression of ethnic populations; environmental degradation leads to intensified ethnic conflict	Migration tensions; hate crimes and ethnic tensions in United States compared with ethnic clashes in the global South; pressures encouraging ethnocentric political appeals; affirmative action policy disputes	Issue-specific cross-ethnic self-help organizations; developing web of NGOs and movements that empower citizens to solve their own problems (vibrant civil societies); projects to preserve ethnic cultures; dialogue and conflict resolution groups
Drug-related violence	Global drug networks become part of global economy, evade enforcement through migration and expansion into new territories	Poverty leads poor farmers in the global South into drug production while poverty leads poor people in United States into drug consumption; gang-related informal governance compared with corruption of formal governments and businesses; traditional use of drugs compared with uncontrolled abuse	Combination of strategies related to factors such as poverty and motivation; viable alternatives to production in the global South; politicized community mobilization and mutual aid models, based on empowerment ideologies and intense peer support; holistic community processes involving prevention, coalitions, treatment

(*Table 14-1 continues*)

Table 14-1
Summary of Observations Concerning Violence *(continued)*

Form of Violence	Global Linkages[a]	Comparative Insights[b]	Best Practices[c]
Violence-related trauma	Ethnic conflict, civil unrest, and mass migration; breakdown of governance; wholesale abandonment of uncompetitive local economic sectors	Family and community breakdown in traumatized areas compared to similar issues in economically devastated U.S. towns and neighborhoods; unresolved trauma perpetuates cycle of violence worldwide	Cultural activities for healing, with grief work to mourn losses, plus self-expression in art, storytelling, drama with music and dance as metaphors for trauma, survival and spiritual rebirth

[a]Problems in global South affect problems in United States and vice versa
[b]Observations of similarities and differences here and in global South
[c]Lessons from experience addressing similar problems in the global South and the United States.

themselves to engage with problems of violence from a global perspective (see, for example, Billups, 1990, 1994; Elliott, 1993; Estes, 1992; Healy, 1988; Hoff & McNutt, 1994; Hokenstad, Khinduka, & Midgley, 1992; Lloyd, 1982; Midgley, 1990; Paiva, 1977; Spergel, 1977, 1982). Nevertheless, serious incorporation of a global consciousness into our professional identity remains an elusive goal and education for social development a marginalized effort. Similarly, although much has been written about social work concerns with violence—primarily domestic violence—the profession has been ambivalent and uncharacteristically taciturn about other issues such as the widespread use of firearms, the global arms race, war and peace, and most forms of institutional and structural violence (Bryant, 1993; Van Soest & Bryant, 1995).

A Professional Peace Consciousness

If we are to expand the context within which social workers address social problems to include a global understanding of the relationship between violence and development, there must be a paradigmatic shift in our professional consciousness. Such a shift in consciousness calls for the social work profession to incorporate within its education and practice a fundamental and comprehensive philosophy of and commit-ment to peace. A professional peace consciousness for social work would be based on a positive peace concept, one that goes beyond the notion of peace as the absence of war (Boulding, 1977) to include an under-standing that violence is present whenever people are not allowed to reach their full potential (Galtung, 1969). Thus, peace is inextricably linked to issues of justice, human rights, and development (Sanders & Matsuoka, 1989). Serron (1980) articulated the links thus: "Justice in-volves . . . a question of development: the development of a population raised to its full creative potential. . . . Justice in this sense is not only the development of the full potential of all that is included under the term human: it also involves the establishment of institutions which are hu-man toward human life itself" (p. 239).

Given the reality that global problems of violence plague the lives of millions of people worldwide, adherence to a peace philosophy would inevitably mean a redirection of professional energies toward people-centered development, empowerment, development of sustainable com-munities, and commitment to social justice and nonviolence. All situa-tions that threaten human life and well-being would be within the boundaries of social work concerns, including the struggles of underde-veloped communities anywhere in the world. By understanding how different levels of violence fuel each other, social workers would come to see in a broader context the causes of—and thus expanded solutions to—violence. Equipped with an overarching framework for understand-ing global problems of violence, the profession could reclaim its roots in community activism and internationalism.

Several facts argue for the feasibility of bringing about such a profes-sional peace consciousness. First, the idea is not new to social work and we have role models from whom to learn. Many of our foremothers understood global interdependence and the interrelatedness of peace and justice and were active leaders in the pursuit of social justice. Some of them, for example, proposed in 1915 not only to demand the right to vote but to transform international relations, end the war, and bring about a new world order (Bowen, 1988). Jane Addams in particular dis-cerned the need for community development informed by knowledge and understanding of international struggles in her work at the Hull-

House in Chicago. Addams expressed moral indignation about the many forms of violence worldwide that victimize primarily poor and power-less people. The message of Bertha Reynolds (1986), another of our so-cial work foremothers who was active in the peace and social justice movements, still eloquently admonishes us:

> How does the world conflict touch us, as social workers, and what do we propose to do about it? . . . Perhaps we recognize that the welfare of people is our business, but accept responsibility for only such portions of it as we can reach with our special professional skills. Beyond that, we say we can do no more than any other citizen, and national and international affairs are not in our range of competence. Nevertheless, we are affected, and deeply, by what is going on in our world. . . . It is not only as citizens, but as an organized professional group that we are challenged to take our place in the movement of today. (p. 90)

Second, social workers are in a position to understand, from first-hand experience, the consequences of violence at the structural and in-stitutional levels. In most countries, most of their clients are poor, dis-advantaged, and disenfranchised people. Wherever they practice around the globe, they do so as peacemakers already:

> In all countries, social workers see themselves as agents of social change and institutional reform. In emerging nations, the social work role is cast in terms of the challenge of nation building; in divided communities social workers are expected to be agents of reconciliation. . . . They organize at the grassroots level and engage in advocacy and community action . . . they share a com-mitment to the values of promoting human dignity and social justice, em-powering poor and vulnerable people, and encouraging intergroup harmony and goodwill. (Hokenstad et al., 1992, p. 182)

Third, the goal of peace educators and activists is essentially the goal of social work practice, that is, conceiving, gestating, and nurturing those conditions in which all can develop their capacity to be fully human (Reardon, 1988). Courage is often required in the service of such a goal, particularly when injustices create barriers to its achievement. Special cour-age is called for when the injustices are found within the social worker's own work environment (that is, at the institutional level of violence), be-cause future career goals may be jeopardized. Courage was one of the char-acteristics of Gandhi—one of the world's greatest peacemakers—who taught that the failure to act or demand justice, in the face of truth, can never be justified and that both individual and societal transformation are necessary for self-realization. Gandhi's ideas could be the foundation for a new professional peace consciousness for social work (Walz, Sharma, & Birnbaum, 1988).

Fourth, the central values of social work (as manifested in practice and articulated in our professional code of ethics, policy statements, and curriculum standards) emphasize social justice, equity, self-determination, and human rights. The premises that the profession accepts are, in fact, the antithesis of militaristic values that are embedded in the structural and cultural level of violence and feed violence at other levels. Crane (1986) pointed out that war and militarism are based on premises about human behavior that are inconsistent with elementary social work principles, knowledge, and skills. Table 14-2 shows some of these inconsistencies (Crane, 1986; Van Soest, 1992).

Finally, social workers are inherently well-suited for the primary role of peacemaking and community activism. In fact, the personal qualities and skills required to be effective social workers are parallel to those needed for peacemaking. Essential for peacemakers and social workers alike are human qualities such as empathy, compassion, a strong sense of self, independent identity, and critical loyalty (which makes it possible to say no to authority instead of just following orders in the face of inhumane demands), strong personal values, generosity, tolerance, the ability to perceive and forgive human weakness, imagination, and self-criticism (Keefe & Roberts, 1991).

Table 14-2
Social Work and Peace

Social Work Values in Approaches to Change	Assumptions of War and Militarism
• humanistic/holistic	• technological fix
• rational, spiritual, and emotional	• rational solutions
• interdependence	• independence
• recognition of mutual vulnerability; empowerment of others	• control; coercion; power over others
• win–win strategies	• win–lose strategies
• peace as justice and benevolence	• peace as absence of violence or war

Implications for Social Work Education

Education is one of society's institutions that can stimulate positive change for the human condition and reduce global violence. The social work profession—students, faculty, and practitioners—is primed for peace education by virtue of its training, employment, and value orientation. People who are attracted to the profession have a broad concern for society and the world. Educators need to find ways to translate that concern into a more profound understanding of global peace issues and prepare future social workers to be community activists and peacemakers.

Growing Support for Curriculum Development

There is growing support for curriculum development in this area. The Council on Social Work Education (CSWE), which sets the standards for social work education, recognizes that effective social work education programs must convey the concept of interdependence among nations and the need for worldwide professional cooperation. The 1994 CSWE *Handbook on Accreditation Standards and Procedures* emphasized the importance of principles of social and economic justice—social work programs are required to include in their curricula information about the consequences of oppression and about those who have been affected by social, economic, and legal bias or oppression.

In addition to support from accreditation standards, several curriculum materials were developed in the 1990s to assist social work educators. Healy's (1992) curriculum manual provides ideas and resources that help social work educators incorporate international development content in their courses, with an emphasis on issues relevant to child and family well-being and the global South. Estes' (1992) guide to resources for internationalizing social work education gives information on a broad range of issues rooted in social work, social welfare, and social development; the guide also provides models of international education that can be used in social work education and ideas about how to incorporate an international perspective in the curriculum. Van Soest's (1992) manual offers curriculum materials and suggestions about how to incorporate peace and social justice in social work education. A curriculum module developed for the Violence and Development Project of the National Association of Social Workers (NASW) presents more global content in social work education concerning issues of violence and is an excellent accompaniment for faculty use in conjunction with this book (Van Soest & Crosby, 1996). Several of the curriculum manuals provide specific ideas and resources about the foundations of social work educational programs: human behavior in the social environment; social work practice; and social welfare policy, research, and field practicum.

International and peace emphases have also been fostered within the profession by collaborative practice and education-based projects of the National Association of Social Workers and CSWE. A Child and Family Well-Being Development Education Project, for example, developed curriculum materials and facilitated partnerships between some state NASW chapters and groups of social workers in the global South (Healy, 1992). A violence and development project expanded professional capacities for community building and global learning through a massive outreach and education effort (out of which came a national teach-in week on campuses of schools of social work); produced two ground-breaking satellite videoconferences hosted by Charles Kuralt; and developed educational resources for students and educators (Van Soest & Crosby, 1996). NASW and CSWE have undertaken a follow-up initiative to further expand capacities for community building and global learning; this one will create model programs for preparing social workers to adopt and use a community and global peace perspective in their work.

Guiding Principles for Curriculum Development

The process of socializing future social workers into a professional peace consciousness could be guided by the following principles:

> Development: Community development is based on tapping into and building the integrity and leadership of the members of the community.... Breaking the cycle of violence is a development process that local people must direct and ultimately sustain. No imported scheme can substitute for bottom-up ingenuity.

> Participation: If violence is an expression of powerlessness, isolation, and exclusion, then participatory community development must seek to counter

it. Sustainable development must have the participation of community members. Successful participation calls for engaging people, unleashing their creativity, building their capacities, and giving them a sense of ownership.

Reciprocity: Successful development calls for an equitable relationship between "the givers of help" and "the recipients of help" and a blurring of who receives from whom. Assisting a community requires one to become involved with it, to learn from it, be influenced and changed by it—in a sense to join it. Home-grown strategies to address violence must be retrieved and exchanged, and new methods must be devised to share learning about what works and why.

Innovation: As budget cuts and managed care change the face of social service delivery, U.S. social workers must become innovative. . . . As in resource-poor developing countries, accomplishing more with less and pooling resources to achieve otherwise impossible goals become increasingly important. The infusion of more community-wide approaches to treating societal issues must become part of the day-to-day jobs of social workers. Innovation demands that social workers review the root causes of problems so that they can begin to institute positive change for more people at less cost.

Global learning: The gap between home and abroad, between "them and us" is rapidly shrinking. Not only do so-called Third World conditions exist in neighborhoods across America, but the globalization of the economy, immigrant flows, environmental degradation, and a host of other factors all combine to make interdependency a fact of life. Armed with a more sophisticated knowledge base to analyze and understand current situations and policies, social workers can enhance their effectiveness. The search for solutions to societal problems should not be limited to U.S. communities and policies. (NASW, 1996, pp. 6–8)

Suggested Curriculum Goals

Development of a curriculum model designed to assist future social workers in acquiring a professional peace consciousness might include the following overall goals (NASW, 1996, p. 4):

- To inspire a return to social work's roots in community activism, peacemaking, and internationalism
- To expand the context within which social workers address social problems to include a global understanding of the relationship between violence and development

- To increase the number of social workers who are comfortable crossing boundaries of culture, race, and class and who are well-versed in the historical roots and current struggles of underdeveloped communities
- To integrate the individual/group/therapeutic and macro perspectives and interventions by applying a simultaneous dual focus to situations involving violence and development issues (Billups, 1990; Hokenstad et al., 1992).

Suggested Learning Objectives

The following student learning objectives (Van Soest & Crosby, 1996) are suggested for curricula designed to encourage a professional peace consciousness in future social workers:

- Students will be able to describe parallel conditions of violence in the United States and in less economically advantaged nations.
- Students will demonstrate a broadened understanding of violence and the role of the social work profession in solving the problem on a global scale.
- Students will demonstrate an increased interest in learning from successful interventions by human services workers in countries in the global South and the United States.
- Students will demonstrate an awareness of social work's commitment to social justice and peace by describing how violence and oppression affect vulnerable populations throughout the world.

Teaching and Learning Processes

Development of educational goals and objectives for a professional peace consciousness is very important and necessary, but it is not sufficient to produce that consciousness. The processes of teaching and learning are as important as the content. Two broad areas require special attention (Klein, 1987). The first is that of faculty–student relations: The educational process itself must help students learn to be nonviolent in their orientation toward, and work with, clients and communities. The second area concerns the social work practice methods that are taught in the classroom: In short, they must emphasize respect for clients' humanity, identity, and abilities. The characteristics in both areas that are listed in Table 14-3 can be summarized thus: To teach peace, nonviolence, and community activism, teaching and practice methods must be consistent with the learning objectives.

Conclusion

The social work profession must find ways to address more adequately the deterioration of communities and the violence that increasingly af-

Table 14-3
Teaching and Practice Methodologies
for Professional Peace Consciousness

Area of Attention	Characteristic
Faculty–student relations	• safe classroom environment • sense of equality • active listening • dialogue rather than debate • shared problem solving and decision making • affirming and supporting students • encouraging critical thinking • asking for feedback • providing direct personal experiences • modeling concepts • removing as much of the power differential as possible • engaging in community development projects and experiences together
Social work practice methods	• egalitarian in nature • client and community self-determination and freedom of action • empowerment vs. social control of clients • positive influence efforts vs. forms of coercion • community building through participatory development projects • reciprocal strategies • humanizing social institutions • consciousness-raising processes • use of cultural activities and processes • emphasis on interdependence • bottom-up social and economic development strategies • conflict resolution strategies

flicts them. The greatest and most important challenge for social workers is to become global professionals who understand the deeply embedded and submerged structural foundation of violence, which feeds violence at the institutional and individual levels in an increasingly interdependent world. A paradigmatic shift in consciousness is required if we are to understand the different layers of violence that plague our world and to reclaim our professional roots in community activism, peacemaking, and internationalism. Since the time of Jane Addams and others of her era who worked with and learned from new immigrants to the United States,

> We have come full circle. . . . Our communities are once again being transformed by a worldwide demographic revolution. Driven by influences beyond our borders, people from many shores arrive here looking for a new start. The United States in general, and the social work profession in particular, are not prepared for this dramatic change. Social workers should be ahead of the national learning curve on how to build hospitable communities, and recognizing the interdependence of nations. As brokers between the old and the new, in assisting people to adjust to change, and in helping communities redefine themselves and build on their strengths, social workers need to be astute global thinkers. (NASW, 1996, p. 6)

References

Billups, J. O. (1990). Toward social development as an organizing concept for social work and related social professions and movements. *Social Development Issues, 12*(3), 14–26.

Billups, J. O. (1994). The social development model as an organizing framework for social work practice. In R. G. Meinert, J. T. Pardeck, & W. P. Sullivan (Eds.), *Issues in social work: A critical analysis* (pp. 21–37). Westport, CT: Auburn House.

Boulding, K. E. (1977). Twelve friendly quarrels with Johan Galtung. *Journal of Peace Research, 16*(1), 75–86.

Bowen, J. (1988, September–October). Of foremothers and feminism: WILPF's heritage. *Peace and Freedom,* p. 1.

Bryant, S. (1993). *Violence in social work literature.* Unpublished manuscript, Northern Virginia Commonwealth University School of Social Work, Richmond, VA.

Council on Social Work Education (CSWE). (1994). *Handbook on accreditation standards and procedures.* Alexandria, VA: Author.

Crane, J. (1986). Potential contributions of social work education to peace studies. *Social Worker/Le Travailleur Social, 54*(3), 102–106.

Dalai Lama. (1994). Foreword. In M. Henderson (Ed.), *All her paths are peace: Women pioneers in peacemaking* (pp. ix–x). West Hartford, CT: Kumarian Press.

Elliott, D. (1993). Social work and social development: Towards an integrative model for social work practice. *International Social Work, 36*(1), 21–36.

Estes, R. (1992). *Internationalizing social work education: A guide to resources for a new century.* Philadelphia: School of Social Work, University of Pennsylvania.

Galtung, J. (1969). Violence, peace and peace research. *Journal of Peace Research, 10*(3), 167–191.

Healy, L. M. (1988). Curriculum building in international social work: Toward preparing professionals for the global age. *Journal of Social Work Education, 24*(3), 221–228.

Healy, L. M. (1992). *Introducing international development content in social work curriculum.* Washington, DC: National Association of Social Workers.

Hoff, M. D., & McNutt, J. G. (Eds.). (1994). *The global environmental crisis: Implications for social welfare and social work.* Brookfield, VT: Ashgate.

Hokenstad, M. C., Khinduka, S. K., & Midgley, J. (Eds.). (1992). *Profiles in international social work.* Washington, DC: NASW Press.

Keefe, T., & Roberts, R. (1991). *Realizing peace: An introduction to peace studies.* Ames: Iowa State University Press.

Klein, R. (1987, March). *Integrating peace and nonviolence in social work education and social work practice.* Paper presented at the Annual Program Meeting of the Council on Social Work Education.

Lloyd, G. A. (1982). Social development as a political philosophy: Implications for curriculum development in social work education. In D. S. Sanders (Ed.), *The developmental perspective in social work* (pp. 43–50). Manoa: School of Social Work, University of Hawaii.

Midgley, J. (1990). International social work: Learning from the Third World. *Social Work, 35*, 295–301.

Midgley, J. (1992). The challenge of international social work. In M. C. Hokenstad, S. K. Khinduka, & J. Midgley (Eds.), *Profiles in international social work* (pp. 13–27). Washington, DC: NASW Press.

National Association of Social Workers. (1996). *The violence and development project: Expanding capacities for community building and global learning* (preliminary funding proposal by the National Association of Social Workers in collaboration with the Council on Social Work Education and the Benton Foundation). Washington, DC: Author.

Paiva, J.F.X. (1977). A conception of social development. *Social Service Review, 51*(2), 327–336.

Reardon, B. A. (1988). *Comprehensive peace education: Educating for global responsibility.* New York: Teachers College Press.

Reynolds, B. (1986). Focus on peace: Social work faces world conflict. *Catalyst,* 5(4), 90–91.

Sanders, D., & Matsuoka, J. K. (1989). *Peace and development: An interdisciplinary perspective.* Honolulu: University of Hawaii Press.

Serron, L. A. (1980). *Scarcity, exploitation and poverty: Malthus and Marx in Mexico.* Norman: University of Oklahoma.

Spergel, I. (1977). Social development and social work. *Administration in Social Work, 1*(3), 221–233.

Spergel, I. (1982). The role of the social developer. In D. S. Sanders (Ed.), *The developmental perspective in social work.* Manoa: School of Social Work, University of Hawaii.

Van Soest, D. (1992). *Incorporating peace and social justice into the social work curriculum.* Washington, DC: Peace and Social Justice Committee, National Association of Social Workers.

Van Soest, D., & Bryant, S. (1995). Violence reconceptualized for social work: The urban dilemma. *Social Work, 40,* 549–557.

Van Soest, D., & Crosby, J. (1996). *Challenges of violence worldwide: A curriculum module.* Washington, DC: NASW Press.

Walz, T., Sharma, S., & Birnbaum, C. (1988). *Gandhian thought as a theory base for social work.* Unpublished manuscript.

Resources

Organizations

Adolescent Violence Prevention Resource Center
Susan Gallagher, Director
Education Development Center, Inc.
55 Chapel Street
Newton, MA 02158
617-969-7100; FAX: 617-244-3436
Assists maternal and child health agencies as they develop new adolescent violence prevention programs and improve current prevention efforts. One of six centers in the Children's Safety Network. Provides written resources as well as consultations. Biannual newsletter.

Alcohol and Drug Problems Association of North America
444 North Capitol Street, NW, Suite 181
Washington, DC 20001
202-737-4340

Alliance for a Global Community
American Council for Voluntary International Action
1717 Massachusetts Avenue, NW, Suite 801
Washington, DC 20036
202-667-8227; FAX: 202-667-8236
Publishes a newsletter called Connections *10 times a year about the links between the United States and countries of the global South.*

American Friends Service Committee/
Immigration Law Enforcement Monitoring Project
5711 Harrisburg
Houston, TX 77011
713-926-2799

American Friends Service Committee
Primitivo Rodriguez, Director
Mexico–U.S. Border Program
National Community Relations Division
1501 Cherry Street
Philadelphia, PA 19102
215-241-7123
Conducts research and promotes justice in Mexican immigration law, policy, and procedures.

Amnesty International
1 Easton Street
London WC1X 8DJ England

Amnesty International of America
322 8th Avenue
New York, NY 10001
212-807-8400

Asian Law Caucus
468 Bush Street, 3rd floor
San Francisco, CA 94108
415-391-1655

Association of Multi-Ethnic Americans
P.O. Box 191726
San Francisco, CA 94119-1726
510-523-2632
Includes local organizations representing interracial and multiethnic families and individuals. It conducts educational programs and promotes the advancement of multiethnic children and adults. Publishes Melange *quarterly.*

Bread for the World
802 Rhode Island Avenue, NE
Washington, DC 20018
202-269-0200
A citizens' lobby movement that works through more than 1,000 local groups to influence U.S. government policies on hunger issues.

Brookings Institution
1775 Massachusetts Avenue, NW
Washington, DC 20036
202-797-6105
A think tank engaged in research, education, and publishing on important issues of foreign and domestic policy. Publishes the quarterly Brookings Review *as well as a catalog of its other publications.*

Center for Democratic Renewal
P.O. Box 50469
Atlanta, GA 30302-0469
404-221-0025
A national clearinghouse for information about the white supremacist movement in general and the Ku Klux Klan in particular. Works to end racial violence and bigotry and offers programs of education, research, victim assistance, community organizing, leadership training, and public policy advocacy. Publishes a bimonthly newsletter, Monitor, *and the manual* When Hate Groups Come to Town: A Handbook of Community Responses.

Center for Immigrant Rights
48 St. Marks Place
New York, NY 10003
212-505-6890

Center for Substance Abuse Prevention
5600 Fishers Lane, Rockwall II Building
Rockville, MD 20852
301-443-0373

Center for the Applied Study of Ethnoviolence
The Prejudice Institute
Stephens Hall Annex, Towson State University
Towson, MD 21204
410-830-2435; FAX: 410-830-2455

Center for Victims of Torture
722 Fulton Street, SE
Minneapolis, MN 55455
612-626-2465
A nonprofit full treatment center that serves victims of torture. The only such center in the United States. Publishes The Storycloth *semiannually.*

Center for Women's Global Leadership
Charlotte Bunch, Director
Douglass College, Rutgers University
27 Clifton Avenue
New Brunswick, NJ 08903-0270
908-932-8782; FAX: 908-932-1180

Center of Concern
3700 13th Street, NE
Washington, DC 20017
202-635-2757
Engages in social analysis, theological reflection, policy advocacy, and public education on issues of peace and justice. Advocates self-determination and economic independence for developing nations. Publishes a bimonthly newsletter, Center Focus, *and books, including* Dialogue on Debt: Alternative Analyses and Solutions.

Center to Prevent Handgun Violence
1225 Eye Street, NW, Suite 1100
Washington, DC 20005
202-289-7319
Publishes CPHV: Rx for Gun Violence; *free.*

Children as Witness to Community Violence
Dr. Hope Hill
Howard University Department of Psychology
525 Bryant Street, NW
Washington, DC 20011
202-806-5199
Program that is developing a culturally based prevention and treatment model for African American children who are constant witnesses to community violence. Goals are to prevent the occurrence of negative psychological symptoms such as PTSD among children exposed to chronic community violence; to lessen the psychological effects of exposure among children already displaying psychological symptoms; and to help children develop coping skills to reduce the likelihood of their involvement in future violence.

Children Now
727 Third Street, SW
Washington, DC 20024

Children's Defense Fund
25 E Street, NW
Washington, DC 20001
202-628-8787
Educates about the needs of children in the United States and encourages preventive investment in children before they get sick, drop out of school, suffer family breakdown, or get into trouble.

Children's Express
1440 New York Avenue, NW, Suite 510
Washington, DC 20005
202-737-7377
A national youth journalist organization that gives children a voice in the media. Collects the voices of children and teens and conducts public hearings. Writes a weekly national column that is researched, reported, and edited by Children's Express reporters.

Coalition against Trafficking in Women
Times Square Station
P.O. Box 2166
New York, NY 10108
212-874-6170

Committee for International Human Rights Inquiry
New York City NASW Chapter
545 8th Avenue, 6th floor
New York, NY 10018
212-947-5000
A coalition of social service unions and organizations that oppose human rights violations against social service workers, other workers performing social service functions, and those whom they serve around the world.

Congress of Racial Equality (CORE)
1457 Flatbush Avenue
Brooklyn, NY 11210
718-434-3580
A human rights organization that works to promote civil liberties and social justice. Seeks to establish true equality and self-determination for all people regardless of race, creed, or ethnic background. Publishes CORE Magazine *quarterly and a monthly newsletter,* Correspondent.

Consortium on Peace Research, Education, and Development
4103 Chain Bridge Road, Suite 315
Fairfax, VA 22030-4444
703-273-4485
email: bwien@gmu.edu
A community of researchers, activists, and educators working for the nonviolent resolution of conflict.

CSWE Commission on International Social Welfare Education
1600 Duke Street, Suite 300
Alexandria, VA 22314-3421
Concerned with internationalizing social work through curriculum development. Publishes Inter-Ed.

Defense for Children International
Marc-Alain Berberat, Secretary General
P.O. Box 88, 1211 Geneva 20, Switzerland
41 22 734 05 58; FAX: 41 22 740 11 45
Environmental Project on Central America
Earth Island International Center
13 Columbus Avenue
San Francisco, CA 94111
415-788-3666
Works to stop ecological devastation in Central America and to educate the
public about deforestation, pesticide use, and U.S.-funded militarization
in the South. Regularly publishes Green Papers *on these issues.*

Equity Institute
6400 Hollis Street, Suite 15
Emeryville, CA 94608
510-658-4577; FAX: 510-658-5184
e-mail: equity@aimnet.com
A national nonprofit agency that teaches people how to reduce racism, sex-
ism, anti-Semitism, classism, ableism, heterosexism/homophobia, sizism,
and ageism. Dedicated to training community and corporate leaders in
developing multicultural leadership skills and helping organizations create
inclusive institutions.

Ethnic Anonymous
c/o F. J. Nubee
1631 Belmont Avenue, #107
Seattle, WA 98122
206-325-8091
EA is a self-help group patterned after Alcoholics Anonymous by applying
a 12-step program to individuals "whose common problem is an inability
to view the self and others as equals and to maintain functional lives." Con-
ducts research and educational programs and publishes the quarterly Ethnic Anonymous Newsletter.

Federation of American Scientists Fund
307 Massachusetts Avenue, NE
Washington, DC 20002
202-675-1018; FAX: 202-675-1018
e-mail: llumpe@igc apc.org
Publishes Arms Sales Monitor*; $20 a year.*

Feed the Children
P.O. Box 36
Oklahoma City, OK 73101-0036

Global Awareness Society International
c/o Dr. James C. Pomfret, Treasurer
Bloomsburg University
Bloomsburg, PA 17815
717-389-4504 or 717-389-4242; FAX: 717-389-3890
Promotes mutual understanding and appreciation to create a cooperative global village.

Global Exchange
2017 Mission Street, #303
San Francisco, CA 94110
415-255-7296; 800-497-1994; FAX: 415-255-7498
Sponsors reality tours and study seminars to Africa, Asia, Latin America, and the Caribbean, which examine topics such as the environment, political situation, economy, public health, women's issues, culture, and human rights. Also publishes excellent books at reasonable prices.

The Hunger Project
1 Madison Avenue, 8A
New York, NY 10010
212-532-4255
An educational organization committed to eliminating world hunger by the year 2000. Educates the public about the worldwide problem of hunger and starvation. Free semimonthly report of facts, trends, and opinion on international development, World Development Forum.

Institute for Food and Development Policy (Food First)
145 Ninth Street
San Francisco, CA 94103
415-864-8555
Provides research and education on world hunger issues. Contends that world hunger can be eliminated if countries of the North such as the United States allow countries of the South to take control of their own food production. Publishes Food First News *quarterly and other materials.*

Institute for Women's Policy Research
1400 20th Street, NW, Suite 104
Washington, DC 20036
202-785-5100; FAX: 202-833-4362
Conducts research and publishes reports on various issues concerning women and poverty in the United States.

Institute on Black Chemical Abuse
2614 Nicollet Avenue
Minneapolis, MN 55408
612-871-7878

InterAction American Council for Voluntary International Action
1717 Massachusetts Avenue, NW, Suite 801
Washington, DC 20036
202-667-8227
An umbrella organization for several hundred international development agencies with programs throughout the world; publishes Monday Developments *biweekly.*

Inter-American Institute of Human Rights
Apartado Postal 10081
San Jose, 1000 Costa Rica

Interfaith Hunger Appeal
475 Riverside Drive, Suite 1630
New York, NY 10015-0079
212-870-2035
Publishes the quarterly newsletter Hunger TeachNet *and other educational materials about development education.*

Inter-Hemispheric Education Resource Center
Box 4506
Albuquerque, NM 87196
505-842-8288
Provides educational materials on issues such as human rights and oil and uranium exploration in underdeveloped areas. Opposes U.S. policies in Central America and the Caribbean. Publishes Central American Factbook.

International Activities Committee
National Association of Social Workers
Peace and International Affairs Program
750 First Street, NE, Suite 700
Washington, DC 20002-4241
202-336-8388
Publishes a newsletter and loans videotapes, curriculum materials, and other resources.

International Association of Schools of Social Work
c/o CSWE
1600 Duke Street, Suite 300
Alexandria, VA 22314-3421
An international membership association representing approximately 1,700 social work programs in 100 countries. Sponsors international conferences and publishes the IASSW Newsletter. *Both individual and institutional memberships are available.*

International Center for Research on Women
1717 Massachusetts Avenue, NW, Suite 302
Washington, DC 20036
202-797-0007; FAX: 202-797-0020

International Council on Social Welfare
Sirpa Utriainen, Secretary General
380 Saint-Antoine Quest, #3200
Montreal, Quebec, Canada H243X7
1-314-287-3280
A global nongovernmental organization representing tens of thousands of smaller organizations in more than 70 countries, as well as more than 20,000 NGOs, with a focus on advocacy on behalf of vulnerable and marginalized groups the world over.

International Labor Organization
Washington Branch
1828 L Street, NW, Suite 801
Washington, DC 20036
202-653-7652
ILO publications, research studies, reports, statistical surveys, and other materials address issues related to improving living and working conditions worldwide.

International Monetary Fund
700 19th Street, NW
Washington, DC 20431
202-623-7000
Promotes international economic cooperation, helps keep a balance of trade among nations, and lends its member nations money when necessary. Publishes the semimonthly IMF Survey *and other materials.*

International Women's Rights Action Watch
Humphrey Institute of Public Affairs
University of Minnesota
301 19th Avenue South
Minneapolis, MN 55455

International Women's Tribune Centre
777 UN Plaza
New York, NY 10017
212-687-8633; FAX: 212-661-2704

Maryknoll Mission Center of New England
50 Dunster Road
Chestnut Hill, MA 02167
617-232-8050
Aims to increase awareness about the global South by providing educational materials on world hunger, the harmful effects of multinational corporations in the global South, and U.S. involvement in Central America. Publishes Maryknoll *magazine monthly.*

Mexican American Legal Defense and Educational Fund
634 S. Spring Street, 11th floor
Los Angeles, CA 90014
213-629-2512

Minnesota Advocates for Human Rights
Domestic Violence in Eastern Europe Committee
400 Second Avenue South, Room 1050
Minneapolis, MN 55401

Narcotics Anonymous
World Service Office
P.O. Box 9999
Van Nuys, CA 91409
818-780-3951

National Alliance against Racist and Political Repression
11 John Street, Suite 702
New York, NY 10038
212-406-3542

NASW National Committee on Racial and Ethnic Diversity
National Association of Social Workers
750 First Street, NE, Suite 700
Washington, DC 20002-4241
800-638-8799
A standing NASW committee to promote equality of treatment and opportunity for social workers and others who are members of various racial or ethnic groups.

National Clearinghouse for Alcohol and Drug Information
P.O. Box 2345
Rockville, MD 20852
301-468-2600

National Clearinghouse on Development Education
c/o American Forum for Education in a Global Age
45 John Street, Suite 1200
New York, NY 10038
212-732-8606
Provides the latest information about programs, materials, and practices in teaching about nations of the global South. Seeks to ensure that American schools achieve and maintain a global perspective in education so that students become responsible citizens in a global age. Publishes Global Resource Book, Global Yellow Pages, *and the monthly bulletin* Access.

National Coalition against Sexual Assault
P.O. Box 21378
Washington, DC 20009
202-483-7165

National Coalition Building Institute
172 Brattle Street
Arlington, MA 02714
617-646-5802
NCBI runs training programs to reduce prejudice in schools and workplaces. Trains leaders in communication and conflict resolution skills. Publishes the newsletter Working It Out *and several manuals.*

National Committee to Prevent Child Abuse
332 S. Michigan Avenue, Suite 1600
Chicago, IL 60604
312-663-3520; FAX: 312-939-8962
Provides information through the NCPCA Monthly Memorandum and other resources and conducts conferences on issues related to violence.

National Foundation to Improve Television
60 State Street, Suite 3400
Boston, MA 02109
617-523-6353

National Institute against Prejudice and Violence
31 South Greene Street
Baltimore, MD 21201
410-328-7551
National research center concerned with violence and intimidation moti-
vated by prejudice. Publishes the newsletter Forum *quarterly.*

National Network of Violence Prevention Practitioners
Education Development Center, Inc.
55 Chapel Street
Newton, MA 02158-1060
617-969-7101, extension 2359
e-mail: kcroke@edc.org
Anyone active in the field of adolescent violence prevention is invited to
join this network. Members represent violence prevention programs, schools,
community-based and national organizations, university faculty, criminal
justice, and public health agencies. Members receive a quarterly bulletin,
fact sheets, a worldwide web home page, reproducible violence prevention
materials, and a membership directory.

National Women Abuse Prevention Project
2000 P Street, NW, Suite 508
Washington, DC 20036
202-857-0216

Oxfam America
115 Broadway
Boston, MA 02116
617-482-1211
Funds self-help projects in the global South, with the goal that recipients
achieve economic self-reliance, particularly in food production. Publishes
a newsletter and other materials.

Panos Institute
1717 Massachusetts Avenue, NW, Suite 301
Washington, DC 20036
202-483-0044
An excellent source of literature and other resources that feature voices of people from the global South.

Program for Trauma, Violence, and Sudden Bereavement
Dr. Robert Pynoos, Director
UCLA Department of Psychiatry and Biobehavioral Science
Neuropsychiatric Institute
760 Westwood Plaza, Box 18
Los Angeles, CA 90024
310-825-0511
A research and clinical prevention and intervention program for children. Responds to requests for assistance after extreme acts of violence or disaster. Follows several populations of children exposed to different types of violence, including spousal abuse, homicide, rape, and suicidal behavior, as well as being victimized by juvenile gang violence and community violence.

Programs for the Rehabilitation of Torture Victims
3239 Bennett Drive
Los Angeles, CA 90068
213-851-0726

Refugee Women in Development
Sima Wali, Executive Director
810 First Street, NE, Suite 300
Washington, DC 20002
202-289-1104

Save the Children
17 Grove Lane
London SE5 8RD England
071-703-5400
Works in more than 25 countries with child victims of wars; trains social workers to carry out family tracing programs; supports treatment for emotional distress; provides care in refugee camps and family centers; and helps to rebuild the infrastructure of countries and the lives of its children and families, which have literally been torn apart by war.

Social Workers for Peace and Justice
National Association of Social Workers
Peace and International Affairs Program
750 First Street, NE, Suite 700
Washington, D.C. 20002-4241
202-336-8388
Publishes a newsletter and loans videotapes and other resources.

Southern Poverty Law Center
400 Washington Avenue
Montgomery, AL 36104
A membership organization that takes on legal and educational work in the cause of justice and tolerance. "Teaching Tolerance," a project established in 1991, produces educational materials (curriculum kits, videotapes, books) and a magazine (Teaching Tolerance) that are available to educators free of charge. Another SPLC project, "Klanwatch," monitors hate groups in the United States and produces reports in a publication called Intelligence Report.

Study Circles Resource Center
687A Pomfret Street, P.O. Box 203
Pomfret, CT 06258
203-928-2616; FAX: 203-928-3713
Promotes the use of study circles on critical social and political issues. Based on the premise that, in order to function at its full potential, democracy requires the participation of a concerned, informed public. Topics include racism and race relations.

Third World Women's Project
c/o Institute for Policy Studies
1601 Connecticut Avenue, NW
Washington, DC 20009
202-234-9382, extension 234
Works toward global education on such issues as women in Third World development and human rights. Provides a critical examination of U.S. policies toward the global South and offers alternative strategies for policy making. Publishes the quarterly Letelier–Moffitt Update *on its human rights project and other materials.*

United Nations Centre for Human Rights
Palais des Nations
CH-1211 Geneva 10, Switzerland

United Nations Department of Public Information
Room S-1040
United Nations
New York, NY 10017
FAX: 212-963-1186
Published a series of issue papers for the World Summit for Social Development, held March 6–12, 1995, in Copenhagen, Denmark. Short, easy-to-read papers full of pertinent information about worldwide poverty.

United States Committee for Refugees
1717 Massachusetts Avenue, NW, Suite 701
Washington, DC 20036

Upper Midwest Women's History Center
Hamline University
Crossroads Center
1536 Hewitt Avenue
St. Paul, MN 55104-1284
612-644-1727

Women's International League for Peace and Freedom
1213 Race Street
Philadelphia, PA 19107-1691
215-563-7110

World Youth against Drugs
100 Edgewood Avenue, Suite 1216
Atlanta, GA 30303
800-241-9746

Further Reading

American Friends Service Committee. (1994, July). *Operation blockade: A city divided* (report from the Immigration Law Enforcement Monitoring Project). Philadelphia: Author.

This is a report about Operation Blockade, an initiative of the U.S. Border Patrol that cut the twin cities of El Paso, Texas, and Ciudad Juarez, Mexico, off from each other by positioning 400 agents and their vehicles along a 20-mile stretch of the border. The report proposes rethinking immigration and border control policies so that they are the product of mutual agreement and respect human rights and dignity.

Bennet, O., & Bexley, J. (1995). *Arms to defend, arms to protect: Women's experience of conflict and its aftermath.*

Oral testimonies from women regarding their experience with conflict and its impact on their lives, families, and communities.

Books on Women and Development, Ink, 777 United Nations Plaza, New York, NY 10017.

Bullard, S. (Ed.). (1991). *The Ku Klux Klan: A history of racism and violence* (4th ed.). Published by Klanwatch, a project of the Southern Poverty Law Center, 400 Washington Avenue, Montgomery, AL 36104.

A special report delineating the background of the Klan and its battle with the law and pointing out why hate groups cannot be ignored.

Burke, A. C. (1995). Substance abuse: Legal issues. In R. L. Edwards (Ed.-in-Chief), *Encyclopedia of social work* (19th ed., Vol. 3, pp. 2347–2357). Washington, DC: National Association of Social Workers.

Describes the resurgence of antidrug sentiment and increased legal action of the "war on drugs" in the United States and the implications for social work.

Cagan, B. (1994). A case study of populist community development in rural El Salvador. *Social Development Issues, 16*(2), 36–49.

El Salvador's civil war has given rise to numerous grassroots communities that offer populist models of social development. This article examines the largest of these, Segundo Montes City, as it attempts to preserve the egalitarian values that shaped the community's development in a refugee camp and that are now threatened by the introduction of market forces.

Cahill, K. M. (1994). *Clearing the fields: Solutions to the global land mines crisis.* New York: Basic Books.

Identifies steps needed to build widespread support for an international agreement on a total ban on the production, stockpiling, transfer, and export of mines and their components. The contributors—all experts in their fields—agree that there must be an unequivocal acceptance of the goal to eliminate the danger of these horrific weapons of indiscriminate destruction.

Carrillo, R. (1992). *Battered dreams: Violence against women as an obstacle to development.* New York: United Nations Development Fund for Women.

Links gender-based violence to development. Based on the thesis that development plans cannot succeed if they ignore the reality that gender-based violence hinders women's participation in the process at many levels. Gives useful direction for programs and policy and includes a comprehensive resource section.

Center for Advanced Study of International Development. (1991, October). *Ethnicity, social justice and development: A selected bibliography.* Prepared by T. Kallio, Center for Advanced Study of International Development, 306 Berkey Hall, Michigan State University, East Lansing, MI 48824-1111.

This bibliography provides an overview of literature published in the 1980s and 1990s on ethnicity, social justice and development, and related topics such as ethnic conflict and conflict resolution.

Center for Substance Abuse and Mental Health Services Administration. (1995). *Curriculum modules on alcohol and other drug problems for schools of social work.* Washington, DC: National Clearinghouse for Alcohol and Drug Information.

BSW/MSW curriculum materials developed by the National Association of Social Workers, the Council on Social Work Education, the National Association of Deans and Directors, and the National Association of Baccalaureate Program Directors. Consists of five modules filled with helpful information and resources: Human Behavior in the Social Environment, Practice, Policy, Research, and Field Practice. To obtain a copy, call 800-729-6686.

Center for Women's Global Leadership. (1993, June). *Testimonies of the Global Tribunal on Violations of Women's Human Rights, at the United Nations World Conference on Human Rights.* Highland Park, NJ: Plowshares Press.

A compilation of 33 testimonies by women from 25 countries. The testimonies highlight the obstacles to women's human rights in both the global North and the global South that stem from violence against women, violations of women in war and conflict situations, and more.

Center for Women's Global Leadership. (1994). *Gender violence and women's rights in Africa.* Highland Park, NJ: Plowshares Press.

Papers that were presented at a symposium held at Rutgers University on April 7, 1993. Focus is on the ideas, activities, and strategies of continentally based African women from diverse perspectives who challenge the abuses leveled against them at familial, communal, and national levels.

Chester, B. (1995). Victims of torture and trauma. In R. L. Edwards (Ed.-in-Chief), *Encyclopedia of social work* (19th ed., Vol. 3, pp. 2445–2452). Washington, DC: National Association of Social Workers.

A concise overview of stress and attendant trauma on conceptual and technical levels. Includes definitions, consequences, treatment modalities, therapeutic issues, and case studies.

Correspondicia. Woman to Woman: 606 Shaw Street, Toronto, Ontario, Canada, M6G 3L6. Mujer a Mujer: A.P. 24-553, Colonia, Roma, 06701, Mexico, D.F.

A bilingual forum for sharing analysis, information, and resources about the impact of globalization and economic restructuring on women's lives and struggles, published three times a year by Mujer a Mujer, a collective of women based in Canada, the United States, and Mexico. A year's subscription for individuals from the United States costs $10, $20 for institutions. Checks should be made payable to Mujer a Mujer/Woman to Woman.

Cozic, C. P. (Ed.). (1995). *Ethnic conflict.* San Diego: Greenhaven Press.

Provides a wide range of suggestions to cap brewing conflict within, between, and among ethnic groups in the United States. Several writers discuss how Americans should reconcile their ethnic heritages, similarities, and differences.

Cummings, B. (1990). *Dam the rivers, damn the people: Development and resistance in Amazonian Brazil.* London: Earthscan Publications Ltd.

Describes the plans for development of Balbina in Amazonas and the Xingu River in Para (which the state attempted to keep secret), the extent to which these projects will destroy the forest, the consequent dispossession of the people of the forest, and, above all, their growing resistance. Illustrates how the outcome of their struggle affects us all.

Currie, E. (1993). *Reckoning: Drugs, the cities and the American future.* New York: Farrar, Straus & Giroux, Hill & Wang.

A perceptive argument about the social roots of the drug crisis and steps we must take to solve it. Draws on a vast body of research, both in the United

*States and abroad, to examine the uses and limits of traditional strategies—
law enforcement, treatment, legalization. Argues that the only hope lies in
a more profound reckoning with the underlying causes of the drug problem: disintegration of our cities' economic and social structures.*

Danaher, K. (1994). *50 years is enough: The case against the World Bank
and the International Monetary Fund.* San Francisco: Global Exchange.

*Excellent critique by 36 authors on the global economic context, country
case studies, women, the environment, tribal people, internal scandals, and
alternatives. Includes a resource section and guide to organizations; $14.*

Davies, M. (Comp.). (1983). *Third World–second sex: Women's struggles
and national liberation—Third World women speak out.* Atlantic Highlands, NJ: Zed Books.

*A compilation of interviews and articles by diverse women from the global
South who share no one approach to women's liberation but who, together,
show the revolutionary emergence of a new feminist consciousness among
women of the global South.*

Davies, M. (Ed.). (1994). *Women and violence: Realities and responses
worldwide.* London: Zed Books.

*Highlights the extent of the problem of violence against women and actions
against such violence taken by individual women and groups from more
than 30 countries as diverse as Papua New Guinea, Argentina, Tanzania,
France, Scotland, Bosnia, India, and Tibet. Their writings examine the incidence of domestic violence and child sexual abuse, sexual harassment in
the workplace, rape and torture in war, genital mutilation, and the effects
of male violence on women's reproductive health.*

De La Rosa, M., Lambert, E. Y., & Gropper, B. (Eds.). (1990). *Drugs and
violence: Causes, correlates, and consequences* (NIDA Research Monograph 103). Rockville, MD: National Institute on Drug Abuse, U.S. Department of Health and Human Services. To order, call 800-729-6686.

*Reports of studies on violence in crack distribution networks in Detroit
and New York City. Shows correlations between drug abuse and domestic
violence and links among gangs and violence; crack and violence among*

juvenile delinquents; violence, drugs, and prostitution; and mental illness, drugs, and violence. Concludes with a conceptual model to be used when studying the relationship between drug abuse and violence.

De Silva, D. (1989). *Against all odds.* Washington DC: Panos Institute.

This book deals with ordinary people and how they have broken through the poverty trap in India, Tanzania, Bangladesh, Kenya, Sri Lanka, Indonesia, and Zambia. Journalists from each country visited development project sites and listened to the people whom the project was intended to benefit. This very interesting book is a compilation of their reports.

Directory of International Networking Resources on Violence against Women. Available from Victimization of Women and Children, P.O. Box 2462, Ada, OK 74820.

Epstein, G., Graham, J., & Nembhard, J. (1993). *Creating a new world economy: Force of change and plans for action.* Philadelphia: Temple University Press.

This book was written by a group of economists who—based on their years of research and their experience teaching activists from community movements, labor unions, environmental, feminist, and other groups—assembled this look into the emerging global economy. The book is designed for those who think that the purpose of knowledge is to change the world for the better.

Estes, R. J. (Ed.). (1992). *Internationalizing social work education: A guide to resources for a new century.* Philadelphia: School of Social Work, University of Pennsylvania.

Provides a wealth of resources that address various international development topics of interest to social work.

Evans, A., & Weiss, B. P. (1995). Developing a violence prevention coalition in Los Angeles. In B. Bradford & M. A. Gwynne (Eds.), *Down to earth: Community perspectives on health, development, and the environment* (pp. 35–42). West Hartford, CT: Kumarian Press.

Violence prevention experts from various disciplines formed a coalition of community-based agencies, including gang and former gang members, to address the problem of violence in Los Angeles County. This book outlines the organizational structure, efforts, and achievements of the "generalized community approach" in the first years of the Violence Prevention Coalition.

Figley, C. R. (Ed.). (1995). *Compassion fatigue: Coping with secondary traumatic stress disorder in those who treat the traumatized.* New York: Brunner/Mazel.

Comprehensive book aimed at increasing understanding, treatment, and prevention of compassion fatigue.

Garbarino, J. (1995). *Let's talk about living in a world with violence.* Available from the Erikson Institute, Children in Danger Resource Center, 420 N. Wabash Avenue, Suite 600, Chicago, IL 60611; telephone 312-755-2250.

A hands-on educational tool written to help children process their feelings, thoughts, and experiences as they relate to violence. The workbook is designed to foster dialogue between child and adult as well as among children in group settings.

Healy, L. (1992). *Introducing international development content in social work curriculum.* Washington, DC: National Association of Social Workers, Office of Peace and International Affairs (call 202-336-8388 for information on ordering).

Provides key concepts and curriculum issues and learning modules on global poverty, hunger, and development; the rights of the child; and inter-country adoption as a field of application.

Journal of Multicultural Social Work. Haworth Press, Inc., 10 Alice Street, Binghamton, NY 13904-1580; 800-342-9678.

Dedicated to the examination of multicultural social issues as they relate to social work policy, research, theory, and practice from an international perspective. The annual subscription rate for individuals is $40.

Kabeer, N. (1994). *Reversed realities: Gender hierarchies in development thought.* New York: Women, Ink.

Lays bare the deeply entrenched biases underpinning mainstream development theory, which lead to the marginal status given to women's needs in development policy.

Macksoud, M. (1993). *Helping children cope with the stresses of war: A manual for parents and teachers.* New York: UNICEF.

An easy-to-read and easy-to-use manual for parents and teachers in communities where children are subjected to the extreme stresses of war and other forms of systematic violence.

Morales, E. (1990). Comprehensive economic development: An alternative measure to reduce cocaine supply. *Journal of Drug Issues, 20*(4), 629–637.

Article uses published information and fieldwork data on Peru, the largest producer of cocaine, to argue that the boom in cocaine production is the result of North–South politicoeconomic relations. Recommends comprehensive economic development to wean Andean peasants from their dependence on the cocaine economy.

National Association of Social Workers. (1997). *Social work speaks* (4th ed.). Washington, DC: Author.

Includes all policy statements, including those approved at the 1996 Delegate Assembly. Policy statement on alcohol and other drugs supports drug addiction as a primary illness, not a symptom of other disorders; recognizes that addiction affects all family members, thus requiring social work attention; advocates including substance abuse knowledge and skill in social work practice throughout the profession; promotes advocacy for client services; identifies civil rights issues; supports public education; and more.

O'Connell, H. (1994). *Women and the family.* Atlantic Highlands, NJ: Zed Books.

The family can be a haven for women or a source of oppression and brutality. This is an examination of family structures worldwide and women's roles within them, particularly in the context of their increasing challenge to men's power in the family.

Omvedt, G. (1990). *Violence against women: New movements and new theories in India.* New Delhi: Raj Press, R-3 Inderpuri, New Delhi.

Essay that focuses on three major writers on women in India who represent the dynamics of the participation of women in the "new social movements" prominent in India: the ecology movement, the peasant movement, and the anti-caste movement.

Ortmann, J., Genefke, I. K., Jakobsen, L., & Lunde, I. (1987). Rehabilitation of torture victims: An interdisciplinary treatment model. *American Journal of Social Psychiatry, 7*(4), 161–167.

A report on various aspects of the work of the International Rehabilitation and Research Center for Torture Victims in Denmark, including a bio-psychosocial treatment model, preliminary research findings, and ongoing teaching, training, and educational activities.

Panos Institute. (1993). *Narcotics and development.* Washington, DC: Author.

A teaching–learning module that argues that international drug policies and programs need to deal with causes of underdevelopment—poverty, unemployment, and hopelessness. Provides an overview and history of illegal drugs and underdevelopment and gives voice to people from the global South who speak about why they grow drugs. To order, call 202-483-0044.

Panos Institute. (1994). *Conflict and development.* Washington, DC: Author.

An educational module that examines social, economic, and political factors within and among countries, especially developing ones, that contribute to violent conflict. It also describes the impact of conflict and the ways in which armed conflict reduces the potential for sustainable human development. Discusses current approaches to conflict resolution, prevention, and peacekeeping efforts.

Philleo, J., & Brisbane, F. L. (Eds.). (1995). *Cultural competence for social workers: A guide for alcohol and other drug abuse prevention professionals working with ethnic/racial communities* (CSAP Cultural Competence Series 4). Center for Substance Abuse Prevention, National Clearinghouse for Alcohol and Drug Information. To order, call 800-729-6686 and ask for DHHS Publication (SMA) 95-3075.

A special collaborative NASW/CSAP monograph that provides thought-provoking, culturally sensitive treatment of alcohol and drug issues related to six major cultural groups—Native Americans, Hispanics/Latinos, African Americans, Asian Americans, Pacific Islanders, and gay men and lesbians—to help social workers become culturally competent practitioners.

Poverty and Race Research Action Council. *Poverty & Race.* 1711 Connecticut Avenue, NW, Suite 207, Washington, DC 20009. 202-387-9887; FAX: 202-387-0764.

The newsletter is published six times a year and includes articles related to issues of poverty and race in the United States and in other countries, PRRAC updates, and resources. There is no charge for the newsletter but donations are encouraged.

Powerful images—A woman's guide to audiovisual resources. Available from Isis International, Casilla 2067, Correo Central, Santiago, Chile.

Premdas, R. (1995). *Fiji: Ethnic conflict and development.* Brookfield, VT: Ashgate.

Examines the link between ethnic conflict and development by providing a detailed background of the evolution of the communal strife in Fiji. It shows in particular the role of ethnic entrepreneurs and outbidders who instigated latent ethnic fears for political purposes. The book argues that the introduction of democratic policies in multiethnic states requires special institutions that do not cultivate zero-sum rivalry over control of the state and its resources. Good case illustration.

Prigoff, A., Abrahams, C., & Adeyeri, C.L.K. (Eds.). (1994). *Social Development Issues, 16*(1) (Special edition on gender and social development).

A wealth of articles that address critical issues related to failure of developmental approaches of past decades to advance the living standards of most of the world's women and their families. Articles present findings of research- and data-based analyses on global concerns of women and are written by social workers from both the global North and South.

Program for Community Problem Solving. (1993). *Facing racial and cultural conflict: Tools for rebuilding community.* Program for Community Problem Solving, 915 15th Street, Suite 600, Washington, DC 20005.

An easy-to-use manual that profiles 25 successful collaborative efforts across the United States in which community leaders worked to solve racial and ethnic conflicts. It offers substantial guidance on how to create communities free of hate and intolerance. Cost is $23.

Prothrow-Stith, D., & Weissman, M. (1991). *Deadly consequences: How violence is destroying our teenage population and a plan to begin solving the problem.* New York: HarperCollins.

Looks at various issues of adolescent violence and cites the need for a comprehensive approach to the problem. Discusses the need to mobilize society through its churches, schools, media, government, community organizations, and industry.

Reardon, B. A. (1985). *Sexism and the war system.* New York: Teachers College Press.

Makes the case that sexism and the war system are two interdependent manifestations of a common problem: social violence.

Rohr, J. (1989). *The Third World: Opposing viewpoints.* San Diego: Greenhaven Press.

Presents differing viewpoints on why the global South is poor, why human rights are threatened in the South, whether U.S. foreign aid benefits the South, what policies would promote development, and how Third World debt can be reduced.

Rothman, J., & Reed, B. G. (1984). Organizing community action to address alcohol and drug problems. In F. M. Cox, J. L. Erlich, & J. E. Tropman (Eds.), *Tactics and techniques of community practice* (pp. 115–130). Itasca, IL: F. E. Peacock.

Authors address the variation in communities regarding types of users, drugs of abuse, source of drugs, and their consequences. They recommend a range of objectives for a community action plan. Examples are given.

Saferworld. (1995). *The true cost of conflict.* Order from the publisher: New Press, 450 West 41st Street, New York, NY 10036; 800-233-4830.

Taking a cost–benefit approach, this book investigates the social, economic, and environmental costs of seven conflicts to the countries and regions involved in the global South, as well as to their trading and investment partners in countries of the global North. The conclusion is unequivocal: Because of the interconnectedness of today's world, conflict imposes costs on the quality of life even of those seemingly remote from it.

Salazar, L. S. (L. Fierro, Trans.). (1993). "Drug trafficking" and social and political conflicts in Latin America. *Latin American Perspectives, 20*(1), 83–93.

Examines information on the production, distribution, and consumption of drugs and the policy instruments designed to deal with their socioeconomic and political effects.

Sen, G., & Grown, C. (1987). *Development, crises, and alternative visions: Third World women's perspectives.* New York: Women, Ink.

This classic book ties the roots of women's oppression with current crises—debt, famine, militarization, and fundamentalism—that threaten women's survival and recommends short- and long-term development strategies.

Shuman, M. (1994). *Towards a global village: International community development initiatives.* Boulder, CO: Pluto Press.

Describes community-based development initiatives that are people centered, multidimensional, and two way and shows how communities can link up with countries in the global South in a new way.

Shuman, M., & Harvey, H. (1993). *Security without war: A post–cold war foreign policy.* Boulder, CO: Westview Press.

A proposal of post-cold war strategy aimed at a future without military conflict and with people-centered development.

Smith, M. L. (1992). *Why people grow drugs: Narcotics and development in the Third World.* Washington, DC: Panos Institute.

Book includes accounts from Thailand, Pakistan, Bolivia, Colombia, and Peru from the perspective of those whose survival depends on narcotics cultivation. Argues that unless the growers' views are taken into account, and viable economic alternatives developed with their particiation, control programs will continue to fail. The war against drugs may ultimately be won not by guns and laws but by sustainable development.

Steady, F. C. (1993). *Women and children first: Environment, poverty, and sustainable development.* Cambridge, MA: Schenkman.

Explores the synergy between poverty and environmental degradation and its impact on women and children. Policies that are adopted in the name of development often result in unsustainable patterns of production and consumption. Book moves women and children to the forefront of policy and is a key resource for those concerned with people-centered development.

Stiglmayer, A. (Ed.). (1994). *Mass rape: The war against women in Bosnia-Herzegovina.* Lincoln: University of Nebraska Press.

Brings to light the abuses of women's rights during the continuing war in the former Yugoslavia: torture, murder, abduction, sexual enslavement, and systematic impregnation of women. Contains interviews with female victims—primarily Muslim but also Serbian and Croatian—and with three Serbian perpetrators.

Study Circles Resource Center. (1992). *Can't we all just get along? A manual for discussion programs on racism and race relations.* Pomfret, CT: Author.

This manual offers guidance for engaging groups in a dialogue about racism and race relations. Provides suggestions for designing a program that can be individualized to meet the needs of particular communities and organizations. It is based on the philosophy of study circles, which encourages respectful listening to everyone's views.

Sudanese People. (1988). *War wounds: Development costs of conflict in southern Sudan.* Washington, DC: Panos Institute.

Eighteen Sudanese people from different sides of the political spectrum come together to tell the world about the development costs of their civil war since 1983. Using interviews, case studies, and photographs, they describe the terrifying consequences for ordinary people caught up in combat and the implications for future development strategy. A good case example of the connections between violence and development or underdevelopment.

Taylor, C. (1992). *The house that crack built.* San Francisco: Chronicle Books.

Author transforms a well-known nursery rhyme into a powerful poem about the tragic problem of illegal drugs and all its victims. From the harvesting of the coca plants to the dealers and gangs on the streets to the innocent crack babies born every day, cocaine's journey is starkly traced from beginning to end.

The Third World Guide 1993/94. New Internationalist, 1011 Bloor Street West, Suite 300, Toronto, Ontario M6H 1M1, Canada; 416-588-6478; FAX: 416-537-6435.

A global survey from the vantage point of researchers, journalists, and academics in the global South. Six hundred thirty pages of facts and information on key global development issues such as arms, children, housing, global warming, transnational corporations, poverty, aid, refugees, the General Agreement on Tariffs and Trade (GATT), and so on.

Toubia, N. (1993). *Female genital mutilation: A call for global action.* New York: Women, Ink.

Provides specific information about female genital mutilation, its effects, the extent to which it is practiced, and its cultural and religious significance. Calls for specific actions and provides list of advocacy groups around the world.

United Nations. (1987). *Methods of combatting torture* (Fact Sheet no. 4) and *Enforced or involuntary disappearances* (Fact Sheet no. 6). Both fact sheets can be obtained at no charge from the Centre for Human Rights, New York Office, United Nations, New York, NY 10017.

Both fact sheets are intended to assist the reader in better understanding basic human rights, what the United Nations is doing to promote and protect them, and the international machinery available to help realize those rights.

United Nations. (1989). *Violence against women in the family.* New York: Author.

Provides an overall picture of violence against women in the family as a world issue rather than as an issue that is confined to one country or cultural system.

United Nations. (1992). *Teaching and learning about human rights: A manual for schools of social work and the social work profession.* United Nations Center for Human Rights, United Nations Office at Geneva, Palais des Nations, 8–14, vanue de la Paix, CH-1211 Geneva 10, Switzerland; (41 22) 917-1530 or 4326 .

A practical manual for social work developed by a diverse group of social workers and social work educators; introduces international human rights documents and explains how to use them in social work education.

United Nations Children's Fund (UNICEF). (1994, January). *Antipersonnel landmines: A plague on children.* New York: United Nations.

UNICEF. (1994). *The progress of nations 1994* and *The state of the world's children 1994.* Order from UNICEF, 3 United Nations Plaza, New York, NY 10017.

United Nations Development Programme (UNDP). (1994). *Human development report 1994.* UNDP, 1 United Nations Plaza, New York, NY 10017.

Provides extensive information and integrates the peace agenda and the development agenda. Makes the point that without peace, there may be no development, but without development, peace is threatened.

United Nations Development Programme. (1994). *Programming through the lens of gender.* UNDP, 1 United Nations Plaza, New York, NY 10017.

This information package is composed of eight booklets that define the gender approach to development. It explains the steps taken by UNDP in developing a strategy for mainstreaming women's issues into programming. Includes information on services to the field, The Fourth World Conference on Women, special initiatives, programming guidelines, key concerns for UNDP staff, a survey of approaches to women in development, as well as an overview and additional reading suggestions.

Van Soest, D. (1992). *Incorporating peace and social justice into the social work curriculum.* Washington, DC: National Association of Social Workers, Office of Peace and International Affairs (call 202-336-8388 for information on ordering).

Two hundred pages of information, course objectives, class assignments and exercises, resources, and bibliography for social work foundation areas.

Vickers, J. (1993). *Women and war.* Atlantic Highlands, NJ: Zed Books.

A look at many present-day wars and conflicts and their increasingly violent impact on civilians, as well as at defense policies and the arms trade, the prospects for conversion from military to civilian production, and peacekeeping attempts by the United Nations. Relationships between disarmament and development and between peace and human rights are brought into focus. The author proposes that women, who, with children, suffer most from wars, have far more power to stop them than most of them seem to think.

Wetzel, J. W. (1993). *The world of women: In pursuit of human rights.* New York: New York University Press.

Distills the multitude of problems facing the world's women into one central issue: human rights. Book examines the social issues and problems that affect women throughout the world, the policies and practices that impinge on their human rights, and the programs around the globe that are successfully changing their conditions.

Wronka, J. (1994). *Human rights and social policy in the twenty-first century*. University Press of America, Inc., 4720 Boston Way, Lanham, MD 20706; 800-462-6420.

This book analyzes the extent of human rights principles, as defined by the United Nations Universal Declaration on Human Rights, in U.S. federal and state constitutions and identifies the implications of this analysis for social policy.

Yanoov, B. C., & Korazim, Y. (Eds.). (1994, July). *Conflict resolution by social workers in Israel: A reader*. Tel-Aviv: Israel Association of Social Workers, 93, Arlosorov St., Tel-Aviv, Israel; telephone (3)6956482, FAX: (3)6964308.

Papers presented as part of a miniplenary on conflict resolution at the 1994 Social Workers World Conference in Sri Lanka. Includes some theories of conflict and the practice of conflict resolution, including case studies.

Young, G., Samarasinghe, V., & Kusterer, K. (Eds.). (1993). *Women at the center: Development issues and practices for the 1990s*. West Hartford, CT: Kumarian Press.

An overview of the vital, diverse, and central roles that women play in solving fundamental development problems. Based on the experiences of practitioners, grassroots activists, and academics from both the global North and the global South, this collection covers issues such as working to reduce the risks of HIV/AIDS infection, to use natural resources sustainably, and to bridge nationalist conflicts through women's activism.

Index

J, K

L

About the author

Dorothy Van Soest, DSW, is associate dean and associate professor, School of Social Work, University of Texas at Austin. She is former director of the NASW Violence and Development Project and was the development education coordinator of NASW's previous international education initiative, the Child and Family Well-Being Development Education Project. She also served two terms as chair of NASW's Peace and Social Justice Committee. Dr. Van Soest has more than 20 years of teaching experience in social work education and has authored several articles and book chapters on issues related to violence, oppression, cultural diversity, social justice, peace, and development. She wrote two curriculum books, *Incorporating Peace and Social Justice into the Social Work Curriculum* (1992) and *Challenges of Violence Worldwide: A Curriculum Module and An Educational Resource* (1997, with J. Crosby).

The Global Crisis of Violence:
Common Problems, Universal Causes, Shared Solutions

Cover design by Gehle Design.

Interior design by Toni L. Milbourne, Wolf Publications, Inc.

Composed by Wolf Publications, Inc., in Minion and Stone Sans.

Printed by Automated Graphic Systems, Inc., on 60# white offset.